T0294206

BLACK
POLITICS

Aboriginal and Torres Straight Islander people are warned that this book contains the names of deceased persons.

BLACK POLITICS

INSIDE THE COMPLEXITY OF ABORIGINAL POLITICAL CULTURE

SARAH MADDISON

ALLEN&UNWIN

First published in 2009

Allen & Unwin
83 Alexander Street
Crows Nest NSW 2065
Australia
Phone: (61 2) 8425 0100
Fax: (61 2) 9906 2218
Email: info@allenandunwin.com
Web: www.allenandunwin.com

The Cataloguing-in-Publication entry is available
from the National Library of Australia

ISBN: 978 1 74175 698 2

Set in 11/16 pt Caslon by Midland Typesetters, Australia

10 9 8 7 6 5 4 3 2 1

CONTENTS

This book is dedicated to the memory of Dr R. Marika—
a leader, a role model and an inspiration to all who had the
privilege of knowing her.

FOREWORD

The epic drama of Australia's colonisation and the contemporary re
lationship between Indigenous and non-Indigenous people that has
been forged by relentless oppression—by the gun and application of
administrative law in a story 220 years in the making—is an extraordinary challenge to write.

Thirty years ago, Kevin Gilbert provided a stage for the voices of
diverse Indigenous people to be heard in his classic book *Living Black*.
That book took mainstream Australia on a journey into the heart of
Indigenous nations, revealing the anger, trauma and hopes of black
people through the searing power of an Aboriginal-held pen. Gilbert
captured an historic mood of Aboriginal Australia's political resurgence
as black men and women throughout the nation rallied to the potential
for change inspired by leaders such as Vincent Lingiari and the people
who set up the tent embassy in Canberra.

This was a time in history when the window of despair for Indigenous Australia opened ever so slightly to allow a flickering vision that
this nation could transcend its history and shape a future where Aboriginal and non-Indigenous people could share this country in respectful
coexistence. For many of us it was that vision, together with a belief that
justice for the dispossessed and the colonised in this nation is possible,
that shaped our life journey. Yet we still faced the power and greed of
people who perceive that controlling the land and its natural resources

through systems of government inherited from British colonisers means keeping the original owners in permanent subjugation. They have acted ruthlessly to frustrate the good that this nation can be.

Much has happened since *Living Black* was published. The hope for uniform national land rights was crushed by the mining industry and state governments; the recognition of our common law rights was corralled and subordinated in a land management system that favoured settler interests; and, more recently, the evil philosophy of assimilation—which Indigenous people thought had been repudiated by a nation determined to address its past—has re-emerged in public policy and been argued with moral righteousness by its proponents.

Thirty years on, Sarah Maddison takes mainstream Australia on a journey to Kevin Gilbert's projected world. This is a timely book. *Black Politics* captures the complexity of Indigenous politics where the reader is challenged to see beyond the power structures of the settler nation-state where Indigenous diversity is treated as conflict for the purpose of diminishing the power of Indigenous political advocacy and narrative. Instead, the reader is challenged to appreciate Indigenous complexity as a political force in the context of imagining a very different Australia—a nation liberated from its colonial chains.

In a world of economic and cultural integration where human rights are increasingly a condition of international respect, the complex reality of Indigenous Australia provides a pathway for national renewal. Beyond the fractured pan-national Indigenous framework manufactured to intersect unequally with Anglo-Australian centres of power, Indigenous and non-Indigenous people coexist in countless locations throughout the nation. Here is the potential for a revitalised Australia with a new philosophy that will transcend assimilation and subordination, in which current relationships are trapped, with a commitment to a functioning partnership of Indigenous societies, governments, industry and civil society.

But such a philosophical approach must be based on the repudiation of assimilation and practices designed to absorb Indigenous people into mainstream Australia. *Black Politics* highlights that within the complexity of Australia's Indigenous polity lies a pernicious peril of Indigeneity that is framed by an Anglo settler society designed to give comfort to Indigenous people about racial continuity while the capacity of people to live on their country and practise their cultural ways, laws and languages is obliterated.

Sarah Maddison has brought together a formidable range of Indigenous voices and sources, and placed their narratives within an analysis to show the depth and complexity of Indigenous cultural and political expression. There is strength to this complexity that is underrated by Australian settler society. While there is a rich diversity of Indigenous political views that advocates of cultural absorption and assimilation will exploit, what connects all Indigenous people is a shared history of violent oppression and exclusion that the Australian nation-state cannot escape. For the vast majority of Indigenous people and a significant number of settler Australians, the substantial recognition of Indigenous people's inclusion as a distinct and unique people is a fundamental condition for a reconciled nation.

At the same time, the forces of destruction inherent in Australia's nation-building project, which have sought to extinguish Indigenous people's society and culture in their own country, are as powerful today as they were in the era of violent dispossession and state-sanctioned human rights abuses. The repudiation of assimilation as a philosophy of Australian nationhood will require a creative dialogue between diverse Indigenous peoples as much as a discourse between Indigenous people and settlers, so that a philosophy of recognition and respect of the culture of the First Peoples can become a foundation principle of Australian nationhood.

Patrick Dodson

ACKNOWLEDGMENTS

The research for this book took place over several years, during which time I have incurred a debt of gratitude to many individuals and groups.

Researching this book has allowed me to truly understand what it means to acknowledge the traditional owners of the land on which I live and work, the Gadigal people of the Eora nation. I pay my sincere respects to the elders and ancestors of the Eora nation, several generations of whom bore the full brunt of the invasion and early settlement of this country.

I offer my deepest thanks to the Aboriginal leaders and activists who agreed to be interviewed for this book. Their generosity of time and spirit, particularly given the many other obligations and responsibilities they all hold, was a great honour. Several of these individuals went above and beyond what was requested in supporting my work. I have enjoyed meals and coffees with many of these fine people since our interviews and deeply, deeply appreciate their ongoing support for—and pride in—this work. Every effort was made to provide each interviewee with the opportunity to review their interview transcript and/or drafts of the book itself. In a few cases this has not been possible. All quotes are taken directly from our recorded conversations, but any errors in interpretation are my own.

I am grateful for the financial and institutional support I received from the Faculty of Arts and Social Sciences at the University of New

South Wales, which provided me with the research grants that funded my travel around the country to conduct the interviews. The Australian Research Council funded the final stages of research through Discovery Project 0877157. These combined funds also provided for the excellent research assistance I received early on from Gemma Edgar and later from Deborah Cummins. Deborah's calm efficiency during the last weeks of editing the manuscript are especially appreciated.

My gratitude also to Elizabeth Weiss at Allen & Unwin for seeing something in the original proposal for this book that she thought was worth pursuing. Her guidance, advice and support have helped me craft a better, and I hope more accessible, book. Thanks are also due to those who read and commented on drafts of the manuscript, including Megan Davis, Alan Kirkland, George Morgan, Tim Rowse and Maggie Walter, and to Rebecca Kaiser at Allen & Unwin for steering this project through production.

Finally, to my family: my teenagers Sam and Eliza endured an absent and preoccupied mum with surprising good grace, although Eliza tells me I did 'nothing else' other than work on the book during the final months of writing. To my partner Emma Partridge—who read every word, supported every crisis, kept the home fires burning during my many research trips, and who still makes every day a good day—big love always.

INTERVIEWEES

Alison Anderson was born in Ikuntji (Haasts Bluff), growing up in a number of communities including Hermannsburg and Papunya. She has a Diploma of Community Management from Batchelor College. A strong community person, fluent in several Aboriginal languages, Alison has spent her life trying to improve the conditions of people living in Central Australia. She has served as a representative for Central Australia on the Aboriginal Development Commission and later as ATSIC Commissioner for the Northern Territory's Central Zone. In 2005, she was elected as the Labor Member for Macdonnell in the Northern Territory government.

Henry Atkinson is an Elder of the Wolithiga people and spokesperson for the Elders Council of the Yorta Yorta Nation. Henry successfully negotiated with the Victorian government to have the Yorta Yorta Nation recognised in a binding agreement through legislation. He is a lecturer and consultant at the Faculty of Education at Monash University and has been inspirational in the setting up of a new compulsory course on Indigenous Education for all student teachers. Henry advises in many areas, including the Aboriginal Cultural Heritage Advisory Committee of Museum Victoria and the Murray Lower Darling Rivers Indigenous Nations.

Muriel Bamblett is a Yorta Yorta woman who has been employed as the Chief Executive Officer of the Victorian Aboriginal Child Care Agency (VACCA) since 1999. From 1997–99, Muriel was the Chairperson of VACCA. Muriel actively serves on many boards concerning children, families and the community. Muriel has been the recipient of a number of awards for her work, and was awarded an AM (Membership in the General Division) in the 2004 Australia Day Honours for her services to the community, particularly through leadership in the provision of services for Aboriginal and Torres Strait Islander children and families.

Larissa Behrendt is a Eualeyai/Kamillaroi woman. She is the Professor of Law and Director of Research at the Jumbunna Indigenous House of Learning at the University of Technology, Sydney. Larissa is a judicial member of the Administrative Decisions Tribunal, Equal Opportunity Division and the Alternate Chair of the Serious Offenders Review Board. She has published on property law, Aboriginal and Torres Strait Islander rights, dispute resolution and Aboriginal women's issues. She won the 2002 David Uniapon Award and a 2005 Commonwealth Writer's Prize for her novel *Home*. Larissa is also a director of the Sydney Writers' Festival and a director of the Bangarra Dance Theatre.

Paul Briggs is a Yorta Yorta man, raised on the Cummeragunja Aboriginal Mission within a strong family environment. Among other positions, he serves as chair of the First Nations Foundation, co-chair of the Victorian Indigenous Leadership Network, co-chair of the National Indigenous Money Management Agenda, president of the Rumbalara Football Netball Club, councillor of the University of Melbourne Council, and founding member of the Koori Resource and Information Centre. In 2005 he was awarded the Order of Australia Medal in recognition of his service to his community.

Tom Calma is an Aboriginal elder from the Kungarakan tribal group and a member of the Iwaidja tribal group. He has worked in the public sector for over thirty years. From 1995–2002, he worked as a senior Australian diplomat in India and Vietnam, representing Australia's interests in education and training. Tom now serves as the Aboriginal and Torres Strait Islander Social Justice Commissioner and Race Discrimination Commissioner. In 2007, Tom was awarded the prestigious number one position in the Indigenous category for the *Bulletin* magazine's Power 100 in recognition of his service in driving change for Aboriginal and Torres Strait Islander people.

Vince Coulthard is an Adnyamathanha man, born at Leigh Creek in South Australia. He has worked for government and private enterprise and has been the Director of Umeewarra Media—the only Aboriginal radio station in South Australia—for over sixteen years. Vince was also an ATSIC Councillor for nine years and has been the elected chairperson of the Adnyamathanha Traditional Land Association for over a decade. Vince is one of the founders of the Iga Warta Community, a cultural tourism enterprise in the northern Flinders Ranges. He has previously been awarded the South Australian Premier's Australia Day Award and the Federation Medal and has been given three NIADOC awards (Male of the Year 2004, Person of the Year 2005 and Elder of the Year 2007) by the Port Augusta Community, which is made up of over 4000 Aboriginal people from some 28 diverse language groups.

Josie Crawshaw-Guy belongs to the Gurindji Nation in the Northern Territory. Josie's mother was part of the Stolen Generations and was removed in 1921 to the Kahlin Compound Institution in Darwin. Josie has spent several decades fighting and advocating for the rights of Indigenous people, including as a member of the Aboriginal Provisional Government, in the National Coalition of Aboriginal Organisations, and as an ATSIC Commissioner in the Northern Territory. In August of 1990, Josie was detained at Darwin Airport for using her Aboriginal passport to gain entry back into her country of birth. Currently, Josie is working for the Aboriginal Interpreter Service in Darwin.

Eddie Cubillo has strong family links in both urban and rural areas throughout the Northern Territory. His mother is of Larrakia/Wadjigan descent and his father is Central Arrernte. In 2001 he obtained a Bachelor of Laws Degree and in 2002 he was admitted as a Barrister and Solicitor of the Supreme Court of the Northern Territory. In 2002 he was elected to the ATSIC Yilli Rreung Regional Council, and subsequently became the Chair of that Council. Eddie has also been a former chair of both the North Australian Aboriginal Justice Agency (NAAJA) and the Aboriginal Justice Advisory

Committee (NT). Eddie is currently working as an Indigenous employment consultant at the University of South Australia while undertaking a Master in Laws.

Mick Dodson belongs to the Yawuru peoples from the southern Kimberley region of Western Australia. Professor Dodson works as Director of the ANU's National Centre for Indigenous Studies. In 1993 he was appointed Australia's first Aboriginal and Torres Strait Islander Social Justice commissioner and co-authored the *Bringing Them Home* report, exposing the plight of the Stolen Generations. Mick serves on a number of boards and is chairman of the Aboriginal Indigenous Leadership Centre and of Reconciliation Australia. Mick has also been active internationally, assisting in the drafting and negotiations for the Draft Declaration on the Rights of Indigenous Peoples in the United Nations Working Group on Indigenous Populations.

Eugenia Flynn is a young Aboriginal (Larrakiah and Tiwi), Chinese and Muslim woman. She holds two degrees in Information Technology and Innovation and Enterprise in Science and Technology. Eugenia is an executive member of the National Indigenous Youth Movement of Australia (NIYMA). Most recently she has worked with other Indigenous colleagues to deliver a set of Indigenous Youth Engagement workshops around Australia in 2007, to culminate in a National Gathering to be held in 2008. In 2005, she attended the First Inaugural National Muslim Youth Summit and in 2007 founded the Indigenous Muslim Support Network.

Colleen Hayward is a senior Noongar woman with family ties throughout the southwest of Western Australia. Colleen is Associate Professor and manager of the Kulunga Research Network at the Telethon Institute for Child Health Research in Western Australia. Colleen is the only Indigenous member of the Western Australia State Training Board, serves as deputy chair of the Ministerial Advisory Council on the Prevention of Deaths in Children and Young People and is a member of the Australian Council of Social Services Indigenous Policy Advisors' Group. In 2006, she was awarded the Premier of Western Australia's Multicultural Ambassador Award and in 2008 was the National NAIDOC Person of the Year.

Kim Hill is a Ngaringman man, the eldest child of Kim (Snr) and Jane (nee Ah Kit). He has also been adopted by the Tiwi people. Kim is the Chief Executive of the Northern Land Council (NLC). He began his career with the NLC representing it at the First World Indigenous Youth Conference in Canada in 1992 and co-chairing the Second World Indigenous Youth Conference the following year. Later he was elected for two terms as ATSIC's NT North Zone Commissioner and served as chair of the ATSIC Board's Economic and Social Participation Committee. More recently he has worked as an adviser to the Northern Territory government.

Jackie Huggins is an historian and published author, of the Bidjara and Birri-Gubba Juru peoples in Queensland. In 2001, she was awarded an Australia Medal (AM) for her work with Indigenous people. She currently works as deputy director of the Aboriginal and Torres Strait Islander Studies Unit at the University of Queensland. Most recently, she co-chaired the Indigenous Australia stream of the Prime Minister's 2020 Summit. Jackie is a former co-chair of Reconciliation Australia and is a director of the Telstra Foundation, as well as a member of the Indigenous Reference Group of the Queensland Centre of Domestic and Family Violence Research. She authored *Auntie Rita* with Rita Huggins in 1994, and *Sistergirl* in 1999.

Sam Jeffries is a Moorawoori man, born and raised in Brewarrina. Sam is chairperson of the Murdi Paaki Regional Assembly. Over the years, he has served as Walgett Shire councillor, ATSIC councillor, board member of the Aboriginal Housing Office, and chairperson of the NSW ATSIC State Council. He is also a board member of the Western Catchment Management Authority, panel member of the NSW Aboriginal Trust Fund Repayment Scheme and chairperson of the National Aboriginal Sports Corporation Australia. In 2001, he was awarded the Centenary Medal in recognition of his service to Aboriginal and Torres Strait Islander people in the Murdi Paaki region.

Jilpia Jones is a Walmadjari woman born in the Sandy Desert in the Kimberley region of Western Australia. She is part of the Stolen Generations and was removed from her mother and sent to Queensland when she was five years old. She worked as a registered nurse with Fred

Hollows on the National Trachoma and Eye Health Program around Australia during the 1970s and 1980s. She is currently a research officer in Aboriginal health at the Australian Institute of Aboriginal and Torres Strait Islander Studies. Jilpia was awarded an Order of Australia for services to ophthalmology and birthing choices in 1995, and an Australian Centenary Medal in 2003.

Alwyn McKenzie is of the Luritja and Adnyamathanha people. He currently works as a principal policy/project officer with the South Australian government's Aboriginal Affairs and Reconciliation Division. Alwyn worked for eleven years as the community executive officer of the Davenport Community Council, an Aboriginal community located outside of Port Augusta. Alwyn served as ATSIC regional councillor for the Nulla Wimila Kutju Regional Council, and was elected as chairperson of the regional council for two three-year terms. Amongst several other commitments, Alwyn is a member of the Social Inclusion Board of South Australia and a board member of Desert Knowledge Australia.

Marvyn McKenzie is an Adnyamathanha Ararru Yura man born in Port Augusta, three years before the 1967 referendum. He grew up on the Davenport Community, an Aboriginal community a few kilometres out of Port Augusta. He has been an activist for the rights of Aboriginal people from a young age, beginning his involvement in Aboriginal Affairs when he was sixteen, working with Aboriginal Community First. He is a well-known figure in his local community, and a regular letter-writer to the Port Augusta newspaper the *Transcontinental*. Marvyn is an artist and photographer, and a founding member of the Yarta Arts Group.

Dr Marika was a member of the Rirratjingu clan, who understood all the fourteen clan languages of the Rirratjingu people and spoke three. She was a participant in the Ganma/Garma Research Project at Yirrkala School, and was responsible for instruction and planning of numerous orientation, induction and Yolngu Matha classes for Balanda staff at Yirrkala and Nhulunbuy, Northern Territory Health Department, Laynhapuy Resource Centre staff, and Northern Territory Education staff from Nhulunbuy. Dr Marika was also a member of Council for the Australian Institute of Aboriginal and Torres Strait Islander Studies.

In 2006 she was named the Northern Territory Australian of the Year. Dr Marika died suddenly and prematurely in May 2008. For cultural reasons her first name will not be used in this book.

John Maynard is a member of the Worimi people of Port Stephens, New South Wales. He is a professor of Indigenous Studies and head of Wollotuka School of Aboriginal Studies at the University of Newcastle. John is an Australian Research Council post-doctoral fellow and a member of Council with the Australian Institute of Aboriginal and Torres Strait Islander Studies and the Indigenous Higher Education Advisory Council. John has worked with and within many Aboriginal communities—urban, rural and remote. He is the author of five books, including *Aboriginal Stars of the Turf* and *The Fight for Liberty and Freedom*.

Warren Mundine is the ninth of eleven children to Olive Bridgette (Dolly) Mundine (nee Donovan) and Roy Mundine. Dolly is a Gumbayngirr woman and Roy a Bundjalung man. Warren now serves as CEO and company secretary of NTSCORP Ltd. He has been actively involved in politics for many years. He is the former national president of the Australian Labor Party, deputy mayor of Dubbo and former chair of New South Wales Country Labor. He has also served as president of the New South Wales Local Government Aboriginal Network, as an executive member of the Local Government Association of New South Wales and is a former member of the New South Wales Attorney-General's Juvenile Crime Prevention Committee.

Tauto Sansbury is a Narungga man whose community is the traditional owners of the Yorke Peninsula in South Australia. He now works as chief executive officer of the Ceduna/Koonibba Aboriginal Health Service. From 2002–05 he served as ATSIC chairperson for the Papta Warra Yunti Regional Council. In 1996, Tauto was awarded NAIDOC's highest honour, the Aboriginal and Torres Strait Islander Person of the Year, and in 2003 he was awarded an Australian Centenary Medal for his work in the Aboriginal justice sector.

Geoff Scott is a Wiradjuri man. He is currently adjunct professor at the University of Technology, Sydney, chief executive officer of the New

South Wales Aboriginal Land Council, and Chair of the Australian Indigenous Leadership Centre. He was formerly the director-general of the New South Wales Department of Aboriginal Affairs and the deputy CEO of ATSIC. He was awarded a Public Service Medal in 1993. He is a founding editor of the *Journal of Indigenous Policy* and has worked as a consultant to various Indigenous organisations, including Reconciliation Australia and the Australian Institute of Aboriginal and Torres Strait Islander Studies.

Ray Swan is from Moree (NSW) and a member of the Kamilaroi nation. He has been a strong activist for the rights of Aboriginal people and in advancing Aboriginal claims to sovereignty and treaty. He is on the working group for the Aboriginal Tent Embassy in Canberra.

Robbie Thorpe is from the Krautungalung people of the Gunnai Nation, the traditional owners of Lake Tyers in Victoria. Robbie has been an activist for the rights of Indigenous people for most of his life. He works with the National Aboriginal and Island Health Organisation, made up of 80 community-controlled health services. He is a lead figure and spokesman for the Black GST (Genocide, Sovereignty, Treaty) Campaign, and the establishment of the Stolenwealth Games and Camp Sovereignty in Victoria. He is also on the working group for the Aboriginal Tent Embassy in Canberra.

William Tilmouth was born in Alice Springs and is of Arrernte descent. William serves as the executive director of Tangentyere Council. Prior to this, he was chairperson of the ATSIC Regional Council. He has served on a number of Northern Territory ministerial boards to address Indigenous policy issues of human rights, land rights, economic development, social welfare programs and housing. He chairs the Central Australian Legal Aid Service, the Alice Springs Institutional Ethics Committee and Alcoota Incorporated. He is a founding member of the Central Australian Indigenous Men's Health Committee and is an elected community representative for the Centre for Remote Health.

Klynton Wanganeen is a Narungga-Ngarrindjeri man who was appointed as South Australia's Aboriginal Engagement Commissioner in 2008. Prior to that he was the general manager of the State's

Aboriginal Access Centre, Technical and Further Education. Klynton is active on many boards and committees and serves as chairperson of the South Australian Congress of Native Title Traditional Owner Group and the Narungga Nations Aboriginal Corporation. From 2000 to 2002, Klynton was elected chairperson of the Patpa Warra Yunti Regional Council (ATSIC), and from 2002 to 2005 was the South Australian Zone Commissioner for the Aboriginal and Torres Strait Islander Commission.

Sam Watson is of the Munnenjarl and Biri Gubba tribal nations and he has blood ties to the Jagara, Kalkadoon and Noonuccal peoples. He co-founded the first Aboriginal and Islander political party ('The Australian Indigenous Peoples Party'). He has been a foundation member of a number of key Aboriginal and Islander community organisations and was a full-time staff member for the Aboriginal Embassy in Canberra. He won the National Indigenous Writer of the Year Award in 1991 for his first novel (*The Kadaitcha Sung*). He is now a deputy director of the Aboriginal and Islander Studies Unit at the University of Queensland. He also works as an adviser and cultural writer for film and television.

Ted Wilkes is a Nyungar man from Western Australia whose professional background includes working for the Western Australia Museum, the Centre for Aboriginal Studies at Curtin University of Technology, and sixteen years as the director of the Derbarl Yerrigan Health Service. He is an associate professor in the Indigenous Research Program at the National Drug Research Institute, Curtin University of Technology. Ted is a member of the Australian National Council on Drugs, is the chair of the National Indigenous Drug and Alcohol Committee, and provides advice and expertise to various other state, national and international committees.

ABBREVIATIONS AND ACRONYMS

AAPA   Australian Aboriginal Progressive Association
ABA   Aboriginals Benefits Account
ADC   Aboriginal Development Commission
AFL   Australian Football League
ALP   Australian Labor Party
ALRA   *Aboriginal Land Rights Act* (Northern Territory)
APG   Aboriginal Provisional Government
ATSIC   Aboriginal and Torres Strait Islander Commission
ATSISJC   Aboriginal and Torres Strait Islander Social Justice
           Commissioner
CAR   Council for Aboriginal Reconciliation
CDEP   Community Development Employment Program
CLC   Central Land Council
CLP   Country Liberal Party
COAG   Council of Australian Governments
DAA   Department of Aboriginal Affairs
FaHCSIA   Department of Families, Housing, Community Services and
           Indigenous Affairs
FCAATSI   Federal Council for the Advancement of Aborigines and
           Torres Strait Islanders
HREOC   Human Rights and Equal Opportunities Commission
ICGP   Indigenous Community Governance Project
ILC   Indigenous Land Corporation
ILUA   Indigenous Land Use Agreement
KALACC   Kimberley Aboriginal Law and Culture Centre

KLC	Kimberley Land Council
NAA	National Aboriginal Alliance
NAC	National Aboriginal Conference
NACC	National Aboriginal Consultative Committee
NIC	National Indigenous Council
NIYMA	National Indigenous Youth Movement of Australia
NLC	Northern Land Council
NNTT	National Native Title Tribunal
NTA	Native Title Act
NTRB	Native Title Representative Body
SRA	Shared Responsibility Agreement

It looks like now—from where I see, from my understanding—I am on the same fight again. Looks like I am going to go back all over again.
It is the same fight.
That's all I got to say.

—Mr Rangiari, 1997

I don't hold the present generation responsible for the past but I will hold it responsible for the present and the future because it is its responsibility and mine to change things for the better.
—The late Oodgeroo Noonuccal, quoted in Watson (2006)

INTRODUCTION

Cabinet is aware of increasing concern in the Australian community and internationally for the social and economic welfare of Aboriginals.

—Cabinet submission 1185, 'National Employment
Strategy for Aboriginals', 1977

I have called this news conference to announce a number of major measures to deal with what we can only describe as a national emergency in relation to the abuse of children in indigenous communities in the Northern Territory.

—Former Prime Minister John Howard announcing
his government's 'emergency intervention' into
Northern Territory Aboriginal communities, 2007

Between 1977 and 2007, the federal political response to deteriorating conditions in many Aboriginal communities escalated from 'increasing concern' to an apparent 'national emergency'. In the intervening three decades, policy had been repeatedly reoriented, from self-determination to mainstreaming, and from reconciliation to intervention. Commentators and politicians had debated the symbolic versus the practical; paternalism and coercion were proposed as antidotes to dependency. None of it made a blind bit of difference. Aboriginal people[1] today occupy the same peripheral political space that they did thirty years ago; if anything, they have become more marginal to an Australian polity captured by a mythical 'mainstream'. Conditions in many remote Aboriginal communities are the same as, or worse than, they were thirty years ago; indeed, Aboriginal people are arguably more disadvantaged and communities are more dysfunctional than they were then. Successive Australian governments have made little or no difference to the life chances of this continent's original inhabitants. How can we explain this failure?

This book explores this question, but is not a book about Aboriginal disadvantage. It is not about dysfunctional communities, welfare dependency, child abuse, alcohol or violence. In recent years, these issues have come to dominate political debate as though they were the sum total of Aboriginal life. This book looks beyond the issues that make the headlines to investigate the real complexity of contemporary Aboriginal political culture.[2] It is concerned with the challenges faced by Aboriginal people today as they grapple with the often-uncomfortable intersection of their fractured (but not abandoned) traditional and cultural life, the legacies of colonisation, and their own diversity across the continent. These intersections of history, culture, experience and identity have produced an extraordinarily complex political culture that, in general, is very poorly understood by non-Aboriginal people.

In negotiating this complexity, Aboriginal people are resourceful, creative and persistent. No other group of political actors faces greater challenges than Aboriginal people in their struggles to articulate a collective identity, connect with the broader Australian population and achieve urgent political outcomes. Certainly, no other group of political actors has as much at stake as does this group. For Aboriginal leaders and activists—terms that do not sit comfortably with many—what is at stake is their material and cultural survival.

Thirty voices, ten areas of complexity: The approach of this book
Mine is not the only voice in this book. Over the past five years, I have interviewed thirty Aboriginal leaders and activists from many parts of Australia, discussing their life histories, their political views, their worries and their aspirations. All of these interviewees, with one exception, have chosen to be named rather than anonymous in this work. I draw on these interviews throughout the book, along with a wide range

of Aboriginal and non-Aboriginal writing, all of which is woven into the analysis. In this sense, I hope this work fulfils Lester-Irabinna Rigney's definition of 'indigenist research'—that is, research that is culturally safe and respectful by virtue of following three principles, namely that the research is guided by resistance as an emancipatory imperative, that it has political integrity, and that it privileges Indigenous voices (Rigney 1999: 116).

Almost without exception, non-Aboriginal people to whom I have spoken about this project have suggested I am 'brave' to be wading into such a fraught and complex field. People are aware, as Tim Rowse has noted, of Aboriginal collectivity as 'a political scene with its own internal dynamics and tensions' (Rowse 1998: 97)—tensions that can sometimes obscure and obstruct political aims. It is inevitable that, as an outsider, I will misinterpret, misunderstand or miss altogether some of the subtleties of these dynamics. Nevertheless, where non-Aboriginal people have emphasised the challenges, the vast majority of Aboriginal people I have met with and interviewed over the past five years have been nothing but encouraging. I have been invited to stay in people's houses and communities, I have been picked up and dropped off at airports, I have been fed and watered, entertained and listened to by Aboriginal people whose response has (almost universally) been, 'That's great that you're doing this work'. Many of the people I interviewed, and others I have spoken with informally, have mentioned how hard it is to look up and consider the whole of the political work they are engaged in when they are working, as Pat Anderson put it, 'at the pointy end of the needle'. For some, the interviews we did provided a welcome opportunity to do just that.

Of course, not everybody responded in this way. There were certain key people I would have liked to interview but who chose not to participate for various reasons. Marcia Langton, for example, accused me of being racist for describing her as an activist rather than as a public intellectual. Noel Pearson simply ignored my repeated requests until I was politely let down by his personal assistant. Michael Mansell told me he felt he had nothing else to offer that was not already on the public record. These are all busy people whose days are often dominated by requests for their time from non-Aboriginal people, of whom I was just one more. At the same time, everywhere I travelled, people I spoke to suggested a list of ten other people I should interview. But the reality is I could have gone on interviewing people indefinitely and never written this book. The interviewees I have included, ranging from the high-profile to the local and community-focused, are not intended to be representative of the diversity of Aboriginal people, communities or leaders. They are merely a snapshot of the range of views, the types of work, the kind of experience and commitment that contribute to this rich political culture.

In part, this book is concerned with what Canadian political philosopher James Tully (2000) describes as 'practices for and of freedom'. Tully makes a distinction between struggles *for* freedom—that is, struggles against continuing political and institutional oppression—and struggles *of* freedom—or those struggles focused on preserving and protecting language and culture and 'keeping Indigenous ways of being in the world alive and well' (2000: 42). The aim of this book has been to capture some of the dynamics involved in these struggles. I have attempted to distil the vast complexity of this field down to ten key areas of tension, each of which is addressed in a separate chapter. In sum, these tensions are between autonomy and dependency; sovereignty and citizenship; tradition and development; individualism and collectivism; Indigeneity and hybridity; unity and regionalism; community and kin; men, women and customary law; elders and the next generation; and mourning and reconciliation.

Diversity and disagreement

A significant barrier to understanding the complexity of Aboriginal political culture lies in the widespread failure to recognise the diversity of Aboriginal people and their aspirations and demands. Historically, Aboriginal people have known and understood far more about non-Aboriginal people than non-Aboriginal people have known about them. Indeed, Aboriginal people have often deliberately limited the sharing of information about themselves with non-Aboriginal people as a means of limiting non-Aboriginal control over their lives (Morris 1988: 49). To some extent, this is still true today. Aside from anthropologists and other researchers, whose knowledge is often contested by Aboriginal people themselves, how many in the dominant culture can say they understand Aboriginal sociality or political culture?

Aboriginal people often lay at least part of the blame for this ignorance at the feet of the mainstream media. There is a tendency in much mainstream media coverage to ignore differences between Aboriginal people in order to limit the full scope of their political demands. In recent years, this dynamic has been driven by the dominance of the idea of 'welfare dependency' as an explanation for all Aboriginal disadvantage. In our interview, Colleen Hayward makes the point that few other issues are represented as simplistically in the media as Aboriginal politics. For other stories, Colleen says, journalists will have 'gone around and tracked down people with different views to present a more rounded argument'. When it comes to a story about Aboriginal politics, however, journalists seem intent on presenting the view that Aboriginal people are 'all like minded' and where there is a difference of views it is interpreted as meaning that Aboriginal people are 'not organised, we don't know what we're talking about, we've got to get our act together, and who cares anyway?' For Colleen, this type of representation is indicative of 'how far Australian society actually has to come in terms of their understanding of us': 'As communities and nations of people—we are different. Our nations are different. Our communities are different. We have different needs. We have different views. That's healthy!'

Maintaining their political and social diversity has always been important to Aboriginal people, as it is for any minority group keen to avoid being swallowed by the dominant culture. Although Australian Aboriginal people are the only collective of Indigenous peoples anywhere in the world to have united under one flag, Aboriginal communities in Australia remain intensely, and proudly, local (Behrendt 1995: 27). As Jilpia Jones puts it simply in our interview: 'We're all black fellas, we've just got different roads.' Debate and disagreement, as Galarrwuy Yunupingu has pointed out, is 'as would be expected from a dynamic and culturally diverse community' (1997: xv). Michael Mansell has also made this point in evidence before the Senate Standing Committee on Legal and Constitutional Affairs during the 1993 negotiations over native title legislation. Mansell told the committee:

> We are no different from any other people anywhere in the world. We have different lifestyles and different communities. We have different political attitudes and we have different aspirations. Even though there are many common threads which run throughout the Aboriginal communities in Australia, we tend to encourage the differences because they are healthy. The worst aspect of political life that can be imposed on Aboriginal people

is that we must all speak with one voice and say exactly the same thing. (quoted in Brennan 1995: 73)

Still, despite Mansell's assertion of the importance of healthy disagreement, there is a strong tendency for Aboriginal people to smother their tensions and disagreements. Given the intense media interest in any sign of trouble in Aboriginal communities, there is pressure placed on communities to appear trouble free, meaning that community issues often remain unresolved. Many Aboriginal people regard this pressure as a distinct double standard, as Jackie Huggins has argued:

> when Blacks publicly analyse and criticise each other it is perceived as infighting. However, when non-Aboriginals do the same it is considered a healthy exercise in intellectual stimulation. Why is the area of intra-racial Aboriginal debate such a sacred site? (Huggins 2003 [1993]: 65)

Larissa Behrendt agrees, suggesting that non-Aboriginal people are 'quick to label any type of internal dispute as evidence that the Aboriginal community is incapable of running its own affairs' (Behrendt 1995: 94–5). But as Megan Davis asks, 'Why is it that blackfellas have to reconcile their views if there is a fundamental, ideological difference of opinion? We should be able to partake in a robust discussion of policy and ideas.' (2005: 1)

There are sound reasons for Aboriginal leaders and activists to display a degree of wariness about revealing their internal conflicts and contradictions. Disagreements between Aboriginal leaders and activists have often been used to embarrass them or to undermine their credibility. Patrick Dodson points out that Australian governments have long attempted to 'divide and rule' Aboriginal people in their efforts to suppress Indigenous resistance (2000: 14). The racialised divisions (for example, by 'degrees of blood') that were imposed on Aboriginal people were, at least in part, a conscious attempt to limit Aboriginal protest and resistance (O'Shane 1998). This dynamic has contemporary manifestations. In our interview, Warren Mundine suggests that debate between Aboriginal leaders and activists has been smothered, in part because 'we were scared that the white people would think that we were divided and take advantage of that'. There is certainly a long history to justify this fear. In our interview, John Maynard told me of evidence he had uncovered that documented the undermining of the Australian Aboriginal Progressive Association (AAPA), the organisation started by his grandfather, Fred Maynard.[3] In the 1920s, the AAPA was mobilis ing Aboriginal people in large numbers and in 1925 succeeded in having 250 Aboriginal people attend a conference in Sydney and another 700 attend a conference in Kempsey, despite restrictions on Aboriginal people's freedom of movement. Once the Aborigines Protection Board awoke to the growing strength of the AAPA, according to John, they started 'hounding' the organisation, intent on 'driving them into oblivion' with a series of threats and other strategies designed to 'turn black against black'.

But while understandable, there are costs to this tendency to smother debate, particularly on controversial topics. Warren Mundine suggests that in the past Aboriginal people 'didn't want to talk about black domestic violence and sexual abuse of children' because: 'Then the racists would go, "Oh look, see, we told you they were bad people, that's what they do to their children, what they do to their girlfriends and wives and that." But by being silent we didn't advance ideas, and the perpetrators just got away with what they got away with.'

Non-Aboriginal Australia has at best failed to recognise, and at worst deliberately silenced, the diversity and differences within Aboriginal political culture. In turn, many Aboriginal people themselves have felt a need to smother their disagreements. But silencing these tensions in the past may well have contributed to the 'emergency' of the present.

Struggle, disappointment, re-engagement

Despite endless political disappointment, it has been a hallmark of Aboriginal politics that Aboriginal leaders and activists are seemingly endlessly prepared to engage with governments that have repeatedly let them down. William Tilmouth suggests that Aboriginal people have always made the best of the political circumstances in which they have found themselves, being prepared to 'participate, negotiate, resist or comply with the pressures imposed on them, as they see fit and within the opportunities provided' (Tilmouth 2007: 231). Geonpul scholar Aileen Moreton-Robinson (2003) makes a similar point, arguing that Aboriginal people have been creative in their engagement with white Australian society, creating cultural forms that 'take account of the ambiguous existence that is the inevitable result of this engagement'.

This ambiguity adds to the complexity of Aboriginal resistance: 'rather than simply being a matter of overtly defiant behaviour, resistance is re-presented as multifaceted, visible and invisible, conscious and unconscious, explicit and covert, intentional and unintentional' (2003: 128).

No period illustrates this point more clearly than the last term of the Howard government. Following Howard's election win in 2004, and with the impending demise of ATSIC (announced during the election campaign), there was widespread concern among Aboriginal leaders and activists about their diminished capacity to be heard on the national stage. Former AFL star Michael Long highlighted this concern by initiating what became known as the 'Long Walk'. In November 2004, Long set out from his home in Melbourne to walk to Canberra to demand a meeting with the Prime Minister. Long had previously rejected a seat on the Howard government's National Indigenous Council (NIC), and he set off on his walk intent on persuading the Prime Minister that he needed to listen to Aboriginal people other than those on the NIC (Gordon 2004).

At around the same time, in a different part of the country, another group of around a dozen Aboriginal leaders attended a two-day meeting at Port Douglas, convened by Noel Pearson. The meeting was an effort to resolve some of their differences, particularly those between Pearson, with his acceptance of the Howard government's position on 'mutual obligation', and Patrick Dodson, who continued to advocate for the recognition of inherent Indigenous rights. The goal in Port Douglas was to develop a more cohesive response to the Howard government, and indeed the meeting seemed to produce what was later described as a 'fusion of two competing paradigms based around rights and responsibilities' (Kelly 2004). Pearson claimed the meeting was a 'turning point in the psychology of the nation's Indigenous leaders', with Dodson and Pearson releasing a joint statement in which they claimed that the group at the meeting had decided to 'combine their energies' to 'advance the situation of Aboriginal people from an abysmal state of social and economic inertia to a circumstance more closely approaching the reality of non-Aboriginal Australians' (Dodson and Pearson 2004). The Port Douglas meeting also prepared the ground for Michael Long to engineer the first meeting in seven years between Howard and the Yawuru brothers Michael and Patrick Dodson, who had been two of the government's more vocal critics. After the meeting with Howard, Patrick

Dodson claimed there was 'a lot of fruitful ground for collaboration' between the government and Aboriginal people (Rintoul 2004).

But despite this behind-the-scenes work to re-engage with the Howard government, early optimism was soon replaced with bitterness. By May 2005, Patrick Dodson was again pointed in his criticism, telling the National Reconciliation Planning Workshop that:

> We offered engagement at every level only to be ushered to the corner and told to wait in the queue of rejected petitioners. We were told to continue to dream, but were given no encouragement of any outcome that would give our children any hope of something better for the future. Michael Long showed humility and leadership for us all in walking from Melbourne to Canberra, only to be part of a photo opportunity and then to be politely ushered out the door of the parliament. (Dodson 2005)

Still, many Aboriginal leaders and activists seem reluctant to permanently close any door. Despite his brother's disappointment in 2005, by 2006 Michael (Mick) Dodson was prepared to try again to engage with the Howard government. In July 2006, Mick shared a platform with Howard at a lunch organised by Reconciliation Australia. During his speech, in which he canvassed current government policy to look for gaps and opportunities for Aboriginal people, Dodson told the gathering: 'I'm here today to tell the Prime Minister that I am ready to walk alongside him in taking the next steps towards reconciliation. I believe that you, Prime Minister, are here for the same reason.'

Dodson's speech was moving and powerful, concluding:

> together we will tell the Australian people what we are doing and why we're doing it. Because it is morally right. Because it is economically sound. And because it is in all of our best interests. The Aboriginal culture is something precious we have in Australia. We will respect that culture and we will invest in the success of our First Peoples. The time is right to take this next step. Together. (Dodson 2006b)

Howard's reply to this speech was a crushing disappointment. He responded to none of the content of Dodson's speech, instead focusing on education policy and outlining a number of his government's initiatives in the area of Aboriginal education. According to people who attended the function, there were shocked faces all around the room as the offensiveness of Howard's behaviour began to sink in. In our interview, Mick divulges that Howard had in fact had a copy of Mick's speech for three weeks prior to the event. Still angry, Mick tells me: 'He knew exactly what I was going to say. I had an expectation he would respond to what I had to say. And he didn't. It was like ships passing in the night . . . It's as if I said nothing . . . But this is the standard of disrespect we've come to know with this government. So very, very, very little respect for us.'

Dealing with this lack of respect and continuing to re-engage seem to be part of the struggle for Aboriginal leaders and activists in Australia. But after 2005 these struggles were increasingly invisible to the wider public, as Aboriginal people were without a national voice. Larissa Behrendt (2003) has suggested that what may be seen as 'seemingly contradictory aspirations' among Aboriginal leaders and activists can in fact 'work together to produce a more comprehensive and representative process of representing rights' (2003: 14). This is certainly true but, as in non-Aboriginal politics, differences that are not managed well can blow apart a fragile capacity to articulate an effective political voice on the national stage. In the aftermath of the abolition of ATSIC in 2005, Aboriginal people struggled without a national voice, and these struggles are an important part of the context of this book.

The 1967 referendum, which gave the Commonwealth government the power to legislate with respect to 'the Aboriginal race', also saw the focus of the Aboriginal movement shift to the national arena in an effort to transform the success of the referendum into real policy commitments (Goodall and Huggins 1992: 400). Aboriginal people have had some form of elected national representation almost continuously since the 1970s, first with the National Aboriginal Consultative Committee (NACC), 1973–77, then its replacement, the National Aboriginal Conference (NAC), 1977–85. Two years after the NAC was wound up, the Hawke Labor government announced its intention to develop another representative body, which eventually began operation as the Aboriginal and Torres Strait Islander Commission (ATSIC) in 1990. ATSIC survived until its abolition by the Howard government in 2005. The void left by ATSIC has been of great concern to many Aboriginal people around the country, and meetings and other discussions concerning its replacement have been held since its abolition was announced in 2004. Key meetings included what has been called the Adelaide Leaders'

Meeting in 2004 and a further gathering in Melbourne in 2006. An anonymous spokesperson for the Melbourne meeting summed up the mood of the group by saying:

> We just want things to get better, we're sick of being booted around at the hands of government. We can all start networking with each other and if we have those regional meetings which people will convene as best they can, we'll get a better idea of the things that people want. (quoted in *Koori Mail* 2006)

But despite these efforts at meeting, no new body was created until several months after the announcement of the Northern Territory 'emergency intervention', during which time the urgent need for a national body to be able to represent views to government had become increasingly obvious (as discussed in Chapter 7). In September 2007, a three-day meeting in Alice Springs, attended by around 100 Aboriginal people from all over Australia, saw the hasty formation of the National Aboriginal Alliance, an organisation unlikely to evolve into a sustainable legitimate or representative body.[4]

These efforts to develop a new national body highlight just some of the complexities involved in contemporary Aboriginal politics. Larissa Behrendt sees the lack of a 'clear view' about 'what a representative body should look like or be like' as a major obstacle that is exacerbated by what many Aboriginal people understand as an Indigenous cultural protocol that prioritises consensus decision-making. In our interview, Larissa suggests that if Aboriginal people are going to wait for consensus on the design of a new national body, they are 'going to be waiting for a long time'. Paul Briggs agrees that there are more difficult conversations to be had to determine a sustainable organisational model that can incorporate Aboriginal diversity, but worries that in the meantime Indigenous energies are wasted in 'setting up structures around crisis intervention'. Paul argues that, without a national body, 'We're working off personalities and individual energies that ebb and flow in their capacity to work with Aboriginal people. The only thing really constant in Aboriginal lives is the consistency of our poor relationships with the broader community.'

Controversial Cape York leader Noel Pearson has, at least in the minds of many in the media and general public, filled the void left by ATSIC. In recent years, Pearson has had what many Aboriginal people consider to be a disproportionate and inappropriate degree of influence over the shape and direction of government policy. His arguments about the ills caused by welfare dependency and his assertions about the restoration of social norms in Aboriginal communities by developing individual capacity to engage in the so-called 'real economy' evolved into much of the content of the Howard government's 'new arrangements' (discussed in Chapter 1). However, as Kerry Arabena (2005) has pointed out, Pearson's influence has 'not endeared him to other Indigenous leaders' (2005: 20, 25), many of whom are angry that he seems to speak for country that is not his own (an issue discussed further in Chapter 7). Pearson's dominance in public political discourse, including in delivering 'the Aboriginal view' of the Northern Territory intervention, left many other leaders and activists feeling 'morally bludgeoned' (Gaita 2007: 12). Pearson himself has offered a simplistic assessment of the state of Aboriginal politics, suggesting that, while there is 'at present no effective *rights* leadership and advocacy', he and Warren Mundine, together with an unnamed group of 'many others', are 'carrying the Indigenous *responsibility* leadership' (Pearson 2007a: 58, my emphasis).

As will be evident throughout this book, Pearson has become a controversial and increasingly reviled figure among other Aboriginal leaders and activists. One reason he generates such hostility among his peers is his apparent disregard for the 'Janus-faced' dynamic of contemporary Aboriginal politics. Tim Rowse (1993) has noted the tendency to speak of Aboriginal politics as though Aboriginal people's most important political relationships were with the state rather than with each other. Rowse instead suggests the need for Aboriginal political leaders and activists to engage in a politics which 'faces two ways'—that is, to engage with both the political mainstream and with each other (Rowse 1993: 66–7). One reason Pearson is criticised by other Aboriginal leaders and activists is because his primary political focus is non-Aboriginal politicians in Canberra.[5] In contrast, this book looks the other way in that it is more concerned with the dynamics *between* Aboriginal leaders and activists.

What's a white woman doing writing about our mob?

In researching this book, I was frequently asked this question by Aboriginal people curious to know why I was sticking my nose into their business. The answer I usually gave involved telling my own story of a typical white Australian upbringing. I lived in a white, middle-class suburb and had white, middle-class friends. Although there may well have been some Aboriginal children in my primary school, I do not recall them. I remember the grainy black and white films of semi-naked Aboriginal people hunting and gathering in the desert as the entirety of my education about the way Aboriginal people lived before Captain Cook 'discovered' Australia. I am sure many white readers will recall childhoods similar to this.

It was not until my first job in the welfare sector, as a youth worker in the inner-Sydney suburb of Waterloo, that I really began to come to grips with what it meant to be Aboriginal in contemporary Australia. The vast majority of the young people who visited the centre I worked in were Aboriginal. They were feisty, challenging, funny, rude, and a whole lot of fun to be around. But being around them was also distressing on several levels. First, I was struck by the fact that these kids simply did not enjoy the civil liberties that I had enjoyed as a teenager. Almost every night after leaving the youth centre, they would be stopped by police, harassed and taunted, and often arrested and charged with what was widely known as 'the trifecta'.[6] Second, their lifestyles—and the amount of damage they inflicted on themselves and each other through alcohol and other substance abuse, unprotected sexual activity, and violence— were disturbing to observe.

Finally, I was also distressed by my own ignorance. It seems shocking to write this now, but at the time I had just not ever really contemplated the impact of our colonial history on the people most affected. As a twenty-year-old, the 200 years since European arrival seemed like ancient history. But I can vividly remember the conversation where all that changed: I was talking to a young person about their family and they mentioned that both of their parents had been brought up in an institution. I had a sudden—if belated—realisation that I was only one generation away from the time when Aboriginal children were removed from their families. I realised I knew almost nothing about this history and started to read everything I could get my hands on. But like many white 'do-gooders' before me, my response to this growing awareness was a paralysing guilt. The more I learned about Australia's colonial history, the worse I felt. In desperation, I went to speak to an older woman I knew and poured out my guilt to her. (I cringe at this memory now as I think of the burden of guilt that white people are forever taking to Aboriginal people. What are we looking for? Absolution?) To this woman's absolute credit, she did not send me away to get over myself. She quietly put her arm around me and said, 'Don't be guilty, daught, just be really, really angry.'

This was excellent advice indeed. I did get angry, and I have stayed angry for twenty years as I have worked in welfare, gone to university, had children of my own, taught Australian politics and finally learnt enough (I hope) to come back and write a book about black politics. My anger has not diminished in this time. I only hope that through this book it is channelled into something more useful than yet another expression of white guilt.

I also take seriously the message I have heard from innumerable Aboriginal people over the years: that they are tired of being asked to educate white people about what it means to be Aboriginal. Jackie Huggins has made this point convincingly:

> The constant demands placed on Aboriginal people to be educators is tiring. Surely it is time for non-Aboriginal people to begin their journey of discovery by themselves. It is too much to be expecting Aboriginal women to be continually explaining their oppression—as if somehow it is their fault and they have to talk and write their way out if it. And do others really listen to their pleas? (Huggins 1998: x)

The paralysis of white guilt can often paralyse the inquirer such that they feel unable to read and think for themselves, a feeling that can seemingly only be alleviated through asking Aboriginal people, 'What can I do? How can I help?' A glance at this book's bibliography will reveal the tip of the iceberg of writing by Aboriginal and non-Aboriginal writers about Aboriginal history, politics and culture. This book is a contribution to an already rich field in which non-Aboriginal people are surely capable of helping ourselves to greater understanding rather than draining the time and resources of already stretched Aboriginal leaders and activists.

The urgency of understanding

No Australian government has ever addressed the complexity of Aboriginal political culture. From the earliest encounters, Aboriginal people have been met with a range of simplistic responses, which have variously attempted to obliterate or assimilate them. When it at last became clear that Aboriginal people were not going anywhere—as decade after decade of Aboriginal protest, resistance and persistence have shown—the damage had been done. Since then, successive governments have looked for the 'silver bullet'—the quick-fix solution to the most complex issues. Underspending and neglect have been chronic, policies and programs have been weak and ineffective, Aboriginal interests have taken a back seat to mining and pastoral concerns, Aboriginal leadership has rarely been supported or legitimated, and the resulting cycle of decline has continued virtually unchecked.

Is Australia a particularly simplistic nation? Certainly it seems that our incapacity to grasp both the historical reality and the modern-day complexity of Aboriginal life and political culture puts us out of step with other decolonising settler-states. We have, according to Stuart Bradfield, 'an enduring mindset that is unusually suspicious of Indigenous rights' (2004: 168). Australian national identity is characterised by a blind insistence that we are 'one nation', that we should in all meaningful ways be monocultural with only the most minimal tolerance of difference to the fantasised white, Christian majority. For Aboriginal people, this response constitutes what Larissa Behrendt describes as 'psychological *terra nullius*', a worldview that continues to deny the presence, let alone the complexity, of Aboriginal people and political culture.

Much about contemporary Aboriginal life is described in terms of disadvantage and dysfunction. While this is far from the totality of Aboriginal lives, it is also true to argue, as Michael Dillon does, that Aboriginal disadvantage in Australia 'remains a weeping sore on the body politic' (Dillon 2007: 227). There really is no acceptable explanation for the life circumstances endured by many Aboriginal people in Australia. For a wealthy, developed country, it is our greatest shame that the first inhabitants, who should by rights hold a special place in contemporary society, instead are subject to outcomes including shorter life expectancy (by seventeen years), higher death rates, higher rates of infant mortality, higher rates of incarceration, higher rates of substance abuse, poor educational attainment, and high levels of individual and community poverty.

Given this, it is a deep irony that the governments that have come closest to understanding the underlying issues germane to perpetuating Aboriginal disadvantage have not matched their rhetoric with the necessary commitment of resources. Michael Morrissey has made this point in relation to the Hawke–Keating Labor governments (1983–96), a period during which the gap between Aboriginal and non-Aboriginal health, income, incarceration, employment and education actually widened despite the 'sweeping rhetoric of reconciliation, atonement and social justice' (Morrissey 2006: 348). It is a further irony that the Howard goverment's 'intervention' into Northern Territory Aboriginal communities came with a more substantial investment of resources than had been seen in the area of Indigenous affairs for some time, but in a context where the underlying policy settings were completely at odds with Aboriginal aspirations.

Certainly the term of the Howard government brought new challenges for Aboriginal people that are likely to leave a long legacy. As Klynton Wanganeen pointed out in our interview, during this period Aboriginal people had to 'come to terms with the fact that they have no one they can go to for support . . . They don't have the media, the media will decry anything that they say. They have no ATSIC. If they think they can go to NIC, they'll be told to nick off because the NIC has got no power to do anything. They're just puppets.'

Enduring this period was difficult and disheartening—although, as Geoff Scott suggests, there is a mistrust of government felt by many Aboriginal people that goes beyond the political persuasion of the government of the day. Years of feeling 'done over' by government are exhausting and depressing. In our interview, Dr Marika expressed a sentiment I heard from many Aboriginal people about the way they perceive they are treated by government: 'They ignore everything about us as a people, human beings. To them we're nothing really, they don't care who we are. The laws they dictate to us make us feel oppressed and down. I hate this you know, the way that they do this. They deliberately do that to belittle us, to make us feel stupid.'

Such feelings of despair have a long history, and it is crucial that the impact of invasion and post-contact history on Aboriginal life is understood, accepted and addressed. It is not possible to simply take a forward-looking approach that neither acknowledges past hurts nor addresses the continuing social problems produced by those hurts. This is not to propose what Peter Sutton has described as a 'sustaining fiction'—that is, the view that 'all Indigenous disadvantage has been caused by external impacts alone'. Indeed, this book is premised on the need to understand the complex causes of contemporary problems in Aboriginal communities, although I maintain that Australia's colonial history is a significant component of this causality. Still, it is worth considering the merits of Sutton's argument when he suggests that silence about some of these elements of complexity, that have been 'promoted and policed by both the Left and a number of Indigenous activists', has allowed a vacuum in public debate to develop, a vacuum that in recent years has been filled 'by those pursuing the agendas of the Right' (Sutton 2001: 128).

It would be far more effective if this void were filled by a deeper understanding of the diverse experiences of Aboriginal life that contribute to Aboriginal political culture. As Colleen Hayward suggests, understanding this complexity will 'make for a more rounded argument . . . The more that we can harness the diversity of views, the more likely we are to be able to move forward with a solution that really is a solution, instead of only meeting the needs of a few rather than the many.'

Coming to grips with this diversity and the challenges it poses may also help Aboriginal leaders and activists work together more effectively. In a 2007 speech, Mick Dodson highlighted the continuing threats to Aboriginal culture and survival, calling for 'strong leadership, from men and women, young and old, city and country, all of us together':

My argument is that we're getting slaughtered by the colonial imperative to steal our land, to strip our culture, and to demoralise us as peoples and nations. What I think I'm on about is self defence—we must defend our identity and our inheritance in the land and sea. And as we resist—and we have always resisted in many different ways—I say that we must pull together as nations, forever connected to the land and fortified by our law and culture, to make decisions for ourselves in determining our future. (Dodson 2007: 5)

What the late political philosopher Iris Marion Young called the 'postcolonial project' entails a commitment to confronting the legacies of colonialism in all their guises as an essential task in creating a more just society (Young 2000: 237). My hope is that this book is a small contribution to this project, that it will facilitate a deeper understanding of what must happen to confront the colonial legacy in Australia. The starting point must be to listen to and to understand Aboriginal voices talking about the complexity of their political culture. Because it is only if we understand that we can support Aboriginal people to determine their own futures.

A HISTORY OF POLICY FAILURE

In policy terms, Aboriginal people in Australia have rarely been seen as anything other than a 'problem to be solved'. Rather than engaging with Aboriginal people and working in meaningful partnership with them, successive Australian governments have looked for a solution to 'the Aboriginal problem'. Racialised views of Aboriginal competence have allowed for often-Draconian policy to be justified as being 'for their own good'. These points were made by Patrick Dodson in a lecture in 2000, where he argued that for all governments, at all stages in Australia's post-invasion history, policy has been about 'their solutions to us as the problem':

> The problem of our being here; the problem of our disposal; the problem of our assimilation; and the problem of having us appreciative of all that governments have done 'for our own good'. (Dodson 2000: 13)

The result of this view has been continual and unambiguous policy failure. Policy programs from protection, assimilation, self-determination and, most recently, intervention have all been delivered with a measure of simplicity that does not match the complexity of Aboriginal political culture. Despite (sometimes) good intentions, none of these policies has actually improved Aboriginal lives, and in many instances they have made them infinitely worse. Indeed, as Tristan Ray, the coordinator of the Central Australian Youth Link-Up Service, has suggested in response to the 2007 Northern Territory 'intervention', if the current situation in Aboriginal communities in the Territory is to be described as a national emergency, it is an emergency 'created in part by decades of inconsistent, incompetent and reactive government policy' (Ray 2007: 195).

Indigenous affairs is acknowledged by experts as 'an extraordinarily complex policy domain'. Policy that is simplistic or doctrinaire, or that ignores the diversity of Aboriginal lives and aspirations, is unlikely to succeed by any measure (Altman 2005: 36). But as anthropologist Gaynor McDonald (2001) has suggested, one problem with much policy in the Indigenous Affairs portfolio has been that it is designed to turn Aboriginal people into 'a certain kind of Australian citizen'. This intention can often sit uneasily with aspects of Aboriginal identity, social life, kin relationships and community authority structures (2001: 2). There is an implicit suggestion in much contemporary policy and public debate that Aboriginal culture is '*in itself* pathogenic', with the further implication that if Aboriginal people could just be more like white people their problems would be resolved (Morrissey 2006: 352). The reality, however, is that many of the challenges facing Aboriginal people in their interactions with government and, more significantly, in the management of their own lives, derive from a complex combination of 'cultural persistence' and the legacy of colonisation (Sutton 2001: 149). These issues go to the heart of the argument in this book—that is, that the bulk of Indigenous Affairs policy has simply failed to respond to the complexity of Aboriginal political culture.

It is not true to suggest that government has no awareness of these areas of complexity. Some, if not all, of the tensions that will be explored in the following chapters have been observed over time in a range of documents, including government reports. For example, in 1988 the then Department of Aboriginal Affairs (DAA) made a submission to the House of Representatives Standing Committee on Aboriginal Affairs in which it discussed 'the federal government's philosophical and practical difficulties in delivering services to Aboriginal people while simultaneously affirming Aboriginal self-determination'—in other words, it had identified the complexities involved in claims for both sovereignty and citizenship. The DAA report also noted that the economic circumstances in many Aboriginal communities made people in those communities dependent on government funding, thereby leaving DAA 'in the unhappy situation of sometimes being seen to limit Aboriginal autonomy', a clear articulation of the complexities of autonomy and dependency. The submission further commented that 'community development sometimes undermined the preservation of traditional cultural patterns'—the tension considered here in Chapter 4, examining tradition and development (all quotes contained in Rowse 1992: 1–2). Clearly there is some knowledge of these tensions that have informed the policy process over time, and yet . . .? Who knows where this knowledge has gone or how it has influenced policy development today. It is certainly little in evidence.

This chapter offers a brief overview of the history of Indigenous Affairs policy, with a focus on the period since the election of the Howard Coalition government in 1996. It would be patently impossible to attempt a comprehensive history of Indigenous Affairs policy here. As this book is concerned with the broad sweep of Aboriginal political culture, it cannot also take into account the differences in policy across Australia's states and territories over the last 220 years. What is relevant here, however, is the frequency with which Indigenous Affairs policy has changed direction, often quite dramatically, in a relatively short period of time. The rapidity of these changes has left Aboriginal people in turmoil. In our interview, Muriel Bamblett described this experience as like being 'caught in a big washing machine . . . You've got change all the time; every time we just get used to something you move to another cycle and the cycle keeps changing and we keep moving and we haven't got used to the last cycle before we're moving on to the next cycle.'

In our interview, Tom Calma discussed at some length the history of failed government policy in this regard. Unfortunately, Tom points out, 'government has never maintained a policy long enough to be able to let any of this stuff bed down':

> The moment something starts, there's a change of government or there's a change of government policy, which then undermines whatever advancement has been happening. So we now have a situation where the government is able to say, 'Well, look, we've tried a whole lot of things and they've failed.' They blame it on the Aboriginal people.

Yet, despite this cycle of blame—a cycle that began with the earliest confrontations between colonisers and original inhabitants—Aboriginal people have continued to struggle for the preservation of their autonomy and dignity, and for control over their own lives.

From dispossession to self-determination

Colonisation in Australia has followed a similar pattern to that in countries such as Canada, New Zealand and the United States. In this pattern, relations between the colonising force and Indigenous peoples have fallen into three distinct periods. Judy Atkinson describes these periods as:

- invasion and frontier violence;
- the intercession of well-meaning but often ethnocentric and paternalistic philanthropic and religious groups; and
- the reassessment of government responsibility to Indigenous needs around the 1930s to 1960s that continues to the present day.

This book is focused primarily on this last period, which Atkinson suggests has been just as damaging as the earlier periods as it has allowed the increasing intrusion of the state into Aboriginal lives, 'creating dependencies and dysfunctions that have re-traumatised Indigenous peoples' (Atkinson 2002: 58).

The early frontier history of the British colonisation of this land has been well documented (see, for example, Reynolds 1982; Elder 2003). This was a violent time that saw Aboriginal people dispossessed of their land, often through armed conflict. The conflict spread across the continent from the southeast, bringing disease and alcohol along with massacres and sexual violence, as colonial outposts were established in what are now Australia's states and territories. In short, during the early decades following white invasion, the political response to the 'native problem' was to contain and dispossess Aboriginal people in order to access land for farming. Despite orders that the establishment of penal colonies take place with the consent of the Indigenous inhabitants, early British arrivals took the attitude that the continent of Australia was *terra nullius* (although this term was not used until much later)[1] and simply took over. It is clear from historical accounts that the invaders' views of the original inhabitants ranged from at best curiosity to at worst outright hostility. The racialised thinking of the time produced a general view of Aboriginal people as 'savages', which was used to justify their brutal treatment.

4

By the time of Federation in 1901, just over 100 years later, the general policy framework had moved towards what became known as 'protection'. Violent conflicts over land had for the most part given way to the creation of reserves and missions on which Aboriginal people were kept separate from white society but accorded no rights to the land on which they were contained (Burgmann 2003: 70). Between 1901 and 1946, all Australian states passed legislation that would control Aboriginal people's independence of movement, marriage, employment and association, and that authorised the removal of Aboriginal children from their families. Protection policies assumed that Aboriginal people were merely an ancient remnant who would inevitably die out. During this period, Aboriginal people were 'protected' in poorly paid or unpaid service, often never even seeing the meagre wages they earned (Brennan et al. 2005: 58–9). As it became evident that Aboriginal people were not dying out, however, national policy changed again, and by 1951 the state had adopted a policy of 'assimilation'.[2] The underlying assumption this time was that, rather than dying out, Aboriginal people would be absorbed into the white population to live like other Australian citizens. Ostensibly, assimilation was a commitment by the state to the 'advancement' of Aboriginal people, rather than a view of their inevitable demise (Morgan 2006a: 15). It was soon clear, however, that 'advancement' was really code for 'more white, less black'. Assimilation policy was also riven by internally conflicting ideas, as Frances Peters-Little (2000) has noted, in that Aboriginal people were often expected to assimilate into white society while still being subjected to segregation laws that restricted them to reserves and missions (2000: 4).

Despite the extraordinary challenges they faced during these discriminatory policy eras, a large percentage of Aboriginal people maintained a degree of independence from the state and prioritised their continuing connections to land and kin (Brennan et al. 2005: 59). Resistance to colonial authority shifted focus during this period, evolving from armed struggle to political struggle as Aboriginal people began to demand their entitlements from the state. New political struggles over land rights began to emerge in the 1960s: 1963 saw the Yolngu bark petitions sent to Canberra in protest over the mining of their land on the Gove peninsula, and 1966 witnessed the Gurindji walk-off from the Wave Hill station. In subsequent years, demands for land rights were fought out in the courts and on the streets, eventually bringing change—for example, through the *Aboriginal Land Rights Act (Northern Territory)* 1976. As a result of these struggles, there are now land rights regimes around the country, bringing some degree of certainty that governments and developers can 'no longer push Aboriginal people off their land to build or mine or run cattle' (Tilmouth 1998: xi). The Central and Northern Land Councils claim that the Northern Territory Act gave Aboriginal people some 'breathing space' to 'develop our land in a way that we choose and at a pace that we choose . . . to help us achieve economic security for the future' (Central and Northern Land Councils 1994: 8). However, legislating for land rights has also had some unintended consequences for Aboriginal people, not least the masking of economic marginalisation and dependency on many small outstations through the primary focus on their political and cultural significance. It was assumed that land restoration would lead to economic development, despite the fact that returned land is generally remote, arid and of low commercial value (Altman et al. 2005: 3).

The issue of land rights underscores the competing voices to which governments must listen in the formulation of policy. The mining and pastoral industries are clearly significant stakeholders in issues of land use and ownership, and have been influential—often to the disadvantage of Aboriginal people—in this domain. Indeed, before the 1992 *Mabo* decision (discussed in Chapters 3 and 7), Australian governments engaged in land and resource management processes as if Aboriginal people had not existed or held any rights before the arrival of the British (Howitt 2001: 202, 203). The mining industry opposed the proposed *Native Title Act* during 1993 negotiations, first seeking to prevent the introduction of the Act at all, and later lobbying the Commonwealth government for amendments on the grounds that the proposed Act was 'unworkable and an impediment to development' (Howlett 2006: 13). Ongoing concerns relate to the social impact of mining crews on Aboriginal communities (Yu in KALACC 2006: 86), which has seen 'small communities overturned by alcohol troubles or the presence of too many white blokes' (Pitjantjatjara letter quoted in Lippmann 1981: 62).[3]

But in the 1970s there was growing optimism among Aboriginal leaders and activists that the Australian state was at last beginning to recognise their status as first nations peoples and to make policy accordingly. In 1972 the Whitlam government introduced the formal policy of self-determination, which was endorsed and further developed by the successor Fraser government. Under Hawke and Keating, there was talk of a treaty (which never eventuated), Native Title became enshrined

6

in legislation (although the promised social justice package component was never developed), the creation of ATSIC meant that Aboriginal people had elected representation for the first time, and the official decade of reconciliation was initiated. By the mid-1990s, however, it was becoming increasingly clear that these changing policy settings were neither improving the quality of, nor lengthening, Aboriginal lives. Defence of existing policies was increasingly half-hearted, and growing despondency meant there was little energy available to develop new policies. This situation provided an opportune moment for the election of a new government, one that would transform the Indigenous Affairs landscape with an aggressive rejection of all policy that accepted current responsibility for past policy failure (Gaita 2007: 10). The Howard government came to power, as Peter Jull has suggested, with some powerful *rhetoric* that it mistook for a *policy* (2005: 1).

The Howard years
Almost as soon as John Howard became prime minister in March 1996, it was clear that he intended to undo much that he had inherited in the Indigenous Affairs portfolio. The first target in the new government's sights was ATSIC, created in 1989 to recognise the unique place of Indigenous peoples in Australian history and contemporary society, and to address both historical disadvantage and ongoing discrimination (Jonas and Dick 2004: 8). Announcing an audit of ATSIC was the first statement made by the new government once in office. ATSIC survived on that occasion, but in 2002 the Howard government set up another review. The review team—consisting of former Liberal MP John Hannaford, Former Labor MP Bob Collins and Indigenous academic and activist Jackie Huggins—released its final report, *In the Hands of the Regions*, in November 2003, making recommendations for structural change to the organisation but not recommending that ATSIC be abolished. Despite this, in 2004 the government followed the lead of the then Opposition leader, Mark Latham, in announcing that it would abolish ATSIC after the upcoming federal election, suggesting that the decision was in accordance with the findings of the review.

ATSIC was blamed for lack of progress in areas where it had never had any program responsibility, and this supposed failure was in turn used to explain the poor living conditions and short life expectancies of many Indigenous people. This political sleight of hand caused outrage

7

among Aboriginal people. As Bill Jonas and Darren Dick have argued: 'It is one thing to suggest that ATSIC could perform its obligations to Indigenous peoples better; it is another thing entirely to suggest that there should not be a national representative body through which Indigenous people can participate in government decision making about their lives.' (Jonas and Dick 2004: 14)

Howard claimed that Aboriginal people supported the decision to abolish ATSIC since they 'felt an absolute disconnect' with the organisation since 'ATSIC was not serving them well' (Howard and Vanstone 2004). This assessment only tells a part of the story, as there was much in the structure and functioning of ATSIC that was always supported by Aboriginal people. It is certainly the case that problems with some members of the senior leadership, including allegations of fraud and other criminal charges, were debilitating for the organisation and damaging to its reputation. Nevertheless, the point has frequently been made that it was inappropriate to do away with a whole level of governance due to the alleged corruption of a small number of representatives. And while Howard was correct in saying that many Aboriginal people were unhappy with ATSIC, it is also true that his decision to abolish the organisation has done much to galvanise support for it in the years since its demise, as Aboriginal people faced a future with no national representation. Indeed, Howard caused great offence by determining that Aboriginal people should no longer be represented through separate institutions. At the media conference announcing ATSIC's abolition, he claimed that: 'the experiment in separate representation, elected representation, for Indigenous people, has been a failure. We will not replace ATSIC with an alternative body.' (Howard and Vanstone 2004)

The description of ATSIC as an 'experiment' underscored the Howard government's lack of commitment to the idea of self-determination. As Larissa Behrendt (2004) has argued:

ATSIC was not just an experiment in public administration. It was an attempt to provide a representative voice to Indigenous people in the development of policy and program delivery. One of its real strengths was that it provided a voice—an independent voice—at the national level . . . In areas such as native title, Australia's obligations under international human rights conventions and the protection of rights within the Australian legal system,

Indigenous people had a view that conflicted with the federal government's. That view was often voiced by ATSIC. (2004: 3)

ATSIC's apparent replacement, the handpicked National Indigenous Council (NIC), was criticised for being both undemocratic (Rowse 2005: 2) and unrepresentative. But although the loss of ATSIC made Aboriginal political struggle more difficult, it did not entirely prevent leaders and activists from having a voice. In our interview, William Tilmouth of Tangentyere Council expressed the view that although the Howard government had 'deliberately chopped off the head of Indigenous Affairs', this was 'not going to stop people from wanting to talk up'.

The abolition of ATSIC also facilitated the introduction of other changes in Indigenous affairs. Dubbed the 'New Mainstreaming', ATSIC's twenty-one programs were divided between six existing federal agencies with new Indigenous Coordination Centres (ICCs) established to manage the transition. Further complicating this transition was the introduction of the new policy of Shared Responsibility Agreements, another part of what the government dubbed a 'quiet revolution' in Indigenous policy (Vanstone 2005b: 1). Shared Responsibility Agreements (SRAs) entail a community making certain commitments towards achieving their nominated goal and the government, in turn, making commitments of its own—usually the provision of services or funding. Following a number of SRAs initiated under the COAG trials,[4] the federal government announced the wider introduction of SRAs in June 2004. The best-known example of an SRA pertained to the tiny community of Mulan (population 150) on the edge of Lake Gregory in Western Australia. In an effort to reduce the incidence of trachoma,[5] the community signed an agreement in which, among other things, it promised to ensure that children showered daily and washed their faces twice daily in return for the federal government's provision of $172 260 for the installation of fuel bowsers.[6] It was later revealed that the Mulan school had already begun a face-washing program and that rates of trachoma had fallen from 90 to 16 per cent of children in the town at the time the SRA was signed. Nonetheless, the government relied upon the old statistics to justify the agreement (McCausland 2005a).

SRAs such as the one in Mulan have been criticised extensively. Rather than the 'grass-roots' initiatives that the Howard government purported them to be, SRAs proved to be quite paternalistic, as the provision of services became dependent on behavioural change (McCausland 2005a). SRAs entailed a shift away from government responsibility for service provision such that failures in areas such as Indigenous health could be seen as the fault of Aboriginal people who had perhaps failed to 'live up to the goodness of their governments' (Rowse 2005: 3–6). And despite government claims that the new arrangements were all about 'main-streaming' Indigenous policy and service provision, the fact that SRAs applied only to Indigenous communities meant the agreements could not be considered mainstream at all. As Michael Morrissey has argued: 'the rhetoric of shared responsibility provides many opportunities for blaming the appalling state of many remote Aboriginal settlements on the people who live in them, and it also casts the government in the role of a benevolent patriarch engaged in community-based behaviour modification' (Morrissey 2006: 352).

But 'new arrangements' such as SRAs were entirely consistent with the Howard government's approach to Indigenous Affairs from early in its tenure. In 1996 the High Court ruled in the *Wik* decision[7] and Howard was quick to respond, developing his highly controversial 'Ten-point Plan' to provide 'certainty' to pastoralists that eventually became enshrined in the *Native Title Act Amendment Act* 1998. Many Aboriginal people saw the Ten-point Plan as an 'attack' on hard-won native title rights and a 'sell-out of their interests' (Sanders 2005b: 153). Mick Dodson believes that the consequences of Howard's response to *Wik* have been far reaching. He suggests that where the government could have used the *Wik* decision to 'draw Australia together . . . educating the nation in a calm and factual way', it instead behaved 'in the style of a colonial power' and 'repudiated any responsibility for land justice' in this country (Dodson 2004: 123–6). In keeping with this approach, Howard moved to further wind back Aboriginal rights in land with his 2006 amendments to the *Aboriginal Land Rights (Northern Territory) Act* 1976. As with the native title amendments, this policy was developed despite little consultation with Aboriginal people.

Howard also radically undermined the reconciliation process, which had originally been developed out of a recommendation in the Royal Commission into Aboriginal Deaths in Custody Report (RCIADIC 1991). The then Labor government, under Prime Minister Bob Hawke, had initiated the formal process through the creation of the Council for Aboriginal Reconciliation (CAR) and set out the timeline for the process, which would conclude in 2001. Although he maintained that he strongly supported the reconciliation process, Howard differentiated his version of reconciliation from previous ways of thinking by emphasising the need to 'adopt practical measures' to address Indigenous disadvantage (Howard 2000). This view was underscored with the handing over of the Final Report of the Council on Aboriginal Reconciliation (including its Declaration Towards Reconciliation) to federal parliament in December 2000. Both the report and the declaration met with opposition from the government, leading them to publish an alternative version (Sanders 2005b: 156). When the then chair of ATSIC used Corroboree 2000 to again call for a treaty, Howard responded by arguing that 'an undivided nation does not make a treaty with itself' (quoted in Sanders 2005b: 156).

Reconciliation under the banner of practicality was primarily aimed at reducing material disadvantage in Indigenous communities—hardly a new approach, given that it had been central to Indigenous policy in all governments since the 1970s. In reality, what differentiated Howard's version of reconciliation was his hostility to the rights-based approach that had been embraced by the majority of Aboriginal leaders and activists and taken up by the grass-roots movement for reconciliation. But despite compelling arguments pointing to the 'false dichotomy' between practical and symbolic reconciliation, Howard remained committed to his view that there was a 'direct tradeoff' between these two approaches (Altman 2005: 39). While many acknowledge that practical outcomes are required, they point out that it is also the job of the prime minister to address the outstanding 'symbolic' issues of sovereignty and self-determination between Indigenous peoples and the state (Dodson 2004: 135–6). Howard's rejection of this role, as former Governor-General Sir William Deane has observed, meant that relations between Aboriginal people and the Commonwealth government 'significantly deteriorated' (quoted in Byrne 2005).

Nothing did more to exacerbate these problems than the Howard government's response to the *Bringing Them Home* report from the National Inquiry into the Separation of Aboriginal and Torres Strait Islander Children from Their Families. The report, tabled in federal parliament on 26 May 1997, concluded that 'between one in three and one in ten Indigenous children were forcibly removed from their families and communities in the period from approximately 1910 until 1970' (HREOC 1997: 36–7). Further, it recommended that all Australian governments should officially and publicly apologise to the 'stolen generation'[8] for the harms done by past policies. The Howard government both disagreed with the figures in the report and rejected the idea of a government apology, responding with a 'defensive, mean-spirited suspicion' (Manne 2001a: 38). Howard later argued that many Indigenous children 'were taken in circumstances where under today's laws they would be regarded as being properly and lawfully taken from their families in the interests of their own protection' (Parliamentary Debate, 2000: 15008). The government also consistently refused to give an official apology on behalf of the Australian parliament to members of the stolen generations. Even during parliamentary debate on the government's own Motion of Reconciliation, Howard argued that: 'The Australian people do not want to embroil themselves in an exercise of shame and guilt'. (Parliamentary Debate 1999: 9205) As Robert Manne has observed, the arguments that Howard and his then minister John Herron used to 'deconstruct' the idea of the stolen generations were 'pedantic and tactless in almost equal measure' (2001b: 83). Indeed, in Mick Dodson's view, nothing that Howard did during his decade in office compares with the 'insensitivity, lack of imaginative depth or simple heart' displayed in his reaction to the *Bringing Them Home* report (2004: 130).

In sum, many Aboriginal leaders and activists have described the tenure of the Howard government as a 'living nightmare' (Graham 2007a), during which many of the hard won rights that were achieved in political struggle over the previous thirty years seemed to slip from their grasp. By 2007, Aboriginal people were angry and despondent in equal measure, and were left to confront an unapologetic and paternalistic government without a national voice. In Sam Jeffries' view, Aboriginal people had seen 'a return to bureaucratic control over our lives' a distressing reminder of 'the bad old days' (Jeffries 2007: 23). It was in this climate that the Howard government launched its final assault on Indigenous Affairs policy: the broad-reaching 'emergency intervention' into Aboriginal communities in the Northern Territory.

The Northern Territory 'intervention'
On 21 June 2007, John Howard announced an 'emergency intervention' into Aboriginal communities in the Northern Territory.

The announcement was a response to the *Ampe Akelyernemane Meke Mekarle 'Little Children are Sacred'* report released six weeks earlier by the Northern Territory Board of Inquiry into the Protection of Aboriginal Children from Sexual Abuse (Wild and Anderson 2007). This report had itself been commissioned by the Northern Territory government in response to allegations of rampant abuse made by the Alice Springs Crown Prosecutor, Nanette Rogers, on ABC Television in 2006 (ABC 2006), and joined a growing list of reports highlighting the same problem in other parts of Australia (see NSW Aboriginal Child Sexual Assault Taskforce 2006; Gordon et al. 2002). The *Little Children are Sacred* report confirmed what many Aboriginal people had been saying for years: that many of their communities had broken down to the point that normally unacceptable behaviour, including violence, suicide, alcohol and other substance abuse, and the abuse of children, had become a way of life. Until this report, however, pleas for help had fallen on deaf ears. As Larissa Behrendt has suggested, this was 'the national emergency that was sitting neglected for over thirty years' (Behrendt 2007a: 15).

That all changed when Howard and his Indigenous Affairs minister, Mal Brough, announced their 'emergency response' to the report, a response that would contain governmental interventions unmatched by anything introduced in the previous forty years (Hinkson 2007: 1). To tackle the issue of child sexual abuse, the Howard government undertook to apply a range of 'emergency' measures to all people resident in remote Aboriginal communities in the Northern Territory. Specifically, it would:

- introduce widespread alcohol restrictions on Northern Territory Aboriginal land;
- introduce welfare reforms to stem the flow of cash going toward substance abuse and to ensure funds for child welfare were used for that purpose;
- enforce school attendance by linking income support and family assistance payments to school attendance for all people living on Aboriginal land and providing meals for children at parents' cost;
- introduce compulsory health checks for all Aboriginal children to identify and treat health problems and any effects of abuse;

13

- acquire townships prescribed by the Commonwealth government through five-year leases, including payment of 'just terms' compensation;
- increase policing levels in prescribed communities, including through secondments from state and territory jurisdictions;
- scrap the permit system for common areas, road corridors and airstrips for prescribed communities;
- marshall local workforces through Work for the Dole to undertake ground clean-up and repair of communities;
- improve housing and reform community living arrangements, including the introduction of market-based rents and normal tenancy arrangements;
- ban the possession of X-rated pornography and introduce audits of all publicly funded computers to identify illegal material; and
- appoint managers of all government business in prescribed communities (Brough 2007).

The intervention was to commence immediately, drawing on police and army personnel and a volunteer workforce of doctors and other professionals. The three Bills comprising the complex 500-page emergency response legislation were introduced to the House of Representatives on 7 August and passed that same day with bipartisan support. Following a hastily convened one-day Senate inquiry on 10 August, the legislation passed in the Upper House on 17 August without amendment.[9] The passage of the legislation required the suspension of the *Racial Discrimination Act* 1975 by prescribing the intervention as falling under the 'special measures' provision of the Act. A further change, which predated the intervention but was part of the emergency response, was the abolition of the Community Development Employment Program (CDEP), set to be phased out by 30 June 2008 with CDEP jobs replaced with 'real jobs' or participants moved on to mainstream Work for the Dole arrangements. The abolition of CDEP (discussed further in Chapter 4) was alleged to be necessary in order to create a single welfare system to streamline the quarantining of welfare payments (Hinkson 2007: 1–5).

Initial responses to the intervention emphasised the relief that many Aboriginal people felt that the issue of child sexual abuse and community decline more generally were at last on the government radar. The large budget attached to the program was also welcomed. However, this early

14

optimism soon turned to anger as many Aboriginal leaders and activists realised the extent of the intervention. In our interview, Mick Dodson described the new policy as 'heavy handed, ill thought out, paternalistic and Draconian', and asked: 'Why do you keep doing this? What's the problem with you people that you always feel you have to come in and fix things rather than support us to fix the things?' Mick, like many others, was angered by the claiming of the moral high ground that meant critics were told, in his words: 'You're a paedophile because you don't want something done about child sexual abuse. Well, of course we do, but we don't think sending troops in and a squad of doctors to examine people are going to fix the problem.'

Rex Wild and Patricia Anderson, the authors of the *Little Children are Sacred* report, were devastated that their report had been used to justify the intervention. They told the audience at the 2007 Garma Festival at Gulkula in Northeast Arnhem Land that when they saw 'the troops roll in' they felt 'betrayed and disappointed, hurt and angry and pretty pissed off at the same time'. Anderson was concerned that, despite government claims the intervention was a response to their report, there was 'not a single action that . . . corresponds with a single recommendation . . . There is no relationship between this emergency protection and what's in our report.' (quoted in Ravens 2007: 3) A resolution signed by more that 400 participants at the Garma festival argued that: 'The government does not have to destabilise communal rights to land to effectively address sexual abuse, social dysfunction or poverty.' (quoted in *Koori Mail* 2007c)

In the weeks following the announcement of the intervention, Aboriginal leaders and activists organised quickly. On 28 June, Arrernte and Guudanji woman Pat Turner, former CEO of ATSIC, spoke on behalf of an alliance of Aboriginal organisations in accusing the government of 'using child sexual abuse as the Trojan horse to resume total control of our lands', and declared the intervention 'totally unworkable'. On 10 July the Combined Aboriginal Organisations of the Northern Territory (CAO) released a comprehensive response complete with their proposals for redesigning the intervention to become a five-year development plan (CAO 2007). These proposals were ignored by the government. Around Australia, Aboriginal leaders and activists expressed their anger and concern. Former Northern Territory MLA John Ah Kit, representing a group of Northern Territory Indigenous leaders, condemned the government for rushing the legislation through, and claimed that the legislation was 'the beginning of the end of Aboriginal culture' and would 'go down in history as one of the bleakest days in the history of the country' (quoted in ABC 2007g). Muriel Bamblett pointed out that the words 'child' or 'children' did not appear even once in the legislation, and argued passionately that:

> This legislation does nothing for children, nothing for Indigenous disadvantage, nothing to actually stop child abuse. It takes control away from Indigenous communities. It allows government bureaucrats to force themselves into our boardrooms. It takes over our land. It takes away our ability to have a say on who can come onto our freehold title land. It places bureaucrats in charge of our lives. And it exempts these and other actions from the *Racial Discrimination Act*, which means it acknowledges that some of its measures may be racially discriminatory. This legislation is an attack on our people. (quoted in *National Indigenous Times* 2007: 16)

David Ross, from the Central Land Council, expressed the view that the intervention would have 'deeply negative consequences for Aboriginal people in remote communities', and argued that it would be 'unconscionable' to support legislation that 'pervades and controls every level of Aboriginal people's lives in the Northern Territory'. Ross suggested that: 'When the army and government business managers are sent in to fix child abuse, one has to wonder at the sheer nonsense associated with the whole exercise.' William Tilmouth (2007g) made the point that the intervention policies were being 'driven by people who do not have to live with the consequences', whereas Aboriginal people were concerned with 'the direct implications for themselves, their families and communities, and for land and culture' (2007: 231). Harry Nelson, a traditional owner from Yuendumu who had been part of a delegation of Aboriginal leaders who went to Canberra to try to stop the passage of the legislation, was distressed at its passing, saying:

> Our dream has been shattered. This is coming from my heart. We can't go home from Canberra and hold our heads up. I've got no answer for my people because the minister wouldn't even meet with us. I feel sad and no good. I fought for my land and they can take away all the houses but they can't take my land. After all these years of fighting for our land and our

freedom, this is where we end up. (quoted in *National Indigenous Times* 2007: 16)

Even those Aboriginal leaders and activists who were broadly supportive of the intervention had some reservations. In the days immediately following the 21 June announcement, Cape York leader Noel Pearson, who had been advising the Howard government on Indigenous welfare, defended the intervention and attacked its critics. He described the negative reaction from many Aboriginal leaders and activists as 'a kind of madness', saying that he was 'just amazed that anybody would put the protection of children secondary to anything else' (ABC 2007a). In his regular column in the *Weekend Australian*, Pearson noted that Brough had telephoned him fifteen minutes before the intervention was announced to explain what the government was going to do. Pearson also outlined his assessment of the intervention strategies:

- The focus on grog and policing is correct, but as well as policing there must be a strategy for building indigenous social and cultural ownership.
- Making welfare payments conditional is correct, but the Howard–Brough plan needs to be amended so responsible behaviour is encouraged. Responsible people shouldn't just be lumped in with irresponsible people.
- The land-related measures are clumsy and ideological, but they are not an attempt at a land grab, and the problems with the land measures are nowhere near as high a priority as action for the welfare of children.
- There is a huge implementation challenge. Based on the performance of the federal and provincial bureaucracies up to now, I am not confident they are up to it. The Council of Australian Governments' trials in the past five years have not delivered meaningful results.

Despite the hint of concern in Pearson's analysis, he concluded that: 'Whatever one thinks of Howard and Brough, their strategy is justified on the basis of the fate of the children.' (Pearson 2007c) Others, such as Warren Mundine and Alison Anderson, agreed and Marcia Langton has since championed the intervention as 'the greatest opportunity we have

17

had to overcome the systemic levels of disadvantage among Aboriginal Australians' (Langton 2008a: 147). As the implementation of the intervention rolled out, there were mixed reports, with some women reporting feeling safer as a result of some of the measures, but others expressing anger at the lack of consultation and the frustrations and additional costs caused by the welfare quarantining measures. Feedback from traditional landowners and community members collated in a briefing paper by the Central Land Council suggested that although people remain supportive of efforts to address child abuse in their communities, they were 'overwhelmingly opposed' to many of the intervention measures and had been upset by the lack of consultation in introducing these changes (CLC 2007). At the same time, Marcia Langton argued that 'those opposed to the intervention are morally and politically wrong' (Langton 2008a: 152). That views of the intervention were so deeply divided in a context where there was little in the way of hard evidence to support either point of view should suggest to any government—and particularly a new government—that great caution is required.

New government, new policy?

The election of the Rudd Labor government in November 2007 brought an end to the Howard years. Evidence from key seats suggested that the change of government was a great relief to many Aboriginal people. In the seat of Lingiari in the Northern Territory, for example, which encompasses all 73 Aboriginal communities affected by the intervention, the so-called 'Aboriginal booths' across the seat delivered votes to the ALP in the 90 percentile range. However, as the editor of the *National Indigenous Times*, Chris Graham, explained, even these figures did not tell the whole story. Graham points to the exact count at certain booths to emphasise the extent of Aboriginal discontent with Howard—and the intervention—in the Northern Territory. Of the 723 people who voted at the Wadeye booth, for example, only 26 voted for the Country Liberal Party (CLP). And at Angkarripa in Central Australia, the CLP received only five primary votes out of a potential 503, or 0.99 per cent of the total vote. Graham makes specific mention of the small booth at Yirrikala in Northeast Arnhem Land, home to prominent Aboriginal leader Galarrwuy Yunupingu, who (as discussed in Chapter 5) greatly upset other Yolngu by reversing his opposition to the Northern Territory intervention shortly before the official start of the election campaign. Of the 266 votes cast in Yirrkala, the CLP secured just two, or only 0.75 per cent of the primary vote. Graham also draws attention to the voting trends in two key Queensland seats. Across Queensland there was an 8 per cent swing against the Howard government, but a striking swing of nearly 11 per cent against Indigenous Affairs Minister Mal Brough, who lost his seat of Longman on election night. Further north, the government secured only 25 per cent of the vote at the booth in Noel Pearson's home town of Hopevale (Graham 2007b).

So what will Kevin Rudd and his government do to reflect what could be interpreted as a clear demand for change in the Indigenous Affairs portfolio? As I write this, nearly twelve months into the Rudd government's term, the messages on Indigenous Affairs policy emerging from the new government are mixed. In a speech in early 2008, the new Indigenous Affairs Minister, Jenny Macklin, acknowledged the 'vast and worsening gulf' between Indigenous and non-Indigenous people in Australia, and argued that her government must 'find new ways of doing things because the old ways have so comprehensively failed'. Macklin emphasised the need to 'engage Indigenous people in developing solutions' in recognition of the fact that effective and sustainable solutions 'have to be developed on the ground and driven by the communities that own them' (Macklin 2008a). One indication of this intended new approach was a substantial commitment to a nine-point plan to provide Indigenous people with access to the same standard of health services as other Australians within a decade. The plan, including a significant commitment to providing decent housing, is the central plank of the Rudd government's promise to close the seventeen-year life expectancy gap by the year 2030 (Parker 2008b: 1). Together with the long-awaited apology to the stolen generations (discussed in Chapter 11), early signs such as these did indeed seem to promise a new direction in Indigenous Affairs.

But the positives have been balanced by some clear negatives and many uncertainties. The new government flatly rejected the idea of a compensation fund for the stolen generations to accompany the apology. And while the controversial National Indigenous Council was quickly disbanded, it was evident that the election promise of a new 'ATSIC-like' body may be a long time coming as the government has struggled to resolve how it might consult sufficiently to develop a workable model (Behrendt 2008: 24). (It eventually initiated a six-month consultation process in July 2008.) This is of great concern because, as John

Chesterman (2008) has argued, the lack of Indigenous involvement and ownership in the development of new policy 'will prove fatal as it always has'.

The Northern Territory 'intervention', which the Rudd government supported in Opposition and inherited upon election, remains the greatest uncertainty. Immediately following the election, the prime minister convened a summit in Darwin with about thirty Aboriginal leaders, where he promised to have quarterly meetings with Northern Territory Aboriginal leaders and promised to take his Cabinet and senior bureaucrats to remote areas to see the issues at first hand. However, he also reiterated that he would be retaining some controversial aspects of the intervention at least until his promised mid-2008 review (*Koori Mail* 2007d). The meeting received a mixed response, with Olga Havnen of the Combined Aboriginal Organisations commenting that:

> It was an attempt by Labor to honour commitments they gave before the election to meet with Aboriginal people, so, from that point of view, I think it's a positive thing. But it's unfortunate that we didn't actually get down to any of the detail of what people are concerned about, in particular the application of the *Racial Discrimination Act* and the income quarantining. (quoted in *Koori Mail* 2007d)

Prior to the election, the most widely criticised aspects of the intervention were the abolition of CDEP, the abolition of the Aboriginal land permit system and compulsory quarantining of half all welfare payments in 73 communities, together with the suspension of the *Racial Discrimination Act* to achieve these things. The new government promised to restore CDEP in some areas and to reintroduce a modified permit system; however, the welfare quarantining measures would continue to roll out across the Territory despite widespread criticism. The new minister asked the intervention taskforce to advise on the data it would need to evaluate the effectiveness of welfare quarantining in 'making sure that families are able to spend more of their money on food, that less money is being spent on alcohol, for example or gambling' (quoted in *National Indigenous Times* 2008a).

In June 2008, the Rudd government announced the three-person review board that would evaluate the effectiveness of the intervention.

The board, chaired by Peter Yu, working with Marcia Ella Duncan and Bill Gray, would invite public submissions and undertake consultations with Aboriginal people in order to address the terms of reference for its inquiry, with a final report expected at the end of September 2008.

In the meantime, however, the Rudd government has supported the implementation of alternative income-management models in Western Australia and through a new Family Responsibility Commission to be trialled in four communities in Cape York, with the minister claiming that this would give the government the 'evidence' it needs to 'find out what works' (Macklin 2008b). This insistence on the continuation and extension of controversial measures that have received a mixed and predominantly critical response from Aboriginal people has contributed to feelings of uncertainty about the new government.

How to make better policy

Quite aside from the complexity of Aboriginal political culture discussed in the rest of this book, it is also important to acknowledge that Indigenous Affairs policy is made in a context of enormous structural inequality where governments hold almost all the cards. As Waanji author Alexis Wright (2005) argues: 'The use of colonial laws and the policies associated with those laws has been, and still is, an abusive weapon, which is rendering more and more Indigenous people powerless, apathetic and tragic.' (2005: 106)

Despite this imbalance, however, there are many ways in which governments are powerless to address the problems and complexity in the Indigenous policy domain, at least as long as they refuse to listen to the people who actually have first-hand experience and the best-informed ideas about how things might be improved—that is, Aboriginal people themselves. Government deafness in this field will mean that policy will continue to ignore the long term, and will remained focused upon the symptoms rather than the causes of Aboriginal disadvantage (Brennan et al. 2005: 43).

In his role as Aboriginal and Torres Strait Islander Social Justice Commissioner, Tom Calma has outlined several key elements that he considers necessary in the development of good Indigenous policy. These are:

- that all legislation, policies and programs are consistent with international human rights standards;

- that policy is made with the engagement and participation of Indigenous peoples;
- that there is a capacity-building and community development approach to policy-making;
- that policy supports sound Indigenous governance;
- that policy fosters and recognises Indigenous leadership;
- that there is a learning framework for planning and implementation;
- that funding and planning occur on the basis of need;
- that there are robust programs in place for monitoring and evaluating policies and programs;
- that there is a culture of implementation and government accountability (ATSISJC 2007a: 3–13).

In relation to the Northern Territory intervention in particular, Tom outlines a ten-point action plan emphasising consent, procedural fairness and protections against racial discrimination that would ensure the policies complied with human rights standards (see ATSISJC 2008a).

In our interview, Tom stressed the importance of a long-term policy vision and a return to bipartisanship. Tom is concerned that 'too much government policy is done for the life of the parliament' with an emphasis on political expedience. The result, Tom says, is that he 'cannot think of one piece of Indigenous policy that's been developed in the last four or five years—or probably longer—that has any hope of sustainability'. Tom expressed his frustration at the ways in which Aboriginal people remain 'guinea pigs' while 'the government changes policy almost at will'. Every time the policy direction changes, Tom says, 'you're undermining confidence and you're undermining people's ability to cope'. Larissa Behrendt supports Tom's view, and urges that Indigenous Affairs policy must 'move away from ideological approaches to policy' towards an emphasis on 'research-based approaches'. Alison Anderson agrees, but expresses a degree of caution about how much research is sometimes needed. Alison warns that there is a long history of government wanting 'report after report after report to verify the same things', and insists that until governments 'stop doing that and start getting things right, things aren't going to change'.

What is clear from my interviewees is that Aboriginal people will be deeply suspicious of, and are highly unlikely to support, any policy decision that is not developed through meaningful consultation with them. Tom Calma, who has been a vocal critic of much government policy during his tenure as ATSISJC, makes it clear that he is 'not always opposed to policy directions' but that he is opposed to the 'lack of consultation and the lack of informed consent that's out there'. Tom expresses the view that: 'If a community decides that they want to go in a certain direction and they've been provided with appropriate levels of information to make an informed decision, well and good. That's their prerogative and it's important that we support them.' However, Paul Briggs worries that 'in the absence of a national agenda and a national governance structure' there is no possibility for the constructive conversations that need to happen to develop a 'collective vision' for Indigenous policy. Without a national agenda, Paul is concerned that individuals such as Noel Pearson may produce unintended consequences for other groups and communities.

Certainly, the road back from the cul de sac of the Howard years will be long and arduous, for government but most of all for Aboriginal people. Debating the pros and cons of the contentious Northern Territory 'intervention', and without a recognised national voice, Aboriginal people will struggle to be heard and to negotiate the complexity of their political culture. Key to these struggles is the recognition of Aboriginal autonomy—a central concern of any successful future policy intervention made more difficult by current levels of dependency in some areas. But, as Pat Anderson (2007) has suggested in relation to the Northern Territory intervention: 'It is not the fact of the intervention, but the kind of intervention that is contentious. No intervention will work if it is an attempt to "turn the clock back", to go back to a past when the non-Aboriginal state was a presence in every Aboriginal person's daily life.'

It is the complexities involved in Aboriginal struggles for autonomy from the non-Aboriginal state that I address in the next chapter.

2
AUTONOMY AND DEPENDENCY

Colonisation creates dependency. In every country where Indigenous people have been subjected to a colonial regime, precolonial autonomy has been eroded. In its place a range of damaging dependencies have manifested themselves. These postcolonial dependencies add complexity to Aboriginal political culture as individuals, families and communities struggle to regain their autonomy as self-determining peoples and as political actors. These struggles take place in political contexts that tend to necessitate at least some degree of dependence on non-Indigenous structures of government.

Australia is no exception to this pattern. Before their country was invaded and colonised, and long before such terms were needed, Aboriginal and Torres Strait Islander peoples had lived autonomous and self-determining lives for millennia. Sustainable social systems with enduring spiritual beliefs, viable economies and recognised legal systems ensured survival in challenging and diverse physical environments (Brennan et al. 2005: 4). Now, however, as has been widely observed, Aboriginal Australians are suffering from various forms of dependency, including both 'welfare dependency' and political dependency. In fact, Aboriginal people in Australia experience less in the way of formal political autonomy than any comparable settler society anywhere in the world (Bradfield 2006: 80). They control 'neither things nor ideas', and

24

have spent much of the past 220 years attempting to negotiate a suitable place for themselves in the new political and socioeconomic order (Howard 1982: 1).

The mainstream political response to the complexities of Aboriginal dependency has been both simplistic and cowardly. Although Australia had a formal policy of Indigenous self-determination between 1972 and 2005, this policy was always more rhetorical than real. No Australian government has ever been prepared to unsettle the status quo sufficiently to afford Aboriginal people real autonomy. Some strategies that have been made to look like self-determination are in fact understood by Aboriginal people to further restrict their political autonomy. In 2005, the 'new arrangements' in Indigenous Affairs, discussed in the previous chapter, replaced even the rhetoric of self-determination with neo-paternalistic policies cloaked in language of mainstreaming and mutual obligation. And in 2007, despite growing international evidence that more rather than less autonomy would improve Aboriginal life chances, the former Australian government initiated the most blatant threat to Aboriginal autonomy yet seen in the post-assimilation period: the Northern Territory 'intervention'. How has this happened?

Creating dependency

The transformation of Aboriginal peoples from autonomous societies to a dependent minority began at colonisation. Dependency arrived with the colonising forces that invaded Aboriginal lands, and developed during periods characterised by dispossession, protectionism and assimilation (Cronin 2007: 186; Palmer 2005: 101). By the time Australia introduced a weak and compromised self-determination in the 1970s, much damage had already been done—meaning that something far more radical would be needed to restore Aboriginal dignity and autonomy.

Darryl Cronin has argued that dispossession is the 'core of Indigenous disadvantage' both because it saw Indigenous peoples lose control of their natural and cultural resources, and because of the trauma that this dispossession engendered—the 'devastating spiritual and psychological impact' it had on Aboriginal people (Cronin 2003: 152). Jiman and Bunjalung woman Judy Atkinson, who spent fifteen years researching Indigenous trauma, agrees. She claims that dispossession 'enforced dependency' as it 'tore families apart' and 'destroyed any sense of self-worth and value in culture' (Atkinson 2002: 67). Many Aboriginal people carried the trauma

25

of earlier periods of violent dispossession with them on to reserves and missions. Here, as colonial governments attempted to 'smooth the dying pillow' of a culture apparently destined for extinction, they experienced further threats to their spiritual beliefs and traditional ways of life while becoming newly dependent on rations and handouts. In many ways the missions did much to entrench a post-invasion dependency. But in the cities and towns too, away from the direct control of missions and reserves, Aboriginal people found themselves increasingly trapped in a 'welfare milieu' that provided 'more subtle forms of domination' but nonetheless denied them their autonomy (Howard 1982: 7).

The racialised thinking of the time allowed non-Aboriginal people to believe that Aboriginal people were not really capable of living autonomous lives. The 'neo-evolutionary' views held by non-Aboriginal politicians, both then and now, endorse a view that Aboriginal people need to be helped or forced to overcome their dependency through paternalistic policies, regardless of the effects these policies may have on Indigenous culture. It must therefore have been something of a surprise and an irritation that Aboriginal people seemed so reluctant to accept this paternalism or to allow their cultures and communities to be eradicated. Aboriginal people from diverse contexts continued to assert their distinctiveness and their autonomy (Coombs and Robinson 1996: 2). By the 1970s, the Aboriginal voices clamouring for recognition could no longer be ignored, and the election of the Whitlam Labor government in 1972 saw the formal introduction of a policy of Aboriginal 'self-determination'.

Self-determination meant many things. In some parts of Australia, it meant the decline and eventual withdrawal of missions; in other places, it meant the emergence of Aboriginal-controlled organisations. Some Aboriginal people gained limited rights over or ownership of their lands. The assumption from the outset was that the new policies would both lessen Indigenous dependency and allow Aboriginal people to make decisions about their own priorities and lifestyles. However, it is worth noting two fundamental problems with the way 'self-determination' was introduced in Australia. The first problem was the assumption that, after nearly two centuries of domination and dependency, Aboriginal people would immediately be equipped to assume greater autonomy over their lives. It is a sad irony that regimes of dependency, such as missions, not only did irrevocable damage to traditional social norms and modes of social control during their tenure, but that their withdrawal also meant that their imposed set of laws was simultaneously revoked, leaving a significant social void (Sutton 2001: 128). Although many communities clearly prized the restoration of their autonomy above all else, in Cape York leader Noel Pearson's view many communities 'threw the baby out with the bathwater' by destroying the 'moral and cultural order that the churches had given to communities' (Pearson 2007a: 28). In our interview, Warren Mundine shared a similar point of view in suggesting: 'When you're fighting against the coloniser and you finally get independence and the coloniser goes home, all of a sudden you have to do what they were doing . . . You have to run the law and order, you have to become the police, you have to become the judges, you have to become the educators.' Muriel Bamblett also raised this issue in our interview. She recalled the Whitlam era as 'a great era' but also feels that Aboriginal people were not prepared for the way in which self-determination was delivered: 'At that time we weren't sophisticated in being able to take all the legislation and the policies and turn it into services. We had all of this great rhetoric around self-determination and self-management . . . [but] . . . we didn't really have very good tools to put those things into practice on the ground.'

In short, the protectionist and assimilationist periods in Australia did not leave Aboriginal communities well equipped for the immediate takeup of these tasks. This lack of readiness to assume administrative and social responsibility for community management also became something of a self-fulfilling prophecy, with governments expressing their lack of confidence in Aboriginal people by continuing to weigh down 'seemingly liberating policy' with continuing government controls (Lippmann 1981: 96). This dynamic was further compounded by the newly dependent relationship in which many leaders and activists found themselves once they had accepted government positions or funding (Jones and Hill-Burnett 1982: 238; Attwood and Markus 1999: 277).

Further complicating the attempted transition to self-determination was the clash between traditional structures of community organisation and control and the newly imposed structures such as community councils, with their elected representatives. Richard Trudgen (2000) observes that there was an assumption that, as the missions withdrew from communities in northeast Arnhem Land, the elders would take control of the new community councils. In most cases, however, this did not happen because the new 'Balanda [white] processes' were only understood by some of the younger, Western-educated Yolngu (2000: 55). As a result, traditional models of social organisation were further undermined at a time when stability was desperately needed. Despite the rhetoric, the new policy of self-determination in fact contained underlying pressures for acculturation that were not all that different to the pressures of the assimilation era (Rowse 2002: 231).

The second problem with the way that policies of self-determination were introduced in Australia concerned their weak and compromised philosophical underpinnings. As Chapter 3 will explore further, Australian governments have never dealt with Aboriginal people 'government to government', but have instead insisted on a 'top-down' approach to self-determination (Brennan et al. 2005: 32)—clearly a contradiction in terms. This approach has meant that aspirations for autonomy have been 'buried in practices that are assimilationist' (Young 2005: 120), thus compromising the capacity of Aboriginal people to actually exercise their individual and collective responsibility. Aileen Moreton-Robinson (2005) suggests that government policies of self-determination have been more concerned with organisational and community management than with placing meaningful political and economic power in Aboriginal hands (2005: 63). This profound *lack* of self-determination at the heart of policies ostensibly espousing self-determination has continued to frustrate Indigenous desires for a more meaningful autonomy.

Living with dependency

Few would dispute the extent of the social crisis being experienced in many Aboriginal communities. It is generally understood that what has now become a 'self-perpetuating cycle of poverty and despair' (Stokes 2002: 196), in which women and children in particular endure horrendous levels of violence, has its roots in Australia's colonial history. This cycle is perpetuated by a present-day sense of powerlessness and lack of control by Aboriginal people over their own lives. As Richard Trudgen (2000) observes: 'When any group of people lose control of the basic things of life, the result is disaster. Normal things become abnormal and the people concerned start to suffer in all sorts of strange ways.' (2000: 58)

For some Yolngu, this has meant a descent into *wulula*, or hell. As one man, John Djatjamirrilili, observed to Trudgen: 'Living in the community is like *wulula*. We sit with sad faces, with nothing to do except watch the Balanda [white people] running around doing everything for us . . . That's what *wulula* is like. It's like living in a [present day Arnhem Land] community.' (quoted in Trudgen 2000: 158) This dependence on non-Aboriginal people for administration and management in communities is certainly troubling to observe. Anyone who visits a remote Aboriginal community will see the multitude of white public servants—CEOs, teachers, nurses, police—who essentially run the place. In many communities there are multiple forms of 'bureaucratic and technical dependency' (Palmer 2005: 104) which have developed due to operational complexity, multiple funding and reporting requirements and the necessary maintenance of inappropriate and overly complex equipment. Both the number of white bureaucrats and the complexity of community administration have been significantly increased since the intervention began.[1] For Warren Mundine, this is something Aboriginal people desperately need to overcome, particularly in the area of law and order. Warren suggests that 'law and order issues in Aboriginal communities are never going to be resolved until such time as we actually have Aboriginal police and Aboriginal judges working in those communities, where we actually take on the ownership of looking after our communities'. From a somewhat different perspective less accepting of the legal framework imposed by the settler state, Larissa Behrendt (1995) has suggested that with greater community autonomy Aboriginal people would be able to restore traditional laws and dispute-resolution processes 'away from the structures of the dominant culture' (1995: 74). From both perspectives, however, the proposed solution is for more rather than less Aboriginal ownership of problems and their solutions—that is, more autonomy, not less.

From around 2000, when his 'Light on the Hill' lecture declared his changed views on Indigenous policy (Pearson 2000b), much public debate about the problem of welfare dependency in Aboriginal communities has been led by Noel Pearson. Pearson has described the 'institutionalised dependency' that he believes has been created by a regime of 'passive welfare' (2007a: 17). Pearson has also claimed that these symptoms of welfare dependency, particularly the collapse of social norms and the rise of ills such as violence, suicide, alcoholism and child abuse, are recent rather than historical phenomena, dated to the rise of 'victim politics' in which the 'increased recognition of black rights' was accompanied by 'a calamitous erosion of black responsibility' (2007a: 26). Pearson argues that three factors have contributed to Cape York Aboriginal communities' 'descent into hell' over recent decades: the equal wages decision in 1966, which saw the collapse of Aboriginal employment in the pastoral industry; the introduction of social security payments; and the attainment of full citizenship, which brought with it the right to drink alcohol (2007a: 26–7). Pearson and his colleagues at the Cape York Institute summarise the situation by arguing that:

> the current problems of Indigenous people are very much the result of passivity problems created by earlier interventions. Passivity, at its core, involves an abandonment of responsibility by individuals, families and communities. With the decline of responsibility comes family and community breakdown and social problems. (Cape York Institute 2007: 44)

It would be a mistake, however, to think that Pearson's diagnosis is anything new. What Gary Foley has described as 'the essence of the Pearson position' is the idea that 'the excuses of the past have got to be got rid of. Aboriginal people have now got to take personal responsibility for their lives, their families, their destiny.' Foley claims: 'That's almost exactly what we were advocating thirty years ago in the self-determination movement.' (ABC 2003a) Writing in the early 1970s, the late Kevin Gilbert observed that 'Aboriginal life is an ocean of suffering, maladjustment, ill-health, dreadful conditions, stunted wasted lives, dying babies and frustration'. (Gilbert 2002 [1973]: 141) Gilbert—like Pearson—also claimed that 'dependence on "handouts" has sapped the initiative and the substance of blacks' and advocated 'the need for community self-discipline and total community organisation.' (2002: 148, 149). However, unlike Pearson and his more paternalistic proposals for restricting welfare payments based on behaviour, Gilbert advocated a more radical autonomy, claiming: 'The only thing that years of white administration have proved to us is that it doesn't work, it can't work.' (2002: 160) Gilbert further argued that 'what blacks really want' is a combination of 'land, compensation, discreet non-dictatorial help and *to be left alone* by white Australia', insisting, 'You'll never heal a wound if you keep picking at it'. (2002: 175, emphasis in the original)

In other words, where Pearson advocates greater community responsibility through individual coercion, Gilbert was calling for a more meaningful form of Aboriginal autonomy that required of Aboriginal people a true range of responsibilities for their communal welfare and well-being. As Foley also argues, the solution to dependency articulated by activists in the 1970s was to 'put the resources into the hands of the communities themselves, cut out the middle man and . . . let the communities make their own mistakes. Create real self-determination.' (ABC 2003a) Many other Aboriginal leaders and activists today still point to paternalism and interference as contributing to ongoing dependency. In the 2006 HREOC Social Justice report, Tom Calma points out that the irony of failing to treat Aboriginal people as 'partners and equal participants in creating a positive life vision' is that this approach 'fosters a passive system of policy development and service delivery while at the same time criticising Indigenous peoples for being passive recipients of government services' (ATSISJC 2007a: 18). In our interview, Mick Dodson made a similar point, arguing that: 'You can't fix community problems, they belong to communities. Communities have got to fix them. What you can do is help them. Give them the power and the resources to do what needs to be done.'

Pearson is correct in highlighting the growing dependence on welfare payments since the advent of self-determination in the 1970s. In many Aboriginal communities, in both remote and urban locations, social security or CDEP payments make up the majority if not the whole of the local economy (a situation that will be discussed further in Chapter 4), leaving Aboriginal people 'hopelessly dependent on the dominant culture' (Trudgen 2000: 160). A problem arises in much current debate, however, with a tendency to 'blame the victim'. The reality is that determining responsibility for the current state of affairs is as difficult as it is pointless. As Tim Rowse notes: 'The attribution of responsibility is often part of the game of politics itself.' (1993: 75) It is, however, worth noting that the CDEP program that was temporarily abolished in 2007 was originally a response to community fears that 'passive welfare' in the form of social security payments would create 'harmful personal and social consequences' (ATSISJC 2007a: 39; Sanders 1998).

Nevertheless, the 'blame the victim' approach, along with Pearson's influential neoliberal arguments, is used to justify the imposition of paternalistic policies, including the 'intervention' in the Northern Territory. But one of the results of the 'top-down' approach to self-determination so favoured by Australian governments is the maintenance of passivity, as Aboriginal people are subjected to the ever-changing policies of governments. Alison Anderson described this process as being like:

> hopping on a merry-go-round, you know but the merry-go-round stops at the same place certain years down the road. All you've got to do is have a look at the history of Aboriginal affairs, ADC, DAA and ATSIC. Our life is dependent on policy. Our life is dependent on other people's direction. And we've got to change that around so our poverty becomes an industry for *our* culture and not an industry for others.

Paul Briggs expressed very similar views, talking about dependency in terms of 'twelve-month cycles of hope that the next level of government will somehow provide us with a way forward'. For Briggs, it is this dependency on government 'to somehow magically give us the answers to the way in which we're going to live', rather than a dependency on welfare, that is the greater problem. Briggs feels that this dependency on government has 'consumed' Aboriginal people, draining them of their capacity to develop their own solutions to social problems.

So while many Aboriginal leaders and activists around Australia agree with Pearson's diagnosis of the disease of dependency that is crippling their communities, Pearson finds himself almost a lone voice (supported by Warren Mundine and Marcia Langton) in advocating his particular cure. The majority of Aboriginal leaders and activists see more, rather than less, autonomy as the answer to dependency. In light of this, it seems tragic that the Northern Territory intervention is precisely the opposite of what the majority of Indigenous leaders and activists know is needed. As Judy Atkinson has noted, there is a long history of 'multiple, protracted and many-layered' interventions by governments and others into Aboriginal lives. These interventions have at many levels 'acted as traumatising agents, compounding the agony of already traumatised individuals and groups' and have 'increased the dependent conditions of the oppressed' (Atkinson 2002: 68). Despite this, Aboriginal people have continued to resist.

Struggling for autonomy
Worimi historian John Maynard points out that Aboriginal people were calling for self-determination as early as the 1920s. It is the later

articulation of these demands under the banner of 'Black Power', however, that is best known and associated with political strategies such as the Aboriginal Tent Embassy. As Gary Foley points out, Black Power was 'always about self-determination . . . we were about Aboriginal people assuming responsibility and control of their own affairs' (ABC 2003a). Black Power became a means of articulating a rejection of white paternalism and an assertion of demands for Aboriginal control and autonomy (Attwood 2003: 322–4). It also provided a space for Aboriginal people to grow in both confidence and community strength (de Costa 2006: 105).

Several interviewees noted the cynical response from governments to these Aboriginal demands for a greater political autonomy. There is a strong belief that many strategies appearing to 'allow' greater autonomy have really been government efforts to derail and demobilise the movement. Representative bodies from the 1970s, such as the NACC and its successor the NAC, have been assessed as 'impotent' bodies designed to contain a threatening political movement (Bradfield 2006: 84). Many government actions have created a 'dependent Aboriginal elite' (Howard 1982: 10)—an elite that perhaps became somewhat lost following the abolition of ATSIC.[2] Several interviewees spoke of the incorporation of Aboriginal organisations under the policy of self-determination as a factor that compounded, rather than alleviated, Aboriginal dependency. Early organisations, such as the Aboriginal Legal and Medical Services, were intended to be as much about autonomy and self-determination as they were about service provision (Briskman 2003: 31, 33, 34). However, Robbie Thorpe claims to have missed this aspect of the 'experiment in self-determination' altogether, because he says: 'You can't get self-determination from Aboriginal organisations because they're corporate bodies. They're counter-productive as far as I'm concerned . . . Originally it started off we were going to do it ourselves . . . Then they got incorporated and went back to square one. We're worse off.' Through the incorporation of Aboriginal organisations, many previously autonomous leaders and activists found themselves 'integrated into the very structure of oppression that they are trying to combat' (Jones and Hill-Burnett 1982: 224).

In mainstream political circles and in the media, ATSIC is generally spoken about as though it really was an organisational model that afforded Aboriginal and Torres Strait Islander people some meaningful autonomy, and there is a perception that this so-called 'experiment in self-determination' somehow failed. However, despite a deep appreciation of many of the things that ATSIC offered, most especially an elected representative body delegated to interact with the federal government, for most Aboriginal people ATSIC was never understood as an autonomous or Indigenous organisation. Rather, it was understood as a 'creation of non-Aboriginal Australia' (O'Shane 1998: 6) that hovered in 'uncertain space' between a dominant state and the possibility of Indigenous autonomy (Bradfield 2006: 88). Nor was it considered to provide for real self-determination. Geoff Scott argues that the organisation was really just 'a normal government department with an elected arm on top', a structure that caused 'significant tensions and frictions, which were never sorted out'. As Mick Dodson has argued in regard to ATSIC and the 'myth' that self-determination failed: 'An approach that has never been tested cannot be deemed a failure.' (Dodson 2006a)

These limitations were understood from the outset. As both Colleen Hayward and Josie Crawshaw explained, ATSIC 'wasn't ever about self-determination'. Josie elaborated: 'How could it be self-determination? You've got a government body. The chairperson's appointed, not elected. At no stage do you control any funds, you've got to work to a minister of the government of the day. It had nothing to do with self-determination.'

Certainly ATSIC had its critics. Sam Watson, for example, put his own view that 'ATSIC made no measurable impact on the lives of the great majority of our Brisbane community', although other Brisbane-ites may well disagree. Others, like Paul Briggs, felt that ATSIC was 'caught up in the politics around service delivery' when it 'needed to operate at a higher policy level that reinforced the accountability of Australian governments to Aboriginal people'. But, regardless of some of the structural problems, there is still much anger at ATSIC's abolition. As Irene Watson (2007) has argued: 'Aboriginal people were given an under-resourced white model to perform the impossible task of caring for Aboriginal Australia. From the beginning the ATSIC project was doomed to fail and, when it did, white racism laid the blame in black hands.' (2007: 24)

Many, like John Maynard, concede that there were 'points of ATSIC that many blackfellas would disagree with', however, he now sees that 'communities are suffering' in its absence. Klynton Wanganeen agrees that 'there were problems with the way ATSIC was structured' but argues that 'it wasn't anything that could not have been dealt with'. Tauto Sansbury goes further, claiming that the abolition of ATSIC 'was really a racist attack on many Aboriginal people right across Australia'. Sam Watson disagrees, but he is in a minority in arguing that 'since ATSIC's gone, nothing's changed'. One former ATSIC commissioner described the abolition as 'a step back into the draconian past of mission mentalities overlorded by bureaucrats whose bottom line is economic expediency' (Rick Griffiths, quoted in Barnett 2005: 11). Even Ray Swan from the Tent Embassy—a noted critic of ATSIC—concedes that 'ATSIC was a devil, but Aboriginal people should have been given the opportunity to fix it. We should have had the right to mend our own wrongs, you know?'

This view is at the heart of Aboriginal people's struggles for autonomy. Being autonomous means making mistakes, being accountable and fixing those mistakes yourself. As Bill Jonas and Darren Dick (2004) have observed: 'It is one thing to suggest that ATSIC could perform its obligations to Indigenous peoples better; it is another thing entirely to suggest that there should not be a national representative body through which Indigenous people can participate in government decision making about their lives.' (2004: 14) Without ATSIC, Aboriginal people were left without national representation, without a recognised body for dealing with the federal government and without a recognised body that was able to express views in Indigenous affairs that were often critical of government (Behrendt 2004: 3). Many of the former ATSIC councillors I interviewed were still acting in that de facto role because, as Tauto Sansbury points out, now 'there's nobody at all to go to and knock on the door'. Aboriginal people, he says, 'can only turn to one another for comfort and ideas'. The National Aboriginal Alliance may attempt to fill this void, but it remains to be seen whether it will emerge as an organisation with legitimacy and influence.

One group of Aboriginal people to whom Tauto and others were unlikely to turn was the Howard government's hand-picked National Indigenous Council (NIC), which Tauto describes as 'one of the most prettiest window dressings you'll ever see'. Kerry Arabena has suggested that the members of the NIC were people who had 'never been given legitimacy from their community to speak about issues', but who were given 'new platforms to infiltrate public opinion' (2005: 39). Anger about the NIC was palpable among some I interviewed. Geoff Scott for example, while acknowledging the 'fine line' in trying to decide when to work with a hostile government and when to walk away, felt that members of the NIC had crossed that line. Geoff claimed he would 'never shake the hands of an NIC member ever . . . they should soon get their breastplates'.[3] Irene Watson was a little more conciliatory, expressing her understanding that their position is determined by 'a hopelessness, a powerlessness, and thought that . . . there is no other choice but to negotiate the best deal for now' (2007: 30). Members of the NIC itself acknowledged that it was in no way a representative body (NIC 2006: 2; 2007).

Separate spaces or separatism?

Given the size of the Indigenous population in Australia (only around 2.5 per cent of the total population), Aboriginal people have a limited support base through which to exercise some degree of electoral leverage. Therefore, Aboriginal leaders and activists have an ongoing need both to mobilise broader support among non-Aboriginal people and to negotiate and possibly compromise with the state in order that it may allow Indigenous groups some measure of autonomy (Russell 2005: 131). However, this need for support from non-Indigenous people is at odds with the desire for autonomy that is a 'defining characteristic' of much Indigenous politics (Burgmann 2003: 58). Indigenous peoples the world over desire autonomy, which for the most part means that they want 'local control over their own affairs *within* the states in which they live' (Maybury-Lewis 2003: 331, my emphasis). Often, however, non-Indigenous people misinterpret this desire for autonomy as a desire for separatism. In reality, separatism is rarely on the Aboriginal political agenda.

There are, however, many Indigenous people in Australia who do express a strong desire for 'separate spaces' in which to discuss their politics and plan their agendas. One woman I spoke to expressed her concern at the number of prominent Aboriginal leaders and activists who are influenced by 'white advisers', many of whom she thinks behave like 'giddy children' around Aboriginal leaders. This woman felt very strongly that Aboriginal people have 'got to be allowed to have a conversation without the white people in the room', particularly in order to facilitate inter-generational conversations, as will be discussed in Chapter 10. Eugenia

Flynn echoes these concerns, expressing a wish that Aboriginal people could 'internalise things' by working amongst themselves and 'really kind of just cutting ourselves off for a while, just to think and take a breather'. However, Eugenia also feels that the opportunity for Aboriginal people to work 'behind closed doors' has now passed, saying with some sadness: 'I don't think we're going to be allowed to have time and space to be able to just be together as a community, behind closed doors [and say] this is what is really happening and this is what we need to do.'

A sense of caution and suspicion about the possibility of engaging effectively with non-Aboriginal people was clear in a number of interviews. Such suspicion is entirely understandable. As Quentin Beresford (2006) observes of the Western Australian situation, 'generations of segregation and the breaking up of families created a mentality among Noongars . . . which resisted intercultural cooperation or negotiation with white society' (2006: 78). Robbie Thorpe expressed a similar view with humour, claiming to have warned the Yorta Yorta of the dangers of engaging in white systems like the native title claims process. Robbie says: 'We wrote a little song for them':

You ought to listen, Yorta
It's no good for your aorta.
To play games with the white man's law
You ought to listen, Yorta

For the majority of interviewees, however, this sense of caution was tempered by a political pragmatism. As Alwyn McKenzie concedes: 'Aboriginal people need non-Aboriginal people too, that's the reality.' For some people, such as Larissa Behrendt, this pragmatism is derived from the recognition that 'the hearts and minds exercise' is crucial if Aboriginal leaders and activists want to 'bring the broader community with us'. Larissa feels strongly that:

At the end of the day it doesn't matter what kind of legal system you have if you don't have a community that's capable of recognising those rights. And we're not going to have a community that's capable of recognising those rights while people feel the way they do about Aboriginal people; where Aboriginal rights are seen as un-Australian, where we're kind of a threat to whatever it is that Australia holds.

In this regard, many interviewees felt that their struggle had gone back-wards during the term of the Howard government. John Maynard points to the fall in support for Aboriginal people from the highpoint of the 1967 referendum to today, when he wonders: 'Could we get even 30 per cent of this country to vote in favour of Indigenous people? I wouldn't think so.' John feels that there has been a concerted campaign by 'the powers that be' to undermine the 'collaboration between Aboriginal people and non-Aboriginal people who supported us' and which has seen anti-Aboriginal sentiment flourish in recent years like 'a massive bushfire'.

Even the sceptical Robbie Thorpe concedes that the 'conscientious ones'—those non-Aboriginal people who 'don't want to live in a state where genocide is not a crime'—are important allies. But Robbie also feels that Aboriginal people 'haven't galvanised and harnessed that support in the right way' and could do more to develop these relation-ships. Paul Briggs is another who recognises that there is more support to be had from non-Aboriginal people, but he is frustrated that 'the vehicles for them to get in and be able to contribute haven't been devel-oped'. Without such vehicles, Paul feels that non-Aboriginal people will continue to 'engage and pick up knowledge and information about the Aboriginal community only through crisis'. Like John Maynard, Paul feels that the term of the Howard government did much to entrench the divide between Aboriginal and non-Aboriginal Australians. Nowadays, he says, public concern about Aboriginal issues 'has been hijacked by the governments', but he insists, 'Other views are important in determining what happens in Aboriginal lives—if we think it's only us and [former Indigenous Affairs minister] Mal Brough then we're in strife'.

An autonomous future?
A significant part of any meaningful Aboriginal autonomy will be some genuine economic autonomy. These issues will be discussed in more depth in Chapter 4, but here it is worth noting the extent to which contemporary leaders and activists express their desire to reduce their economic dependency on government.

For several interviewees, economic autonomy is an important precon-dition for greater political autonomy. Klynton Wanganeen suggests that government should 'pay the rent' and then allow Aboriginal people to use these funds to run their own organisations. In this way, governments could not longer say: 'You are misusing taxpayers' monies . . . They will only be able to say, yes, we paid you your rent, you use it to the benefit of Aboriginal communities.' Alwyn McKenzie suggests that Aboriginal people must be able to 'sit, talk, think, argue all the issues and make recommendations to whoever', but that these processes have 'got to be paid for. Whether it's paid through the taxation system or a portion of the state's gross profit.' Henry Atkinson shares these concerns, pointing out that although he and others like him already pay for a lot of political activity out of their own pockets, they have limited resources, which 'makes it very hard for Indigenous Australians to even get down into Parliament House and speak to a minister or to make contact with a minister. You've got to have resources to even make contact with those people that want to help.' Dr Marika suggests that government should just give Aboriginal people *ruppiya* (money) and 'leave us alone', a view shared by Gary Foley, who claims the only sort of Indigenous Affairs bureaucracy that Canberra needs is 'a single public servant with a cheque book and a pen'. Foley suggests that government should just 'send the money direct out to the communities and let the people make their own mistakes' (ABC 2003a).

Complicating the view that government should provide funds through reparations and by 'paying the rent', there is also a sense that a meaningful future autonomy must somehow be self-funded. Alison Anderson argues that 'while you go cap in hand to government, you're controlled by government. You're controlled by government legislation. You're born out of legislation, so you're born out of that piece of paper and your mother becomes the pen and your father becomes your minister.' Mick Dodson agrees, while also acknowledging the expense of developing an autonomous political organisation:

> The key question is the resources. You've got to run these things, and they take resources. You've got to get resources for getting the body together, you've got to have resources for the representatives to engage with their constituents, to be able to travel around the regions they represent. These are very important things. And they cost money.

Nevertheless, for Mick, the 'ideal' would be an autonomous national organisation 'totally unconnected to government' so that 'government can't dismantle it because it's not a creature of the parliament'. In Mick's view, 'the less reliance on government the better'. Gularrwuy Yunupingu also agrees, emphasising that the Mala Elders group he has formed in Arnhem Land (as a part of the memorandum of understanding signed with the Howard government in September 2007) 'will not be a construct of government but self-forming and self-funded' (Yunupingu 2007). The issue of funding for a new national representative body is addressed in the HREOC discussion paper examining this issue discussed in the conclusion to this book (ATSISJC 2008c).

Like the majority of my interviewees, Warren Mundine is also frustrated by an ongoing dependence on government, claiming that 'with Aboriginal affairs in Australia, when we try and do things, we always tend to go to governments to fix it'. For Warren, the bottom line in thinking about the future of Indigenous representation is that: 'Governments can't empower people . . . We don't need government sanction or white people's sanction or anyone's sanction on our governance. We need to work that crap out ourselves. We shouldn't be going to governments and saying, "Hey, give us a national body." Why aren't we forming our own national body? Why don't we just do it?'

For many, the obstacles on the road to this sort of autonomy at times seem overwhelming. Jackie Huggins is one who, despite her endless preparedness to engage with hostile governments, has really felt the pain and offence of recent neopaternalism. Jackie recalls that her parents were 'put on missions and reserves', where they were essentially 'treated like children'. For Jackie, little has changed today:

> We're treated like children, you know, [under Howard] we were just being put on a big reserve, that's how I feel. With permission to do this, and do that. Yes sir, no sir, three bags full sir. And the sad part is about it—I love to be optimistic, and I am in certain ways—but it's just such a blanket there now. Show me how to find a way out of it.

Paul Briggs expresses very similar sentiments, saying: 'People are floundering at the moment.' Like Jackie, he feels that there is 'still a bit of mission mentality . . . You know if you do this then we'll take the tea and sugar off you.' For Paul, it is time for Aboriginal people 'to come back together because I think we were just *too* reliant and dependent on the way government operated'. Eugenia Flynn agrees that Aboriginal people need to stop 'constantly responding to non-Indigenous ideas about how we should behave or who we should be and who should be our leaders'. Sam Watson expresses the same idea more bluntly:

> Aboriginal people don't need outside resources, don't need outside help. We've got everything there within our own communities. Aboriginal people have to open their eyes and look at what we've got. Instead of forever castigating ourselves for the weakness within our own community, let's build on the strengths that we've always had there.

While the rhetoric is somewhat different, Sam's meaning is not dissimilar to Noel Pearson's argument that one of the most significant problems facing Aboriginal communities 'is that our lives are dominated by our dependency on and relationship with government' (Pearson 2006a: 4). It is ironic, then, that in what Irene Watson (2007) calls 'the classic so-called "decolonisation" scenario', conditions in many communities have now become so oppressive that Aboriginal people themselves, including Pearson, are calling for greater protection. As Watson observes, what was once considered colonialism is now referred to as 'humanitarian intervention' (2007: 30–1). However it is described, though, it is the opposite of autonomy.

Moving beyond paternalism

Complex debates about Indigenous autonomy and dependency have been almost overwhelmed by the 'Noel Pearson-versus-the-rest' debate over rights and responsibility. Noel Pearson is quite correct in diagnosing passivity and dependency as significant social problems in Aboriginal communities all over Australia—indeed, many other leaders and activists concur. But Pearson's diagnosis is nothing new. Kevin Gilbert pointed out over three decades ago that 'the toughest thing that blacks are going to have to come to grips with' is the 'psychological damage done to individuals and communities' as a result of postcolonial dependency. Gilbert argued that, even though 'the white man put you there, psychologically', even if he wanted to 'he can't get you out' (Gilbert 2002: 200).

Nor are Pearson's proposed solutions as innovative as he would like to think. In essence, Pearson's proposed solution to passivity and dependency is more paternalism and coercion. But paternalism—the insistence that disadvantaged groups must be coerced into greater individual responsibility—is not an original idea. Pearson's rhetoric here is slippery.

When he talks about Aboriginal people's 'right to take responsibility' (2000a), he is in fact talking about the quarantining of welfare payments of 'irresponsible' individuals. It is difficult, therefore, to assess the reality of his claim that he finds 'widespread resonance with the responsibility agenda' in Aboriginal communities (Pearson 2007a: 56). It is certainly evident that, over many, many years, Aboriginal people have been struggling for forms of autonomy that would increase their responsibility for themselves. As Lowitja O'Donoghue has pointed out, Aboriginal people have never been 'content to play the role of helpless victim' (1997: 30). However, there is a wide gulf between the type of meaningful, self-determining autonomy articulated by the majority of Aboriginal leaders and activists and Pearson's neopaternalistic proposals.

Many Aboriginal people believe that Pearson's new iteration of paternalism will do nothing to relieve Aboriginal dependence on 'the beneficence of government' (Cronin 2007: 199). Where Pearson is most at odds with his peers is in his rejection of what he calls 'victim politics', otherwise understood as the argument that until some of the wrongs of Australia's colonial past are properly addressed and corrected, Aboriginal people will be forced into relations of dependency with governments. Autonomy is, after all, about more than just 'where the money comes from'; it is more fundamentally about the sense of ownership and control people have over their lives (Rowse 1992: 35). Larissa Behrendt (1995) argues that it will only be through the recognition of Aboriginal autonomy that Aboriginal people will experience dignity and respect (1995: 104).

As Aden Ridgeway (2003) has noted, Australian governments have had 'report after report' that consistently advocate the same principle—that is, that 'Indigenous disadvantage can only be improved when Indigenous people are given greater control over the decisions that impact on their daily lives' (Ridgeway 2003: 188, emphasis in original). Rex Wild and Patricia Anderson, the authors of the report into child sexual abuse in the Northern Territory that allegedly prompted the federal government's intervention, have added to this list of reports, pointing out that the continuing failure to find solutions to the problems in Aboriginal communities is exacerbated by 'an ongoing paternalistic approach' that fails to address the problem (Wild and Anderson 2007: 9). International evidence also supports the view that paternalism exacerbates rather than ameliorates social problems in Indigenous communities (Cornell 2004;

Fournier 2005; Harvard Project 2008), as does the evidence from the Indigenous Community Governance Project (Hunt and Smith 2007). As Alexis Wright observes, Aboriginal people have been left with the 'chaos' caused by two centuries of non-Aboriginal 'solutions' proposed by 'the good, the bad and the incompetent'. In light of all that has been tried and has failed, why, Wright wonders, can non-Indigenous Australia not just embrace 'the Indigenous vision' (Wright 2005: 107)?

So, rather than self-determination having 'failed' as Pearson and the former prime minister would have us think, advocates of Aboriginal autonomy would say that *real* autonomy, *real* self-determination, has never been tried in Australia. Gularrwuy Yunupingu has argued that: 'Governments must stop babysitting us because we are not children. But if treated like children, people will behave like children. It is time for us to be given responsibility in the right way.' (Yunupingu 2007) The right way means recognising that real autonomy will not be achieved until the legal basis of relations between Aboriginal and non-Aboriginal Australians is resolved. While Darryl Cronin emphasises that the right to self-determination is 'not a right to secession' but rather a 'right to some form of autonomy *within* the Australian nation' (Cronin 2003: 158, emphasis added; Ivanitz 2002: 133–4), for others—like Lester-Irabinna Rigney (2003)—a treaty would at least provide a form of inoculation from ongoing assimilation, without which Indigenous people will continue to be 'forced into government care and obligation with its associated paternalistic practices' (2003: 76). ATSIC was making a similar point over a decade ago, arguing that Australia: 'must make a quantum leap, from patronising and condescending welfarism and the dependency and sense of inadequacy it engenders, to a policy foundation of full recognition of the rights of Indigenous peoples' (1995a: 23). Such a leap—suggesting a radical reconceptualisation of Aboriginal–non-Aboriginal relations in this country—has never been made. This challenge, essentially one to do with the sovereignty of Aboriginal peoples, is an issue I take up in the next chapter.

3
SOVEREIGNTY AND CITIZENSHIP

Are Aboriginal people citizens of Australia or members of sovereign Indigenous nations? The nation-state of Australia may have sovereign legitimacy in the eyes of the world, but in the eyes of many of its Indigenous inhabitants it remains an illegitimate interloper on their territory, still trying after 220 years to usurp a sovereignty that they have never ceded. Aboriginal leaders and activists who hold this view believe passionately that this 'unfinished business' will not be resolved until Indigenous sovereignty is accorded proper respect, and until the sovereign Indigenous peoples of Australia are dealt with properly by way of a treaty or some other type of formal recognition.

But as with so much else in Aboriginal political culture, the question of sovereignty is not straightforward. Leaders and activists often engage in 'sovereignty talk' while simultaneously demanding their citizenship entitlements from the settler-state. There is a history of Aboriginal activism directed towards both these goals, separately and together. Treaty and land rights campaigners, who may identify themselves as belonging to Indigenous nations rather than to the Australian state, insist that Aboriginal peoples have never ceded their sovereignty to the British Crown. At the same time, many have engaged in civil rights campaigns, struggling for their full entitlements as Australian citizens, including access to state-provided services such as health and education. So how do these strands of political culture work together? As Roger Maaka and Augie Fleras (2005) ask, 'how does the concept of citizenship apply when Indigenous peoples see themselves as members of fundamentally autonomous political communities rather than as citizens of the state?' (2005: 42)

For some, this situation produces confusion over whether it is possible even to speak of a singular Aboriginal political movement or whether it is more appropriate to understand Aboriginal political culture as comprising two distinct movements. For John Chesterman, 'it does not make much sense to talk of a "civil rights movement" in contrast to an "Indigenous rights movement" or a "land rights movement"' (Chesterman 2005: 27–8), even though these strands clearly have, at the very least, quite different goals. According to Chesterman: 'These two sets of rights entail two sorts of belonging: to one's community, and to the state. For Indigenous Australians these two relationships often require quite divided loyalties, which will occasionally come into conflict with each other and will raise quite complex issues.' (2005: 31) The reality, however, is that many Aboriginal people are struggling for both types of belonging. Aboriginal people understand citizenship and its rights, obligations and services as essential for improvements in their quality of life. But citizenship and government programs directed at bringing about formal equality will never achieve the more fundamental justice that Indigenous people pursue (Bradfield 2004: 167). For justice, Aboriginal people seek sovereignty—in many forms.

Sovereignty has many meanings

The colonising forces that arrived in *terra australis* failed to recognise existing forms of Aboriginal social organisation and sovereignty. Indigenous kinship groups were not seen as nations, and their sovereignty over specific territories was invisible to European eyes. Rather than being dealt with by way of a treaty or treaties as other Indigenous peoples had been, Indigenous peoples in Australia were physically brutalised and legally ignored. Australia remains the only former colony that has not dealt with its Indigenous peoples by way of a treaty.

With no treaty, Indigenous claimants have been forced to test the legality of British assertions of sovereignty in court, notably by the Wiradjuri barrister Paul Coe in *Coe vs Commonwealth* (1979). In what many consider to be something of an ambit claim designed more for media attention than likely legal success, Coe claimed that Captain James Cook's 1770 declaration of English sovereignty over the east coast of Australia was illegal in that it did not recognise the existing sovereignty of Aboriginal people. The claim was rejected by a majority of the High Court, who countered that the Australian colonies had become British possessions 'by settlement and not by conquest'. In 1983, a Senate Standing Committee reported on its investigation into Aboriginal sovereignty, which concluded that 'sovereignty does not now inhere in the Aboriginal people' and recommended constitutional change that would permit the negotiation of a new relationship between Indigenous peoples and the Australian state (Senate Standing Committee on Legal and Constitutional Affairs 1983). Aboriginal people then had to wait until the 1992 *Mabo* judgment to have some degree of legal recognition for the fact that they had never relinquished their land nor ceded their sovereignty. However, the *Mabo* decision also found that the acquisition of Australia had been an act of state that rendered future claims to Indigenous sovereignty 'non-justiciable'—an issue unable to be heard in any court. This decision has been interpreted by some as *Mabo* essentially dumping the question of Indigenous sovereignty in the 'judicial "too-hard basket"', leaving Aboriginal people without a legal avenue to pursue their claims (Falk and Martin 2007: 34). Gary Foley further argues that the legislative response to the *Mabo* decision—the 1993 *Native Title Act*—was a 'sell out' (particularly by Aboriginal negotiators) that amounted to 'an absolute denial of Aboriginal sovereignty' (2007: 118). Frank Brennan has claimed that Aboriginal sovereignty can now be 'at best' a political rather than a legal claim (1995: 127).

Despite these legal limitations, however, 'sovereignty talk' remains important in Aboriginal political culture, although it is not universally supported. Pat O'Shane, for example, argues that it is 'nonsense' to suggest that the different clans and tribal groups who were 'thrown together' as a result of colonial and assimilationist policies have any 'sense of common purpose, or interests, sufficient to constitute a national identity' (O'Shane 1998: 8). Noel Pearson (2007a) dismisses talk of sovereignty as arising from the 'acquisition of an undergraduate command of some key ideas in international and human rights law' (2007a: 41), preferring to discuss what he calls 'peoplehood issues' (2007a: 43). However, despite these occasional rejections, calls for sovereignty are widespread, although it is a term that appears to have many different meanings. For Murri legal scholar and international law expert Megan Davis (2006a), the continuing ambiguity around the concept of sovereignty gives the word 'its power and its strength' (2006a: 139).

North American political philosopher Iris Marion Young distinguishes between the 'factual situation of state powers' and 'the *idea* of sovereignty' (2000: 247). According to Young, the legal, factual situation of sovereignty involves centralised and final authority within territorial borders, clear distinctions between inside and outside, authority over lesser jurisdictions and external recognition of state legitimacy (2000: 247–8). This understanding of sovereignty is also known as 'external sovereignty'. It refers to the recognition of a sovereign nation-state by other nation-states and in international law. The 'idea' of sovereignty to which Young refers is something quite different, and opens the possibility for recognition of 'internal sovereignty', which focuses on 'where power is distributed within a nation's boundaries' (Brennan et al. 2005: 71). Many writers are at pains to differentiate Indigenous calls for sovereignty from the *real* sovereignty of international law. For Maaka and Fleras (2005), Indigenous sovereignty 'is not about secession or separation' (2005: 58); Larissa Behrendt is also clear that Indigenous people do not use the term 'sovereignty' 'as it is used in an international legal context' (Behrendt 2003: 18).

However, Behrendt also suggests that deciphering the various meanings that Indigenous leaders and activists do attach to terms such as 'Aboriginal sovereignty' is 'key to understanding the Indigenous political agenda', arguing that 'just because non-Aboriginal Australia refuses to recognise our sovereignty does not mean that it does not exist' (Behrendt 1995: 99). Behrendt articulates the aspirations of many when she writes:

> In the heart of many Aboriginal people is the belief that we are a sovereign people. We believe that we never surrendered to the British. We never signed a treaty giving up our sovereignty or giving up our land. We believe that we are from the land, that we are born from the land. When we die we return to the land . . . Land, in our culture, cannot be bought or sold. It always was Aboriginal land. It will always be Aboriginal land. (Behrendt 1995: 97–8)

A deep belief in their prior and continuing rights as sovereign beings is a source of identity and strength for many Aboriginal leaders and activists. Alwyn McKenzie suggested that his belief in his people's sovereignty is an antidote to 'self-doubt': 'I'm proud of the fact that I've got inherent rights and that my people were here for thousands of years. That keeps me going and gives me the link to my country. And no matter what happens in this world, for better or worse, at least I know that.' Colleen Hayward says simply: 'When I describe myself, I describe myself as a member of the Noongar nation. That's sovereignty.'

Larissa Behrendt has also written about what she calls the 'colloquial sense' in which Aboriginal sovereignty is discussed, where the term has become something of 'a catch-phrase for Indigenous people in expressing their vision for the future' (Behrendt 2003: 94–5). In our interview, Larissa explains that this idea of sovereignty:

> is all about how we structure Australian society to accommodate the rights and aspirations of Aboriginal people. I don't see it as being something that challenges the Australian state in terms of wanting to be separate. I see it as something that challenges the Australian state to say, as a democracy, how do you accommodate the rights of the culturally distinct and the historically marginalised, especially when there is a particular legal and moral claim by those people?

In emphasising this more 'colloquial' sovereignty, Behrendt claims that only 'very few activists' pursue a version of sovereignty that 'embraces notions of statehood and secession' (Behrendt 2003: 96). Tom Calma articulated several different positions on sovereignty from 'the extreme to the most moderate view and in between' that he hears around the country. He suggests that:

> Some argue it's a sovereignty that we put to organisations like the UN through the draft declaration, that sovereignty means the recognition that we are the traditional owners of land in Australia and with that we need to be recognised through various forms of compensation . . . Others say: 'Look, we're a sovereign nation, we want to set up our own country as Little Australia or whatever we call it. This is Aboriginal land, we take total control and issue passports.'

In Tom's opinion, this second more 'extreme' position could never be workable because it would mean that 'an Aboriginal person must disenfranchise themselves from their own country to go to somebody else's country to become a sovereign nation. That's not going to happen.' He also feels that, because 'there's no common view', governments are able to 'play the game':

> They will pick on the extreme views of sovereignty and of self-determination and say that self-determination means sovereignty and they want to secede from Australia and set up their own home nation, which is all bullshit. But politically, that's the way that they can push things.

Nevertheless, despite this potential for political exploitation, Tom believes the language of sovereignty—including in its more 'extreme' expressions—remains an important component of Indigenous political culture. A so-called 'radical' such as Michael Mansell has been necessary for Aboriginal people to assert themselves. In Tom's view:

> Whether we love or hate Michael Mansell, it doesn't matter, we needed somebody to be up there making a lot of noise, raising issues with the general population to make them understand more about Indigenous affairs and our plight. If we just tried to do it as a moderate, like I often try to be, you don't get listened to. But you get listened to if you come out with it, and that's what I respect and what Michael's done.

So what are we to make of the few activists, like Mansell, who still articulate a demand for a secession-based sovereignty? Should they be dismissed as merely the radical fringe of the Aboriginal rights movement with little contribution to make to the citizenship-focused agenda? What are we to make of groups such as the Aboriginal Provisional Government that have called for the creation of a separate Aboriginal state?

> Let it be clearly understood: the Aboriginal Provisional Government wants an Aboriginal state to be established with all of the essential control being invested back into Aboriginal communities. The land involved would essentially be Crown land but in addition there would be some land which would be needed by the Aboriginal community other than Crown land . . . (APG quoted in Attwood and Markus 1999: 327)

These more 'extreme' claims to sovereignty are not a thing of the past. Ray Swan asserts that the Tent Embassy mob maintain their occupation of the embassy site because Aboriginal people 'have never acquiesced or ceded our sovereignty in any legal shape or form'. Original Tent Embassy activist Michael Anderson agrees, suggesting that people need to look at why the Tent Embassy was established in the first place. Anderson has argued that: 'In 1972 back when we first started the protest there was a single sign saying "Sovereignty"; you can't be recognised as people without sovereignty . . . That is why the Tent Embassy is still there and should remain there until that happens. Nothing has changed.' (quoted in Giles 2005a: 3)

As recently as 2006, Tent Embassy activists declared 26 January (officially Australia Day, but long known as Invasion Day to Aboriginal people) 'Sovereignty Day', issuing a call for 'Aboriginal Sovereign nations to stand up against the illegal occupation of our country'. Michael Mansell also still insists that Aboriginal people 'have to give up the idea that a sacred site here and a small reserve over there can form the basis of an Aboriginal government. The only way we can survive as a people is to have enough land to provide for a quality living standard, and with hard work, a thriving and lively set of Aboriginal communities.' (Mansell 2005: 88)

Mansell's claims to sovereignty quite specifically involve 'the right to have enough land given back so that Aboriginal communities can realistically have their own government, raise their own economy and entirely run their own affairs' (Mansell 2005: 83). Yet Behrendt claims that these calls for a state are 'not in the sense of a separate country', despite a 'clear claim to jurisdiction at a community level' and a vision of 'Indigenous representation at the national level that would take responsibility for the coordination between communities . . . and for negotiations with other governments' (Behrendt 2003: 97–8). There is a tendency by some, including Behrendt, to downplay calls for the return of land and the creation of separate and autonomous jurisdiction. Others emphasise the 'rhetorical and political effect' of such claims, which they argue are 'impractical and utopian' (Mulgan 1998: 190).

But sovereignty talk is more than just a rhetorical move. It is a deeply felt and sincerely expressed belief about self and place in the world. Behrendt herself has written of the 'passion with which Aboriginal people believe in their nationhood' (Behrendt 1995: 98).

As we have seen, sovereignty activists do voice a demand for secession at times, and these 'few' are as important as their more moderate
cousins.

Clearly, however, there is a strategy in play to articulate a 'softer'
version of sovereignty, one that emphasises recognition, inclusion and
negotiation. It is this that Behrendt argues is the 'unique' Indigenous
interpretation of the term, which has 'leaked' into Aboriginal political
rhetoric and been transformed in the process (Behrendt 2003: 101–3). In
some ways, this rhetoric has also leaked into the mainstream, as Colleen
Hayward suggests, with 'more and more of that language creeping into
the vernacular'. Colleen observes that every time a non-Aboriginal
speaker acknowledges the traditional owners of the land they are on,
they are acknowledging Aboriginal sovereignty: 'While we've got a very,
very long way to go, when people get up and acknowledge that they're
on country and acknowledge traditional owners, it's a big step forward.
When they actually know the nation name of those traditional owners,
that's another step forward . . . They don't know that they're talking
about sovereignty, but in fact they are.' Colleen is referring to the indis-
putable aspect of Aboriginal sovereignty claims. Aboriginal people *are*
the traditional owners of the land, they *are* the first nations of Australia.
Sovereignty is 'embodied' in Aboriginal people, it is tied to their country
and 'performed' in 'everyday living' (Bunda 2007: 75; Birch 2007: 107).
As historian Henry Reynolds notes, Aboriginal people may be 'citizens
of the state', but they remain citizens of Aboriginal nations rather than
the Australian nation (Reynolds 1998: 214). Wendy Brady (2007)
describes this as living her life 'on two levels' in relation to sovereignty.
On the one hand there is her *'existence'* within the Australian nation,
while on the other hand she is a *'functioning* sovereign Indigenous being'
(2007: 140, emphasis in original). In this way, Aboriginal people live
both as members of a multiplicity of sovereign Indigenous nations and
also as citizens of Australia.

Where does citizenship fit?
In contrast to the alleged radicalism of some sovereignty claims, civil
rights activism has often been seen as 'the more earnest and less radical
sibling of the search for the recognition of Indigenous rights' (Chesterman
2005: 26). Citizenship has long been a central component of Indigenous
struggles for justice, but at no point in history have civil rights for

Aboriginal people simply been handed to them by a benevolent state. Rather, citizenship rights have been wrested from governments over decades of activism that has often been rendered invisible in history. Indeed, as John Chesterman has argued, in examining the history of advances in Aboriginal civil rights one is led to believe that these rights were gained 'as a result of a slowly developing governmental mindset that gradually and simply came to see the existence of racially discriminatory laws as unjust' (Chesterman 2005: 3). This is far from the truth.

Early demands for full citizenship emerged in the 1920s, motivated by the experiences of poor treatment meted out to Indigenous ex-servicemen returning from World War I. Activists such as Fred Maynard, who established the Australian Aboriginal Progressive Association at the end of 1923, were dismayed to find that even upon their return from active service they were denied full citizenship. In our interview, Fred Maynard's grandson, historian John Maynard, spoke of his grandfather's political motivation, which grew out of the period known as 'the second dispossession' following World War I. From the 1880s through to the 1920s, Aboriginal people in several southern states had developed 'independent farms' on reserve land where they 'built their own homesteads, they planted their own crops, they had live stock, and they did very well'. According to John, however, following the war this land was 'handed over to soldiers, and what did they take? Aboriginal land already cleared, already cropped, already homes built on it. The black fellas were thrown off.' Maynard here refers to white soldiers; Aboriginal soldiers who had served in the war were not only denied access to the soldier resettlement schemes offered to their brothers in arms but, in the greatest irony of all, Maynard points out that 'while some of these fellas were away fighting in Gallipoli or the Western Front, they were having their children taken off them'.

These issues prompted the first wave of citizenship struggles, which continued during the interwar period with the 1938 Aboriginal Day of Mourning conference. By 1948 the *Nationality and Citizenship Act* had created the category of Australian citizen, which included Aboriginal people by virtue of the fact that they had been born in Australia. In reality, however, citizenship status remained 'in name only' (Chesterman 2005: ix), a 'formal shell' (Chesterman and Galligan 1997) that did little to conceal the 'systematic exclusion of Aboriginal people from the rights, entitlements and privileges of citizenship through a mosaic of discriminatory laws and administrative practices' (Cunneen 2005: 48). More substantive changes to the citizenship status of Aboriginal people did not emerge until the 1960s when the restrictions that had been enshrined in various 'protection' Acts began to be wound back (Peterson and Sanders 1998: 14). The 1960s were the culmination of the thirty-year period that had gradually extended to Aboriginal people full citizenship rights and formal equality before the law, in the context of an official social policy of assimilation. The high point of these struggles was the 1967 referendum, which saw the Australian Constitution amended to permit the Commonwealth Government to make laws in relation to (although not necessarily for the benefit of) Aboriginal people, and to allow Aboriginal people to be counted in the census.

The development of Aboriginal citizenship was the result of civil rights activism that broke new ground in Australian politics. Despite these advances, however, for many Aboriginal people citizenship remains an 'ambiguous achievement' reliant on forfeiting the possibility of sovereign recognition (McDonald and Muldoon 2006: 210). Aboriginal people have resisted and continue to resist their classification as 'just another category of needy citizens' (Rowse 1992: 100), wanting instead to be recognised both as 'fellow human beings' and as 'a race' with a special claim to a set of rights that are unique to them (Attwood 2003: x). Citizenship, however, is often understood as reproducing existing inequalities in Indigenous–state relations. During the assimilation era, citizenship was offered as a 'reward' to Aboriginal people prepared to renounce their Aboriginality and embrace the dominant culture. Mick Dodson notes that even though the 1967 referendum 'provided a ticket of entry into the political system', this was only a 'concession ticket' with entry to 'the back stalls at some of the shows' (Dodson 1997: 57). There are implications in the achievement of citizenship for Aboriginal identity, as for many it remains vitally important to still be seen as a 'race apart' with distinct sovereign rights. As Stuart Bradfield suggests, the message to Aboriginal people is still that 'you can be "one of us" as long as you deny who you are' (2004: 168).

Citizenship does not mean the same thing for Aboriginal people as it does for non-Aboriginal people. Aboriginal people may not, in the first instance, even identify as Australian. For example, when I put this to Yorta Yorta elder Henry Atkinson, he replied: 'I can't class myself as a whole Australian in a sense. And I can never ever class myself solely as a Yorta Yorta person. First of all I'm a descendant of Wollithiga, which comes under the umbrella of the Yorta Yorta nations . . . I identify myself as Aboriginal or Indigenous Australian. Last of all I would class myself as an Australian.' For Henry, Australian citizenship is a necessity, but it does not describe who he is. His citizenship is always partial and provisional. Yura man Marvyn McKenzie makes a similar point when he says: 'I vote in state elections and the federal elections, but there's a big joke at home when I go against an Australian team because they don't represent *us*.' For Marvyn, the fact that he was born prior to the 1967 referendum, when Aboriginal people were 'still classed as flora and fauna', continues to influence his views about citizenship. Jilpia Jones has a similar perspective, saying in our interview:

> I don't consider citizenship a big drama because I was born in my country and my people recognise me as their own, I'm recognised for who I am and where I come from. I'm a Walmadjari. I'm a blackfella. This is my country. When I was born, I didn't have recognition of citizenship so how can I recognise something that wasn't recognised when I was born? I don't even have a birth certificate.

Wendy Brady (2007) takes a similar view, writing that she thinks of herself as a Wiradjuri person rather than as Aboriginal or Australian, pointing out that it is only when she is outside Australia that she is identified by her Australian citizenship (2007: 149). Sam Watson is more blunt, arguing: 'There's no fucking thing as Australian . . . It says nothing about the land. It says nothing about our culture or what happened on this land, how it was created, the dreaming stories, the cultural pathways that criss-cross this land, the ceremonies, rituals.'

But citizenship is also understood in the context of the appalling social circumstances in which many Aboriginal people live. For some leaders and activists, these circumstances make the exercise of citizenship rights a matter of some urgency. Ted Wilkes, for example, insists that improving these circumstances must come before any recognition of sovereignty. As he argues:

> Before you can actually get sovereign rights and before you can actually walk on the land with your sovereign rights you have to be healthy and able and mentally alert enough to be able to enjoy what your sovereign rights are.

I don't think you can do it the other way. I don't think you can get your sovereign rights before you get to do that other stuff.

Here Wilkes is at odds with others who are more focused on the *dangers* of citizenship for Aboriginal people in terms of both assimilation and complacency. As has been noted, the granting of full citizenship to Aboriginal people came during a period in which assimilation was official government policy. For many, there remains a deep suspicion that civil rights were granted as part of this assimilationist program. As long-time sovereignty activist Michael Mansell notes: 'There is indeed a fine line between gaining equality through citizenship, and succumbing to assimilation forces.' (Mansell 2003: 9) Kerry Arabena (2005) suggests that citizenship still implies a process of redefining Aboriginality so that Aboriginal people may be better integrated into the 'colonial, corporate, globalised culture' of modern Australia (2005: 50). These risks are also something to which Pat Dodson is alert; he argues that Aboriginal people must have the right to maintain their cultural identity and distinctiveness, without having their 'entitlements as Australian citizens held hostage to the social imperatives of governments' (2000: 17). Aden Ridgeway has made a similar point, arguing that:

Of course, we want the same opportunities for our people as everyone else gets . . . But having the same opportunities is different from being the same . . . Defining us as 'disadvantaged citizens' masks the structural and systemic barriers that have contributed to the situation we now find ourselves in . . . We need to be careful not to be coopted into over-simplified debates about our need which are based on language which is benign in appearance, but loaded in meaning. (Ridgeway 2005: 4–5)

Beyond concerns with assimilation, there is a further consideration of the ways in which acquiring citizenship rights may in fact 'inhibit the recognition of Indigenous rights' (Chesterman 2005: 28). As Michael Mansell argues:

[citizenship] is not offered without strings attached—it comes at a heavy price. The price to be paid . . . is the abandonment of indigenous sovereignty, and with it the loss of self-determination. Any rights would be limited to those granted by the parliaments or recognised by white law. There would be no inherent rights. (Mansell 2003: 8)

Several interviewees expressed concern at the way in which some of the 'new arrangements' in Indigenous affairs further eroded the emancipatory capacity of citizenship for Aboriginal people. Of particular concern were Shared Responsibility Agreements and the provisions for ninety-nine-year leases over Aboriginal land. In negotiating SRAs, Colleen Hayward warns that citizenship rights are a bottom line that 'Aboriginal people have got a right to expect and insist upon'. This means communities 'shouldn't be negotiating on the provision of adequate health care. That's a right.' Similarly, Alison Anderson points out that many Aboriginal people are 'really, really scared' that they may have to 'give up their land on a ninety-nine-year lease in order to receive essential services'. Like Colleen, Alison maintains that 'housing is a citizenship right for anybody', and the perceived coercion of the new arrangements is 'the factor that's really holding many negotiations from happening'. Alison questions why an identified need, such as for improved housing and other services, is not being met 'without a gun being held to these people's heads in order for them to relinquish their land'. Eddie Cubillo also wonders why leases can be made a condition of the provision of basic services. As he says: 'If we have to give up land to get a school there's something awfully wrong.'

Despite these risks, however, Michael Mansell sees the struggle for citizenship as appealing to certain Aboriginal leaders precisely because it is 'less confrontational', and therefore 'much more acceptable to the majority'. For Mansell, citizenship as an end is simply not 'good enough'; he highlights the 'doubtful merits of Aborigines being content to be Australian' at the expense of continuing struggles for the recognition of their sovereignty (Mansell 2005: 83). This view is shared by others such as Black GST activist Robbie Thorpe, who feels so strongly on the issue that he has taken himself out of the citizenship framework as much as possible. Robbie says that he has 'already got an identity' and he is not what he calls 'A-stray-alien'. Robbie argues that he has 'rights over and above the invaders', and that citizenship is 'a backward step for Aboriginal people. As soon as we say we're Australian we're giving up our identity. So I don't want your dole. I don't want your welfare. I want my human rights recognised.'

For others, citizenship is not only inadequate or disempowering, it has also failed to produce better outcomes for Aboriginal people. Speaking at the Aboriginal Tent Embassy's Day of Protest and Mourning for the 25th Anniversary of the 1967 Referendum in 1992, sovereignty activist Kevin Gilbert argued passionately against citizenship for Aboriginal people:

> Twenty-five years after this citizenship, which was supposed to give us some sort of rights and equality we see that instead of lifting us to any sort of degree of place or right it has only given us the highest infant mortality rate, the highest number of Aboriginal people in prison, the highest mortality rate, the highest unemployment rate and so on. (quoted in Attwood and Markus 1999: 321)

For Gilbert and others who share his view, citizenship for Aboriginal people has failed.

Accommodating citizenship and sovereignty

At times, political strategies oriented to both sovereignty and citizenship have come together. Several of my interviewees explained their vision of how sovereignty and citizenship can work together. Colleen Hayward, for example, described the way that sovereignty and citizenship might be accommodated in the practice of developing education policy in Western Australia. Colleen insists that 'all kids, regardless of their cultural background, need to be literate and numerate' as a minimum standard. This is a right of citizenship in a developed country like Australia. At the same time, however, Aboriginal people have a sovereign right to see education delivered in culturally appropriate ways that may differ from community to community, nation to nation. So, as Colleen argues:

> This community might say that's fine, but we want our kids to be literate and numerate in *our* language as well . . . What then varies from community to community is that [some will say], 'We want that to happen while the kids are at school, so we want some of our elders to come in and teach that', and others will say, 'Well, our kids are going to do it too, but it's got nothing to do with you, that's our business. We're going to do it out bush.'

In this vision of Aboriginal policy development, Hayward is claiming both citizenship rights (through a demand that all children be educated to a standard of mainstream literacy and numeracy) and sovereignty (through enabling different communities or nations to determine the context and basis for cultural education). Dr Marika (1999) makes a similar point in relation to education and curriculum development, which she says is 'all about power' and can be used to strengthen Yolngu culture and avoid 'an intellectual *terra nullius*' (1999: 7, 9). Lester-Irabinna Rigney also suggests a link between sovereignty and education, arguing for Indigenous jurisdiction and control rather than a view of Indigenous people as merely 'consumers' (2003: 77).

Sam Jeffries describes practices in the Murdi Paaki region, where the Regional Assembly model is based on communities 'leading the process, leading government along with us'. According to Sam, this model of community governance is 'a tool that returns responsibility to us, to be in charge of our own development and our own destiny'. For Mick Dodson, there is hope that this sort of 'local sovereignty' is already being accommodated, or at least shared, to some extent although 'people may not recognise it as such'. Mick sees organisations like the Murdi Paaki Regional Assembly 'making decisions that affect our lives'. These decisions, he says, could be described as 'sovereign decisions'. Such aspirations suggest that sovereignty is about the activity of Aboriginal people, not the activity of governments. Paul Briggs agreed with this view, saying:

> We can live as sovereign people and we can practice our own elements of sovereignty in the way we look after ourselves and the way we take care of Aboriginal culture and identity within Aboriginal life. That's a little bit different to waiting for an agreed relationship with the broader Australian people. I think we've been waiting for the Australian people to give us approval to live as Aboriginal people and I think that's just a mindset that's been inflicted on us over many generations.

One response to the assimilationist potential of a common citizenship has been the developing notion of 'Indigenous citizenship', in which Indigenous people enjoy their entitlements to state support combined with the responsibilities of Indigenous people *and* government to reproduce Indigenous culture and collectivity (Rowse 1998: 98). In some senses, this way of bringing sovereignty and citizenship together can be understood in Michael Mansell's (2003) definitions of 'Aboriginal Australians' as opposed to 'Australian Aboriginals'. According to Mansell, 'Aboriginal Australians' are 'the original people who lost their country and consented to be citizens of Australia. Their lost rights are replaced with those of other Australians.' This, in other words, is a view of Aboriginal citizenship in the Australian state which has lost any acknowledgment of the persistence of Aboriginal nations. By contrast, Mansell defines 'Australian Aboriginals' as 'the original people whose lands were invaded and are now occupied. All past rights are not lost, although they are unable to be exercised. [They] can still enjoy all rights of Australian citizens without losing their inherent rights.' (Mansell 2003: 5) In this second definition, sovereignty and citizenship can be understood as coexistent components of a complex political culture.

Recognising sovereignty

For the majority of Aboriginal leaders and activists, the formal recognition of sovereignty remains a deeply important goal. Mick Dodson speaks of sovereignty as 'part of that unfinished business that we keep talking about'. He longs for the day when Australia has a government that is 'interested in talking about sovereignty as part of the unfinished business', a government that is 'prepared to put the sovereignty question beyond doubt', a government that says: 'Right, we will deal with this unfinished business. Let's have that final honourable settlement with Indigenous Australia about this.' But Mick wonders whether Australia will ever see such a government. In a 2007 speech, he expressed his doubt that the Australian state even had the 'capacity' to support Aboriginal aspirations and respect Aboriginal people's 'sovereign status' (2007a: 5). Politically, he says, governments do not need to deal with the question of sovereignty 'in practical terms, because no one's challenging them'. It certainly seems that, as Stuart Bradfield (2004) has noted, Australia has 'little appetite' for a renewed dialogue on issues of how we, as a nation, may accommodate Indigenous political aspirations (2004: 165). Eddie Cubillo shares this pessimism:

We know non-Indigenous people aren't going to give us sovereignty. There's no chance of it. They can't even give us native title in its pure form. They've just got to change it straight away . . . I don't think it's ever going to come. I really don't . . . I read books about it all the time just to see if we've missed something, but I think things like native title are enough to show that this country is not ready to embrace Aboriginal people.

Others are in no way prepared to give up the fight for the recognition of sovereignty. Robbie Thorpe's organisation, the Black GST, stands for Genocide, Sovereignty and Treaty. For Robbie and his comrades, these are the 'fundamental legal questions that remain unresolved, the unfinished business'. Ray Swan agrees, pointing out that 'the recognition of Aboriginal sovereignty' will give Australia 'a true legal base'. Through this recognition, it will be possible to 'take this country forward on legal truths instead of continuously living on under illegal occupation, on illegal fictions'. Aileen Moreton-Robinson (2007) suggests that the continuing refusal of Aboriginal sovereignty shapes an Australian politics that is driven by 'white anxiety of dispossession' and 'white colonial paranoia' (2007: 101, 102)—further simplistic responses to political complexity. Moreton-Robinson (2007) asks: 'If Indigenous sovereignty does not exist, why does it constantly need to be refused?' (2007: 3)

The recognition of Indigenous sovereignty in Australia cannot be understood as some sort of 'fix all'. In many ways, recognising sovereignty may only serve to reveal the full extent of other underlying complexities in the Aboriginal domain—complexities that are discussed in the following chapters. Equally, until such imagined future time that Aboriginal people have achieved sufficient autonomy, including economic autonomy, to be able to properly exercise their sovereign duties to care for one another, governments are not off the hook. Until sovereignty is recognised and the institutional foundations of the nation are appropriately reformed, Aboriginal people will be forced to continue 'pulling on the weak moral heart strings of Australia' in order to have their needs met (Barnes 2004: 15). Without proper structural recognition, Aboriginal peoples' position within the Australian polity will remain subject to the whims of politicians and the goodwill of the government of the day (Davis 2006b: 130).

Ethicist Stephen Curry has argued: 'whatever indigenous sovereignty is, it is more than the right to autonomy or regional self-government where this is possible. It has something to do with the whole country that once belonged to indigenous people and now contains them.' (2004: 147) This is an issue that will not go away. All over the world, notionally postcolonial nations continue to struggle with the 'unresolved contradiction and constant provocation' at the heart of Indigenous–state relations—that is, that states continue to exercise jurisdiction over land that Indigenous people refuse to surrender (Tully 2000: 40). Australia is no exception to this pattern. Until this contradiction is properly recognised, Australia will only ever be chasing its tail in Indigenous affairs.

4
TRADITION AND DEVELOPMENT

As the previous two chapters have suggested, autonomy and sovereignty are important, if contested, goals in Aboriginal political culture. Despite their importance, however, a complex mix of historical circumstance and current reality combines to keep them out of reach. One significant factor in this dynamic is the relative, and in many cases extreme, poverty of many Aboriginal individuals, families and communities. Without an economic base, Aboriginal people cannot be autonomous. Not surprisingly, however, there are complexities that get in the way of economic development for Aboriginal people. One is the communal nature of Aboriginal ownership, which will be discussed in the next chapter. Another is the tension between the need for economic development and the importance of traditional connections to land.

In some parts of Australia, tensions to do with tradition and development are primarily concerned with the extent to which Aboriginal groups wish to preserve their traditional way of life—thus protecting land, language and culture for future generations—versus the extent to which these groups exploit their traditional lands for the economic opportunities they offer. The demand for economic development sits uncomfortably alongside one of the 'arts' of Indigenous resistance— that is, the acts of 'protecting, recovering, gathering together, keeping, revitalising, teaching and adapting entire forms of indigenous life that were nearly destroyed' (Tully 2000: 59). Making decisions about mining and other potentially destructive industrial practices entails asking fundamental questions such as 'How should we live?' (Davis 2005: 53) This is an unenviable task for Aboriginal leaders concerned about both economic and cultural survival, who risk being charged with 'saving the village by destroying it' (Havemann 2000: 25). This challenge has been exacerbated in recent years by a new policy paradigm designed to stimulate market forces in order to 'lift' remote communities out of their 'social and economic malaise' (ATSISJC 2007b: 3). The desire to insert mainstream economic thinking about development into diverse Indigenous community contexts, regardless of the cultural fit, is inherently problematic.

Poverty and inactivity in Aboriginal communities are far from the whole story. Aboriginal enterprises on Aboriginal land include mud brick manufacturing, crocodile farming, road and building construction, aeroplane and helicopter charter, 'bush tucker' and art material wholesaling and retailing, mustering of wild cattle, horses and buffalo, and participation in the commercial fishing and pearling industries. These activities allow Aboriginal people to combine income generation with land management, 'using their land and traditional skills in ways that both help look after the country and provide employment' (Central and Northern Land Councils 1994: 9–10). But in visiting remote communities, it is also clear that, even given a meaningful alternative for relocation, many Aboriginal people would still choose to live on their own country in poverty than move off their land for economic gain. As Robert Tonkinson (2007) notes, Aboriginal people living on country want to be able to visit towns and cities, but primarily as sites of consumption rather than as places for temporary employment (2007: 52). Many display a 'tenacious commitment' to preserving their way of life, even in the face of abject poverty (Martin 2005: 110).

Nevertheless, there is widespread recognition among Aboriginal leaders and activists that improving economic well-being and creating greater capacity for economic development are urgent tasks (Dodson and Smith 2003: 5). A decade ago, Tracker Tilmouth argued that Aboriginal people would continue to be politically marginalised unless they developed an economic base (Tilmouth 1998: xi). More recently, Marcia Langton has described 'economic justice' as 'the new frontier in Aboriginal and settler relations', crucial so that Aboriginal people may live 'as well as other Australians do for the same effort' (2002: 18). Tom Calma, writing in the 2006 *Native Title Report*, agrees that sustainable economic development is 'essential' for well-being 'now and into the future' (ATSISJC 2007b: 1). In our interview, however, Tom stressed that while development is 'critically important' to Aboriginal health and well-being, there is 'no one answer' to the challenges it poses. Australia has a long history of misguided effort in this area.

A history of failure?

There is a widespread assumption that traditional Aboriginal culture was and is unproductive. Aboriginal ways of life are generally considered far removed from dominant understandings of 'market', 'economy' or 'production'. However, as Mick Dodson has pointed out, the assertion that Aboriginal people in Australia did not and do not have economic interests in land is 'simply wrong' (Dodson 1997: 43). Contrary to the view that Aboriginal people were primitive people who did not exploit their land's potential, the real history of pre-invasion economic life included complex, nationwide trade routes along which ochre, bush tobacco and stone were exchanged; a developed industry in eel aquaculture in the Western District of Victoria, which involved hundreds of kilometres of stone walls, weirs and tunnels (Pascoe 2007); and international trade in trepang, tamarind and turtle shell between Yolngu and Macassans from Indonesia[1] (Stephenson 2007). Land and its resources provided an economic base for Aboriginal people for many thousands of years prior to colonisation (Goodall 1996: 2).

Even in traditional life, however, there could be tension about the relative merits of preservation versus exploitation. In our interview, Alwyn McKenzie explained that the different ways in which people gained their attachments and obligations to certain areas of country could create difficulties. As Alwyn explained:

> You have certain responsibility that you get from being from the country your mum comes from and other responsibilities from where your dad comes from too. So maybe on your dad's side you can exploit things like the red ochre and extract that from the land. But on your mother's side you've got a responsibility to look after the land in an environmental way. So that's the tensions there, see? Even in traditional society that was a tension, but it was balanced.

The arrival of British colonisers unsettled this balance. In the ensuing decades, Aboriginal people were dispossessed of their land, relocated on to reserves and missions, and denied the capacity to maintain their traditional livelihoods. As industry developed, Aboriginal people were coerced or coopted into labour. In many cases they received rations rather than wages, and where payments were made they were often 'kept in trust' by governments in practices that literally amounted to slavery (Highland, in Kidd 2007: 8).

It was not until the land rights campaigns of the 1960s and 1970s, 180 years after the invasion, that attention began to be paid to economic development on land that was slowly being returned to Aboriginal communities. However, the hostile environment into which land rights were born did not help economic development. In the Northern Territory, for example, the CLP government (in power from 1974 to 2001) opposed every single land claim made by Aboriginal groups, engaging in litigation estimated to have cost over $10 million. The Northern Territory government's attitude turned something that was intended to be beneficial for Aboriginal economic development into a 'legalistic battlefield' (Central and Northern Land Councils 1994: 4). A forced engagement on this battlefield was a frustrating distraction from the economic development that *could* have been occurring. As Sean Brennan points out: 'Who knows what greater partnership and socio-economic development might have been possible during that time if Aboriginal Territorians and their land councils had not been regularly pitted against the Northern Territory government in litigation.' (Brennan 2006: 21)

The terms of land ownership under the Northern Territory *Land Rights Act* still limit the capacity for economic development. To start with, ownership of subsurface minerals in Aboriginal land is retained by the federal government (Howitt et al. 1996: 14). Mick Dodson argues that although nearly half of the land mass of the Territory is now 'under Aboriginal ownership and control', this means 'very little in commercial terms':

I mean, it's enormously important to people in terms of acknowledgment and recognition, the spiritual and cultural aspects of it. But as a commercial vehicle, it's virtually useless because the traditional owners, the native title holders, don't have any real property rights. There is no property in the natural resources, all the property in that is held by the government who flog it off to developers of all sorts, particularly the mining industry. And the original owners of that property, they get very little from it.

Mick also identifies significant problems with the ways that mining royalties in the Northern Territory are distributed. Under the current scheme, the mining companies pay royalties to the federal and Northern Territory governments. The federal government then determines royalty 'equivalency' payments, which are paid into the Aboriginals Benefits Account (ABA), the funds from which are legally tied to use only for the benefit of Aboriginal people in the Territory.[2] Mick argues that this way of distributing revenue from Aboriginal lands means that even where there is some recognition of Aboriginal property and mineral rights, Aboriginal people 'don't have control over that resource'. A related problem is that Aboriginal landowners only have a power of 'veto' in relation to mining on their land at the time that exploration is proposed. If the landowners agree to minerals exploration on their land, they are deemed to have agreed to any subsequent mining activity. In other words, landowners are expected to make a decision about whether to allow mining on their land when very little information about the type and scope of the potential project is known (Central and Northern Land Councils 1994: 4). This situation, as Mick Dodson observes, is 'unfair to everybody'. Not surprisingly, mining proposals are often knocked back at the exploration stage because Aboriginal landowners fear the loss of control that could result if they agree to allow exploration on their land.

The native title regime introduced in 1993 has also produced mixed results as far as helping Aboriginal people to resolve these tensions. Native title provides the crucial 'right to negotiate' without which, according to Kimberley leader Peter Yu, Aboriginal people would not have the capacity to even begin developing economic projects (Yu 1997: 175). However, a grant of native title can produce very different outcomes in different parts of the country, depending on the history of the area.[3] Jackie Huggins highlights the fact that although 'people say it's great to have an economic base' as a result of a successful native title claim, 'It doesn't happen like that for most of us . . . It doesn't happen over here, or in the urban areas.' The extent to which native title can even create the sort of economic base to which Jackie refers is also highly questionable. Even when native title rights are recognised, they are rarely economically productive, as Tom Calma has explained:

The right to fish under traditional laws has not translated into commercial fishing rights; the native title right to take flora and fauna is not able to be used to sell bush foods or native wildlife as of right. The traditional use of minerals has not become a native title right to exploit minerals such as through mining enterprises. (quoted in Dick 2007)

Much of the current debate about economic development for Aboriginal people remains focused on the extreme poverty of some remote communities. However, Larissa Behrendt points out that development is needed in urban areas as well, where Aboriginal people still find themselves excluded from the 'mainstream' of economic life. For her, Howard-era policy that explicitly redirected resources away from urban to rural and remote areas was 'very flawed'—a flaw recognised by the Rudd government which, in April 2008, announced a new focus on fighting Indigenous poverty in cities (Franklin and Karvelas 2008).

The most recent change of direction in debates about Indigenous development centres on the issue of welfare dependency, discussed in Chapter 2, and particularly the controversial Community Development Employment Program (CDEP). Marcia Langton (2002) claims that CDEP was generally regarded 'by informed Aboriginal leaders' as being the 'principal poverty trap for Aboriginal individuals, families and communities' (2002: 10). In our interview, Ted Wilkes agreed with this perspective, arguing that he was 'in favour of closing all the CDEPs down' which he saw as being 'worse than being on the dole'. Ted says that many Aboriginal leaders and elders are worried that 'all our young warriors are all working on CDEP' when they should be properly employed. Like Ted, Marcia Langton would prefer to see Aboriginal labour redirected to what she calls 'the productive economy' (2002: 13).

Others, however, are concerned that abolishing CDEP in order to move people to 'real jobs' is merely fanciful in many areas. Geoff Scott agrees that tension between 'economic development issues and welfare agenda' is 'the biggest debate at the moment', but he worries that the abolition of CDEP is 'ideologically driven', even if it does appear to be 'sadly backed by some Aboriginal people'. Like many other critics of the change in policy, Geoff points out that 'most Aboriginal people live in areas where the industries aren't there, the markets aren't there. You're not creating an industry in one that doesn't exist.' The abolition of CDEP means that Aboriginal people have to comply with mainstream 'work for the dole' requirements or risk losing their benefits. The application of this regime in remote communities where little 'real' employment exists is likely to produce an array of unintended consequences, including a drift to already struggling regional towns.[4]

But increasingly, a distinction is being drawn between the 'real economy' and the 'Aboriginal economy', with a growing insistence that all Aboriginal people should engage in the real economy in order to develop a sound economic base. Many Aboriginal people, however, remain sceptical about what development such as mining might actually bring them. As Henry Atkinson asks: 'What benefit does Indigenous Australia really get from the resources that are taken off of our lands, whether it's gold, silver or uranium, water, trees or what?' Sam Jeffries also suggests that people 'check out in five years' time' what increased mining on Aboriginal land will actually deliver to Aboriginal communities and suspects that the 'real agenda' is about 'exploiting property rights'. Yet, despite this scepticism, much effort is being expended to consider options for development on Aboriginal land.

Opportunities for development
In the face of ongoing, extreme and seemingly entrenched poverty, Aboriginal groups and communities are always examining their options for economic development. Many groups have chosen to negotiate resource development agreements and establish enterprises on Aboriginal land, although making these choices creates new challenges for land and resource management (Dodson and Smith 2003: 5). In the past, many such negotiations have been the result of bullying and harassment from government and industry, although more recently some mining companies and pastoralists have learned to appreciate the land rights regime and have negotiated the use of Aboriginal land more appropriately (Central and Northern Land Councils 1994: 4). Mining companies have had to accept that Indigenous rights cannot be considered 'externalities' to their industry, but instead must be seen as 'an integral component of the decision making landscape of resource management' (Howitt 2001: 203). Still, Mick Dodson claims that the mining industry 'gets it easy' and that industry and government still demonstrate 'a reluctance to fairly deal with Indigenous people'.

Historically, the pastoral industry has been a significant area of Indigenous employment and economic activity, although these relationships have at times been highly exploitative. Currently, the Indigenous Land Corporation (ILC) is involved in purchasing pastoral property for Indigenous groups, a strategy that Tom Calma says has 'partly worked'. Many properties have depreciated rather than appreciated in value due to significant under-investment. As an increasingly automated industry, pastoralism does not offer the same levels of employment it once did. While still a feature of Aboriginal economic development strategy, pastoral possibilities are limited. Pastoralism can also create tensions within Aboriginal land-owning groups through the isolation of pastoral land from the traditional social practices and communal bonds that are characteristic of Aboriginal land ownership (Davis 2005: 53).

Some economic opportunities in Aboriginal communities provide limited scope to combine Indigenous culture with the market economy. Tourism on Aboriginal land—of the 'eco' and 'cultural' varieties—has been pursued by both Aboriginal and non-Aboriginal interests with varying success[5] and with a mixed response from Aboriginal people. For example, Luritja man Ben Clyne has commented that, while he is 'not against tourists', he observes that 'they just come and go away again'. In contrast, he says Luritja people 'want to go [to their land] and stop there, to look after our country forever' (Clyne, quoted in Central Land Council 1994: 6). The Aboriginal art industry has also offered economic opportunities; however, these have been undermined by exploitation, theft of intellectual and cultural property, 'carpetbagging' and significant inequities between the original sale price and subsequent resale values (Janke and Quiggin 2006; Rimmer 2007; Senate Standing Committee on Environment, Communications, Information Technology and the Arts 2007). Much of the high-priced Aboriginal art now on display in urban galleries and homes was produced in conditions that would be 'very confronting to the affluent city dwellers on whose walls it hangs' (Martin 2005: 110).

Without doubt, the most contentious area of development on Aboriginal land is in the mining sector. Proposals for mineral and gas extraction, such as those to extract gas on the heritage rich Burrup Peninsula and uranium at Jabiluka in the Kakadu National Park, have sparked heated debates in both Aboriginal and non-Aboriginal forums. Across affected Aboriginal communities there is an array of responses to mining projects, ranging from opposition on the grounds of cultural and environmental protection to enthusiasm based on the potential for economic benefits that may flow to Indigenous communities (Trigger 2005: 41). In some communities, mining may offer the only opportunity for the generation of independent wealth (Howlett 2006: 3). Tom Calma, for one, sees 'plenty of potential' for Aboriginal people in negotiating with the mining industry, and is impressed by what he sees as the industry's commitment to 'putting into practice a lot of the government rhetoric'. The most important thing the mining companies are doing, according to Tom, is that 'they are engaging. They're looking at proactive ways in which they can engage Indigenous companies.'

These improvements in relations between the mining industry and Aboriginal people are relatively recent (and far from consistent, see note 7 on page 246). The industry was long opposed to greater Aboriginal economic autonomy, evident through its vehement opposition to the Hawke government's proposed national land rights legislation. Aboriginal people have seen successive governments as complicit in their relationships with mining companies in this regard. For example, writing an (unpublished) letter to the *West Australian* newspaper, the Yungngora community protested the coercion to which it had been subjected in relation to the highly controversial Noonkanbah mine and demonstrated the gulf in understanding between the parties:

> The government said we will benefit from this mining. How can we if our people's lives are in danger from our people and our spirits? Whiteman does not believe our story, our tribal law. But we know it is the right way to live . . . You say we are breaking the whiteman's law, but you, the government, break our law and ask us to break our law, which you don't know or care about. How can our people live a strong life if you take our sacred away? You say you need money from mining. We give you land elsewhere for mining. You say you must have sacred area for mining. Why? (quoted in Lippmann 1981: 183)

In some areas of Australia, there is still much more to be done to build Aboriginal trust in the mining industry. Dr Marika, whose father led the Gove land rights case (*Milirrpum v Nabalco Pty Ltd*) in 1971, remained deeply suspicious of the mining industry, and of Alcan in particular.[6] In our interview, she remembered the complete lack of consultation with Yolngu in 1963 when the mining company's bulldozers rolled in after negotiating a deal with the Methodist mission and the federal government. The contemporary relationship between Alcan and Yolngu remains highly complex. Dr Marika was angry that the company tends to deal almost exclusively with high-profile Yolngu leader Galarrwuy Yunupingu, who Alcan recognises as 'the landowner'. She pointed out, however, that in fact there are 'many landowners. We own communal title to land.' The land that the mine is exploiting is Gumatj land belonging in the cultural way to Galarrwuy's father's daughters. But according to Dr Marika, Alcan only see Galarrwuy as 'the important person, not all the other old people or the old ladies . . . Just Galarrwuy is seen as being important.'

One particularly controversial mining project is the Xstrata-owned McArthur River zinc mine near Borroloola in the Northern Territory. In March 2007, the Northern Land Council and a group of traditional owners from the McArthur River area initiated court proceedings to stop the Territory government-approved expansion of the mine, which would necessitate a 5.5 kilometre diversion of the river itself. One traditional owner from the area was quoted as saying they would be 'sick if they cut that place, because my spirit is there. All my songs are across the river.' (quoted in Wright 2007) The ensuing victory in the Territory Supreme Court was subsequently 'sidestepped' by the Northern Territory government, which intervened with new legislation to provide Xstrata with 'certainty' (ABC 2007d). But, despite three Aboriginal government MLAs crossing the floor over the passage of the legislation, not all Aboriginal people involved share their anger. Kim Hill, for example, is more pragmatic, and accepts that 'Xstrata may not necessarily be a community friendly organisation' but still argues that the company is 'looking at ways of building the region' by 'digging a very big hole'. Kim explained his position on Xstrata as being 'if you can tick off a number of boxes in regards to the environment and how they're going to go about it, which the Territory government has done, and then [have a] a monitoring component, I don't see it as being a problem'. Kim is comfortable with the river diversion going ahead, 'as long as all the sites have been addressed, sites of significance, sacred sites'. The bottom line for Kim is that 'each economic development opportunity on Aboriginal land needs to be looked at on its individual merits. You can't have a blanket over this and over that.'

Despite the current emphasis on mining as a key component of development on Aboriginal land, Geoff Scott argues that this is only 'a transitory phase'. Whether it is passing or not, its impact is certainly being felt. Ted Wilkes describes the miners as 'little white ants' running all over the world—not dissimilar to what he calls 'the agricultural encroachment' of a century ago. Then it was 'the sheep and the cows', now it's 'the shovels and the picks and the trucks'. Traditional owners, such as Neil McKenzie from the Broome/Fitzroy Crossing area of Western Australia, are struggling to make decisions about deals such as the proposed natural gas processing plant on the Maret Islands. McKenzie says traditional owners have to 'live with the decision that we try to make collectively in good faith, that we know it's not going to hurt the next generation, and the country . . . won't be destroyed or desecrated' (quoted in ABC 2007b).[7] For as long as there are minerals to be taken from Aboriginal land, traditional owners are going to have to make these difficult decisions.

Maggie Walter (2007) notes the 'rising intensity' with which market-based policy solutions to questions of Indigenous development are being proposed (2007: 161). Noel Pearson has been active in promulgating the view that the only way to end welfare dependency is to engage in forms of economic development that see the 'overwhelming majority' of working age people in communities engaged in 'real economic activity' (Cape York Institute 2007: 27). This approach, taken up enthusiastically by the federal government, seems to conflate commercial activity with economic activity, and offers an extremely narrow view of what constitutes an economy. Larissa Behrendt suspects this is a 'Trojan horse' of economic development, in that she sees market-based development solutions being used as cover for government desires to 'open up Indigenous land to non-Indigenous interests' (Behrendt 2007b: 10). These approaches pose questions of development as purely economic in nature, obscuring their social and political implications. Development is as much to do with Aboriginal people's need for control and decision-making power as it is to do with policy settings, market ideology or cash.

In contrast to the increasing dominance of market-based 'solutions', Jon Altman and his colleagues at the Centre for Aboriginal Economic Policy Research have argued that market engagement will never provide opportunities for all Aboriginal people in remote Australia. Consequently, mainstream understandings of development will never deliver equality in remote and very remote areas. Recognising this reality gives policy-makers four 'non-exclusive broad choices':

maintain the status quo and allow people to continue to live in poverty; force people to move, although where and what for remains unclear; build an economic base at remote communities . . .; or shift our thinking to a new, different, fourth way that focuses on indigenous livelihoods and the recognition of new forms of property. (Altman 2006: 9)

The new 'fourth way' that Altman proposes would see state support of Indigenous livelihoods through welfare support and CDEP undergo a paradigm shift towards an approach that 'actively supports and lauds indigenous participation in eco-services provision and forms of market engagement (such as in the arts) that are not only sustainable but would enhance indigenous wellbeing' (Altman 2006: 10).

Altman calls this the 'hybrid economy' (Altman 2005; 2006: 9), and argues that limiting the vision of Aboriginal economic futures to a consideration of only the private and public (state employment and welfare) sectors not only denies the culturally informed aspirations of many Aboriginal people, but also neglects a third sector—what Altman describes as the 'customary sector' of the economy (Altman et al. 2006: 139). In ways very similar to feminist economists' attempts to 'feminise the economy' by quantifying the market value of housework, Altman and his colleagues 'seek to include and quantify a predominantly unpaid and unrecognised Indigenous component in the economy', to 'Indigenise' the economy by acknowledging various aspects of customary activity as work. They further point out that a lack of data and wider understanding of the customary element of the hybrid economy tends to erase productive Aboriginal participation and perpetuate poorly informed criticism of state support for the customary sector in remote communities (Altman et al. 2006: 140). In response to Noel Pearson and those in the Howard government who declared remote communities unsustainable, Altman and his colleagues describe this 'hybrid' economy as the 'real "real economy"' and insist that Aboriginal futures in remote Australia must move beyond the 'false binary' between the so-called 'real economy' and welfare dependence (Altman 2006: 10).

Altman's ideas concerning an economic model that recognises customary activity have also been expressed, albeit in less developed form, by some Aboriginal leaders and activists. A decade ago, for example, Tracker Tilmouth argued that: 'Economic development does not have to mean commercial development in the usual western sense. It can also mean maintaining Indigenous economic processes and cultures, and building on them so people have the resources to enjoy land rights.' (Tilmouth 1998: xi) Mick Dodson has also recognised that activities such as hunting, fishing and harvesting are 'neither merely economic or cultural activities', but afford communities a combination of economic participation, environmental protection and cultural preservation (Dodson 1997: 43).

Land and culture

Layered underneath the challenges of contemporary economic development are the traditional relationships to land that are central to Aboriginal culture and identity. These layers, and their implications for development, tend to be poorly understood by non-Aboriginal people who either romanticise Aboriginal culture as some sort of universal, anti-capitalistic spirituality or deride its significance as primitive, anti-development ignorance. Neither view captures the reality of the complex ways in which Aboriginal people balance their obligations to country with their need for economic development (Brock 2001: 6). Aboriginal land ownership is, as Sean Brennan notes, a 'conservative institution'; however, as an institution that has survived harsh conditions across millennia, it also demonstrates a strong capacity for adaptation (Brennan 2006: 22). Integrating new forms of economic activity with social concerns and cultural priorities within a framework of limited legal rights and developing governance systems is one of the greatest challenges facing Indigenous people today (Dodson and Smith 2003: 6). Getting the balance right will be central to achieving real self-determination (Young 2005: 119).

Within the 'hundreds of reports' that have been written about these issues, 'culture' is often discussed as an 'influential factor' that complicates Indigenous responses to development. However, as Mick Dodson and Diane Smith point out, these reports have tended to assume that Aboriginal cultural values are 'at odds with western ideas of capitalism and the market place', reducing a diversity of Indigenous views to an understanding that all Aboriginal people are opposed to development 'because it undermines their culturally based behaviours and values' (Dodson and Smith 2003: 6, 8). Legislation and policy that do not come to grips with the real complexity of Indigenous culture, and that instead rely on 'outmoded frameworks of "the traditional"', will have the effect of constraining rather than advancing economic development (Taylor et al. 2005: xiii).

There is no doubt that, for the majority of Aboriginal people, the protection of culture is crucial and will often take precedence over economic development. Tom Calma, as Aboriginal and Torres Strait Islander Social Justice Commissioner, conducted a survey of traditional owners regarding their attitudes to land and development which confirmed that, although the majority of respondents agreed that economic development was important, they ranked 'custodial responsibilities' as the most important use of their land (ATSISJC 2007b: 1). There was considerable concern among the leaders and activists I interviewed about the way in which government policy was pressuring Aboriginal people to 'go mainstream', as Henry Atkinson put it. This is worrying because, in Henry's view, 'mainstreaming' is really 'another way of genocide': 'There's different ways to genocide, especially when you're denied your rights to your own land and your own culture, your own language and the likes. To me that is genocide . . . I'm not saying people shouldn't be able to evolve also, but for sure, the culture should be protected and preserved for the younger generations.'

Custodianship of the land is a central element of Aboriginal cosmology and cultural practice, in which land is seen to embody religious and philosophical knowledge (Goodall 1996: 2). Alwyn McKenzie describes the emotional response that Aboriginal people may experience when learning of a new development on their country. For example, Alwyn says the non-Aboriginal reaction to the planned dam expansion at Roxby Downs in South Australia was one of excitement about a possible 'economic boom', whereas for a lot of Aboriginal people 'there's a feeling of dread . . . especially if they come from that country'. For some, this means development is completely off limits. Plangermairreenner elder Jim Pura-lia Meenamatla Everett, for example, claims that too many Aboriginal organisations:

> are silent on the environmental issues of this country, about the destruction to our lands and waters—these so-called leaders are lost . . . If we think we need white man's money to develop our culture into our communities, then we ought to throw our culture away, because we're lost if we need money to keep culture alive! (quoted in McConchie 2003: 62)

Aboriginal Law, expressed in songs, dance and paintings, contains extensive and detailed guidance about caring for country and the management of particular areas of land (Goodall 1996: 4). Maintaining these cultural obligations to care for land is highly skilled and time-consuming work that is poorly recognised as an economic contribution (Altman and Whitehead 2003). While concerned with the ubiquitous portrayal of Aboriginal people as 'super-conservationists', and of Aboriginal land as 'wilderness' despite millennia of Indigenous habitation, Fabienne Bayet-Charlton also considers relationships to land as 'the main difference between Aboriginal and non-Aboriginal cultures' (Bayet-Charlton 2003 [1994]: 173, 174). Aboriginal leaders have to weigh the potential economic benefits of development against the cost of even temporary impacts on aspects of Aboriginal land and culture (Kauffman 1998: 157). Tom Calma suggests that many Aboriginal people want to claim back land 'not for economic gain', but rather 'to be able to maintain the land' as traditional owners. Robbie Thorpe, along with several other interviewees, suggested that non-Aboriginal Australia would do well to learn from Aboriginal attitudes to land, arguing that Aboriginal people 'have a sustainable system and society because we looked after the land'. In contrast, Robbie says, non-Aboriginal Australia is 'ripping off and raping' the land in ways that are not sustainable. Dr Marika made a similar point, suggesting:

> *Ngapaki* [white] people should learn from us, you know. This place would be a beautiful sanctuary if it wasn't for that. The Yolngu have cared for the land and have been custodians of the land for millions of years, since time began. And everything now . . . you look at climate change and all those things, everything's starting to fall apart. If people would learn from us then things would be better . . . But it's all that materialism and industry, the pollution, gas emissions and all that. It's destroying the earth now.

In this light, there are some aspects of proposed 'development' that are deeply challenging for some leaders and activists. There is caution about using Aboriginal land for development projects that are not ecologically sustainable, as there is a cultural imperative that they also sustain the land for generations to come. Economic development should not take precedence over this mandate (Bayet-Charlton 2003: 179). Eddie Cubillo, for example, is horrified by the proposal to develop a nuclear waste dump on Aboriginal land in the Northern Territory, and the reported decision by the traditional owners at Muckaty Station to accept $12 million for a 1.5 square kilometre site to be developed for this purpose in a plan backed by the Northern Land Council (Ravens and Peters 2007). Eddie says the idea of nuclear waste on Aboriginal land 'guts' him and 'just goes against the grain of everything that I've been brought up with'.

Uranium mining and nuclear waste are both highly contentious areas of 'development' among Aboriginal communities. Jeffrey Lee, the sole surviving member of the Djok clan and senior custodian of the Koongarra uranium deposit, has decided never to allow his land to be mined despite the wealth it would bring him, insisting that his responsibility to look after his land is more important (Murdoch 2007). William Tilmouth and David Ross have been vocal in their opposition to a dump site anywhere near Alice Springs (SBS 2005). In South Australia, Eileen Unkari Crombie from the Kupa Piti area suggests that her people know 'don't touch that one' about uranium as their cultural knowledge tells that it causes sickness. Unkari Crombie also rejects the money on offer for nuclear waste, saying, 'We don't want money, we want life' (quoted in McConchie 2003: 18–19). Kim Hill, however, has no problem with nuclear waste being dumped in the Territory as long as 'the traditional owners have been consulted and they're fully across the issue and what's going to be there'. While acknowledging that non-Aboriginal people 'find it very difficult' that a small number of traditional owners can have ownership and decision-making powers over a very large area of land, for Kim such decisions are 'an expression of Indigenous sovereignty'.

One effect of colonisation is that Indigenous people find themselves trying to hold on to some of their more traditional ways of life in the face of relentless opposition. If Australia had not been colonised, there is no doubt that Aboriginal culture would have changed in the intervening 220 years. In a postcolonial context, however, the defence of traditional culture itself becomes an act of resistance. The maintenance of custodial relationships to land is a key part of this, as the Central and Northern Land Councils have argued:

> We have taken from non-Aboriginal Australia some of the good things that help us to carry out our responsibilities to our land, like motor vehicles and two-way radios, and they have changed our lifestyles a lot. But nothing has

changed our identity with our land. Our land is our life . . . For us, land isn't simply a resource to be exploited. It provides us with food and materials for life, but it also provides our identity and it must be looked after, both physically and spiritually. If we abuse our land, or allow someone else to abuse it, we too suffer. (Central and Northern Land Councils 1994: 8)

This need to protect traditional culture leaves some people in a quandary. Warren Mundine argues that it took European and Asian societies '500 years to go from hunter-gatherer societies, [to] agriculture, industrial revolution, then on to the other technology, communication revolutions', and insists that Aboriginal people must now 'jump the 500 year gap' between traditional culture and modern Australian society. While Warren also accepts the need to 'rebuild the stuff that was knocked over and kicked around and roughed about through the invasion process', he is concerned that Aboriginal people 'need to pick up on the modern world and pick up all those skills and technology stuff that we need'. Warren worries that holding on to tradition at the expense of development can mean that 'when the bus of opportunity goes past, you don't recognise it . . . The world moves on.' For Warren, the answer is to try to find a middle ground that recognises the constant state of change that occurs in intercultural interaction:

People who are saying that you let go of [culture] are wrong, and people who are saying that we just cocoon ourselves against the world are wrong. What human beings have been doing for thousands of years is that they've been interacting with each other. As soon as you meet another person, it changes you, whether you like it or not. That's why you see a lot of people driving around in Toyotas in the Central Desert and Aboriginal people who are flying in aeroplanes and that now. What you've got to do is use those tools for your own benefit . . . reject some things and keep some things. That's just normal human behaviour. As things change in the world, then you change.

A bottom line for many is the protection of Aboriginal sacred sites, those areas most special and important in Aboriginal cosmology. The Northern and Central Land Councils (1994: 14) have argued that protecting sacred sites 'is one of the most important issues in the Northern Territory'. Indeed, it was a low point in the Northern Territory intervention when some building workers built a toilet on a sacred site after failing to consult with the traditional owners. Many other sacred sites have already been destroyed due to a combination of ignorance, neglect, greed and arrogance, and many non-Aboriginal people still fail to understand exactly what is lost in the destruction of a sacred site (Behrendt 1995: 25). As Parry Agius has argued, although the 'whole of Australia loses when a site is destroyed', still the 'myriad of laws which purport to protect culture' continue to allow the lawful destruction of much that is sacred (Agius, quoted in *Koori Mail* 2005a: 4). Understandably, these practices do not engender in Aboriginal people a greater openness to development, but neither does the protection of sacred sites necessarily preclude development possibilities. Topsy Nelson Naparrula once explained her response to a mining industry representative who was 'talking sweet' to her in the hope of being able to mine a sacred site at Kunjarra. Nelson Naparrula explained to the representative, 'I'm sorry, he cannot have that sacred site'; however, she also 'showed him other stone he can have that are not sacred' (quoted in Central Land Council 1994: 89). The Pitjantjatjara people made a similar point in acknowledging that they 'understand that oil and gas and things in the ground are important to everyone', but insisting that they must have control over decisions as they 'cannot allow our country to be damaged or our sacred places to be interfered with' (quoted in Lippmann 1981: 62).

Openness to negotiation is present in both of these comments, but such negotiation will only be successful when Aboriginal people are listened to with respect. Too often, presumptions about Aboriginal culture lead to a lack of understanding of Aboriginal views on development, with the result that conversations about development possibilities are stymied by suspicion and mistrust.

The cultural bottom line

In recent years, new policies about what should happen on Aboriginal land have narrowed understandings of development and constrained debate. For example, pressure on communities to enter ninety-nine-year leases over their land created a false and unfair dichotomy between those who were seen as wanting economic development in Aboriginal communities and those who allegedly did not (Brennan 2006: 23). Aboriginal culture in general is regarded as an obstacle to economic development, which in turn is understood in a conventional market-based sense. This obscures the fact that Aboriginal people are deeply interested in options for economic development, not for its own sake but to improve their communities' well-being (Cronin 2003: 159). Many Aboriginal people are interested in development as a potential way out of the grinding poverty their communities experience. But they want this development on their terms, and in ways that do not compromise their cultural integrity or obligations to country (Mudrooroo 1995: 226; Kauffman 1998: 3). As Larissa Behrendt pointed out, there are many areas in which Aboriginal people are participating in economic activity that fit with their cultural activity—'things that they're already doing well'. Misunderstanding this situation merely perpetuates the over-simplification of another complex area of Aboriginal political culture.

Many Aboriginal people speak of economic development on their land with a degree of pragmatism and acceptance that some would find surprising. Peter Yu suggests that Aboriginal people should bypass governments to deal directly with the private sector, setting their own terms and conditions for any investment in their land (quoted in KALACC 2006: 164). However, there is always a bottom line below which Aboriginal people are unwilling to compromise, although the issues below the line do vary around the country. Alison Anderson, for example, reported that, in the remote areas of her Central Australian constituency, 'the talk is that people are saying there's scope for us to embrace economic development without relinquishing any rights to other citizens, and they want that balance'. In other words, economic development is fine, but it should not be a substitute for the provision of citizenship entitlements. Dr Marika saw development as a possible pathway to greater autonomy, but her bottom line was that Aboriginal people must have greater ownership and control over natural resources. Dr Marika aspired to the sort of economic independence she observed in Aotearoa New Zealand and in Canada, where Indigenous peoples 'own the land and they can do whatever they like with their land, like have their own fishing rights and commercial rights'. She felt strongly that: 'Yolngu can live off their land. Yolngu can make money out of their land and be successful and be autonomous . . . create their own wealth just like *Ngapaki*, have their own businesses. Like fishing industry or mud crabs or prawns, you know? All the things that's there on our land and sea.'

Ted Wilkes also accepts that 'this is a modern world now' and that Aboriginal people should share in the economic bounty from the current mining boom. For Ted, however, the bottom line is that 'the customary law and the culture takes priority'. The essential point, as Peter Russell has observed, is that Aboriginal people 'should be able to choose how to live on their traditional land'. For some, this will entail development in one form or another; for others, the choice will be to preserve a more traditional way of life (Russell 2005: 174).

In short, Aboriginal people want control over decisions about economic development on their land and in their communities—a shift to a development paradigm that is characterised by 'respect rather than imposition' (Webber 2000: 82). For Paul Briggs, this imperative is 'linked to sovereignty issues and vision'. Paul thinks questions must be asked about 'what it is we as Aboriginal people need to sustain ourselves and for what purpose' so that Aboriginal people can properly understand 'the cultural challenges in trying to mirror the way the economic systems work in Aboriginal lives'. Paul sees many risks in economic development, and he is concerned that Aboriginal people are unprepared to face them and to 'actively protect ourselves against assimilation and abuse'. Again, the concern is with autonomy and ensuring that Aboriginal people are equipped to negotiate and understand the consequences of their decisions. Policy and practice that support these aspirations would provide a sound framework for achieving 'more just, sustainable, equitable and tolerant' development outcomes for Aboriginal people (Howitt 2001: 203). This is certainly not an anti-development vision. Rather, as John Ah Kit has argued, Aboriginal people can envision a future in which the 'sovereignty of Aboriginal people is marked by control over our lives, lands and communities *through a serious engagement with capitalism*' (Ah Kit 1997: 53, my emphasis).

Marcia Langton has observed that 'Aboriginal poverty is not the political property of any party but an historical legacy that brings no honour to those who suffer it nor to those who play politics with it' (Langton 2002: 17). Regardless of one's political ideology, the question of economic reform and development that brings real justice and wealth to Aboriginal communities must be seen as a key area of political effort. It is a central component of addressing all the other areas of complexity outlined in this book. It is absolutely necessary if Australia as a nation wishes to avert the intense social crisis that is occurring in many Aboriginal communities as a result of 'under-development' (Langton 2002: 17). However, the sort of development that is necessary may not look like mainstream development, and it will need to begin by recognising Aboriginal people as already active participants in various forms of economic life. As with all other areas of Aboriginal life, there is a diversity of views and aspirations about economic development. As Tom Calma has suggested, 'not all of us will be or will want to be home owners or entrepreneurs' (2007b: 14). The search for a one-size-fits-all solution to the challenges of economic development is, as Sean Brennan has noted, 'dangerously naïve', even in the face of the acknowledged urgency of this work (Brennan 2006: 16). Unless Aboriginal people themselves are central to determining development goals and agendas, and those goals and agendas are consistent with their unique cultural aspirations, policies directed at economic development for Aboriginal people will simply join a long list of failed policy from the past.

5
INDIVIDUALISM AND COLLECTIVISM

Mainstream political culture understands leadership and success in individual terms. Many Aboriginal people, however, have a very different worldview. Aboriginal value systems are often at odds with liberal democratic philosophy, creating tension between those committed to ideas of individual political equality and those who maintain that the foundational unit of society is the Aboriginal group or community. Pat Dodson, for example, has argued that models of 'the individual as the essential unit of society' as advocated by successive Australian governments are not the Indigenous way (2000:14). Megan Davis has also suggested that much Western human rights discourse, which promotes the individual as paramount, is 'at odds with Indigenous communal and collective cultural practice' (Davis 2003: 140).

Aboriginal social relations are in many ways constituted within this tension between individualism and collectivism. This is the dynamic identified by the anthropologist Fred Myers in his seminal study with Pintupi in the Western Desert. Myers described the tension between autonomy and relatedness: a constant negotiation of shared identity and communal and familial obligations with a desire for individual autonomy (Myers 1991: 159). Myers understood these two forces in Indigenous social life as 'inseparable', and as being in a dialectical relationship with one another (Fajans 2006: 103). Diane Smith suggests that this tension between autonomy and relatedness is a 'fundamental tenet' of Aboriginal social and political life, which operates on several scales, from the individual struggling for autonomy in small-scale local groups to broader questions of local autonomy in the context of a wider political momentum concerned with larger-scale groups and interests (Smith 2007: 30). These broader tensions are discussed further in Chapter 7.

In contemporary Aboriginal political culture, the tension between individualism and collectivity plays out in two key areas that will be discussed in this chapter: land and leadership. Since 2005, there has been a push from both Aboriginal and non-Aboriginal political leaders to individualise land tenure, which traditionally has been held collectively. At the same time, questions of leadership and legitimacy have been brought to the fore in the wake of the abolition of ATSIC. The capacity of Aboriginal people to negotiate these tensions has come under increasing challenge from the political trend towards neoliberalism, which strongly privileges the individual.

Individualising the collective

Central to Aboriginal political claims are claims to group rights. These demands may be at odds with liberal democratic tradition that privileges the right of the individual to own property and gives primacy to individual rights over collective interests, whereas the Aboriginal worldview is based on 'non-ownership of property and the subordination of the individual to the collective' (Ivanitz 2002: 127). As Tim Rowse notes, however, Aboriginal people experience their struggle for rights and recognition in more than one way. Rowse agrees that the sense of collectivity is strong, but he also observes that, as with other Australians, the sense of individual entitlement (to rights such as voting and receiving welfare benefits) is also evident. Rowse sees this dualism as 'a lasting result of the assimilation era', concluding that the modern political culture of Aboriginal people is a 'complex layering' of these elements (Rowse 2002: 18, 19). Wendy Brady also suggests that Aboriginal identity is both individual and communal, a situation that she says is 'not schizophrenic' but represents a 'duality of being' (Brady 2007: 141). Aileen Moreton-Robinson is more pragmatic, suggesting that some of the collective rights that Aboriginal people pursue may also 'overlap' with their individual rights as Australian citizens (Moreton-Robinson 2005: 64). Certainly it would be a mistake to ascribe to all Aboriginal people everywhere in Australia the same levels of attachment to a collective philosophy.

Nevertheless, collectivity does underpin much Aboriginal political culture. This philosophical commitment to collectivism should not, however, be confused with the struggle for pan-Aboriginal national unity. The notion of one 'Aboriginal community', often interpellated in government policy, is at odds with the hundreds of Aboriginal communities all over Australia. The work of defining 'the community' in a national sense is often difficult, particularly in a postcolonial context where traditional families and communities have been broken apart, an issue that will be discussed further in Chapter 8. For the majority of Aboriginal people, the collective is most often constituted by the extended family, although relations of reciprocity and obligation extend beyond blood ties (Mudrooroo 1995: 31). This is one of the ironies of policy-making in Indigenous Affairs. On the one hand, liberal ideas that privilege the individual tend to denigrate Aboriginal collectivism. On the other hand, governments have continually applied uniform policy and legislation to diverse Indigenous collectivities regardless of their unique histories or contemporary circumstances (Tonkinson 2007: 42).

It is certainly true, however, that many Aboriginal people wish to defend their cultural collectivity, which they see as being fundamentally as odds with Western liberalism. Ray Swan, for example, claims that 'liberalism is an enemy to collectivism': 'You know, liberalism's all about individual rights, and Aboriginal people since time immemorial, we've never functioned at an individual level. It was always a collective level . . . It's liberalism that's killing us.' Mick Dodson agrees that 'many societies' do not support the 'neo-liberal view that the individual is the centre of the universe'. Gary Foley has also argued that 'the individual is a notion that belongs in white Australia', suggesting that: 'The basic ethos of many Aboriginal communities is . . . [that] . . . the welfare of the group is more important than the welfare of the individual . . . That's a fundamental core component of Aboriginality.' (ABC 2003a)

But the collectivity of Aboriginal social life is not something to be romanticised or idealised. While the sense of mutual caring and support is strong, so are the obligations to kin and community. Film director Rolf de Heer has written of the toll these obligations have taken on actor David Gulpilil, who:

became a virtual Centrelink in his community. He'd go away for a while on an acting job, and come back with money. As it was his obligation, responsibility and desire to share, all of it would be gone within days. The clothes he'd be wearing on his return went the same way as the money, so that each time he ventured out, he'd have to have new clothes bought for him on arrival. (de Heer with Reynolds 2007: 62)

These kin obligations bring considerable pressure with regard to maintaining familial relationships. The extent to which an individual is prepared to care for and share with kin who are less well off is often interpreted by the wider family as a statement of that individual's level of regard for their family relationships (Myers 1991: 115). Kim Hill believes that these types of kin and communal obligations can 'eat you from the inside out'—something he has witnessed in many up and coming Aboriginal leaders who have struggled to find a balance in their own lives. Kim stresses that these obligations are 'not all about money', but says sometimes the demands for 'a bit of love and a bit of leadership and a role model' can be almost overwhelming.

The other side of this equation, of course, is the knowledge that others will look after you in times of need. William Tilmouth comments: 'Yeah, we live a collective life, don't we? So you know when you haven't got anything you can go and ask family and the family will give to you and you square them up next week, you know?' In a sense, this reciprocity underlines the fact that the sorts of economic development discussed in the previous chapter will not be measured by improvements in individual socioeconomic status, but by improvements for whole communities and family groups (Walter 2007: 162).

Insisting that the mainstream political norms that privilege the exercise of individual rights must also be norms in Aboriginal communities seems a pointless exercise. It should not be the aim of government policy to change Aboriginal cultural and political values, but rather to be creative in response to these values, to imagine new ways of respecting this aspect of cultural difference within certain policy constraints. For much of the second half of the twentieth century, Indigenous Affairs in Australia has shown some level of engagement with this complexity through a push towards the recognition of equal, individual rights combined with struggles for the recognition of unique Indigenous group rights. As Will Sanders (2006: 47) notes, this duality of political aspiration was 'not always easy' to accommodate and often involved 'considerable tensions'. Nevertheless, some creative policy solutions that could combine these two goals have existed.

One such solution is CDEP. CDEP is, of course, a *Community Development Employment Program*—a kind of work for the dole program, but more a 'work for your community for the dole' program. The CDEP emphasis on community development was distinctly at odds with the more mainstream individualised notion of employment. Instead, it 'effectively converted the individual right to unemployment payments to a group right of Indigenous self-management and part-time employment' (Sanders 2006: 47). The abolition of CDEP by the Howard government fed a widespread view that the government was 'anti-collective', with Sam Jeffries saying that the 'community development aspect of CDEP' was 'taken right out of the equation' because the government had 'this notion that everybody's got to have a job'.

The abolition of CDEP is just one example of how the growing influence of neoliberalism in mainstream Australian politics has placed such creative policy solutions under threat. Time and again, Aboriginal structures of governance have been denigrated by government ministers who have labelled representative arrangements such as clan-based councils 'communist collectives' and 'gatekeepers', supposedly perpetuating defunct and dysfunctional communities and hindering economic development (Smith 2007: 35). Once again, Noel Pearson has proffered a controversial point of view with regard to this area of complexity. One of Pearson's ideas in this regard—that of 'orbiting'—highlights the contrast between current thinking and the thinking that underpinned policies such as CDEP. Orbiting is a plan whereby Aboriginal people in remote communities are enabled to leave their communities to pursue education and employment opportunities 'in the wider world' while being encouraged to make 'active contributions' to their home community through remittances. Pearson argues that for orbiting to work, 'communities cannot be parochial: they must value those who have gained connections and experience in the wider world' (Pearson 2005: 13). Orbitors themselves, according to Pearson, must have 'the confidence required to leave their communities, just as they have the confidence required to return' (Cape York Institute 2007: 99). This idea of orbiting redefines the idea of community to focus not on those who live there but on those individuals who are connected to it 'in some way' (Manne 2007: 39). The significance of orbiting is that it makes sense only if one understands orbitors as atomised individuals, and if one understands success as the achievement of individuals who may or may not return to their communities and who may or may not send remittances home.

Pearson wants to develop Cape York communities individual by individual, and many of his ideas were adopted by the Howard government, which in turn attempted to move away from the recognition of Indigenous collectivity towards a more liberal conception of individual rights and responsibilities. But to Pat Dodson, the resurgent neoliberalism that drives such initiatives are anathema to Aboriginal aspirations. Dodson argues that, even with regard to the well-known problems in many Aboriginal communities, the answer is not to 'attack the foundations of our community by putting the individual before the community' (Dodson 2000: 14). Others have argued that the individualisation of Indigenous collectivity is one of the 'essential aims of assimilation', despite the fact that much government effort in this direction has in fact stimulated the collective sense of identity among Aboriginal people resistant to further assimilation (Morris 1988: 52, 53). Proposals to individualise Indigenous land tenure have certainly had a galvanising effect.

Land and home ownership

The view that Aboriginal culture is 'inherently communitarian' is based in part on the collective ownership of land (Davis 2006c: 36). Around Australia, variously composed collectives of landowners, native title-holders and community elders make the majority of decisions about development on Aboriginal land, as discussed in the previous chapter. In contrast to European understandings of property rights, Aboriginal land 'ownership' confers obligations of custodianship and stewardship, determined by (among other things) place of conception and birth (Goodall 1996: 9). These responsibilities to land are held collectively as a part of the Aboriginal cosmology that underpins socio-political relationships (Ivanitz 2002: 128). Traditionally, Aboriginal people do not see the land as a commodity to be bought and sold for profit, although they do exploit its resources in a variety of ways.

Today, what is known as the 'Indigenous estate' (lands that are owned or controlled by Indigenous people through both land rights regimes and the recognition of native title) comprises around 20 per cent of the Australian land mass. This figure is set to increase as further native title claims make their slow way through the system. However, recent years have seen the communal nature of Aboriginal land tenure come under fire. Rather than being seen as improving the socioeconomic status of Aboriginal communities, communal ownership of land has been nominated as a possible barrier to development, particularly because it is unattractive for loans and capital investment that may increase home ownership. The suggestion has been that these communal holdings should be converted to private interests in order to increase Aboriginal wealth (Bradfield 2005: 2).

Such a change threatens decades of struggle for the recognition of the distinct nature of Aboriginal landholding in Australia. In the 1971 Gove land rights case, Justice Blackburn accepted that the eleven claimant clans had a 'subtle and elaborate system' of land ownership but determined that because of the communal nature of that ownership, which bore little resemblance to Western property law, it was incapable of being formally recognised. This view was maintained until *Mabo*, where the High Court determined that although the communal ownership of land by Aboriginal people could not be recognised as a proprietary interest in common law, it did constitute a unique form of title to land that had existed prior to colonisation. The 1993 *Native Title Act*, the legislative response to the *Mabo* decision, created collective rights to land in the Australian legal system (Davis 2006c: 37). Because native title recognises a system of land ownership that is part of traditional Aboriginal culture, it follows that this form of title is not held by any individual but by Indigenous communities (Russell 2005: 266). Interestingly, however, the communal nature of this title is itself a recognition of Indigenous autonomy, which does not, in and of itself, prescribe internal landholding practices (Webber 2000: 71). In other words, native title does not create legal barriers to stop Aboriginal communities deciding for themselves to organise a system of individual landholding within an area of communal title. Prior to the 2006 amendments, the *Land Rights Act* already contained leasing provisions, as long as the lease was on reasonable terms that satisfied the relevant land council and had been developed with the consent of traditional owners (Brennan 2006: 11).

Despite this reality, however, new debates about individualising land tenure in the name of increasing rates of Aboriginal home ownership were advanced by former prime minister John Howard in 2005. In a speech at the Wadeye community, Howard proclaimed his belief that 'there is a case for reviewing the whole issue of Aboriginal land title, in the sense of looking more towards private recognition . . . all Australians should be able to aspire to owning their own home and having their own business' (quoted in Wilson and Hodge 2005). Although Howard later told the National Reconciliation Planning Workshop that he was 'committed to protecting the rights of communal ownership' (Howard 2005), his government's subsequent amendments to the Northern Territory *Land Rights Act* raised questions about his real commitment to this issue. The essence of Howard's proposed reforms were to amend the Act to enable ninety-nine-year leases over communal Aboriginal land in the Northern Territory, which would then allow landholders to attain mortgages with greater security. The Northern Territory government would also be able to use the security of a ninety-nine-year lease to borrow money for public housing. Aboriginal landholders would be able to charge a maximum of 5 per cent of the unimproved value of the land for the lease—which, ironically, would be paid for out of the Aboriginal Benefits Account.

Howard's ideas on the individualising of land tenure were strongly influenced by Noel Pearson (see, for example, Pearson and Kostakidis-Lianos 2004) and particularly by the work of Helen Hughes and Jenness Warin from the Centre for Independent Studies (CIS) (Hughes 2005; Hughes and Warin 2005). In reports that reflect the deep conservatism of the CIS, these authors suggest that the communal ownership of Aboriginal land is the result of 'underlying socialist principles' aimed at creating a 'hunter-gatherer utopia' but which in fact have 'prevented the evolution of private property rights' and thereby perpetuate Aboriginal disadvantage (Hughes and Warin 2005: 1; Hughes 2005: 10, 11).

Howard's 2005 comments received a mixed reaction. Former democrat Senator Aden Ridgeway suggested that they illustrated 'a profound cross-cultural misunderstanding' because they were 'drawn purely from a western perspective that prizes individualism and make no attempt to understand the cultural perspectives of Indigenous peoples' (Ridgeway 2005: 8). Ian Munro, Chief Executive of the Bawinanga Aboriginal Corporation in Maningrida, made a similar point, suggesting that Howard believed that 'if you squeeze a blackfella tightly enough a whitefella's going to pop out ready to buy a house'. Munro insisted that this was 'simply not the case because Indigenous Australians are not white Australians. They have a different value system and a different culture.' (quoted in ABC 2007f). In our interview, Mick Dodson put the view that the emphasis on leasing in order to attract lending institutions was just 'really old thinking': 'To think that the only way you can get economic development is to go into mortgage debt is a reflection of lazy thinking. We need to be a little more clever than that and try and persuade financial institutions that there are ways of securing investment monies other than hocking their land.'

Critics also noted the economic 'unreality' of proposals to increase individual home ownership, given the low incomes and marginal employment status of Aboriginal people in very remote areas (Sanders 2005a). Mick Dodson agrees with this argument. He asks how people with new individual titles to communal land will pay their new mortgages. Mick points out that the 'average cost' of a house in 'so-called remote Australia' is around $450 000. Governments would have to substantially subsidise the cost of building new homes for individuals or families to be able to afford a more modest mortgage of around $100 000. Mick remains sceptical that governments are going to be willing to provide this level of subsidy for property that will end up in individual hands.

Despite these clear limitations, however, a range of high-profile Aboriginal people were active in promoting the leasing arrangements. The NIC was a particularly controversial agent in debates around the individualising of Indigenous land tenure. In 2005, the NIC released its 'Indigenous Land Tenure Principles' as its advice to government on this issue. While these principles did recognise that 'underlying communal interests in land' are 'fundamental to Indigenous culture', they went on to advise the Australian government that implementation of new leasing arrangements may require 'involuntary measures' such as 'compulsory acquisition' of land in the event that consent of the traditional owners was 'unreasonably withheld' from those seeking leases. Not surprisingly, there was considerable concern that the NIC appeared to be advising the government to weaken Indigenous rights under the *Native Title* and *Land Rights Acts*. Further, the NIC's advice seems to leave the federal government with the power to define the 'unreasonable' withholding of consent, the terms of 'just' compensation for compulsory acquisition, and whether 'subsequent return' of land is possible (Bradfield 2005: 9). Fortunately, the Howard government did not proceed with measures to allow forcible acquisition of land, at least until the 2007 intervention.

Warren Mundine is another who is considered to have played a leading role in proposing the leasing of communally held Aboriginal land. In our interview he explained his thinking, which involved the idea of leasehold arrangements as a 'tool' to help Aboriginal people 'break out' of poverty. In Mundine's view, traditional owners would be able to benefit from arrangements not unlike a public–private partnership deal, in which investors take out a lease over Aboriginal land in order to develop it. At the end of the lease period—which Warren insisted did not have to be for ninety-nine years but could be for as little as ten or twenty years—'the infrastructure and everything that was built by the private investor then returns back to the community'. Warren saw the plan as also helping to cut public housing waiting lists. He acknowledged that people in remote areas would not be able to afford a mortgage, but suggested that every person in a wealthier area—such as near a mining project—who could afford to buy their own home made the waiting list shorter for others who did not have that option. Warren feels that the political response to his ideas on leasing was that they were unreasonably seen as 'a panacea of all Aboriginal ills'. He responded: 'Of course, that's not the case at all. It is just one tool.'

Other Aboriginal leaders and activists, however, have expressed strong concerns about land leasing. Some have objected to offers of large sums of money in exchange for ninety-nine-year leases. Dr Marika argued that it was 'wrong' to offer impoverished people money in exchange for agreements over land. For her, these deals were 'like being back in the days of giving natives glass beads and trinkets for their land' (Parker 2006). Central Land Council director David Ross branded the scheme a 'waste' and 'highly insulting', suggesting that few people would take up the leasing option once they realised they would be 'handing over the decision-making and control over their land for the next 99 years for a few dollars, particularly when they work out it's already Aboriginal money' (Graham 2005: 7). Tom Calma has consistently highlighted the international evidence that suggests individualising Indigenous land tenure leads to significant losses of land (ATSISJC 2006a, 2007b). Calma expresses the view that leases of ninety-nine-years, essentially four generations, with the possibility of back-to-back leases, will have the 'practical effect' of alienating Indigenous communal land (Calma 2007a: 4). Noel Pearson also warned that a balancing act was required in order to 'reconcile these two apparently contradictory principles—

communal ownership and transferable property rights'. Pearson argued that the challenge would be to 'preserve the culture of communal tenure whilst enabling maximum individual and private economic use of the land' (Pearson, quoted in *Koori Mail* 2005b: 13).

For Pat Dodson, such a balance seemed unlikely. In his view, the idea of a ninety-nine-year lease has become 'the practical and symbolic instrument of [the Howard] Government's crusade to make Indigenous people culturally invisible in a world where the aspirations and desires of each individual are seen as the binding mortar for the functioning of civil society' (Dodson 2007).

Despite these considerable reservations, in 2007 the first leases were signed. In May the traditional owners of the Tiwi Islands were the first group to sign a ninety-nine-year lease under the new policy arrangements. The deal, which saw traditional owners sign over the town of Nguiu in return for $5 million and twenty-five new houses, was controversial, allegedly dividing the community amid threats and intimidation (ABC 2007e). As with so many postcolonial Aboriginal communities, the recognised traditional owners of Nguiu are not the only residents. Other residents, no matter how long they had been living in the area, are not part of the landholding collective and therefore did not have any authority in the decision-making process. The lease deal was strongly criticised by Tom Calma, in his role as Aboriginal and Torres Strait Islander Social Justice Commissioner. He claimed that the deal made Nguiu 'open for business to anyone who wants to set up shop'.[1] In his view, the communal rights of landholders had been undermined and the 'Tiwi People will now have a limited say in what can occur on their land' (Calma 2007b).

Another controversial lease deal involved the high-profile Yolngu leader Galarrwuy Yunupingu, who agreed to sign a ninety-nine-year lease over the township of Ski Beach on the Gove Peninsula. The deal was arrived at after secret meetings between Yunupingu, Noel Pearson and the then Indigenous Affairs Minister Mal Brough, designed to counter Yunupingu's opposition to the Northern Territory intervention. The resulting memorandum of understanding offered far better terms than the Tiwi lease by enabling Yunupingu's Gumatj Clan to retain considerable control over their land. The deal also included the development of a Mala Elders group, which would 'advise government' on its dealings with Yolngu. In a newspaper opinion piece, Yunupingu stated that the deal satisfied his concerns about leasing, and would 'empower traditional owners to control the development of towns and living areas, and to participate fully in all aspects of economic development on their land' (Yunupingu 2007).

Other Yolngu traditional owners were unhappy, however, claiming that it was 'unacceptable' for the government to deal with individuals. Djapu Clan leader Yananymul Mununggurr referred to provisions in the *Land Rights Act* which mandate that all traditional owners in a region must be consulted before any agreement is approved. Mununggurr claimed the government was 'cherry picking' the leaders it wanted to deal with, saying 'they think they know who our leaders are but they don't'. In broader terms, Pat Dodson described the deal as revealing the 'dysfunctional relationship between Indigenous Australia and the Federal Government as well as the tragic public policy mess that embroils that relationship' (Dodson 2007).

Despite the heat in much of the debate around ninety-nine-year leases, there is considerable support for the need for policy to support more Aboriginal people into home ownership. Geoff Scott, for example, recognises that the 'Australian dream' of home ownership is 'no different for Aboriginal people' who want economic security and a better way of life for their children. Geoff points out that while Aboriginal rights to land are gained 'at the collective level', he believes they can only be enjoyed 'at the individual level'. At the same time, however, Geoff insists that they still 'want to be Aboriginal people' and retain their culture and communal associations. Like many people, Geoff is unsure why these realities are considered incompatible. Similarly, Colleen Hayward does not see individual home ownership as incompatible with collective landholding. In her research, she sees a correlation between home ownership and better outcomes across a range of indicators, including health, education and employment, which suggests to her the need to explore 'innovative designs' and to 'equip people to do it properly'. In our interview, Colleen spoke of her own townhouse in suburban Perth, where the body corporate has some collective ownership over the development as a whole, including responsibility for maintaining the property. Colleen suggests that this sort of idea could work on collectively owned Aboriginal land as long as there were regulations about the sale of the property, limiting future sales to another member of the community. Colleen concludes that the question of home ownership is 'being made harder than it needs to be'.

Whether Colleen is right or wrong on this score, it remains true that many traditional owners are fearful of losing their land under the new leasing arrangements. The Northern Territory 'intervention' saw townships forcibly acquired for a period of five years. The new Minister for Indigenous Affairs, Jenny Macklin, indicated early in 2008 that she would explore leasing options shorter than ninety-nine years in some areas, initiating the first such arrangement with Anindilyakwa Land Council on Groote Eylandt with a township lease for a period of forty plus forty years (Macklin 2008a, 2008c). Nevertheless, there will always be anxiety about the long-term implications of such policy for collective landholding.

Leadership

In traditional Aboriginal culture there is a direct relationship between responsibilities to land and an individual's cultural seniority and leadership. While power was not evenly distributed throughout traditional Aboriginal society, neither did the patterns of social organisation allow for an absolute monopoly on power or cultural knowledge (Howard 1982: 2; Myers 1991: 246). Political authority is accorded to senior men and women who gain ceremonial standing and political autonomy by fulfilling their obligations. These leadership rights do not extend beyond a leader's own country or nation (Goodall 1996: 10; Cronin 2003: 161). Power was often exercised communally, with ultimate authority resting with a group of elders and delegated authority being carried by those with particular relationships to kin and country (Brady 2007: 142). Leadership in these terms was not seen as a reward but as a responsibility, in contrast to many non-Aboriginal notions of leadership, which are more focused on 'winning' office (McConchie 2003: 110–11). While these social practices remain strong or have been revived in many parts of Australia, in other areas they have broken down due to colonial policies.

Today, while many leaders still base their authority in traditional communal recognition, new forms of leadership are also drawn from a range of other contexts. Janet Hunt and Diane Smith have documented contemporary Indigenous leadership contexts that include:

- leadership of language groups, extended families, clan groupings and coalitions of groups;

- leadership of Indigenous knowledge and resource systems (including not only cultural systems but information, technological and financial capital);
- leadership of organisations at local, regional, state and national levels; and
- age- and gender-specific leadership roles (Hunt and Smith 2007: 8).

Part of what makes contemporary Aboriginal political culture so complex is the way these various forms of leadership can, or cannot, translate to legitimate and widely supported leadership on the national stage. National leadership is important to ensure that Aboriginal people can deal with the federal government on issues of national policy. But leaders must have the respect of other Aboriginal people who are prepared to support rather than undermine them in their interface with government. Muriel Bamblett suggests that the complex nature of Indigenous nationhood makes these leadership questions almost impossible to resolve: 'There are so many nations of people it's very difficult to have one leadership group to represent one particular issue . . . I don't believe that there would ever be a leader that would have the capacity to be able to represent all of the issues that Aboriginal people are continually facing on a daily basis.' For Muriel, part of the answer is to develop 'better systems' for recognising 'different leaders', including local leaders, community leaders and matriarchs.

Just what those better systems might be, however, remains highly contentious, and the challenge of finding processes by which individual leaders can be endorsed by the collective is a significant barrier to forming a new representative body at the national level. Klynton Wanganeen sees this need for bottom-up, community-endorsed leadership potentially stalling the process of forming a national body, because that process itself will need some form of top-down leadership. Klynton sees the criticism of some high-profile leaders—on the basis that they are not representing their communities—as a waste of precious human resources, arguing that 'you can't throw out that wealth of experience and knowledge to focus wholly and solely on the bottom-up process'. As a result of previous policies of assimilation and child removal that have broken down traditional structures that would once have endorsed an individual's leadership role, many potential leaders now have to figure out who they should answer to for their decisions.

For the most part, Aboriginal leadership is endorsed at a community level, drawing on people's cultural identity—an issue that will be discussed further in the next chapter. This form of cultural endorsement remains far more significant to a leader's legitimacy than their individual ability. At the same time, there is great wariness about the tendency for mainstream politics to appropriate Aboriginal leaders by picking out one individual who is anointed as the 'authoritative archetype of Aboriginality' and used to justify controversial policy decisions (Dodson 2003a: 39). Richard Trudgen has observed some Yolngu leaders who have been handpicked by government, rather than chosen by their own people, become 'oppressors' themselves, sowing the seeds of cronyism and corruption in their own communities (Trudgen 2000: 197). Those seen as too close to government—or too far removed from their communities—are criticised as 'uptown blacks', 'Jacky Jackys', 'nine-to-five blacks' or 'coconuts' (brown on the outside, white on the inside).

Individual leaders have never had an easy time, especially when they have been attempting to step onto the national stage. Once a leader steps outside the bounds of their own community, their capacity to speak on any issue is immediately under challenge. Writing with characteristic bluntness, Kevin Gilbert observed that:

> Aborigines have not taken kindly to those in their midst who have assumed to be 'leaders.' A strong reason is a uniquely Aboriginal individualism which does not accept the right of anyone to speak for them without long and exhausting prior consultation. Decisions tend to be arrived at by group consensus and are then adhered to—no matter how idiotic or impractical they may be. (Gilbert 2002: 137)

After the abolition of ATSIC, the absence of a national body exacerbated this dynamic. John Maynard observes that there are 'commentators' around Australia who 'speak on everyone's behalf', but he thinks that everyone is 'speaking in isolated ways and there is no united voice'. There is considerable frustration at the way certain high-profile individuals are used to 'represent' Aboriginal points of view in the media. Noel Pearson stands out in this regard and comes under strong criticism for accepting this role. Robbie Thorpe, for example, describes Pearson as 'an Uncle Tom' who is 'rolled out' by governments to endorse their legislation. Gary Foley has suggested that 'most blackfellas south of the

Tropic of Capricorn ain't got as much respect for Pearson as what people in the Murdoch media and other places seem to have' (ABC 2003a). Like many others, Sam Jeffries is angry at the way Pearson's proposals for reform in Cape York have been taken up as a nationwide solution to the 'Aboriginal problem':

> If Noel Pearson wants to grow trees and sit under them in the Cape, fine, great, I've got no problem with that. But don't expect me to grow the same trees to try and create the same shade and sit under them in western New South Wales, because it won't work. And that's the problem I have with the government thinking that what Noel does in the Cape can be replicated right across the country.

Sam finds it difficult to see people like Pearson 'privileging their own individual success over the success of the collective', suggesting that while Noel's leadership is 'certainly doing Noel a lot of good', it is 'not doing a lot of other people a lot of good'.

Pearson seems to fit the mould of what Michael Howard has described as 'cultural brokers'—those Aboriginal elites who attain power through engaging in closed political systems that exclude broader Aboriginal participation. According to Howard, Aboriginal brokers may believe that they are helping other Aboriginal people when in fact they are legitimising a façade of political participation that allows non-Aboriginal interests to maintain control over Indigenous affairs (Howard 1982: 159–79). The criticism directed at Pearson over his failure to engage with the wider Aboriginal leadership at a range of meetings—behaviour I observed first hand at the 2020 Summit—seems to endorse this view of him.

Muriel Bamblett makes a similar point about Pearson's behaviour, saying that when he is at a forum with other Aboriginal people, 'he hardly speaks'. This has been pointed out to him quite forcefully at times, including in a fiery clash with Lowitja O'Donoghue and the rest of the black caucus at the 2005 National Reconciliation Planning Workshop (see Debelle 2005; Davis 2005). Muriel Bamblett says Pearson does not respond to these challenges: 'He just sits there. And he gets up and talks straight to the prime minister or he talks to the bureaucrats. He does not talk to the Aboriginal people.' For Muriel, this type of individualism in the face of a collective challenge 'just defies all understanding'.

Another significant factor in complexities surrounding Aboriginal leadership is the often blatant jealousy of individual success. Warren Mundine claims with a laugh that Aboriginal people are 'the most jealous people in the world'. Tom Calma feels that the level of competition and in-fighting among Aboriginal people 'adds fuel to the fire' by draining the confidence of government and fragmenting any sense of political cohesion. Larissa Behrendt is one who has both had this jealousy directed at her, and who has thought hard about its roots. Larissa reflects that: 'It's almost like we don't acknowledge there's a successful element within the community because somehow it counters our claim that we're impoverished, which it doesn't at all.' Yin Paradies has suggested that this dynamic is the result of an Aboriginal 'group cohesion' that is, at least in part, premised on the impossibility of transcending colonial subordination. In this light, individuals who achieve success put this cohesion at risk (Paradies 2006: 359). In our interview Kim Hill expressed a similar view, pointing to the fact that when Aboriginal people leave their communities for an education they are often 'not welcome back' because community leaders feel 'threatened'. Geoff Scott agrees that people who manage to 'break out' of the poverty cycle afflicting so many Aboriginal communities then tend to be 'ostracised and criticised by those who are still there', including through 'pressure to come back and not achieve'.

Muriel Bamblett has a different understanding of this dynamic, describing it as fear that people will become 'lost to their culture':

> As soon as an Aboriginal person starts to do really good we have this theory that we should bring them back down to earth and ground them. People see that as negative and us hating each other. I don't think it's hating each other, I think it's about us sometimes not wanting to have that person lost to us. If you're a crab in a bucket and you get out of the bucket then we've lost you forever, so sometimes we don't want people to get out of the bucket and go too much mainstream . . . Just the challenge of getting out of the bucket might mean that they're going to be lost to the community and lost to their Aboriginal culture . . . So is it a negative to keep them in communities?

Whether it is jealousy or a real fear of 'losing' people to the mainstream, this dynamic is fuelled to some extent by the scarcity of material resources in many Aboriginal communities. Warren Mundine suggests that 'the jealousy factor' is driven by the fact that most Aboriginal people are still 'living on the fringe', where they are 'only getting the crumbs from the table'. In such circumstances, Warren sees it as inevitable that people 'fight among themselves for those crumbs'. According to Warren, people forget that 'the main game is not fighting amongst yourselves over the crumbs on the table, it is actually sitting at the table and having the meal'.

A level of discomfort about identifying as a leader was palpable in many of my interviews, precisely because of concerns about illegitimately representing a broader collectivity of Aboriginal people. Larissa Behrendt, for example, described herself as 'somebody who's vocal but not somebody who's representing anybody else'. Eugenia Flynn spelt out the view that: 'If you are labelled a leader or you consider yourself a leader there are so many people that are willing to bring you down.' Eugenia insisted she would 'never' think of herself as a leader, saying: 'I'm someone that does work and that's about it.' Kim Hill asserted that, even during his six years as an ATSIC commissioner, he did not see himself as a leader, but rather as 'a facilitator representing Aboriginal nation groups in the northern zone of the Northern Territory'. During his tenure, Kim stressed that he was at pains to always say to people: 'I don't have the cultural authority to make these decisions, you need to go back to the land owners and talk to the relevant people.' He believes the lack of mainstream understanding of the difference between 'legislative powers' and 'cultural powers' means that individuals are 'branded as a leader' and seen as having 'some kind of authority over your people'. Even very senior people like Lowitja O'Donoghue have expressed the view that they are 'not comfortable' being described as a leader.[2]

Aboriginal leadership is an unenviable task. Leaders have to juggle Aboriginal and non-Aboriginal demands with their cultural obligations and responsibilities to immediate and extended family while attempting to achieve consensus outcomes in all areas of their work and life (ATSISJC 2007a: 10). Eddie Cubillo is one of the few people I interviewed who willingly acknowledged the difficulties faced by those who take on a national leadership role. Eddie has been reflecting deeply on these issues since leaving the Northern Territory for Adelaide in order to develop new skills and recover from his own feelings of exhaustion and burnout. He sees that leadership 'takes a toll' on people's friendships and family obligations, and asks: 'Who would really want to get into this business?' In Eddie's own case, there are times when he wishes he had not pursued a law degree and further leadership responsibility but had 'stayed ignorant' because of the stress this has caused in his own life. Of the high-profile national leaders, Eddie says people should realise that 'everyone wants their time and they've got no time and the only ones suffering are them and their families'.

Despite these challenges, Paul Briggs sees resolving questions of leadership as important for the survival of Aboriginal culture. Paul argues that Aboriginal people 'can't remain isolated as individuals sitting in Yorta Yorta country or Wirrundjuri country or with Noel up in the Cape or wherever'. For the sake of a strong future with appropriate representation on the national stage, Aboriginal people must 'come together collaboratively'. These are issues to which I will return in the conclusion to this book.

Redefining collectivity

Aboriginal leaders struggle to exercise their continuing obligations to their country and to each other in the face of over two centuries of colonial onslaught (Wright 2005: 105). Maintaining and reviving traditional culture have been important strategies in resisting European domination in decolonising movements around the world. The complexity of this is that tradition may come to be seen as the only 'authentic' representation of Indigeneity, hampering recognition of new and developing systems of leadership and landholding. For example, leaders who access university education and live 'Westernised' lives may find that their legitimacy is questioned by both Aboriginal groups and by non-Aboriginal politicians (Russell 2005: 136).

In the face of these challenges, Aboriginal people have been struggling to redefine ideas of individual leadership and landholding while in a void of collective national leadership. The Northern Territory 'intervention' highlighted this void and prompted the formation of the new National Aboriginal Alliance. Paul Briggs sees the mixed success with which 'individual voices are trying to be heard' but, like many others, he worries that these voices are being heard as nationally representative when they are not. Individual voices, Paul says, are 'not necessarily the voice of the leaders'.

Communalism and collectivity are likely to remain important foundations of Indigenous leadership and decision-making, based as they are in ancient and enduring cosmology and relationships to land. This fact, however, places additional pressure on Aboriginal leaders, in ways that are often not recognised in mainstream political processes. Aboriginal leaders must mobilise consensus in ways that both constrain and sustain their leadership. Leaders are often 'only as powerful as their last successful exercise of consensus', and failure to achieve consensus can permanently undermine leadership credibility (Hunt and Smith 2007: 10).

This strong emphasis on communality and consensus should not, however, obscure the importance of individual agency. Warren Mundine recognises the importance of charismatic leaders who can not only 'drive forward' and 'think for themselves', but can also 'drag the rest of us with them'. Understanding and respecting Aboriginal collectivity does not mean that we should only understand 'Aboriginal people' as a collective subject, as if the 'collective mind' of Aboriginal Australia could be invited into a dialogue with the collective mind of non-Aboriginal Australia (Rowse 2002: 178, 180). Such recognition of the individualism within Aboriginal collectivity highlights the diversity of Aboriginal selves inherent in the idea of Aboriginal self-determination. I turn to these complexities of Aboriginal identity in the next chapter.

6
INDIGENEITY AND
HYBRIDITY

Before colonisation, Aboriginal people did not exist. There was no 'Indigeneity' or 'Aboriginality' in the sense that there is today (Langton 2003: 118). As discussed in earlier chapters, before colonisation Aboriginal people identified themselves according to their nation and language group, and within these their clans and kin groups. People were Wiradjuri, Yanyuwa, Goreng Goring, Jawoyn, Pitjantjatjara, Wongkadjera, Yawaru and all the other 500 nations that existed on this land before the invasion. The idea of 'Aboriginal' or 'Indigenous' identity is a distinctly postcolonial construct invented to both name and contain the 'natives' of *terra australis*.

In light of this, there is immense complexity concerning questions of Aboriginal identity today. On the one hand, much Aboriginal political culture assumes a politicised pan-Aboriginal identity as an important resource in political struggle. The construction of this national unity will be discussed in the next chapter. This chapter considers the significance of asserting an 'Aboriginal identity' in a postcolonial context. Kevin Gilbert has suggested that 'There is no Aboriginal cultural identity as such' and that the only things linking Aboriginal people are 'their black skin, their poverty and their shared experiences of persecution and horror' (Gilbert 2002: 179). For some, this shared identity is drawn in opposition to the dominant stereotype of Aboriginality—

that is, the 'tribal' Aboriginal person, living a traditional lifestyle in a northern desert. For the vast majority of Aboriginal people, who live in suburbs and towns and who hunt and gather at their local supermarket, 'identity' can be fraught with demands to prove their 'authenticity'. Both non-Aboriginal politicians and, at times, other Aboriginal people will question an Aboriginal leader's racial credentials on the suspicion that they may not be 'Indigenous enough'.

Larissa Behrendt (2003: 79) argues that Aboriginal people's shared experiences of colonisation 'validate and provide an enclave of inclusion and solidarity, detached from the wider community', becoming 'defining aspects of Indigenous self-identity'. Ray Swan agrees, saying that he has spent time in urbanised, semi-traditional and traditional communities and, while he acknowledges that 'colonisation has affected one more than the other', he also sees much that is shared both in the 'social diseases' like alcoholism, but also more fundamentally in the 'underlying stuff'. This sense of solidarity and sameness, however, is complicated by more hybrid identities 'less rooted in tradition and place' than the identities of earlier generations (Havemann 2000: 24). Aboriginality is (and probably always was) complicated by other layers of identity based around gender and age (to be discussed in Chapters 9 and 10), sexuality, class and increasingly by urbanisation. Aboriginal identities are neither essential nor fixed. As with all other cultural groups, Aboriginality evolves, adapts and changes, not least in response to the assault on traditional society and culture since colonisation. While Noel Pearson rejects the idea that the deep connection between Aboriginal identity and traditional social organisation means that Aboriginal people cannot 'embrace modernity' (Pearson 2006b: 7), many others still experience challenge from those who consider the embrace of modernity to be a 'sell out' to 'whitefella ways'.

Many Aboriginal people find in their cultural identity a sense of belonging and acceptance that they do not experience in the wider community. A part of this is a feeling of connectedness to other Aboriginal people, even strangers. Tom Calma speaks of the 'beauty' of being able to 'walk past a thousand people and spot an Aboriginal person' in the street. Regardless of skin colour or lifestyle, Tom feels there is a fundamental 'affinity' among Aboriginal people, and he enjoys the slight raise of the chin or nod of the head that acknowledges something shared. For Tom, 'it doesn't matter what your parentage is, most often you'll be able to identify, or be identified as an Aboriginal person and be accepted'. Nevertheless, this simple acceptance is not always so uncomplicated. Many, like Eugenia Flynn, see the importance of resolving issues around identity because of the way that a lack of acceptance from other Aboriginal people can often prevent people from 'standing up'. Like so many other issues discussed in this book, however, the complexities of today's experiences cannot be divorced from the past.

Tradition, identity and 'authenticity'

As previous chapters have made clear, 'tradition' in various forms is a crucial aspect of both Aboriginal history and contemporary political culture. Claims of the possession of culture are a claim of survival, resistance and connection to the past (Myers 2005: 5). Traditional beliefs and practices form the basis of Aboriginal spiritual life, social relations and, fundamentally, identity. There are also ways, however, that tradition has been used to divide Aboriginal people, or at least to create a hierarchy of authenticity. Tom Calma sees the diversity of circumstances in which Aboriginal people seek to have their identity recognised, suggesting that for people who 'come from a community background' or who 'still have a close association with land', identity is not so much of an issue. For those who have been 'disenfranchised' in various ways, however, particularly if they have been removed or taken off their land, identity can be far more ambiguous. Once this ambiguity becomes intergenerational, according to Tom, and where people have no capacity to go back to their country or maintain their relationship to land, these issues can become very difficult. Differing experiences of Aboriginality have often been exploited by bureaucrats eager to ensure division between 'those living in so-called traditional communities ("real" Aborigines) and those living in urban or fringe communities ("ersatz" Aborigines)' (O'Shane 1998: 11–12).

Traditional Aboriginal identity is attached to a particular language group, which in turn is connected to a specific area of country. In simple terms, an Aboriginal person's country is their fundamental source of identity (Myers 1991: 151). This produces an intensely localised form of identity that dictates a range of social relationships, marriage rules and cultural obligations. These traditional systems produced identities that were 'rarely ambiguous' (Schwab 1988: 77). In the southeastern regions of Australia, which endured the earliest onslaught of invasion, many family groups had their traditional connections to areas of land severed, requiring the construction of new social and cultural identities less closely tied to land (Rowse 1993: 84). Nevertheless, the importance of land and kin relations in asserting and authenticating identity is evident today in the way Aboriginal people most commonly greet each other: by asking 'Who's your mob? Where are you from? Who is your family?' (Brady 2007: 148; Taylor 2003).

The arrival of the British brought new systems of 'classifying' Aboriginal people. Complex systems of classification and control were an intrinsic part of the colonial administration aimed at 'exterminating' one type of Aboriginality and replacing it with a more acceptable, 'sanitised' version (Langton 2003: 116). One type of classification involved descent or 'degrees of blood', and is the familiar, overtly racist trope of half-caste, quarter-caste, octoroon and so on. For much of the twentieth century these terms were used as a guide to an Aboriginal person's character, and were the foundation of policies such as child removal. For example, a child with 'less Aboriginal blood' was considered more likely to assimilate and was therefore at greater risk of removal. The other mode of classification concerned the degree to which an Aboriginal person had become 'civilised' or remained 'tribal' (Goot and Rowse 2007: 31). Aboriginal people have been typecast as the 'noble savage', the hopeless fringe dweller, the violent abuser of women and children, and the primitive, childlike native in need of paternalistic 'care' (Morgan 2006a: 141). These imposed definitions of Aboriginality were, according to Louise Taylor, 'a blatant attempt to manipulate and disempower, a way to divide and confine, a chance to restrict and deny' (Taylor 2003: 90). Many Aboriginal people today still understand these classificatory regimes as attempts to eliminate both the physical and social reality of Aboriginal people in what was being constructed as a 'pure white nation' (Birch 2007: 110).

There can be no denying the damage done to Aboriginal lives by these past policies, which have variously attempted to 'convert, destroy, displace, isolate and eventually assimilate' Aboriginal people all over Australia (Schwab 1988: 77). A large part of this damage has been the postcolonial fracturing of previously intact identities, in ways that have had intergenerational effects. Kevin Gilbert has suggested that colonial policies combined over many years to 'leave the Aboriginal psyche shattered, ripped, tattered', while also allowing group distinctions to emerge between 'government reserve blacks, church blacks, fringe-dwelling blacks and part assimilated town blacks who looked down on what they regarded as their more backward brothers' (Gilbert 2002: 6, 7). These divisions have been evident throughout postcolonial history— for example, the 1976 submission to the government inquiry into the role of the NACC from the Committee of the Aboriginal Cultural Foundation (representing 'tribal' groups) specified that 'Tribal Law is not the business of City Aborigines' (Department of Aboriginal Affairs 1976: 262). Similar claims had been made several decades earlier by David Unaipon, described in the media as 'a full-blooded aboriginal, and a prince of his tribe', whose letter of objection to the 1938 Day of Mourning protest, quoted in *The Age* newspaper, claimed that the protest was sponsored by 'sympathetic white people and half-castes' but that 'full-blooded aborigines' would play little part, preferring instead to 'stoically and silently await the coming of a new day' (quoted in Attwood and Markus 1999: 115–16).

In our interview, John Maynard raised the issue of the complicity of white anthropologists in the construction of the stereotypical 'real blackfella' in the 1920s, a classification John believes was deliberately contrasted with the southern activists of the period.[1] The real blackfella was 'up there somewhere' (i.e. north) and 'harmless', unlike the 'eloquent, articulate, educated' southern activists the stereotype was intended to 'erase'. Irene Watson argues that these anthropologically created identities were something constructed from 'a place beyond' Aboriginal power (Watson 2007: 27). Several of my interviewees saw governments as complicit in these efforts to create a divide between north and south. Jilpia Jones suggests governments put a 'wedge' between north and south, challenging southerners' authenticity with the charge that if 'you don't stand on your leg and show your spears' then 'you're not a real blackfella'.

Skin colour also played a part in the assessment of an individual's authenticity. Skin colour is an emotionally charged issue, replete with cultural knowledge of the sexual exploitation of Aboriginal women and the removal of lighter skinned children from their black mothers. During the course of researching this book, I heard several Aboriginal people speak of their lighter skin as a 'prison' in which they were trapped, representing so much of the history of what had been done to their people. Children who were removed for reasons of skin colour often found themselves caught between two cultures: taken from their families for not being black enough but still subject to racial abuse for being too black to physically assimilate. William Tilmouth experiences this still, being told by 'traditional people' that he is a 'half-caste fella', a painful label he places in historical context: 'The half-castes were taken away, the traditional people were left. The whitefella kept raping the Aboriginal women, making half-caste kids, sending them away. And you ended up with this mistrust between Aboriginal people: "Hey, this yella fella, you've got to watch him."'

It is hard to comprehend the sort of trauma experienced by these children, an issue to which I will return in Chapter 11. The targeting of lighter skinned children for removal was certainly abusive then, and is recognised as abusive now (for example, in the policies of SNAICC—see Briskman 2003: 41). In the context of identity, however, removal and institutionalisation created much confusion. Sue Gordon, formerly the chair of both the NIC and appointed to head up the Northern Territory Intervention Task Force, was herself a stolen child who grew up in Western Australia's Sister Kate's Home. Gordon recalls that: 'We weren't Aborigines in the Home, but when we went across the road to school we were Aborigines. We were natives and darkies and all that sort of thing.' (quoted in Beresford 2006: 46)

Tauto Sansbury described his view that skin colour still creates class division between Aboriginal people along the traditional/non-traditional axis. However, Tauto also rejects the idea that Aboriginal people with lighter skin get any advantages over their darker-skinned counterparts, an idea he dismisses as 'a lot of bullshit' that governments 'use very effectively' to maintain divisions among Aboriginal people. Ray Swan agrees, arguing that skin colour has been used by non-Aboriginal people to 'put a barrier up between full-blood people or traditional people and urbanised people'. This constant assessment of Aboriginal authenticity based on skin colour is distressing and exhausting—not to mention offensive to many. Tom Calma sees that lighter-skinned people are 'challenged a lot more about their Aboriginality' and are often told that they are 'more white than Aboriginal'. Josie Crawshaw remembers the light-skinned, blue-eyed Michael Mansell being marginalised by some of the Top End leaders in the 1980s, who challenged his Aboriginal background and mandate until they heard him speak and were impressed by his political analysis. Jackie Huggins sees this issue from both sides. On the one hand, she accepts that lighter skinned people 'cop it all the time, especially from white people', but at the same time she accepts that darker skinned people experience more overt forms of racist abuse. For Jackie, skin colour is irrelevant. She points out at least one of her blond-haired, blue-eyed Aboriginal friends who 'knows more about his culture, his people, his history, his language than I will ever know'. As Colleen Hayward suggests, 'Aboriginality is something that goes beyond the external physical appearance. It's actually something from inside.'

Marcia Langton has argued that these issues of identity and resolving who is and who is not Aboriginal are located uneasily 'between the individual and the state' (Langton 2003: 116). Debra Hocking, herself a part of the stolen generation, suggests that restoring a sense of personal and cultural identity is 'one of the most hurtful and painful parts of healing'. Hocking believes that many Aboriginal people who were affected by these policies go on to spend much of their lives asking, 'Where do I fit in?' (Hocking 2006: 98). These feelings were captured most vividly in the *Bringing Them Home* report, which documented the effects of child removal policies. One member of the Stolen Generations is quoted in the report as saying: 'You spend your whole life wondering where you fit. You're not white enough to be white and your skin isn't black enough to be black either, and it really does come down to that.' (HREOC 1997: 21) William Tilmouth is one who has found this process of what he calls 'assimilating back' very difficult. Taken as a child and growing up away from his land and his family, William says he 'learned a lot of white fella traits' on the missions, which now leaves him at times feeling in a 'no-man's land', 'torn' between the black and white cultures.

One person I spoke to, who did not wish to be named, spoke of the feelings of displacement that resulted from her own personal circumstances. Adopted as a baby, and still researching her birth family, despite many years of involvement in Aboriginal politics this woman feels she is 'just not black enough', a feeling that goes beyond skin:

It's more about the way I was brought up in the fact that I'm not part of a community in the same way and I don't know in fact who my family is and therefore I've got no right to speak. And those criticisms are things that I've had to think really carefully about and have influenced my decision not to take on more prominent roles. I've struggled with that stuff around my identity and whether it's appropriate for me to be playing certain roles and

I've made the decision to not put myself in that position until I feel more confident about doing that. And that may never happen, you know.

At certain times in postcolonial history, Aboriginal people have also experienced pressure to 'pass' or to hide their Aboriginality,[2] an issue well known to many due to the success of Sally Morgan's novel *My Place* (1987). Paul Briggs expresses considerable empathy for families who experienced this sort of pressure, and the 'despair' many have experienced at the 'dismantling' of their culture. He says:

> You've come out of country, you've come on to mission stations, you've come to live on the edge of town on the river banks and the tip sites, you've come into public housing, and it's slowly just pulling families and identity and culture apart because of the pressure to conform and live white, act white, think white, so that you can get on and get access to services.

Paul feels that this dynamic is still a 'strong element of stress in Aboriginal leaders' lives'. Others have also recognised the terrible bind that families find themselves in once they try to pass in white society. The late Isabel Flick observed that, in the case of one Collarenebri family that agitated to get their kids into the local school during a period of segregated education: 'people would say, "Oh, they're uptown niggers," and all this and that, you know. And I think, well they were people with white skin. They couldn't be black. To get into the school they had to act like whites. And then they had to live up to that. It must have been a terrible strain.'

Not everyone is so understanding, however. Jackie Huggins has recorded her view of the 'act of passing' as 'a horrendous crime'. Given the struggles so many Aboriginal people have faced to retain their identity under assimilationist policies, Jackie argues that many Aboriginal people will 'never forget nor forgive' those 'traitors' who have passed as white. Jackie further rejects much of the complexity of identity discussed below, claiming her identity is 'fixed' and suggesting that 'fluidity is nothing more than a sell-out of Aboriginal heritage, values and identity' (Huggins 2003: 62, 63). Jackie told me she has emphasised to her son John that if there are occasions when people do not recognise him as Aboriginal he should 'never take it as a compliment . . . Don't ever deny who you are.'

Hybrid modern identities

With greater recognition of connections to land—through land rights and native title regimes—Aboriginal people have developed increasing confidence in the possibilities of assuming multiple identities. One important development has been that Aboriginal identity is no longer controlled by the state (Stokes 2002: 206–7). Since the 1970s, the government-endorsed definition of Indigeneity accepts that an Aboriginal or Torres Strait Islander person is any person of Aboriginal or Torres Strait Islander descent who identifies as an Aboriginal or Torres Strait Islander person and is accepted as such by the community in which they live (for a discussion of this, see Gardiner-Garden 2000). Although conservative opponents of the idea of self-definition considered the new policy to be dangerous precisely because it took the power of definition away from white bureaucrats and gave it to Aboriginal people themselves (Bennett 1989: 59), this definition is, unsurprisingly, preferred by the 'vast majority' of Indigenous Australians (Gardiner and Bourke 2000: 44).

This capacity for self-definition, however, does not deal with the hybrid nature of contemporary Aboriginal identities. Noel Pearson suggests that it is 'simply not possible to understand traditional Aboriginal identity in a singular reductive way'. Pearson (drawing on Amartya Sen) suggests that there are 'layers of identity' and describes his own layers as including the traditional kinship layers of Guugu Warra and Guugu Yimithirr (on his father's side) and Kuku Yalanji (on his mother's side). Being a Queenslander, he considers himself a Murri, as well as Bama, which describes Aboriginal people from across the Cape York Peninsula. Layered on top of these traditional or cultural identities are the postcolonial identities of Lutheran, mission-grown, private-school educated, lawyer, and lover of rugby union. Connected to these layers are his complex feelings about Australian patriotism, identifying as 'Australian, but not necessarily a proud one', and feeling alienated from nationalistic rituals such as the ANZAC Day commemorations, which 'feel too white' for him (Pearson 2006b: 3–5; 2007). These complex layers of identity are a simultaneously universal and diverse component of contemporary Aboriginal political culture.

The question of religious faith other than Aboriginal spirituality is one area of complexity. The missionary regimes that peppered the colonial landscape were a significant influence on many people's

111

identities. Bain Attwood has noted the attraction of the 'redemptive vision of Christianity' for many Aboriginal people, which was then translated into a potent subjectivity that adapted colonial political discourse to their own ends (Attwood 2003: 78). In some cases, this involved the successful interweaving of Indigeneity and Christianity—for example, in the case of Percy Mumbler from the New South Wales south coast. Mumbler understood land rights as being a gift from Jesus: 'This land that I speak about is belonging to us and we was put here by the Maker, the Lord Jesus . . . And we know our heavenly Father walked amongst our people. This is right! "This is your land, and everything I put in this land is for you to make use of".' (Percy Mumbler, quoted in Chittick and Fox 1997: 14)

Mudrooroo[3] has argued that, for many Aboriginal people, this sort of modification of Christian belief to fit with Indigenous spirituality was a form of resistance to cultural domination (Mudrooroo 1995: 45). For others like Marvyn McKenzie, however, Christianity has been rejected in favour of what he calls his 'Aboriginal beliefs' (see also Dodson et al. 2006). This is a difficult issue in Marvyn's family, where some people still hold Christian beliefs and tell him that he 'shouldn't believe all that stuff'. Marvyn is one of many Aboriginal people who have deliberately set out to recover and practise the spiritual aspects of traditional culture, pointing out that many elders 'gave up' traditional knowledge in a time when ethnocentric missionaries were proselytising that 'their culture was more advanced than ours'. Others, such as Gadjai Frank Sebastian, have also experienced the divisive effects of missionary regimes on their families:

We bin brought up as a Roman Catholic there in Beagle Bay, when they took us there, the Stolen Generation. And when you come out of there believing that you a Roman Catholic, next thing you know your sister's over there believing some other Church and your brother's over there in another Church. And I don't know if any blackfellas are Mohammed or all them mob today, but that's the divisions we got today and we facing up to that and there's argument between our families. (quoted in KALACC 2006: 70)

Sebastian would be interested to know that 'Mohammed's mob' are indeed becoming part of some hybrid Aboriginal identities, driven in part by a rejection of Christianity as a colonial religion (Morris 2007).

Eugenia Flynn converted to Islam several years ago, and in our interview explained how her religious beliefs fit with her Aboriginal culture:

> For me it comes in the place of knowing those two things really, really well. You really need to know Islam the religion very, very well and you need to know your Aboriginal spirituality very well in order to let those things gel. There are some things that conflict, but because I have knowledge of both of those things I'm able to resolve them in a way that makes me satisfied . . . When you contemplate the spirituality of Islam you see the way that it fits together with being spiritually tied to country.

Eugenia is also very clear, however, that for her Islam must come first. She tells me that she would never 'do things that contradict Islam because in Islam we believe that everything comes from one creator and God'. For her, this means she can never have 'trust and faith' in the spirits of Indigenous cosmology, but that does not mean she does not 'acknowledge that those spirits are there'. While some Aboriginal converts view Islam as 'a rejection of Christianity and a rejection of whiteness', Eugenia stresses her belief that the stereotypes of Aboriginal converts as men who convert while in gaol to become militant Muslims is just a media fiction. Eugenia's beliefs have withstood a considerable backlash from other Aboriginal people, particularly with regard to her claim that Islam and Aboriginal spirituality fit together.

Perhaps the most consistently challenging area of Aboriginal diversity concerns the majority (70 per cent) of Aboriginal people who live in cities and towns. Despite this reality, the image of the 'traditional' desert-dweller continues to dominate the public imagination. There is a widespread conception that urbanisation is 'bad' for Aboriginal people, either because it confronts ideas of what is 'natural' for Aboriginal people or because it is seen as a destructive end-phase of the long process of assimilation. Certainly urbanisation has its positive and negative effects. For some, living in towns and cities results in a loss of status among people living a more traditional lifestyle (Shaw 2007: 37). As Sydney artist Jonathon Jones (2002: 54–8) notes in frustration, the dominance of 'traditional' Aboriginality means that if an Aboriginal person does not fit with this stereotype they are 'stripped by the mainstream community of having that identity'. Some respond to this process of erasure by attempting to adopt a more 'traditional' identity, while others—like Jones—struggle to create a 'contemporary urban Aboriginal identity'.

The other side of urbanisation, however, is what it has offered to Aboriginal people, most notably the formation of political networks that have been significant in the rise of a nationwide Aboriginal rights movement, to be discussed further in the next chapter. Urbanisation was a 'profoundly transformative and politicising experience' that created a new consciousness among an otherwise marginalised minority (de Costa 2006: 97, 98). Protest activity, particularly in the 1970s, offered many urban Aboriginal people a way of 'becoming' Aboriginal in a publicly identifiable sense around which they constituted their identity (Merlan 2005: 484). Urbanisation did not 'deplete' Aboriginality as is so often assumed, but rather facilitated new forms of cultural production 'combining the old and the new, the traditional and the modern'. Ties to communities of origin were combined with 'new solidarities' that would not have been possible outside of the city (Morgan 2006a: 63).

Despite these positives, however, it remains the case that urban Aboriginality is seen as unauthentic and 'unacceptable' to many non-Aboriginal Australians (Shaw 2007: 40). As Mick Dodson has argued: 'There would be few urban Aboriginal people who have not been labelled as culturally bereft, "fake" or "part-time Aborigines", and then expected to authenticate their Aboriginality on terms of percentages of blood or clichéd "traditional" experiences.' (Dodson 2003a: 28) The move away from a 'traditional' or 'community' identity is used by some non-Aboriginal people to perpetuate distinctions not dissimilar to the full-blood/half-caste dichotomy of days gone by (Taylor 2003a: 93). These views are clearly offensive to many, demonstrating a lack of understanding of the way Aboriginal identity is constituted: 'They talk about urbanised Kooris having no traditional culture in them. Well, they should think about that! . . . Koori people today still have got traditional in them through that [kinship] structure.' (Sandy Patten, quoted in Chittick and Fox 1997: 137)

Tom Calma recognises that Aboriginal people in urban areas 'have a stronger sense of need to assert their identity' than do their 'traditional' counterparts, whose identity is less often challenged. There is particular risk, as Alwyn McKenzie points out, that this lack of recognition will mean that Aboriginal people in urban areas will not have their needs met. Alwyn says, 'we know there's great need there', but the overwhelming policy and service focus on remote communities can sometimes obscure this fact. This dichotomy was reinforced under the Howard government's policy of 'practical reconciliation', which redirected resources away from urban-dwelling Aboriginal people and towards those living in rural and remote areas (Morgan 2006a: xiii).

More challenging even than the non-Aboriginal response is the rejection of Aboriginal identity by other Aboriginal people, an experience that can be 'devastating'. According to Debra Hocking (2006: 99), it is a factor in 'many lives' in Tasmania.[4] It is one thing to have your Aboriginality challenged by non-Aboriginal people, but it is quite another to have to fight for acceptance from other Aboriginal people. Larissa Behrendt has experienced this antagonism first hand, telling me in our interview:

> I can't tell you how many times I've been in meetings with people who aren't from the southeast who like to imply that because I'm from here, I'm not as culturally legitimate as they are because I haven't lived on an outstation and I don't speak my language fluently. And it's very hard not to resent the way that your Aboriginality, which I feel inherently no matter where I am, is somehow being dismissed.

This has not deterred Marcia Langton (2008a: 158), herself an urban-based academic, from drawing a political distinction between remote and urban Aboriginal people, which she says also reflects divisions about concerns to do with the 'practical' versus the 'symbolic' in debates about the Northern Territory intervention. Langton draws a distinction between 'those who have lived through the many tragedies and their aftermath in remote Australia, committed to preventing the destruction of their societies in a haze of alcohol and drug abuse; and those with cosmopolitan urban experience who have allowed libertarian leanings, and deep political disappointment, to confuse their logic'. Langton here is relating urbanisation to the class differences that have emerged as a relatively new cleavage among Aboriginal people as many have taken up opportunities for education and training available in cities and towns. While status differences have long been a feature of many rural towns, with differences in lifestyle and values evident between 'town dwellers' and 'fringe dwellers', these categories have been somewhat porous and poorly defined (Keen 1988: 8). Recent years, however, have seen the emergence of what Larissa Behrendt refers to in our interview as 'a middle-class black Australia'. Larissa sees this new class structure as something that will be a 'huge challenge to Indigenous politics and identity' for several reasons:

> First of all the emerging middle class completely breaks the stereotype that is dominant within—and is actually quite a dominant *reality* within—the Aboriginal community, of people who are socioeconomically disadvantaged . . . There's a real challenge in seeing people who are middle class, who have successful careers in professions that are quite influential in mainstream society, whether they're doctors or lawyers or accountants or business analysts, and then having to figure out, well, what does self-determination mean for an Indigenous person who has that profile?

It is apparent that the emerging black middle class is, in part, fuelling the jealousy discussed in the previous chapter, and quite understandably so among the less well off majority. However, even successful people like Noel Pearson—himself an educated lawyer—have attacked the newly emerging middle class for manufacturing 'black urban glamour' through, for example, the launch of a new Indigenous television network (Pearson 2007b). Such criticism seems to fly in the face of the knowledge that elites are an important resource in political culture. Geoff Scott agrees, pointing out that 'a substantial portion of the Aboriginal population has yet to realise the potential benefit [a middle class] can have'. Warren Mundine also acknowledges the importance of the emerging middle class, claiming it is hard to 'name a revolution that was started without your middle class'. Deep suspicion about the new black middle class remains, however, with Gary Foley declaring in a radio interview that: 'They're screwing us.' (ABC 2003a)

One further layer of complexity in the area of Aboriginal identity concerns the relationship between black and white—in families and within individuals. Drawing on the discussion of skin colour above, the question of black–white relationships remains challenging for many. Several of my interviewees had at least one white relative, whether a parent, a spouse or partner, or a more distant relationship. Sam Watson is one who finds considerable joy in his relationships with non-Aboriginal Australians, most particularly his wife Catherine who has been his partner since they were both fifteen. Sam feels that his relationship with Catherine, with whom he lives in 'the broader white community', helps him to keep some 'distance from the Murri community', which in turn makes him 'an effective community operator'. Colleen Hayward understands both the complex history and the contemporary reality of these relationships, saying: 'Were too many of our women raped? Yeah, they were. So lots of the initial instances of babies who became children who became adults who became parents of mixed cultural heritage was violent and not by choice.' Yet Colleen has a simple response when she is asked by colleagues whether any of her experiences with non-Aboriginal Australians have been positive. Colleen says simply: 'My mother is white. Absolutely every experience I have with her is positive.'

Despite the growing confidence with which many Aboriginal people negotiate multi-layered identities, there is still a degree of what several people described as 'internalised racism', which manifests itself in the charge that someone is 'not black enough'. Kim Hill sees the question being asked 'in most communities' about 'who's a real blackfella?' In the Tiwi Islands, where Kim grew up, the lease signed with the Howard government raised new questions about 'Who's real Tiwi?' Since colonisation, Kim says, 'people have married the wrong way, and married people who are from the mainland' creating a situation where 'white people judge us' but, more crucially, 'our own mob judge us'. Eddie Cubillo strongly rejects this sort of internalised racism, pointing to his own cultural mix of Filipino and Chinese, along with his Aboriginal family background. Eddie finds it really upsetting to hear 'one mob say they are more black than another', a view he says is 'just ignorance'. Eddie's response is to say: 'Look, we're all the same. We're just lucky [in the North] that Captain Cook didn't rock up on our gate first.' Still, Eddie is optimistic, believing that many Aboriginal people are 'getting over that hurdle'. If Eddie is right, it seems an important step for Aboriginal people to insist that more than a 'traditional' Aboriginal identity is recognised.

Recognising Indigeneity, resisting assimilation

Claiming Indigeneity—that is, claiming to be the first occupants of a country with rights of prior occupancy—is central to Aboriginal political culture (Maybury-Lewis 1997: 7). Questions of land ownership, autonomy and self-determination are inextricably linked with questions of identity and recognition. The transformation of the idea of Aboriginal identity, from a colonial construct to a politicised identity, a 'badge worn with pride', has occurred through generations of political struggle for recognition (Niezen 2003: 3, 11).

Many Aboriginal people experience their Aboriginality as being under constant challenge from non-Aboriginal people. Being light-skinned can sometimes mean experiencing a type of 'invisibility' in the wider culture, an experience that Paul Briggs describes as 'stifling'. Muriel Bamblett has also experienced challenges to her Aboriginality, recalling with frustration: 'When I say I'm Aboriginal people feel that they have to say that I'm half Aboriginal . . . or people say "Oh, you're only a quarter caste" and I say, "What's a quarter caste? And which quarter of me is Aboriginal?"' In the face of these challenges, claiming an Aboriginal identity is an act of resistance to forces of assimilation. This is certainly the way that several of my interviewees explained their reasons for identifying first and foremost as Aboriginal, even when they are from a more culturally diverse family background. Colleen Hayward was eloquent on this point:

> Because we are so small in number in this place, it goes beyond cultural identity. It goes to the heart of cultural survival. If we cannot claim, or if we stop claiming for ourselves, our Aboriginality, how long do we last as people? . . . This is our place. This is our place forever. How can we not identify and claim that? I don't understand how we couldn't.

Henry Atkinson agrees strongly with these sentiments, claiming that: 'If you want your race to survive you have to identify who you are. Otherwise you're a failure to yourself and you're a failure to your younger generations.' Tradition will always be an important part of Aboriginal identity. Some, like Alwyn McKenzie, want to focus on maintaining and preserving the traditional aspects of identity, prompting him to reflect on the work that he does and whether he is 'actually enhancing white-ness' in ways that will mean 'the dominant culture just flows through our people'. Ted Wilkes agrees with this view of the importance of tra-ditional culture, pointing out that the children surveyed in the Western Australian Aboriginal Child Health Survey were all saying: 'We want our culture.' For Ted, it is important for Aboriginal health that children are able to feel safe and proud in their identities, knowing that 'they're brown-skinned and they're beautiful and they can play sport and they have a knowledge about the land which is theirs'. For Paul Briggs, this confidence in their Aboriginality must be something that children and young people can take with them into the white community, where it is currently devalued. Paul sees that there are too many children who 'feel okay at home, they go off to school in the morning and they don't feel okay until they get back home again'.

For those who are lucky enough to have retained or regained the security of their identity, this knowledge is a great comfort and a source of confidence. For Jilpia Jones, even though she was taken from her family as a child, rediscovering her mob and being recognised and accepted by them means that she feels 'at home' wherever she goes, secure in the knowledge that every year she will go home to the desert, making time for that 'connection' with her Walmadjari people. Tom Calma makes a similar point. Although his job is based in Sydney, he still has the opportunity to visit his traditional land several times a year, where he can 'maintain some of my obligation' to his mother's land. Gooniyardi man Neil Carter has also expressed the confidence that came with returning to his country: 'I gained my sense of identity in my place back up here. I know who my people are and I know where I fit in. And that sense of belonging gives you a sense of satisfaction and confidence to go and do things for your people.' (quoted in KALACC 2006: 75)

But while some can appreciate the certainty of identity that comes with this connection to land, the advent of land rights and native title regimes has in many ways created new challenges for the recognition of Aboriginal identities. Under the Northern Territory *Land Rights Act*, for example, Aboriginal people must 'produce' an identity that meets the requirements of the Act and that allows a white judge to decide 'whether or not they are who they say they are'. In what John Bradley and Kathryn Seton (2005: 35, 43) describe as 'a theatre of tragic farce', Aboriginal people must '"prove" their identity according to an alien means of determining truth and falsehood'. Native title claims processes have also imposed a new 'traditionalist framework' on to Aboriginal communities, requiring that claimants must demonstrate their 'traditional' connections to country in ways that are increasingly at odds with the 'complex intercultural realities' and layers of identity that constitute their contemporary lives (Taylor et al. 2005: xi, xii). Fred Myers has described this process as requiring Aboriginal people to 'stitch culture and tradition together into some kind of wearable garb' in order that their claims to land might be recognised as 'authentic' (Myers 2005: 22). By contrast, Warren Mundine suggests that these processes have helped to dispel the myth of the 'authentic Aborigines' only living in the north, suggesting that native title success in the south is 'dispelling that myth'. For Mundine, issues of 'self-esteem, pride, the recognition of people and how they define themselves' are '100 per cent better' under native title than they previously were (quoted in Dick 2007). To some extent that is true, and the declaration that a certain area of land is traditionally theirs is an important validation.

The other side of the native title coin, however, is the pain and hurt that comes from a failed claim. No case demonstrates this more clearly than the Yorta Yorta claim, finally resolved on appeal in the High Court in 2002 when it was determined that the claimants' traditional connection to their land had been washed away by the 'tides of history' (see Cutliffe 2006; Seidel 2004; Reilly 2001). Elders like Henry Atkinson, who believes that the outcome of the case effectively stripped the Yorta Yorta of their identity, feel the loss very keenly. For Henry and other elders, this was 'a terrible, terrible feeling'. Fellow Yorta Yorta man Paul Briggs agrees, claiming native title recognition is fundamentally about 'validation' of claimants' identity. However, Paul thinks the Yorta Yorta:

> weren't prepared for the Native Title era and we weren't prepared for the debate ... The fallout for Yorta Yorta was the validation by the white mainstream and the 500 odd respondents against Yorta Yorta that we don't have an identity. We don't have a legitimate claim as Aboriginal people to the lands on which we lived. As a people we weren't ready for that.

The lack of logic in the native title claims process, and the lack of acknowledgment of the history of colonisation and the dispossession of Aboriginal people from their lands, continue to confound Paul, who says: 'Well, we don't understand the argument. We're Yorta Yorta, we're still on our land. We understand that people have built fences and are using it for other purposes but there's a belief in the spirituality of Yorta Yorta people that we're still connected and we still belong there.' Aboriginal people in other parts of the country also expressed anger at the Yorta Yorta decision and what it meant for the recognition of Aboriginal identity. Noel Pearson suggested that, in the court's eyes, 'southern traditional owners' are perhaps 'not quite Aboriginal enough' (quoted in Dick 2007).

Given Pearson's views in 2002, some wonder why he is now a leading proponent of adapting cultural practices (that he sees as impeding economic development) despite the potential cost of these policies to the future recognition of identity and native title. Noel Pearson's idea of orbiting, discussed in the previous chapter, is one idea that causes considerable anxiety for this very reason. For Yorta Yorta elder Henry Atkinson, this is a strategy full of dangerous implications in terms of the recognition of native title claims. One of the tests for native title is the continuous association with the land over which a group is claiming title. Henry wonders what the implications of such tests will be if a significant proportion of the community leave to gain employment or education. Henry points out that 'one minute governments are telling you get out there, get an education, get in employment. But if you do that, you're going to lose your culture and your identity.' Some who have moved off their country for reasons of career and employment already feel they have jeopardised their identity. Eddie Cubillo, for example, worries: 'I'm not a real black-fella . . . I'm exactly what John Howard wants. I've got a law degree, I've got two houses and I'm living off my country. I'm assimilated.'

Identity and control
Aboriginal people in Australia, like Aboriginal and non-Aboriginal peoples everywhere, draw on their history and traditions in asserting their right to define their identities, their cultures, their modes of governance and their rights to land. Tradition, in this sense, is an important resource in Aboriginal political culture. At the same time, this recourse to tradition creates tensions for those whose identities are less rooted in the traditional, and is challenging to ideas of freedom and emancipation that foreground the right of the individual to make a destiny of their own choosing (Havemann 2000: 23, 24). The labels 'Indigenous' or 'Aboriginal' function both to distil a complex, politicised identity and to obscure the diversity of people who may wear that label (Dean and Levi 2003: 13). For most Aboriginal people, these layers of identity—that is, the local/traditional, the hybrid/individual and the national/pan-Aboriginal—will be 'activated' at different times depending on context and need (Brennan 2006: 6).

Noel Pearson (2006b: 8) has stated his continuing conviction that it is the 'correct policy for Australia' to recognise Aboriginal identity and 'peoplehood'. But while this claim seems straightforward—and there would be few Aboriginal people who would dispute it—complex questions remain about what Aboriginal identity *is* and how it might be recognised. Mainstream politics continues to see Aboriginality as 'a deficiency, a burden that handicaps Aboriginal people in the modern world and should be shed' (Wootten 2004). Marcia Langton has suggested that one of the central problems facing Aboriginal people is 'the failure of non-Aboriginals to comprehend us' or to 'find the grounds for an understanding'. Langton sees that successive policies directed at Aboriginal people—'protection, assimilation, integration, self-management, self-determination and, perhaps, reconciliation'—have each been ways of 'avoiding understanding' (Langton 2003: 122). Indeed, the tendency in much mainstream policy and politics to focus *only* on the 'traditional' aspects of identity lets governments off the hook by not requiring that they also recognise those complex postcolonial aspects of identity that bring with them particular socioeconomic problems that may require special services and specific policies (Behrendt 2006: 8).

So, in part, this issue of complex Aboriginal identities is one for governments and non-Aboriginal people to come to terms with in order to deliver policy and services to all Aboriginal people. On the other hand, however, questions of identity and the acceptance of both traditional and non-traditional identities are primarily the concern of Aboriginal people themselves. There is concern that, as one person put it to me, unless Aboriginal people 'come to some conclusion and agreement' about how to deal with people of mixed or uncertain heritage, then 'the government will do it for us and it will be another form of the caste system'.

What is certainly true is that Aboriginal people want to define their Aboriginality for themselves, as is their human right. Jackie Huggins has written that she 'detests' the 'imposition' that 'anyone who is non-Aboriginal can define my Aboriginality for me'. Any such definition, she says, is an insult to her 'intelligence, spirit and soul' and, further, 'negates' her heritage (Huggins 2003: 60). At the heart of the violation of Indigenous rights has been what Mick Dodson describes as 'the denial of our control over our identity and the symbols through which we make our cultures and ourselves' (2003a: 31). As Louise Taylor has argued, Aboriginal peoples' 'right to formulate our own identities is tightly bound up in our right to self-determination' (2003: 90):

we must assert ourselves as the gatekeepers of our culture and our identity. The construction and resolution of our individual and collective identities are distinctly Aboriginal areas and must remain exclusively ours. We must attempt to confront issues surrounding Aboriginal identity with compassion and honesty . . . (Taylor 2003: 99)

The challenge will be to assert 'distinctly Aboriginal' identities that at the same time are freed from what Yin Paradies describes as the 'prison of romanticisation', so that it is possible to recognise a diversity of identities that are all 'equally but variously Indigenous' (Paradies 2006: 363). Addressing these questions around identity may help revitalise a sense of national unity in Aboriginal political culture, an issue I consider in the next chapter.

7
UNITY AND
REGIONALISM

To non-Aboriginal Australians, Aboriginal politics is most visible when played out on the national stage. Since the 1967 referendum, which gave the Commonwealth government power to legislate with respect to Indigenous affairs, the Commonwealth has also broadly set the agenda in terms of policy and service delivery. State and territory governments have also played an important role in service delivery and in sub-national land rights regimes, but it is at the national level that the most crucial issues are debated. For this reason, Aboriginal leaders and activists have long seen the need for national representation, and have expended considerable energy in efforts to develop and sustain national bodies over many decades.

This need for national representation is, however, extraordinarily challenging to some of the foundations of Aboriginal political culture. As previous chapters have discussed, much Aboriginal political culture is constituted at the local level. Ronald Niezen has observed that it is a characteristic of Indigenous movements internationally that they are free of 'centralized dogma', coalescing instead around a multitude of 'micronationalisms' oriented to small communities or regions connected by loose networks of communication (Niezen 2003: 13). Attempting to organise political representation at the national level thus risks obscuring the diversity of Aboriginal nations and community groups, leaving many feeling invisible or unrepresented.[1] This emphasis on localism can make national unity seem fragile or even impossible. In the absence of a credible model of national political representation, however, there can be tension between Aboriginal groups and communities who may find themselves competing for recognition and entitlements (Bern and Dodds 2002: 164).

Regional representation, both independent of government and through structures such as ATSIC, is seen as one means of attempting to bridge the local and the national. Tim Rowse has suggested that the effort to develop an effective means of articulating the national with the local by means of regional representation 'has been the primary problem in the politics of Indigenous representation since 1973' (Rowse 2001: 133). Aboriginal people have experimented with various means of determining regions, from the geographic to the social and political, recognising both contemporary political and economic ties as well as the historical foundations underpinning such alliances (Smith 2007: 29). At times, these regional aggregations have coalesced successfully into a strong national voice, despite intense debates about what constitutes 'a region' and exactly who should be included within regional borders.

Despite this emphasis on regionalism, however, there remain compelling political reasons for also prioritising the pursuit of a united, national voice. Michael Mansell points out that gains in Aboriginal rights and freedoms—such as those achieved in the 1967 referendum, the recognition of land rights, and inquiries such as those into deaths in custody and the removal of Aboriginal children—have all been achieved by political action with a strong national voice (Mansell 2007: 82). John Maynard acknowledges that while it has been important for more people to know and identify by their Aboriginal nation name, this has also taken Aboriginal people 'a little bit far from the national mood that we had'. John now feels that there is a need to 'push back towards that national identity', arguing: 'We're not going to make change in this country as isolated groups. Even together we're still a minority and we're still extremely marginalised, so we've got to mobilise as a whole.' Tauto Sansbury suggests that underneath all the complexity discussed in this book, Aboriginal people have 'all got basically the same problem and that problem is ignoring Aboriginal people's rights to their own inheritance'. For this reason, Tauto says unequivocally: 'We've got to be a united voice.' Roderick Bennell-Pearce of the Yamatji Nation argues that family groups and clans in each Aboriginal nation need to 'sort out their differences and then stand united under the umbrella of their Aboriginal nation'. Bennell-Pearce is concerned that until Aboriginal people tackle this tension for themselves, governments will continue to see them as 'an unorganised minority' who are 'no threat to their power base' (Bennell-Pearce 2005).

The announcement of the federal intervention into the Northern Territory certainly crystallised the need for a united, national voice. In the absence of a national body, the weeks following the announcement saw Aboriginal people all over the country struggle to digest the full implications of the plan and to coordinate a response. Non-Aboriginal organisations and individuals like the Australian Council of Social Service and Western Australian Greens Senator Rachel Siewart were instrumental in providing support to Aboriginal groups in the absence of any national organisation or institutional capacity. These efforts facilitated the July 2007 production of a statement by the Combined Aboriginal Organisations of the Northern Territory (CAO), which included an alternative response plan to the issues raised in the *Little Children are Sacred* report (CAO 2007). Writing around this same time, in a rapidly produced collection of responses to the intervention (Altman and Hinkson 2007), Michael Mansell proposed that:

> Now may be the time to consider establishing another such national body. It would give Aboriginal people more than just a voice. It would signal our national struggle. It could encourage respect between Aborigines and help to focus debates. It could help to reformulate and disseminate Aboriginal positions on white rule and our survival as distinct peoples under the domination of another culture . . . (Mansell 2007: 82)

Following the passage of the intervention legislation, the National Aboriginal Alliance (NAA) was formed at a meeting in Alice Springs in September 2007.[2] It remains to be seen whether this new body will be sustainable, whether it will have legitimacy in the wider Aboriginal polity and whether it will remain relevant if the Rudd government fulfils its promise of creating a new national representative body. While forming a new alliance in the midst of a crisis is particularly challenging, negotiating a strategic unity across regional differences is always a complex and delicate process. This chapter considers some of the challenges involved.

A pan-Aboriginal unity?

Following the abolition of ATSIC, it was evident that Aboriginal people were suffering without a national voice. Visiting communities in various states and in the Northern Territory, I heard people express anger and frustration at their lack of representation in policy debates, feelings that were compounded by the extent of other policy changes. As Geoffrey Stokes, convenor of the Coalition of Goldfields Aboriginal People, commented it had become 'impossible to get first-hand advice to the Federal Government on our needs and aspirations' (Stokes 2005: 24). Aboriginal people were silenced in this context, an experience that heightened their desire to create a new national body. A significant obstacle to such a body, however, is the challenge involved in creating a pan-Aboriginal unity.

Efforts to construct a sense of national solidarity are not new. While the earlier periods of political protest (from the 1840s onwards) remained intensely local in focus (Attwood and Markus 1999: 9), over time this changed. By the 1930s, activists such as William Cooper and his organisation, the Australian Aborigines' League, were working to develop a national movement, although these efforts eventually 'stagnated', in large part due to the continuing restrictions on Aboriginal people's movement under protectionist regimes (Jones and Hill-Burnett 1982: 221). The impulse to develop national representation remained, however, and was enhanced in forums such as Federal Council for the Advancement of Aborigines and Torres Strait Islanders (FCAATSI) conferences where, in the 1960s in particular, an emerging national solidarity among Aboriginal delegates was fostered through a growing recognition of their shared experiences of colonisation and dispossession. Delegates understood that each other's first loyalty was to their local community, whether that be defined by kin group or mission experience, but in the late 1960s and early 1970s there was a growing recognition of the need to connect these local affiliations to a national consciousness as Aboriginal people (Taffe 2005: 228). Indeed, Pat O'Shane has suggested that the period of FCAATSI's greatest strength, from the mid-1960s to the mid-1970s, is the only period in which there has been a demonstrable national organisation or Aboriginal movement (O'Shane 1998: 10).

The land rights campaigns of the 1960s and 1970s were a crucial element of the emerging pan-Aboriginal movement. The 1963 bark petition from the Yolngu at Yirrkala and the 1966 Wave Hill strike by the Gurindji people created a surge of national mobilisation and pan-Aboriginal sentiment (Merlan 2005: 484). Urban-dwelling Aboriginal people were at the forefront of the more militant expressions of this movement, linking the land rights struggles in the north to protest events such as the establishment of the Aboriginal Tent Embassy in 1972, considered to be the first nationwide Aboriginal political protest (Jones and Hill-Burnett 1982: 222). Indeed, it was primarily in southeastern cities that a pan-Aboriginal consciousness began to emerge during this period. The work of constructing a pan-Aboriginal identity was in large part driven by urban-dwelling Aboriginal people's interest in history as a basis of shared identity (Keen 1988: 21). For these leaders and activists, history was an important resource through which to develop their knowledge of traditional culture, and a source of identity around which to organise a movement. Activists in the south who had lost their land in the earlier waves of dispossession began to identify with other people's land by laying claim to Australian land in general (Attwood 2005: 45; 2003: 321). Paradoxically, however, the struggles of land rights activists in the southeast were often eclipsed by the more sweeping demands of activists in the north. Southern leaders and activists seeking farming and residential land did not capture the public imagination of the non-Aboriginal population in the way that, for example, the Gurindji strike did. Over time, the demands from the Northern Territory were seen as emblematic of all Aboriginal struggles, virtually erasing the ongoing struggles in the south from the public mind (Goodall 1996: 324–7).

During this period, leaders and activists in the south argued that Aboriginal people in the north would share a common fate with southerners if they failed to unite. Robbie Thorpe says: 'We warned them up there. They're going to end up like us, over time, us yella fellas. They're going to get done over just like we did.' Muriel Bamblett echoes Robbie's thoughts, claiming that activists in Victoria told those in the north:

If you don't support Victoria now you will be where we are in ten or twenty years' time. If you think that what we're going through is a Victorian thing and that all the real blackfellas live up there, let me tell you that if you don't fight for us to have our culture recognised *now*, you in ten or twenty years will be in exactly the same situation.

The implications of some aspects of the Northern Territory 'intervention' suggest that Muriel's prediction may well have been right. In a similar vein, Paul Briggs feels that 'a collective approach' is needed to ensure 'the retention of Aboriginal identity in Australia', pointing out that attempts at assimilation in the north today are 'challenges that we've already gone through down in this part of the country'. Paul maintains that these shared experiences should be the basis of a stronger national solidarity. Robbie Thorpe agrees, stressing that while relationships exist and he has 'some great friends up there and great allies right across Australia', he worries that this unity is not as strong as it needs to be.

An obstacle to the sort of solidarity that Paul and Robbie are advocating is the cultural protocol that prohibits an individual from 'speaking for' another group's country, even if they have lived there for many years. William Tilmouth explains this protocol as something 'that goes right back to cultural law where you don't talk about someone's country. You have no right to.' The rules are clear and strict, according to William:

> You cannot talk about that family mob and their country next door to yours because you have no right to . . . It goes right back to those days when you worked within your family boundary, your family grouping, your family's country. That was your country. You dare not impose yourself or prescribe something for someone who's outside of that.

Many Aboriginal people experience a degree of discomfort when they are on someone else's country. Marvyn McKenzie suggests Aboriginal people experience 'homesickness' and 'feel strange in someone else's country', and are certainly highly mindful of the protocols of that group to avoid causing any offence. Views differ about whether these protocols inhibit a pan-Aboriginal unity. Henry Atkinson thinks they do not, arguing that because traditional owners 'speak only and solely for our country' that means they can also 'support one another' and ultimately 'be a voice that people take notice of by coming together'.

However, it is this protocol that explains much of Noel Pearson's unpopularity, as he is so often accused of speaking for country that is not his own. Pearson's disproportionate influence leads some, like Jackie Huggins, to stress the need for 'a filter on the national scene' that will allow a range of voices to speak 'rather than one or two individuals doing it all the time'. Sam Jeffries despairs at the growing influence of what he calls 'the so-called leadership of Noel Pearson', asking: 'What hope do we have as a population of Aboriginal people when one person, *one person*, can be even more influential to the government than what the NIC is?' Sam was particularly disturbed to learn that former Indigenous Affairs Minister Mal Brough had rung to inform Pearson of the government's plans fifteen minutes before announcing the Northern Territory 'intervention' and asks: 'What would Noel say, what would the people in the Cape say, if Mal Brough rang *me* about what he was going to do in the Cape?' Tom Calma considers that 'probably the greatest fear amongst Aboriginal people was the advice that the government's getting off the Cape York Institute', given the Howard government's stated intention of using the Cape York Agenda 'as the model for the rest of Australia'. Tom sees this plan as 'totally ridiculous', arguing that 'Noel Pearson only represents Noel Pearson and maybe a few people on Cape York' and has no right to speak for anyone else.

Dr Marika was also disturbed by Pearson's singular influence, which she said, 'doesn't mean he's talking for us mob'. But, like many others, Dr Marika also observed that all the Commonwealth government hears is 'one voice, not all voices':

> And that's what we want to try and change so that voices are heard according to who is represented from what area, like Western Australia, Northern Territory, Queensland, you know all those places. Not a *Ngapaki* voice but a Yolngu voice. We're not all the same, we're all different. We come from different communities, we have different experiences, we have different languages, we have different ways of dealing with things.

The challenge is in balancing the needs of diverse communities and considering, as Tom Calma does, whether 'geography plays a part in how effective a representative body might be and how peculiar issues are to a geographic area'. In particular, the geographical, cultural and historical differences between the north and south of Australia have at times created a significant obstacle to a broader pan-Aboriginal unity.

The north–south divide
As the previous chapter has suggested, there have long been tensions between leaders and activists in the north and those in the south, in

part based around questions of 'authenticity'. These divisions, often referred to as the 'north–south divide', have a long history and are a very real source of discord. Several people identified this dynamic as a significant obstacle in the way of developing a sustainable national representative body. At meetings to discuss a new body, however, Larissa Behrendt considers that the issue of the north–south divide is not even 'on the table' for discussion, despite her view that it 'can't not be talked about because it defines every discussion that's had at those levels'. For Larissa:

> The big divide is between the agendas in the north and the agendas in the south and the fact that they are really quite distinct now. Resources flow much quicker to the north than they do to the south and the issues that affect people, particularly in the urban areas, are becoming much more distinct from the issues affecting people who live in rural and remote areas, especially now the government has eliminated services in the urban areas. So as a result of policy changes the southeast has now got a particular set of problems that the north doesn't have, and vice versa. They're quite distinct. And we don't seem to have developed the capacity to look at the big picture in a way that accommodates both of those things. We don't seem to have the language or the ability to step back and look at that as part of the problem.

The 1993 negotiations over the *Native Title Act* have to some extent cemented the divide between north and south in Aboriginal political culture. Negotiations over the legislation saw a small group, known as the 'A Team', reach an agreement with the Keating government that many Aboriginal people believe compromised the native title rights recognised in the *Mabo* decision. Josie Crawshaw, for example, considers it a 'sell out' that the A Team 'went behind closed doors' to negotiate a deal that 'actually lost rights'. What was particularly difficult for Josie in that instance was that the members of the group that signed off on that deal—from the Northern, Central, Cape York and Kimberley Land Councils, and from ATSIC—were, in her view, merely bureaucrats and CEOs. In Josie's words: 'All they were, were employees. They were employees that sold the rights of this country. It was like having CEOs of the public service being able to pass Australian legislation.'

The split over the *Native Title Act* negotiations represents the fragility of pan-Aboriginality when it collides with the realpolitik of Australian pluralism. The Keating government was dealing with the A Team on the one hand, and with powerful state governments and mining and pastoral interests on the other. Meanwhile, a second group known as the 'B Team', led by Michael Mansell and Aden Ridgeway, was negotiating with the Greens and Democrats in order to secure amendments to the proposed legislation in the Senate. In simple terms, the split was between the A Team's pragmatism and determination to negotiate the best deal possible in the political climate, and the B Team's more radical and uncompromising belief that *all* Aboriginal people (including dispossessed southerners) should benefit from the principles laid down in the *Mabo* decision (Beresford 2006: 285). As Noel Pearson wrote at the time:

> The political difficulty for [the negotiators] was that in most areas of the country people have got nothing to lose: they've lost the bloody lot. It has been difficult for the Aboriginal political movement to combine the strategies of people who have nothing to lose and who are getting almost nothing out of the legislative response with the strategies of those who have something and are in grave danger of losing it. (Pearson 1993: 184)

This disunity in the parliamentary negotiations contrasted sharply with the unity that had emerged at large meetings of Aboriginal people to discuss the proposed native title legislation: 400 people at Eva Valley in August 1993 and 700 in Canberra in September of that year. The Eva Valley meeting had produced a unanimously endorsed statement that rejected the government's proposed legislation on the grounds that it did not address the issue of veto rights over proposed development on native title land. These criticisms were subsequently attacked by Prime Minister Keating, who was in turn defended by Noel Pearson (who had not attended the Eva Valley meeting) (Brennan 1995: 54; Russell 2005). Keating resumed negotiations with the more moderate group and on 19 October 1993 the government and the A Team announced that they had reached an agreement and that the *Native Title Act* would proceed. This announcement was attacked in a joint statement from Paul Coe and Charles Perkins, who argued that:

Attempting to legitimise the proposed Commonwealth native title legislation by having the Prime Minister negotiating with five Aboriginals so
as to say Aboriginal Australia has been consulted is not acceptable . . . We
stress that these Aboriginal negotiators have acted in direct contravention
of the resolutions passed by two national meetings of Aboriginal people.
(quoted in Foley 2007: 136–7)

The impact of the native title debates, particularly the split between
the A Team and B Team, cannot be under estimated. Once the legislation
was in place, long-term friendships and professional relationships—for
example, that between Rob Riley and Peter Yu—were challenged by
painful divisions brought about by the new task of representing claimant
groups (Beresford 2006: 305). Alwyn McKenzie has observed the way
that native title has 'turned families and language groups against one
another', particularly in areas where overlapping claims are made by different groups of people. Alwyn points out that these conflicts are 'to be
expected when you intentionally break up the people's culture, rights to
their country, ship them from this part of the land to another part and
put them back again. It's no wonder people are mixed up and shook up
and it's caused a lot of stress.'

Even today, according to Geoff Scott, 'the differences are stark and
the wounds are deep and they're still open'. Geoff believes the A Team
negotiators 'should be held to account for what they did'. Gary Foley
agrees, suggesting the A Team are 'ducking for cover now that the
real nature of the *Native Title Act* that they created has been exposed'.
Foley describes native title as 'a joke', 'almost meaningless' and 'the most
inferior form of land tenure under British Law' (ABC 2003a). Robbie
Thorpe, who wryly notes that he was in neither A Team nor B Team
but 'F Troop', shares a similar view, suggesting that native title is 'the
greatest crime since *terra nullius*': 'It's justifying the occupation of white
people and Aboriginal people end up with the lowest form of title known
to mankind. Less that pastoral leases. Pastoral leases are for white man's
animals and we have a lesser title. So why would you be jumping up and
down and saying hooray?' B Team leader Aden Ridgeway considers it
'hard to argue' that the *Native Title Act* 'has been anything other than a
spectacular failure', which has 'established processes that are alienating
and disempowering for most Indigenous people': 'At the end of the day,
the onus of proof always rests with traditional owners to prove descent

and ongoing, unbroken connection to country, guaranteeing that many Indigenous people will never "qualify" as traditional owners in the legal sense of the word.' (Ridgeway 2003: 187)

Stark differences in the way that native title has been recognised around the country have underscored the divisions that emerged in the negotiating process. In New South Wales, for example, the Dunghutti won a little more than 12 hectares in 1997, which was the first native title win on mainland Australia. But fifteen years after the *Mabo* decision first raised the hopes of Aboriginal people all over Australia, those in the southern states have found little to celebrate. The failed Yorta Yorta claim confirmed what many who had opposed the native title legislation had feared, namely that the Act effectively 'penalises those who have been most severely dispossessed' (Brennan et al. 2005: 118). Although Kim Hill issues a reminder that this is not always the case, contrasting the (initial) success of the Noongar (Perth) claim with the loss of the Larrakia (Darwin), he also acknowledges that disparities in land rights and native title regimes have seen 'people on the southeastern coast shed a lot of blood' for the benefit of Aboriginal people in the Northern Territory. Around the country, hundreds of claims still languish unresolved in the purgatory of the native title system in a system that Tom Calma acknowledges in the 2007 *Native Title Report* tends to 'exacerbate old conflicts and create new ones' (ATSISJC 2008b). In New South Wales, many claims are simply 'non-starters' because the vast majority of the state is out of reach of the claims process by virtue of its freehold status. Tasmania and the ACT have no native title, Victoria has about 400 square kilometres, and the Dunghutti and recent Githabul and Wiradjuri agreements remain the only three recognised areas in New South Wales. Compare this with the north and west of Australia where nearly 30 000 square kilometres is recognised in Queensland, and some form of native title covers a quarter of Western Australia. As journalist Tim Dick has argued, 'This is the obvious paradox of native title as the deliverance of justice for the dispossessed: where Aboriginal dispossession was most extensive it is least likely to exist.' (Dick 2007: 29)

The north–south divide is not something that needs to be perpetuated in Aboriginal political culture. As Kado Muir has argued, 'there is no imaginary line there': the divisions are constructed from historical experience and maintained by the contemporary impact of the native title regime. The answer for Muir is 'to get completely away from that concept' and instead 'start looking at nations' (quoted in Paul and Gray 2002: ix).

Balancing regionalism and unity

Despite the challenges of the north–south divide, there have been strong developments in regional representation in recent years. Regionalism can be a moderating force between the localism of small communities and the broader sweep of national pan-Aboriginality. Sensitivity to the significance of localism in Aboriginal political culture, and the growing recognition of this fact in mainstream political culture, have underpinned efforts to develop greater regional aggregations in some areas (Coombs and Robinson 1996: 14–15). The enormous diversity among communities makes representation difficult and some, like Geoff Scott, suggest that regionalism provides the 'middle ground' needed to 'get some agreement or aggregation on what the issues are and how you address them'. Many Aboriginal people recognise that localism can have political and practical drawbacks, and have thus come to the view that their needs and aspirations may more effectively be represented at a regional level (Reilly et al. 2007: 131). These efforts have often been compromised by non-Aboriginal views of what constitutes 'a region', which is often determined by governments based on an aggregated population size that can produce economies of scale. Such artificial construction of regions will never have internal legitimacy (Martin 1999: 159). By contrast, an aggregation of local groups into a 'region' that is legitimate in Aboriginal eyes must, first and foremost, address questions of 'cultural geography', or who rightfully belongs in that region (Smith 2007: 28). In other words, those areas that have successfully developed regionally representative structures have done so by keeping kinship, language group and spiritual associations as the basis of organisation (Bern and Dodds 2002: 175).

The benefits of regionalism are obvious. Land claims in the north have been far more effective when advanced through the regional representation of the land councils[3] than they could possibly have been if advanced by traditional owners with no aggregation of political representation (Webber 2000: 85). Shortly before the end of his term in parliament, former senator Aden Ridgeway suggested that the major land councils could do more with their regional strength, calling for them to 'come together and have some common cultural goals to put forth for the rights agenda' because they 'have a lot of power and resources they could be using' (quoted in Giles 2005b: 9).

There are some outstanding examples of the strength of representation that can be developed at the regional level. One that is often cited is the Murdi Paaki Regional Assembly in western New South Wales. The assembly was developed as what was intended to be a first step in a transition from regional council to a regional authority model—much like the one in the Torres Strait. The assembly chairperson, Sam Jeffries, works to ensure that all sixteen communities in the assembly region are able to act as autonomously as possible. When ATSIC folded, Sam went to the communities to consult them about the future of the assembly model:

> We gave the option to our communities. What do you want to do? This is all about you. This is all about you as Aboriginal people. If you want to keep this, it's up to us to decide whether we keep it going or not . . . And they've decided to keep it going because it works for them. And I think that that's been the key aspect of success is that it's Aboriginal people making decisions about these things that are important to them.

What has been important for Sam in deciding what happens next for the assembly without the protective umbrella of ATSIC is whether they would seek 'legislative legitimacy' or whether they would remain unincorporated. After 'a long conversation' they decided to remain unincorporated in order to retain their autonomy because, as Sam says, 'once we become legislated, politicians can't help themselves but put their fingers over it and change things'.

Not all such efforts at regionalism have been as successful as the Murdi Paaki Assembly. Groups in the Kimberley also attempted to develop a regional decision-making and administrative structure based on a long history of cooperation between language groups in the area (KALACC 2006: 101). For many in the Kimberley, the ATSIC regional structure was inadequate—based, as Peter Yu has argued, on regional council areas that did not 'in any way correspond to cultural boundaries or traditional land ownership patterns' (Yu 1997: 176). Yu believes the ATSIC structure was actually divisive in the Kimberley region because it failed to engage the three key organisations in the region—the Kimberley Law and Culture Centre, the Kimberley Language Centre and the Kimberley

Land Council—in any of its initiatives, and in fact 'undermined those organisations' (Yu, in KALACC 2006: 115). ATSIC did endorse the Yirra statement—developed at the 1994 Yirra Festival, attended by 1200 people from eighteen language groups—which requested federal support for the development of a regional authority. The then Minister for Aboriginal Affairs offered his in-principle support for this assertion of regional autonomy, but this backing did not go any further (KALACC 2006: 117). Although regional networks in the Kimberley remain strong, it has not been possible for them to develop into a regional assembly model like the one in Murdi Paaki.

A more (briefly) successful example of Western Australian regionalism is the outcome of the single Noongar native title claim, where Justice Murray Wilcox ruled that the Noongar people continue to have native title of more than 6000 square kilometres, covering Perth and its surrounds. This was the first native title win in any capital city and came about, in the words of *National Indigenous Times* editor Chris Graham, 'after a nation of dispossessed, disenfranchised and dirt poor people set aside their differences and competing interests and united to fight a common enemy—white law' (Graham 2006: 5).[4] The single claim eventuated when the South-West Aboriginal Land and Sea Council (SWALSC) managed, in 2003, to unite the majority of competing, overlapping claimant clan groups to the area in question in southwestern Australia, some of whom had individually been seeking native title since the mid-1990s. In the Federal Court, Justice Murray Wilcox found that the Noongar people were indeed 'one people' and that they were the original inhabitants of the land of southwest Australia. He also found that, despite more than a century and a half of colonial devastation and some of Australia's most brutal assimilation policies, the Noongars have continued to observe traditional customs and laws connected to their country.

This decision was exciting and inspiring for many Aboriginal people in other parts of the country, causing some to question ongoing factionalism and disunity. John Maynard, for example, suggested that the Noongar decision might be 'an awakening' for other groups, who might be encouraged to 'move past' their divisions and factions, because the Noongar showed that unity 'can move mountains'. It should go without saying that the April 2008 decision of the full Federal Court to overturn the decision on appeal from the Western Australian and Commonwealth governments, on the grounds that there had been no continuous acknowledgment and observance of the traditional laws and customs by the Single Noongar Society from sovereignty until recent times, nor a proven connection with the land or waters, was a crushing blow.

Some, like Ted Wilkes, place far more importance on regionalism than national representation, arguing that 'the need to have a national body isn't the be all and end all', and that far greater attention should be paid to the local and regional levels of representation: 'Today there are Aboriginal leaders at the regional level who are quite competent and able to represent people at the regional level. That's where we've got to focus our energies. There is no real need for a national focus.' Ted envisages a process whereby different regions could learn from one another's 'best practice' through a process of 'knowledge transfer' in a 'domino effect' from one region to another. Ted sees this as far more effective than 'trying to fix it all up in one big sweep right across Australia' because, as has so often been observed so far in this book, 'one size does not fit all'. Ted's belief is that Aboriginal people have tried 'the national perspective' and he now thinks it is time to 'allow the regions to get on with their business'.

A way forward for national representation

Despite the possibilities that regionalism offers, many Aboriginal people still express a strong desire for a new national representative body. Jackie Huggins maintains that: 'What our people are telling us, at every meeting you go to, is that they want a national voice.' While co-chair of Reconciliation Australia Jackie took this message to government, telling them 'because our people want that so much, we think that's an essential ingredient of reconciliation'. For Jackie, the essential ingredient is for people to have the capacity to 'speak from the community'. It was evident in my interviews that much thought had gone into how such a body would be structured, how representatives would be selected and what role it would play. I will return to some of these issues in the conclusion to this book, but it is worth considering here some proposals that specifically address the challenge of national unity among a highly localised polity.

The first point of reference for many Aboriginal people in considering these issues is the now-defunct ATSIC. ATSIC attempted to bring the local and the regional together in what Will Sanders has described as 'an experiment in Commonwealth-sponsored regionalism'. Its creation followed criticism that its two predecessors, the NAC and the NACC, were not sufficiently connected to, or representative of, Aboriginal communities and organisations. The ATSIC model attempted to correct this situation by creating an 'elaborate hierarchy' of representation, originally spread over 60 regions, with nearly 800 positions for elected representatives in an attempt to connect local governance to national representation through the intermediate level of regionalism (Sanders 2004: 56–7). Perhaps inevitably, however, the regional structure of ATSIC was only a limited expression of Indigenous diversity that did not ever adequately reflect the complexity of local communities (Smith 1996: 28–30). Nor did the ATSIC structure deal effectively with the representation, needs or status of Aboriginal women (see ATSIC 1995b; Davis 2008). Further, as Colleen Hayward notes, the reduction in the number of ATSIC regions from 60 to 35 following a 1993 review further undermined its capacity to represent local diversity, causing resentment that the restructure was based primarily on 'administrative convenience'. Despite these flaws in the regional structure, however, the 2003 review of ATSIC that recommended simplifying the national level structure emphasised that the regional councils were 'the foundation of ATSIC' (Hannaford et al. 2003: 5).[5]

Like many of my interviewees, Alwyn McKenzie would like to see another democratically elected body like ATSIC, despite 'all the flaws in the democratic process'. Alwyn acknowledges the alternate view, that representatives should be selected 'on cultural ways of doing things', and thinks that in 'certain locations' that would be appropriate, suggesting that 'people can work it out there'. But Alwyn, like many others, sees the necessity of balancing the selection of national representatives with regional and local representative legitimacy. Geoff Scott argues that what he calls 'the regional issue' has got to be 'taken on' or else 'people aren't going to actually acknowledge there's any leadership from their point of view'. Geoff draws a comparison with mainstream politics, and says: 'That's why you have local government. That's why you have state governments.' However, without a national organisation attempting to balance the regional and the national, too many Aboriginal people remain wholly unrepresented.

The ATSIC model is still held up by many as a good and workable model. Larissa Behrendt suggests that one of the reasons that ATSIC 'worked as a representative body' was because the 35 regions 'gave every-body a voice at the national level'. Without this range of voices, Larissa says, there is a regional imbalance with 'very, very influential voices from the north, particularly Cape York, and no influence from the southeast'. Vince Coulthard appreciated the way the ATSIC elections brought together a wide range of representatives with 'all these different experi-ences and knowledge of different areas' chosen by popular vote 'to be our leaders at the highest level'. Others, like Colleen Hayward, felt that ATSIC worked as a structure precisely because it was 'underpinned by a regional base'. For Colleen, this meant that: 'Even people who were players in the national arena were still active at a regional level, and that was a good thing, because it meant that they weren't too distanced from their own community and sense of place.' Former ATSIC Commis-sioner Alison Anderson also believes ATSIC was 'a really, really good structure, that really did deliver to remote Aboriginal communities'. Alison argues that ATSIC:

> really gave capacity to remote Aboriginal people to understand how govern-ments operate and that capacity has now been taken away . . . Aboriginal people will tell you today that ATSIC was the best structure ever delivered by any government to remote Aboriginal people because it really, really gave them that opportunity from a community level to go into a regional level and if they wanted to go further, to get to that national level.

But ATSIC is not the only model on the table that could allow local and regional representation in a national body. Mick Dodson is a strong advocate of the assembly model of representation, similar to the Canadian Assembly of First Nations.[6] For Mick, this model allows rep-resentation to begin at the local level and build up to a national structure, while maintaining decision-making and control at the local level. Mick explains how this approach would work:

> You start assemblies locally—it might be all the adults in the local community who then send delegates up to a district committee, the district sends to the regional, regional sends to state and then the state sends it to a national. I think that way you at least get people to believe that someone from their local community could eventually become the head of the national body. And they will feel as if they had a say, which

would help deliver that absolutely necessary characteristic of legitimacy. And they can pick their own method of selection, even the small communities.

Marvyn McKenzie mirrors Mick's words, suggesting that representation has 'got to start from the community first. Local voices become regional voices and become state voices and become national voices, build it up like that.' Dr Marika also saw national representation starting at the local level where 'each of those clans have their own representation', with representatives selected through 'choosing or voting'. It was important for Dr Marika that any new national body avoids being 'one super power', an over-arching structure that she feels would be 'taking away autonomy, taking away rights from the people'. Dr Marika suggested a combination of local community representation and seats in parliament as a way of recognising that 'Yolngu standing up for our own rights should be seen equally like the government'. Paul Briggs is another who agrees that nation groups like the Yorta Yorta need to 'design our own level of governance that works for us' while simultaneously working with others across the country to 'design a model that best meets our needs in a very contemporary modern Australian sort of society'. Important for Paul is that Aboriginal people have a sense of 'ownership' over any new model, and that the development of any new body is in Aboriginal, not government, hands.

Like Mick Dodson, Jackie Huggins also favours the Assembly of First Nations model, which she sees as 'really, really powerful'. As one of the panel members on the final ATSIC review team, Jackie considers that ATSIC 'didn't work for all kinds of reasons'; however, rather than continuing to look back at past failures, Jackie acknowledges that to develop a new national body 'we're going to have to start from scratch and build up our way through':

> Well, the first thing is try to get us all together to speak about it. We've been talking about it ever since ATSIC folded. And so we've got to get together . . . and we've just got to go out to communities and listen to what we're told. People will have their own set of values about what's working in their regions and that's fine. But the difficulty is the process of how you get what people are doing in regions up to this national level where voices can talk about any Indigenous issue . . . How's it going to work?

Towards sustainable representation

New challenges—such as the Northern Territory 'intervention'—can produce new expressions of unity. The announcement of the intervention took the vast majority of Aboriginal people by complete surprise, and in the absence of an established national representative body it was several weeks before anything resembling a coordinated response was produced. During those weeks, there were many who regretted that the creation of a new national body to fill the void left by ATSIC had not been more of a priority, or that the various meetings to discuss this issue that had been held since 2004 had not been more productive. It is almost universally understood that the protocols of local politics add a layer of complexity to Aboriginal culture that makes national representation difficult. But as the intervention made clear, without a strong, united national Aboriginal voice life for many is more difficult still.

Larissa Behrendt has argued that addressing these issues is an 'important dialogue' that needs to take place within Aboriginal communities (Behrendt 2003: 86). As Eddie Cubillo suggests, people participating in this dialogue have 'got to do a stocktake on the realities of everything' so that when they come to the conversation, 'you don't just come for north or south, you come for everybody'. For Warren Mundine, the 'debate that needs to happen' is about whether 'people want an Aboriginal nation' or whether Aboriginal people remain 'a nation of nations'. John Maynard agrees that the debate needs to happen, but cautions that 'it's going to take an awful lot of very brave and courageous people to step into that and try and confront that because it's so divisive and so difficult to deal with'.

Unless these questions are resolved in a sustainable way, however, some—like Colleen Hayward—worry that people will 'take the fight to the local level, and we end up fighting amongst ourselves': 'That sets us up against each other, and if we rise to that bait against each other, we're actually doing their work for them. It's hard to resist, but we've got to resist. What we've got to do is not cut each other's throats in the process.' The bottom line in these debates must be, as Michael Mansell has argued, the need to create new political representation 'that unashamedly promotes Aboriginal needs and aspirations'. Mansell argues that: 'Even in weakened and diminished form, a national black voice could defend Indigenous institutions against the cold dogma of the assimilationists, reinforce the values of Indigenous cultures, maintain hopes, and present a counter to the well-paid converts to assimilation.' (Mansell 2007: 82–3) In the absence of these debates and an ongoing examination by Aboriginal constituencies of the impact of representative structures on their various interests, these constituencies will risk having their interests constituted, and represented, by outsiders (Bern and Dodds 2002: 179).

Alongside the imperative of developing a strong national voice, strengthening regionalism as a bridge between local and national representation seems to offer strong possibilities for the future. While Will Sanders points out that regionalism will not be 'a panacea for organisational and geographic scale problems in Indigenous community governance', he agrees that it may be 'a useful tool for managing resources and participation more effectively' (Sanders 2004: 61). Indeed, regionalism may even help to negotiate some of the complexities of representation that are evident at the community level, an issue I take up in the next chapter.

8
COMMUNITY AND KIN

What is an Aboriginal community? Aboriginal groups outside of urban areas are often referred to as 'communities' as though they were a homogenous group built on inherent allegiances and natural solidarity. Urban groups too are often referred to in this way—for example, the 'Redfern Aboriginal community' or the 'Fitzroy Aboriginal community'. The reality, however, is that the majority of Aboriginal communities are a fiction, or at least a creation, comprising a number of kinship groups that, prior to colonisation, would have occupied different territories and that in many cases still retain different languages and systems of law. The dispersal and dispossession that resulted from colonisation often threw these groups together, on missions, in settlements on the fringes of rural towns, and increasingly in the urban Aboriginal diaspora.

The implications of the historical creation of Aboriginal communities remain poorly understood among non-Aboriginal people despite its continuing significance in Aboriginal political culture. Anthropologists have long observed the degree to which 'settled' or 'community' life has placed strain on Aboriginal people (Myers 1991: 259). Even today, tension between different clans or kinship groups is endemic in many Aboriginal communities. Community organisations are often seen as representing the whole community when in reality they may only represent key families, and divisions between traditional owners and others who have had a long historical association with a particular area often

144

complicate leadership and decision-making structures. It is evident that there are significant challenges in attempting to represent the diversity of Aboriginal society in the simplified language of 'community', yet at the same time government is resistant to proposals from Aboriginal people themselves that are aimed at alleviating community tensions.

In the mainstream media, Aboriginal communities are commonly demonised as being riddled with dysfunction, welfare dependency, violence, alcoholism, petrol sniffing and child abuse. While these behaviours are certainly significant problems in some Aboriginal communities, it should go without saying that these behaviours are not uniformly experienced in Aboriginal communities across Australia, just as they are not uniformly experienced in non-Aboriginal communities. Everywhere I travelled in researching this book, I heard Aboriginal people express anger and bitterness at the overwhelmingly negative portrayal of their communities in the mainstream media. The media, it seems, do not like good news stories about Aboriginal people, preferring instead to misrepresent and overstate Aboriginal problems in ways that are rarely, if ever, corrected by politicians. As Sam Jeffries argues:

> There's this uncanny ability by the media and by politicians to create a perception that dysfunction is rife in a community when it's an incident that involved ten or twelve people maybe, you know? And there's a whole community there that gets the same stereotyped image that that story creates. And that is a great failure just in terms of good government.

But at the same time as Aboriginal communities are demonised by some, they are romanticised by others. Those who would defend community life represent communities as caring and sharing places in which Aboriginal people stoically endure their inevitable poverty, at all times privileging the good of the community over their individualistic, materialistic interests, in an environment in which everyone shares the same cultural opinions, experiences and expectations. Some have described this view as the romanticism that can only be enjoyed by those who do not actually live in a community (Peters-Little 2000: 13). In reality, romanticisation is often used to mask systemic community problems. The romantic view of 'community' as an inherent good creates an imagined deficit in Aboriginal people themselves, who are somehow perceived as having failed to live up to the romantic ideal.

But neither the demonised nor the romanticised representation of Aboriginal communities tells the whole story. Despite the appalling social conditions in many communities, they are nonetheless *home* to many Aboriginal people who would not live anywhere else. As much as reserves and missions have been damaging to traditional kinship structures, they also, over time, have become places of genuine community solidarity. And as much as Aboriginal lives were damaged by their dispossession and displacement onto artificially created communities, so too, according to Irene Watson, community has become a call to 'the gathering of broken and shattered pieces' (Watson 2007: 15). Many Aboriginal people claim communal identities that are real and meaningful, regardless of underlying conflict and heterogeneity. For Frances Peters-Little, it is important to remember that:

> While Aboriginal people did not passively accommodate new and imposed, introduced and artificial colonial boundaries, it is clear that missions, reserves and pastoral stations have become Aboriginal communities which are now an integral part of Aboriginal people's heritage and are fundamental to Aboriginality. (2000: 3)

But Peters-Little also describes the ways in which Aboriginal people have used the language of 'community' and the funding of Aboriginal community organisations to play what she calls 'the community game'. She suggests that Aboriginal people have become so good at playing the game—that is, they have become so good at *representing* themselves as a community—that many have come to believe it (2000: 10). While governments have certainly played a key role in creating concepts of Aboriginal community, Aboriginal people themselves have actively played 'the community game' to their own advantage.

Addressing these complexities in Aboriginal political culture means recognising that while many Aboriginal communities are indeed troubled and unhappy places, that is not their totality. Nor is it possible to understand the contemporary dysfunction in many communities without understanding their creation. As Gary Foley has argued: 'I've got no problem with Pearson wanting to draw attention to the dysfunctional nature of so many communities but you can't separate those communities from the history that's created that.' (ABC 2003a) Some of these issues were touched on in Chapter 2 in considering the issue of welfare dependency. Here I look more closely at the creation of Aboriginal communities and the conflict this creation has engendered in many places.

Creating communities

The term 'community' has become central to both Aboriginal and non-Aboriginal political rhetoric. As a concept, community is both vague and idealised, drawing on a desire for solidarity and social anchorage (Morgan 2006b: 19). Frances Peters-Little has pointed to the ways in which the idea of the 'Aboriginal community' is used to suggest a unity of purpose and action among groups considered to share a 'common culture' (Peters-Little 2000: 2). Increasingly, Australian governments have applied the language of 'community' to represent an ensemble of local living arrangements, including town camps, ex-missions and ex-settlements, despite the fact that, as Tom Calma has suggested, this language is 'misleading' (ATSISJC 2006a: 89).

The language is certainly important. Mudrooroo has suggested that sometimes 'community' is used when really what is being described is an Aboriginal 'nation' (Mudrooroo 1995: 78). In our interview, Ted Wilkes observed how the significant difference between the language of 'community' and 'town' marked a racialised difference in infrastructure and service provision. Travelling around the country in 1988 while developing the National Aboriginal Health Strategy, Ted was struck by the 'masses of human beings living on some of these communities' and thought:

> These should be little towns! These places should have a post office, they should have a community centre, they should be like little towns! But because they were all black people and there were very few white people amongst them they would call them communities . . . Community means you don't get the same sort of infrastructure as you would if it was a town. You don't get the bitumen right to the end of the town, you don't get proper electricity and you don't get proper water facilities.

The disadvantage evident in contemporary Aboriginal communities has a long history. Lorna Lippman has argued that the early government settlements and church missions onto which Aboriginal people were herded were 'the antithesis of traditional living'.

Aboriginal people were often cajoled and at times brutally relocated to these areas, where several large, frequently unrelated groups lived under the 'petty autocracy' of white staff in substandard conditions not dissimilar to refugee camps (Lippman 1981: 93). Warren Mundine sums up the history of trouble in communities as arising from the colonising process, which saw:

> A whole heap of people trucked in from all over the country and forced to live on reserves or missions. You had people who in normal day-to-day life, traditionally, probably wouldn't come in contact with each other or who would have very limited contact with each other. And so then you had these conflicts happening. And of course when you have a whole heap of people living together then you start having the breakdown of law and order . . . And then you have the mental breakdown as well and that's where the alcohol and drugs and everything come in and you get a very destructive society.

In the 1970s, Kevin Gilbert wrote of the social problems these conditions had caused on what were then still known as reserves:

> Reserves are split into factions and the splits are deep and bitter. Families may have lived near each other for generations, but one lot is, say, Catholic and the other lot is Protestant. Groups may have different racial origins. Or one group may have been in the area three generations less than the other group and is never allowed to forget it . . . On reserves, whatever one group decides to do will almost certainly be automatically opposed by another group. (Gilbert 2002: 155–6)

'Community' as a term to describe areas with a predominantly Aboriginal population only came into common usage in the early 1970s. The introduction of the Whitlam government's policy of self-determination saw a move away from the more assimilationist language of 'missions' and 'reserves' and the increasing use of 'community' as a term that was assumed to be universally culturally appropriate (Peters-Little 2000: 10). Tom Calma expressed his concern with the problems in communities created by past government policy, particularly the big ex-mission or ex-government settlement communities that were created when 'people from all over were plonked in an area because of government policy'. These communities are often maintained, according to Tom, because—

148

despite the fact that people are 'outside of their own country'—over time, and 'for reasons of intermarriage and other relationships', 'histori-cal people' as they are often known have 'maintained an interest in that land'. Problems with conflict and violence in these communities are difficult to resolve because the different clans and family groups do not have a uniformly accepted system of customary law or dispute resolu-tion (Brennan 1995: 145). Further, as people began to be enticed off reserves and into towns and cities, important community members were separated from their families, with negative effects for both a sense of community and for individual well-being (Mudrooroo 1995: 133).

Contemporary Aboriginal communities are defined by Janet Hunt and Diane Smith from the Indigenous Community Governance Project[1] as 'a network of people and organisations linked together by a web of personal relationships, cultural and political connections and identities, networks of support, traditions and institutions, shared socio-economic conditions, or common understandings and interests' (Hunt and Smith 2007: 4). Such communities have formed in a variety of historical circum-stances, leading inevitably to a variety of needs, interests, representative arrangements and political views. These complexities have been dis-cussed in the public realm at least since the publication of the final report of the Woodward commission into land rights in the Northern Territory in 1974. While Woodward's first report had recommended the creation of community councils the final report did not, citing the complexities of drawing community boundaries, difficulties in developing councils in small, new communities, the under-valuation of the clan structure, and the possible interference with traditional authority structures if the role of community councils were to extend to landholding (Woodward 1973: 45–6; 1974: 12–23, and discussed in Peterson 1999: 28). Geoff Scott points out that, despite the fact that 'the concept of community' has been the focus of government policy since the 1970s, the reality is that 'keeping people lumped together who never liked each other in the first place—never have and never will—doesn't generate a community in anyone's language'. Noel Pearson goes further, arguing that the focus on communities over the last several decades has contributed to the abrasion between community and family in contemporary Aboriginal society (Cape York Institute 2004).

Marvyn McKenzie describes the sort of jealousies that exist around his community of Davenport near Port Augusta in South Australia. As a desert frontier town, Port Augusta experiences a regular influx of visitors from the 'Pit Lands', the Anangu Pitjantjatjara Yankunytjatjara lands to the north. Marvyn says trouble usually starts among individuals from different language groups, with some people saying: '"It's my country, you go back to your country", and that sort of thing.' These disagreements are exacerbated by economic circumstances because, as Marvyn explains: 'There are limited jobs and all that stuff in the community, so they're sort of competing against each other for Indigenous jobs. So that sort of creates a bit of a division if you see maybe one language group getting all the jobs or one particular family getting all the jobs and that causes a bit of an argument.'

Aside from competition and jealousy, other complexities have also arisen with the creation of communities. Identity, leadership and authority, for example, have become far less straightforward due to new complexities in kinship structure arising from intermarriage among language groups, meaning that many Aboriginal people now include a number of language groups in their cultural heritage. The diversity of language groups in a particular community can also have implications for education. In areas where more than one language is spoken, the decision to teach, or include in teaching, one language rather than another has implications for the status of various language groups in a community (Mudrooroo 1995: 62). The *Little Children are Sacred* report stresses that Aboriginal communities should not be seen as a 'whole', but rather as an often-divided collection of language groups, clans and families. Within this context, the Inquiry's authors were warned that members of one clan may be prevented from speaking out in the presence of members of another clan. Wild and Anderson emphasise the importance of understanding these dynamics in communities to ensure the appropriate delivery of services and resources. They report, for example, that failure to properly act through clan and family structures has led to the failure of Shared Responsibility Agreements in some communities (Wild and Anderson 2007: 15).

Conflict and violence are distressing realities in many Aboriginal communities, as they are in many non-Aboriginal communities. One of the distinct features of Aboriginal communities, however—a feature that inhibits community attempts to manage conflict—is the disruption to traditional methods of conflict resolution. These problems have been exacerbated further by the introduction of alcohol into communities (Behrendt 1995: 26). Historically, conflict (outside of significant breaches of customary law) among kin groups living communally on shared country would see one or more kin group move away from other groups until the conflict had blown over. As time and space worked to lessen the memory of the conflict, disagreement would give way to a renewed recognition of communal ties and shared identity (Myers 1991: 157, 165). As communities became more sedentary and fixed, however, and as Aboriginal people themselves became more dependent on rations, this solution became less feasible. Indeed, large sedentary populations only became possible in desert areas due to the provision of resources in a limited number of areas, which for decades also constrained the growth of the decentralised 'homeland' communities discussed below (Myers 1991: 261). Today, many of these same communities have become mired in what Diane Austin-Broos calls 'the violence of the everyday', which she defines as 'the abusive conditions that come within and between families in milieux shaped by fraying social fabric and the collapse of authority' (Austin-Broos 2008).

Marcia Langton has suggested that fighting is a form of 'cultural knowledge' that comprises part of a distinctly Aboriginal mode of processing community disputes (Langton 1988: 221). However, there is no doubt that others are disturbed and upset by this dynamic. Anthony Phillip Petrick, for example, has written of his decision to become involved in Aboriginal politics through the Central Land Council in these terms:

> You get a lot of fights on the communities over a lot of different issues and the only thing I was interested in was trying to work something out. I have seen community arguments sometimes and I try to sort things out with family groups and try to get them to try and understand and get something for them. (Petrick 1998: 105)

One community that has received a disproportionate level of media attention is Wadeye, also known as Port Keats, 400 kilometres south-west of Darwin. Among other things, Wadeye is famous for its gangs, the Judas Priests and the Evil Warriors, allegedly based loosely on old clan divisions but with inexplicable contemporary associations to white heavy metal bands. The gangs are responsible for much of the violence and unrest in the community. Wadeye was described in one media report as 'so dysfunctional it copped the Mal Brough treatment a year before other Aboriginal towns in the Northern Territory' (Whittaker 2007). The history of Wadeye has been described by journalist Graham Ring in the following terms:

> Wadeye is not a failed nation state. It's a remote Indigenous community whose people suffered grievous mistreatment at the hands of the Europeans, and the dispossession from their traditional lands. Subsequently they were herded together by a doubtless well-intentioned Catholic church to be fed, clothed and protected at the Port Keats mission. (Ring 2006: 7)

Today, over 2300 people live in Wadeye, including the Kardu Diminin people, who are the traditional owners of the area where the Wadeye township now sits. The Kardu Diminin share the town with members of nineteen other clan groups now resident in the Thamarrurr region, some of whom first moved into the township with the establishment of the mission there in the 1930s. The traditional owners now find themselves a minority in the township, a fact that contributes to continuing tension in the region (ATSISJC 2006b: 53). In light of this all-too-common history, and the contemporary population mix it has produced in Wadeye, conflict should really not be surprising. As Tom Calma explained in our interview, 'from an Aboriginal point of view' the traditional owners of the Wadeye township should have primary responsibility for what happens in the community. Instead, the community council is made up of twenty-one different clan groups because government is trying to 'orchestrate' a situation where all clans can 'have a say over that township'. Tom is very clear that this 'unacceptable' situation is a direct contributor to 'the tribal warfare that exists within the groups in Wadeye. The rioting is based on a construct that was created by government policy rather than policy by Indigenous people.'

Rather than acknowledging the complex traditional relationships that exist in communities like Wadeye, however, the mainstream political response has been an emphasis on the external imposition of 'law and order'. While it is certainly true that some members of some communities have demanded greater policing, others are concerned that bringing in an external force to resolve disputes will only entrench community problems. Kim Hill, for example, argues:

152

A lot of it is just a lack of understanding in regards to people's roles within communities . . . I don't think you need police officers in most instances. You know, people can deal with it themselves . . . A third party will take the autonomy out of the community and place it somewhere else, and the decisions will be made outside the community. So it's best that the communities make the decisions for themselves rather than others making those decisions.

One issue that hinders that decision-making capacity is the place of traditional kinship and ownership in contemporary communities.

Kinship, ownership and governance

Kinship ties are the basis of Aboriginal sociality and political culture, although their significance varies across regions and generations (Rowse 2002: 14). Kinship is a 'core structuring principle' in Aboriginal social life, which sees strong distinctions between those considered family and those who are not. These distinctions are significant in determining moral and political priorities (Martin 2005: 111). In Fred Myers' study of the Pintupi, he observed a social world that was divided into categories of 'kin' and 'non-kin', where kin terminology was used to stress closeness and suppress difference. Considerable effort was expended to sustain the appearance of relatedness, of being 'from one camp', to produce the political solidarity as 'one mob' that underpinned political diplomacy and the recognition of mutual involvements (Myers 1991: 164, 181–2). The nurturing of kin relationships and the fulfilment of kin obligations today remain an 'inescapable' component of Aboriginal politics that is often hidden by the language of community in the Aboriginal political vocabulary (Stokes 2002: 207; Morgan 2006b: 20–1).

Family identities are also inextricably bound to relationships to country. Social, political and spiritual life are embedded in kin relations, which in turn are linked to particular areas of land (Ivanitz 2002: 128). Land is a central component of Aboriginal identity because it forms the basis of relatedness: to kin, to the wider society, to history, to religious knowledge and to the economic resources to which an individual or family is entitled (Goodall 1996: 8). Jackie Huggins observes the way that land-based kinship ties 'come across those invisible [state] borders, left, right and centre'. However, Jackie also stresses the 'very definite kin structures' that persist for those who have been dispossessed of their land, even for 'those of us who probably only have a smattering of our own Aboriginal words', noting what she calls the 'renaissance of culture and family history' as displaced people reconnect to their country, kin and traditions.

Aboriginal people still make a clear distinction between those with formal, traditional affiliations to country and those who are associated with country through residence on missions or settlements, no matter how long such associations have endured. These two forms of association do not create equivalent rights and interests in land, and attempts to blur the two have been met with considerable opposition (Sutton 1999: 41; Martin 1999: 157). Like many other Aboriginal people, Henry Atkinson supports this continuing distinction, emphasising that the proper recognition of traditional ownership means 'putting more responsibilities back to the elders to look after the cultural heritage and the land'. The challenge to this idea is that the reality of Australia's colonial history means many groups do not have traditional owner status. For people who are now unable to return to their traditional lands, the old mission sites and ex-government settlements now called communities have taken on enormous significance as successive generations of families have lived and died there (Behrendt 1995: 26). Urban communities, such as those in Fitzroy or Redfern, or even large rural towns like Dubbo, would find it hard to govern in the traditional ways as there are so many residents of these areas who, despite generations of connection to those communities, are not traditional owners. When presented with these concerns in our interview, Henry replies that even in those areas that bore the first brunt of colonisation, traditional owners remain and that these people must be 'recognised and respected'. According to Henry, everyone else residing in an area must connect with their own traditional country, where they will be represented by their own elders.

Henry is far from alone in his view. Quenten Agius, spokesperson for the Adjahdura Land Traditional Owners Group in South Australia, outlined the frustrations of many traditional owners in a 2006 letter to the editor of the *Koori Mail*, writing:

Aboriginal people living on this country (Adjahdura Land, Yorke Peninsula, South Australia) are made up of:
• Traditional owners—with cultural knowledge.
• Traditional owners—with little cultural knowledge.
• Non traditional owners—with little or no cultural knowledge.

The truth is, non-traditional owners whose families were herded like cattle to Point Pearce in the late 1800s and early 1900s, when other Aboriginal missions from around the State closed, have a connection to Point Pearce lands, there's no doubting that. But it's the traditional owners—the direct descendants of this country—who have the knowledge and connection to the entire country of Adjahdura Land. It's the traditional owners who know the Dreaming stories, traditions and cultural landscapes and have the right to call Adjahdura Land their country. White fellas don't understand the difference between non-traditional and traditional owners. The direct descendants of the traditional owners are the true traditional owners of this country. (Agius 2006: 23)

John Maynard commented in our interview that traditional ties to country mean obligations 'to look after your own family' that have 'continued on for generation and generation'. John observes that these issues are always 'lying beneath what goes on' in communities today. While wholly supportive of the traditional law underpinning traditional ownership, Alison Anderson also recognises the 'tension of infighting' with 'people that come from different areas and are just residents always in battle with the traditional owners'. Alison sees this dynamic as 'a really, really big problem'. Kim Hill observes the same dynamic in the Tiwi Islands, and the same tensions between three groups of people: 'You've got the traditional owners, you've got people who have been placed in the community because of past policies, and the third person is the people who have married into those two other groups.' In Kim's eyes, however, the emphasis on traditional owners can create an 'imbalance', particularly when negotiating issues as complex as the Nguiu lease discussed in Chapter 5. However, Kim is also unperturbed by the tension that is produced in such negotiations, suggesting: 'That's a natural occurrence. I don't think people should be all too frightened about it. They just need to respect it.'

It is important to acknowledge that these arguments for the privileging of kin relations and the recognition of traditional owners are based on entitlement, not ideas of equity (Martin 1999: 158). 'Historical people', with connections to a particular area of country that may span several generations, are not traditional owners and are not entitled to speak for country. While this is an accurate reflection of pre-invasion landholding practices, in the light of all that colonisation has done to traditional Aboriginal culture, particularly with regard to dispossession and relocation, the call to maintain recognition of traditional owners' entitlements over all others may seem unfair. Those who strongly defend these claims, however, argue that it is only through the restoration of the rights of traditional ownership that stability will be restored in Aboriginal communities. Henry Atkinson argues that, in too many areas, 'Responsibility has been taken away from the elders to be able to keep up some of the culture or respect from some of the younger ones'. According to Henry, traditional owners should be able to say to other residents:

> This is our country and we respect you being on country and we love to have you on country, but first of all we are the traditional owners, and we're going to have that recognition as such . . . If those people really respect one another, they would be able to live side by side. But leave the tradition to the first people who are the traditional owners and are the ones that have the right of saying what happens to their culture.

Henry sees no way around this protocol as a means of restoring order to Aboriginal lives.

Further complicating this situation is the way the language of community perpetuates the development of 'community representation' through structures like community councils. These structures in turn obscure important lines of kin-based solidarity, often described as factions (Rowse 1993: 68, 71). Several of my interviewees pointed to the manner in which community organisations are often understood by non-Aboriginal people to *be* the community itself. Muriel Bamblett describes the way in which this dynamic can work:

> Say, for instance, a local cooperative knows that the government minister is coming to town and he wants to talk about representation, someone will get together all their family and bring them around and say, 'Now we need to be saying this . . .' It's not a fair process . . . Quite often there's factions that are involved in it and those things are realities.

Similarly, John Maynard witnesses the way that non-Aboriginal people engaged in research or consultation will say "'Oh, we're going out working in the community, we're going to the Aboriginal Medical

Service or the Land Council" or wherever.' John makes a point of replying: 'That's not the community. You've got to go outside of those organisations as well because that is just not the community as a whole.' The way that government funding flows to communities, or rather the way funding flows to organisations where the idea of 'a community' is assumed, is also problematic in situations where organisations in fact represent the interests of only a few families. Such funding arrangements inevitably create conflict.

There is no question that the persistence of kinship ties within communities can be problematic for community governance. Frances Peters-Little describes community organisations dominated by prominent families as 'gatekeepers' that can create tension by ensuring that their family members enjoy benefits not shared equitably with other families in the same community. These families can be very adept at using the language of community 'for their own advantage and to the disadvantage of less powerful language groups and families' (Peters-Little 2000: 10). The result is a perception common to many non-Aboriginal bureaucrats, and perpetuated in the media, that Aboriginal organisations are incompetent and corrupt. Many Aboriginal community organisations are seen as failing to live up to government expectations of both their manner of operation and their success in overcoming community disadvantage (Morgan 2006b: 19). In fact, the history of many community organisations reflects the banding together of certain extended family or kin interests in a community (Hunt and Smith 2007: 4). The result is that key families in a community can dominate community organisations and deprive others of equal access to services, jobs, transport and so on.

More often than not, Aboriginal governance in these circumstances is labelled 'nepotistic', a loaded word that obscures issues of kin obligation and responsibility, as Geoff Scott argues: 'Looking after your family is called obligation, not nepotism. It's a very important point to make. People talk about culture and how bad nepotism is in our culture. Actually, if you remember how you were brought up, you *have* to look after your own. If you didn't, you were in trouble.'

The point has been made earlier in the book that poverty increases competition for scarce resources. Poverty also accentuates the need to care for kin. Funding for Aboriginal organisations has rarely been enough to really create change in communities, and in many instances inadequate funding has only increased conflict and deepened division within communities (Flick and Goodall 2004: 163). Competition over the few resources available to many communities tends to create factionalism among families that is more a product of the present than the past. Paul Briggs suggests that nepotism has become 'an ugly word' in relation to Aboriginal organisations because of questions about 'who actually gets access to services'. Paul acknowledges that these are serious issues about 'delivering public assets out into the community' but suggests that governance models 'need to be refined' not 'thrown out'. Paul suggests that dealing with the tension between 'a democratic process' and 'the internal political issues' is a 'challenge', but one that has rarely been taken up, either by governments or by communities themselves.

Geoff Scott suggests that having strong communities is an important step in building human capital in Aboriginal life, but points out that:

> You only build human capital by having strong communities that aren't fighting day to day just to survive and therefore try to pick at the meagre sort of offerings that are there. That divides communities. It's only when people get to a position where they don't have to do that every day that they can actually focus on making their whole community better. At the moment you have to look after yourself and your family.

Maintaining traditional, kin based associations with land is a crucial element in the composition and stability of the sort of wider, regional groupings discussed in the previous chapter (Sutton 1999: 50). The closeness of family can successfully be invoked in developing regional networks and solidarity as much as it can be used to exclude or to dominate (Smith 2007: 41–2). While negotiating these relationships is fraught with difficulty, undermining kin groups and focusing only on behaviour that through Western eyes is seen as corrupt or nepotistic is unhelpful to community development in the longer term.

Town camps, homelands and community development

Three modes of contemporary settlement illustrate the ways in which Aboriginal people are coping with the disruption of their traditional ways of living together. The first is the development of town camps, such as those around Alice Springs, in which displaced people from a diversity of clans have congregated over many decades. The second is what is known as 'the homelands movement', which has seen kin groups from the sort of constructed 'communities' discussed above return to their traditional land. The third is the development of dispersed yet distinct urban communities.

The town camps on the fringes of Alice Springs developed during the long period (1928–47) that Aboriginal people were prohibited from being in the town after dark. White residents of Alice Springs were vehemently opposed to the camps, and there were several attempts to round up camp residents and remove them from the town area altogether. At different times, groups from the town camps were moved out to Artlunga and Hermannsburg. These efforts were unsuccessful, however, and the population in the camps continued to grow. The collapse of Aboriginal employment in the pastoral industry following their inclusion in award conditions created an influx of former pastoral workers, and contributed to further growth in the camps. By the 1970s, the diverse language groups resident in the camps—including Warlipiri, Luritja, Pitjantjatjara, Pintupi, Arrernte, Kaytetye and Anmatjere—were struggling to secure tenure over town camp land in order to obtain basic services. Leaders in the camps formed Tangentyere Council to represent camp residents in these struggles because, in the words of the Council's first president Mr E. Rubuntja, 'They tried to push us away. But this was our country . . . We wanted our land so we could sit down and not worry about whitefellas pushing us off.' (quoted in Tilmouth 2007: 236) Over time, sixteen of the eighteen town camps were granted leases in perpetuity. Each camp now has a housing association, representatives of which make up the executive of Tangentyere Council (Tilmouth 2007: 235–7; Tangentyere Council 2004: 4–14).

Despite the appalling and overcrowded conditions in the town camps residents have been, and remain, resistant to suggestions they move into public housing in Alice Springs itself, preferring to remain in independent family groups in the camps. They also resisted Commonwealth government efforts to turn the camps into 'normal suburbs', in May 2007 rejecting $60 million in funding from the Howard government that would have required them to relinquish their leases. In our interview, William Tilmouth, CEO at Tangentyere, talks about what was an extremely difficult decision: 'You know I went to every town camp when Mal Brough brought out the $60 million idea, and *every* town camp said no. They all said no to me, "We're not going to take that money" . . . They said, "No, we'll fight these mob."'

The reason for the town camp resistance to government takeover is about retaining control over their communities. Each town camp is a distinct community, and while many residents are Arrernte and therefore traditional owners of the land on which Alice Springs is built, many others from more far-flung language groups now also feel a strong sense of ownership of their town camp communities as 'their own place' (Tilmouth 2007: 238).[2] A new $50 million deal brokered by Minister Jenny Macklin in June 2008 was unanimously supported by Tangen-tyere Council. While the Rudd government deal still sees a government takeover of the town camp leases, the terms allow for continued involve-ment by the council and residents (Maher 2008).

A different settlement strategy, which can in part be understood as Aboriginal people 'pushing back' against government desires to merge kin groups into large communities, is the homelands movement. As Kimberley leader Peter Yu has argued:

> The administrative desire to centralise people in large communities is com-pletely out of step with the reality of Aboriginal aspirations. Aboriginal people do not want to live in large towns—we are all only too aware of the problems caused by living in someone else's country with too many other people. (Yu 1997: 171)

The homelands movement has seen many Aboriginal people in remote parts of Australia move out of troubled communities and back to their traditional lands, in an effort to become more autonomous and self-sufficient (ATSISJC 2007b: 55; CLC 1994: vii; Lippmann 1981: 94). The move to homelands was also explicitly an attempt to avoid conflict and violence in some of the larger Aboriginal communities (Behrendt 1995: 26).

Homeland communities are not without their problems, most notably a lack of employment and basic services. This lack of services led former Minister Amanda Vanstone to describe small homeland communities as 'cultural museums' and the most recent past Minister Mal Brough to declare that those choosing to live on homelands should not expect government services to follow them out to remote areas (Vanstone 2005a; Brough 2006). Government criticism of homelands has been strongly influenced by work from the right-wing think tank the Centre for Independent Studies, most notably the work of Helen Hughes who has dismissed homelands as 'socialist', 'exceptionalist' and 'separatist', ultimately describing them as 'lands of shame' (Hughes 2007, also discussed in Chapter 5). While rejecting the ideologically based critiques of authors such as Hughes, some Aboriginal people also question the long-term viability of homeland communities, with Geoff Scott arguing in our interview that they were 'never created to be sustainable communities'. Geoff claims that governments 'have to make a decision: you have to make them sustainable and support industries and support services there which are the same as elsewhere, or you change them'.

On the other hand, evidence from recent research by the Menzies School of Health Research, which demonstrates improved health and well-being in outstation communities around Utopia in the Northern Territory, suggests that greater support for these communities should be considered (see Rowley et al. 2008). Alison Anderson is a strong supporter of the homeland movement, arguing:

> If you go and have a look at those communities, they actually operate better because they're people that have formed their own community according to their Dreaming and their law on country and they've just got their immediate families living there . . . Elderly people have been taken out to these outstations by their nephews and grandsons and the harmony of those people living on those little outstations is just absolutely wonderful compared to a major community say 25 kilometres away.

Tom Calma also believes that supporting people to 'go back to their own country' will take pressure off communities like Wadeye, even if homeland residents are still reliant on larger communities for some services. Tom is frustrated that there has been 'conflict in government policy that's not going to support people to do that'. Despite this, however, there is much anxiety that many such communities will be deemed 'unviable' and that residents will be forced to move back to larger communities and towns. As one member of a small community told me, however, this will never happen: 'People will get a scrap of tin and build a humpy in the bush over there rather than leave their country again.'

At the other end of the 'community' spectrum are urban communities, which are also significant in contemporary Aboriginal life. Robbie Thorpe is one who identifies his urban home, Melbourne's Fitzroy, as an area that has 'been an Aboriginal community from the seventies'. Muriel Bamblett also sees a community in Melbourne where:

> Even though families are not living on missions or reserves or in communities, they know where other families are all around here. They'll go from house to house visiting and they have a network. It's just not as seen as if you're on a mission where you can see people connecting and visiting each other. But Aboriginal people know where Aboriginal houses are all around, they go and visit, there's family support, there's systems of support. They think that in Victoria here because we don't live in missions and don't live a cultural life that we don't actually have a culture, whereas I say that we do have a culture.

These urban communities may be harder to identify, but they are not without their own particular needs—reflecting the diversity of culture and circumstance in which they find themselves (Behrendt 2003: 87). Larissa Behrendt points out that even urban communities are tied together by family and kinship networks that reinforce traditional connections. In Sydney, for example, which Behrendt notes has the second largest Aboriginal population in Australia (behind the Northern Territory), there are 'clusters of Aboriginal communities' spread across areas as diverse as Redfern, La Perouse, Marrickville, Mount Druitt, Penrith and Cabramatta. Despite the distances involved, kinship keeps these community enclaves tied together (Behrendt 2006: 7). The divisions within urban communities based on their region of origin seem to have mattered less to younger people in the cities than they did to earlier generations of urban residents (Morgan 2006a: 63–4).

So what can be done to improve life for Aboriginal people in these diverse contemporary communities? What alternatives are there in considering the complexities of kin-based struggles in often troubled communities? The answer lies in community development that is led by Aboriginal people themselves. The Murdi Paaki region has engaged in such a community development process, which (with some Commonwealth government funding) enabled them to produce community plans for each of the sixteen communities in the region. These plans produced around 1200 action items, which were then put in a matrix to produce ten priorities that were consistent throughout the communities. Sam Jeffries points out that 'the number one priority that came through was community—not health or education—it was community. It was about our relationships with each other.' Sam believes that 'if we can get that right, I think that there's a lot of other things that we can get right also'. Frances Peters-Little would agree, arguing that:

> The use of the term community without Aboriginal consultation, self-analysis and definition has in fact acted as a barrier to their own self-determination, setting communities up for administrative failure, thus denying Aboriginal people the opportunity to work through the development process, with specialised professional support, and in their own time. (Peters-Little 2000: 10)

The way forward, in this view, is for Aboriginal people themselves to 'identify and define their community' while also acknowledging 'the input they have had in the shaping of their community and identity' (Peters-Little 2000: 16). In this way, communities may arrive at a future in which they have far greater capacity to negotiate kinship obligations without conflict and violence.

Finding a balance between kin and community

The dynamics between community and kin are complex indeed. As Tim Rowse has observed, for every advance made by 'community solidarities', such as the development of community councils and sporting teams, there seems to be a strengthening of 'segmentary affiliations', such as outstations and kin-based ceremonial networks (Rowse 1992: 96–7). Clearly, both dynamics are important in Aboriginal political culture and both need to be understood, supported and resourced.

Even so, negotiating a balance between kin-based obligations and community accord will be important for future stability. According to Tom Calma, these issues must be addressed before there can be 'any sort of harmony'. Tom has been critical of the emphasis on policing in troubled communities, pointing out that while that strategy 'might create some law and order for a short time' it is not 'resolving the problem'. What will solve the problem, according to Tom, is supporting community development that allows 'local traditional owners and community groups to come up with ideas'. Nevertheless, as Frances Peters-Little acknowledges, it is not realistic to expect these tensions to disappear without concerted effort and without reform of some of the community governance arrangements that support continuing conflict. As Peters-Little suggests: 'It is particularly unrealistic to expect all loyalties to kin and tribe to disappear when the structure of "community boards" is based on Western notions of representativeness.' (Peters-Little 2000: 10)

One significant obstacle in the way of effective community development lies with the problems of leadership discussed in Chapter 5. Leadership is further compromised in the tensions between community and kin, and the expectations of government that do not fully appreciate these complexities (Bern and Dodds 2002: 175). One of the end results of ignoring kinship structures in communities, according to Paul Briggs, is that 'Aboriginal authority has been dismantled and discarded'. Despite this historical fact, when trouble in communities occurs 'people expect Aboriginal authority then to fix it'. But even with these challenges there are solutions emerging from communities, particularly in new dispute resolution structures developed by younger community members in consultation with elders (Behrendt 1995: 270). In the absence of traditional authority structures, however, relations between the generations are not easy. It is to tensions in the authority structure between elders and the next generation of leaders that I turn in the next chapter.

9
ELDERS AND THE NEXT GENERATION

Little children are sacred. The title of the report that sparked the 2007 Northern Territory intervention alludes to the special place that children and young people hold in Aboriginal society. But despite their special status, Aboriginal children and young people are also expected to know their place in the hierarchy. Aboriginal political culture is still based on a gerontocracy in which elders command the most potent authority and influence. Elders are holders of special and sacred cultural knowledge, and it is their responsibility to hand this knowledge down to the younger generations. The breakdown of traditional authority structures, however, means that this transfer of knowledge can no longer be assumed. In place of this hierarchy of cultural seniority, younger leaders now emerge from the ranks of political activists, from community organisations, and from the developing class of young, university-educated professionals.

With the weakening of traditional authority structures, issues of leadership and succession have become vexed, particularly as younger activists demand their right to be heard and to participate in decision-making processes. Jackie Huggins acknowledges the 'real tension' that this produces, although she also observes that 'people try to sweep that under the carpet'. Some senior leaders express ambivalence about vocal younger leaders and activists, suggesting they need to 'earn their stripes' and wait their turn. Others, like Sam Jeffries, worry that not enough is being done now to support the emergence of the next generation of leaders. Sam tells me that 'for some time' he has been pointing out 'the gap between us that's involved now, and the next lot coming through. Or the next lot *not* coming through.' He worries that the political struggle for Aboriginal rights and justice is 'recycling the same people', which has the inevitable effect of burning people out. Geoff Scott agrees, and applauds young emerging leaders who are 'prepared to put themselves on the line' even though they get 'discouraged and threatened' by the 'old leadership'.

This issue periodically comes to a head at conferences and in meetings. Jackie Huggins describes the discussion in the black caucus held during the National Reconciliation Planning Workshop in May 2005 where, in the middle of discussion, one young man interrupted:

> This young man said, 'When is it my turn to speak? When am I going to be heard?' You could actually feel the whole tension in the room . . . And one of the fellas from a land council got up and he said, 'What do you want? What do you want from us?' He said, 'I never heard such crap in my day.' And actually he was right, there wasn't that whole debate, because we all knew our place. But he said, 'If you want my job, come and take it. I don't care. My job's a very hard job to do.' And one of the kids got up later and she said, 'We don't want your jobs, we don't want that. We just want to be heard.' And he said, 'But aren't you being heard now?' But they didn't feel they were. But then Linda [Burney, who was facilitating] said, 'Look, where is all this stuff coming from? It hasn't come from us. I still talk to young people, mentor young people—every one of us in this room does that. I don't even know why we're having this argument, I'm sick of it, and I don't want to keep persisting with the discussion of what's wrong or when you get a voice. You'll know it when you've got a voice.'

Jackie agrees with Linda's point of view on this issue, saying: 'I know the young people are impatient, they want to do stuff, but they've got to stand in line like the rest of us.'

But there is more to this issue than intergenerational rivalry. Past government policies have drastically undermined traditional authority structures in ways that leave both younger and older people less sure of their roles. At the same time, more young Aboriginal people are accessing higher education and wanting to use their qualifications to assert political influence. Part of the problem has been that so many elders have necessarily been focused on their own political struggle in their communities, which has sometimes led to the neglect of the younger generation. The well-known South Australian activist Yami Lester admits to having been so focused on his own work there was little time left to train the next generation. Lester is still willing, however, saying: 'There is time, though, to train them up, if they are willing to listen. There is much more to be learnt about our past that will help guide us in the future.' (quoted in Liddle 2006). Another common perception is that too many young people do not know or understand the history of political struggle that has gone before them. Part of what Jackie sees as the process of 'waiting in line' involves learning the history of Aboriginal political struggle as a resource to draw upon in the future.

Learning politics

Political awareness is a precondition for leadership, but it is generally something that develops over time. Tracker Tilmouth acknowledges that very few young people jump out of bed 'with revolutionary zeal', suggesting that for most there is 'a growing awareness of political differences and inequality'. For some, the awareness comes through work and wider experience. Tilmouth believes that for him, although it took time for 'the huge gap between the political rights of Aboriginal and non-Aboriginal people to filter through', his early working life in Alice Springs was significant in this process: 'when you pick up drunks and see the desperate conditions people are living in you don't forget it. Seeing that chasm made a huge impression on me, and I've felt driven to fight it ever since.' (Tilmouth 1998: x) Alison Anderson suggests that 'leaders can't be made' but are 'born and bred from the knowledge and the experience of being with your people, understanding the struggles and participating in the struggles'. Alison insists that: 'You can't be a leader if you haven't participated or understand the struggles.' In part, this is about 're-learning the true history of what happened to Indigenous people in this country'.

For a huge number of contemporary leaders and activists, both older and younger, political awareness began in their families. As we saw in the previous chapter, kin relations are central to Aboriginal sociality. So too they are central to the creation of political awareness among younger people. Anthony Philip Petrick, for example, started learning about politics through attending meetings at the Central Land Council with his father. There, 'sitting in, listening and just learning a bit more and more', he developed an understanding of 'the problems everyone had' (Petrick 1998: 105). Dr Marika also remembered learning her politics from her father. She recalled:

> I watched my father; my father was a political figure in my community and he was one of those old people who instigated the land rights struggle. And he worked with all of the people and then in our communities but he was the one who was actually pushing . . . I grew up seeing him . . . Yeah I grew up in the forefront of the land rights struggle. My growth came from that you know, understanding politics and learning and watching my father.

Robbie Thorpe is another with strong political roots, telling me: 'My mum helped establish the community controlled Aboriginal Health Service, and I learnt all those politics and learnt about the condition of Aboriginal people on a national level because I used to hang with Mum, go travelling with her and that. I learnt a lot and met a lot of Aboriginal people in very similar situations.'

Jackie Huggins sees this pattern continuing in the present day in the work she does with young people in leadership programs. Jackie observes that if young people 'have political parents who speak about Aboriginal affairs every day of their life, they grow up knowing that things were very different in the old days'. This appreciation of all that has changed is an important part of their politicisation: 'They're always reminded about when grandpa or grandma was on a mission or a reserve.' Unfortunately, Jackie also sees too many young people who she says 'grow up and don't even know who Charlie Perkins was. They say, "Who's he?" And it's so sad.' Marvyn McKenzie agrees, blaming what he sees as a lack of politicisation among younger people on their lack of direct experience of social change for Aboriginal people. Marvyn says of his own children:

> My kids haven't experienced what I experienced living in tin sheds. I live in a house now and they think that's just a normal everyday thing but it's not, it's only just happened in the last thirty years or so. And they've forgotten that, or we failed to inform them. They've got to realise that it's been hard fought and won, they've still got a long way to go and they've got to take up the struggle for the next step.

Eddie Cubillo is another who is concerned to educate his own children in the politics of Aboriginal struggle, highlighting to them the fact that they are reaping the rewards of previous generations of activism. Eddie says he tells his kids that 'those that lived before us have allowed us to do what we're doing. They allowed me to go and get a degree.' Eddie impresses on his children that it is now their 'right' to get a university education and that it is his expectation that they 'be a really educated mob and be able to combat those issues'.

Leaders and activists who were young in the 1970s, like Sam Watson, were aware of the need to learn from the past and pass on that knowledge. Sam recalls the weekly 'rap sessions' at the Brisbane 'Panther Pad', which had as its goal the need to:

> just bring young blacks into that room and get people talking so that when they came off the missions, absolutely filled with hatred and violence because of what they'd been through, they at least understood the machinery behind the *Protection Act* and the history of that oppression. Then they could understand how to break that oppression down and how to eventually defeat that oppression.

Sam is proud that 'the people who learnt from the Panther experience' went on to use the knowledge they gained 'and apply it to their own work within their own communities'.

But the 1970s also saw growing divisions between older and younger activists in the movement. The radicalism of many of the younger activists, like Sam, was challenging to many of their elders while the 'new guard' of the movement 'chafed at the prevailing cultural protocol which dictated that the elders did all the talking and all the representations to government'. When younger activists, like Rob Riley in Perth, were given the opportunity to speak, their peers were impressed. Ted Wilkes says that when Riley started talking, 'a lot of us said, "That's better, that's what we need, we need to have our younger men, our younger leaders saying the words for us because they know what's going on in the world"' (quoted in Beresford 2006: 81). Kevin Gilbert also expressed the view that 'real leadership' would have to come from 'younger Aborigines who are more sophisticated in their understanding of how to manipulate the mechanisms of the white society' (Gilbert 2002: 135). At this time, Gary Foley was convinced that the earlier generation of political leaders had 'failed in the struggle for justice' while he and his peers were 'young and impatient and we thought we could change the world' (ABC 2003a).

The younger activists of the 1970s were distinctly different from their forebears in some significant ways: they were more educated, tended to be urban-based, and were interested in refocusing the movement away from social welfare concerns and towards issues of identity and self-determination. The younger activists' political style was also different, generally more assertive and aggressive than those who had gone before, more militant in their language and demands and intent on distancing themselves from white organisations and leadership (Attwood and Markus 1999: 21; Bennett 1989: 7–8). These divisions between generations of activists have their roots in the decline of traditional authority structures in Aboriginal society. Some older activists considered the new political style offensive, and were concerned that the new generation was insufficiently anchored in culture (Jones and Hill-Burnett 1982: 223). The need to ground political action in cultural knowledge remains important today.

Learning from elders

Elders have a special and unique role in Aboriginal society and political culture. They are charged with particular responsibilities and obligations to care for land and to hand down the songs and stories that tell the Law of their country to future generations (Behrendt 1995: 15). Jilpia Jones explains that, in Aboriginal society, 'you're not an elder until you're old enough to *know*, until then you speak when you're spoken to'. The intergenerational transmission of knowledge and Dreaming stories is an important part of maintaining social stability and order, and is essential to the social and cultural reproduction of Aboriginality (Rowse 1993: 44). But elders not only possess knowledge, they also possess authority: to pass on secret and sacred ritual knowledge, to initiate younger members of a language group, and quite literally to 'make' the next generation of leaders in a particular area (Myers 1991: 182, 224–5). Maintaining these practices is a crucial part of what self-determination means for Aboriginal people (Rowse 1992: 98).

One impact of colonisation has been the loss of fully initiated elders in many parts of the country. Members of subsequent generations, like Ossie Cruse, feel 'unfortunate' to have been born at a time when most of these elders were gone, with Cruse pointing out that he was among a generation that 'saw the last of our initiated men die' (Cruse, quoted in Chittick and Fox 1997: 117). With the loss of fully initiated elders, people began to look outside their communities for cultural knowledge. Ted Wilkes experienced his own cultural education not through elders in his own community but through time spent with 'culture men' from the north of Western Australia, who he described as 'very dark-skinned men, very, very profound Indigenous elders in their own right—the real story-tellers of our culture'. Travelling through the Kimberley and the Pilbara opened up another world to Ted, a world in which he learnt 'what the artwork on the caves really meant, about the significance of the sounds, the significance of the shape, the significance of the movement of animals, the significance of hearing, the significance of smell in an Aboriginal context'. Ted believes these experiences made him a 'more complete human being' who was 'more capable of understanding and relating to cultural significance in the Aboriginal world'. For Ted and many others, the declining capacity for this sort of intergenerational transmission of cultural knowledge is a tragedy with political implications.

Today, the destruction of traditional authority structures means that there are many diverse definitions of what constitutes an elder or leader (Peters-Little 2000: 5). In parts of the country where the destruction of culture has been felt most harshly, some—like Jackie Huggins—make a distinction between elders and what she calls 'senior people'. Jackie points out that she will never be an elder because 'traditional knowledge was never passed on to me by my mother'. However, Jackie does feel she is approaching the status of 'senior Aboriginal woman', a position she has earned through observation, wisdom and experience. Jackie also highlights the diversity among elders, challenging assertions from younger people about what is, or is not, 'the way of the elders':

> Well, I don't know what the way of the elders is actually. I have seen elders who will be nasty, aggressive and not allow other people to talk. They will say, 'You're not allowed to talk. You just shut up.' And then there are those elders who do include, and I hope to be one of those senior people who will include and mentor and allow for discussion and collaboration with young people.

Although there are many people like Jackie who want to support young people, in some areas these intergenerational relationships now rely on individual goodwill rather than a strong social structure. The authority of elders has been undermined since colonisation and by the many waves of destructive policy that have followed. The destruction of Aboriginal languages, for example, has drastically undermined the capacity of elders to pass on their cultural knowledge (Rigney 2003: 80). The theft of sacred objects in years gone by has heightened the distress of many elders, who worry that they will not have anything to 'show' the younger generation. Speaking of the objects collected by T.G.H. Strehlow, and now held in the Strehlow Research Centre in Alice Springs, Max Stuart has said:

> We need those things. We need them for ceremony and schooling our younger generation. And after, when they learn, they can school their young ones . . . What are we going to do if we don't get those objects? What's going to happen? The old people and the old people after me, they'll be lost like an old mob of sheep just roaming around the country with nothing, nothing to show their kids. (quoted in CLC 1994: 100)

More recently, the growing influence of Western culture has further fractured many intergenerational relationships as young people experience more 'distractions' from cultural life (KALACC 2006: 43). Writing of the Mardu, Robert Tonkinson observes that 'ritual activities' have diminished because 'elders complain that they are "too tired" and that the young men are too preoccupied with sex and drinking; in turn, younger men accuse the elders of being lazy and failing to pass on vital knowledge' (Tonkinson 2007: 48).

The most devastating policies of all have been those involving child removal, the most radical attempt to erase the authority of senior members of a family or community (Rowse 1993: 44). The traumatic effects of these policies have already been touched on in this book and will be explored further in Chapters 10 and 11, but here it is worth briefly noting the effect of child removal on the transmission of cultural knowledge. Larissa Behrendt summarises these impacts clearly:

> Children that were taken away were not taught their own stories by Indigenous Elders. Instead, they were taught the white culture and the white system. They were taught that they were inferior and that their culture was inferior. If children did not have a strong cultural background

they tended to be persuaded by the cultural propaganda preached within the institutions they were confined to, or by the families into which they were adopted. The policy of resocialisation was one of cultural genocide. (Behrendt 2003: 68)

One outcome of these destructive policies is that the maintenance of Aboriginal customary law and authority structures has become 'an optional way of living for the new generations', who revel in the prospect of being able to 'move freely between two worlds'. Many community elders see this as the younger generation 'running away from ceremony' (Brennan 1995: 147). But this is not the whole story either. Many younger people today are saddened by their grandparents' reluctance to pass on their culture due to experiences of cultural shaming. At the same time, many elders express suspicion and mistrust about young people's ability to respect and protect important cultural traditions (Morgan 2006a: 22).

Quite aside from the implications for future political leadership, it must also be acknowledged that the breakdown of traditional authority structures contributes to the challenging life circumstances faced by many Aboriginal young people today. As Judy Atkinson notes, many young people, whose families should be places of learning and nurturing, are instead growing up 'in places of pain and disorder' (Atkinson 2002: 236). Younger people themselves are demanding support from their elders. For example, a group of young people from NIYMA (discussed below) has written:

The sense of hopelessness that exists in the young community is unbearable for some, leading to suicide and substance abuse. Young Indigenous people need role models and most importantly and simply, love, in order to grow with support and self-esteem . . . Parents, aunties/uncles, grandparents— many who consider themselves to be 'leaders'—need to lead the way in this respect, because a young person's first perspective on life is given to them by such guardians, and that responsibility needs to be maintained. (Phillips et al. 2003: 110)

Alison Anderson agrees that the rights of senior or elder status in Aboriginal communities bring with them responsibilities to 'get the future generations right' by making sure that 'communities are safe for our children to grow up in'. Paul Briggs also believes that the 'dismantling of Aboriginal families' and the 'dysfunction within Aboriginal families' is in part due to problems in Aboriginal leadership 'at an elders level'. But Paul makes an important link between this issue and the relative brevity of Aboriginal life expectancy, arguing that because Aboriginal people are 'dying too soon', elders—grandfathers and grandmothers— 'are disappearing from Aboriginal kids' lives long before Aboriginal kids go looking for them'. One result of this breakdown, according to Muriel Bamblett, is that there has been a loss of cultural 'transitioning' or initiation practices, with negative impacts on the lives of many young people. Muriel suggests that young people have lost their 'rights' to initiation ceremonies, with one outcome being that 'they don't transition as well as other young people'. For Muriel, this is 'a critical failing of the system for young people'.

The mainstream education system is also implicated in the breakdown of traditional authority structures. Mainstream education, which has 'interrupted the natural course of traditional education' (KALACC 2006: 43), cannot by itself meet the cultural learning needs of young Aboriginal people. Ted Wilkes sees the need to 'rearrange' the education system so that Aboriginal people have 'the right to educate our kids about what's right or wrong'. Ted argues that: 'Not too long ago we taught our own young fellas . . . taught the young kids what to expect when they become older. Now that's all changed.' He would like to see the restoration of elders' authority to pass on cultural knowledge through the education system and in other forums, and gives an example of the sort of contemporary experience by which traditional knowledge is being passed on to a new generation:

> Today men are taking some of their young fellas out to men's camps. I've been to those and I've taken my young boys too and they're absolutely wonderful. We put the boys all inside of a circle and the older men stand around the outside and we get them to walk around and shake hands with the old fellas. And if the old fellas want to stand there and have a yarn with them they can ask some questions and tell them what's going down.

For Ted, education and this transfer of knowledge are crucial for the health and well-being of future generations: 'If we get that right we start to make inroads.'

Henry Atkinson is also working to reform the education system so that it places more emphasis on the transmission of cultural knowl edge to children. Henry believes that if 'Indigenous educators are able to bring in the cultural side of their particular country, to their own Indigenous children', this 'may help to make things survive and be a bit stronger than what they are'. Delivering culturally appropriate education that involves elders has already been successful in some areas. In our interview, William Tilmouth spoke about the school that Tangentyere Council runs in the Larapinta town camp. Children from Larapinta were not going to school because 'kids would tease them because their brothers and sisters sniffed [petrol] or they sniffed'. William tells me:

> The community of Larapinta sat down and said, 'Well, we're going to have to come up with something ourselves.' And they said, 'Oh, why don't we have grandparents learning with the grandchildren?' And so they set up the intergenerational learning centre. And now some of those kids are bridging directly into mainstream school like ducks to water, you know.

But as much as some children and young people are struggling to access education that meets their cultural needs, the academic success by other Aboriginal people is creating new tensions in the void left by the collapse of traditional authority structures. While there is no doubting the incredible importance of these educational achievements, it must also be noted that in some ways they are also increasing the gap between young and old.

Stand up, sit down

In Aboriginal society, age is relative to seniority. As Larissa Behrendt points out, 'the good thing about being Aboriginal is that you're a young thing until you're about fifty-five'. But where Larissa sees the positive in this, others like Eugenia Flynn are frustrated with the view that 'unless you're an elder, or unless you've been working since the 1970s and 1980s, you're a young person'. Sam Watson points out that traditionally it was the elders, who he calls 'the grey beards', who 'dominated the decision-making process by age alone'. Some, like Sam and William Tilmouth, do not mind the dominance of the gerontocracy where this still exists. William, for example, was prepared to do what he was told well into his own adulthood. Describing himself as 'a very reluctant leader' who really wanted to be an artist, William tells of being 'dragged' into the leadership of Tangentyere Council by former CEO Geoff Shaw:

> The old man says, 'All right you young fella!' . . . I was the ATSIC regional chair then and I said, 'No, I want to learn more about how government works.' But Geoffrey said, 'I'm pulling up stumps. You've got to get back home to Tangentyere.' I told him I liked being the ATSIC chair, I wanted to stay being the ATSIC chair, but he says, 'No, you get back!' So I only did eighteen months as the ATSIC chair and had to step over this way. But I've never looked back.

Kim Hill believes that there is still a strong practice of elders noticing and encouraging future leaders, pointing out that 'sometimes you don't necessarily have to open your mouth' to be noticed. By 'being involved in community activities', you can gain the elders' attention: 'You can go to meetings and show a bit of interest you know and people do watch.' Eddie Cubillo agrees, recalling his own experience where 'people pretty senior to me—if they feel you're ready, they'll anoint you, they will pull you aside and talk to you'. Kim argues that: 'You've also got to get the support from your elders [or] really you will have no authorisation to speak on behalf of anyone.'

Despite their continuing influence in some areas, however, the overall decline in the authority of elders creates complexity in light of the simultaneous demands that emerging leaders and activists must wait in line. There is a definite sense in these arguments that young people should know their 'place', although the young people concerned do not necessarily experience this as a bad thing. Larissa Behrendt, for example, feels she has learned humility from older people in her community who have grounded her in what really matters. She argues:

> I think it's very easy for Aboriginal people who come through with a bit of a profile to get caught up in the press about being a leader and a role model. I've been very lucky that I've been taught that it's not the quick accolades that mean anything; it's what you actually do with your life that makes the difference. That's meant that I never get too carried away with it. And it's not that people are rude and say, 'Oh, you're not a leader.' Nobody says that to me in my own community. But nor do I go out there and say I'm a leader.

For Larissa, this message was summed up in her community's response when she became the first Aboriginal person to be accepted into Harvard Law School. Despite the articles in the paper and the deserved accolades, Larissa says the response from the old people in her community was to say, 'You know, that's really great Bub. But what are you going to do when you get back?'

Not all emerging leaders are so tolerant of being put back in their place, however. Eugenia Flynn spoke to me about what Mark Yettica Paulson has dubbed the 'stand up, sit down' phenomenon in which: 'Young people are told they need to stand up, and then it's like "No, no, no. Sit down and wait your turn." It happens all the time! . . . It's really strange watching it happen in meetings or forums or whatever and I've even seen people do it to their own children.' Gangalidda man Murandoo Yanner has described younger leaders as being 'more like war chiefs' who, although they go into battle, are 'not really in charge'. According to Yanner, the older leaders 'just throw us in the roughest part' (quoted in Rintoul 2002: 24). Although appearing to tolerate being held back by her elders, Larissa Behrendt also resents the sorts of arbitrary barriers that are put in the way of emerging leaders, saying that she has heard 'ridiculous things', including the suggestion that 'if you haven't worked at a land council you can't be a leader'. Larissa speculates that: 'It's almost like people want to set up the requirements to be a leader that fit exactly their own profile.'

The message to young and emerging leaders and activists is confusing indeed. On the one hand, there is an acknowledgment that entering the sphere of Aboriginal politics is not necessarily appealing to many young people. Muriel Bamblett recognises that many young people coming up through the ranks 'are really scared' and suggests that someone like Tania Major, the young Kokoberra woman who is a protégé of Noel Pearson and was 2007 Young Australian of the Year, must experience enormous pressure. Muriel asks: 'What kind of pressures will be on her to fulfil that role as a leader into the future?' Aden Ridgeway, a great supporter of young people's political participation, has also warned emerging leaders: 'You don't do it lightly. It is not a nine-to-five thing. It is seven days a week, every day of the year. It's tough, it's hard, it's extremely draining and sometimes it does not give the rewards that you would like.' (quoted in Liddle 2006)

Colleen Hayward worries that the stand up, sit down dynamic that frustrates emerging leaders is contributing to their 'growing absence' in Aboriginal communities. Colleen sees two groups of young people opting out of future leadership. She observes one group put off by the gatekeeping of older leaders who say, 'Well, I'm not going to wait. I'll go and do something else.' The other group Colleen observes is looking at the current generation of leaders and 'seeing that people are pulled in ten different directions, that you're spread really thin because every-body wants a piece of you, and everything's important and it all needs doing'. This group, according to Colleen, is put off by 'the early deaths and ill-health that go with all that stress', and opts out of leadership altogether.

At the same time as these deterrents are recognised, however, there is definite resistance from many older leaders to giving space to those younger leaders who *do* put their hands up. Jilpia Jones feels that part of the tension between older and younger Aboriginal people arises from the fact that 'the young ones have to learn respect'. Tauto Sansbury recognises the importance of youth representation, but is cautious about tokenism, warning: 'Don't have somebody there just because they're younger than you. You've got to have somebody that's going to have an opinion and stick by that opinion, that if they don't like the way that you're saying something then they tell you straight out.' And, despite her sympathies for their situation, Jackie is also among those older leaders who feel that younger people need to 'earn their stripes':

> This idea of young versus the rest; there's always been a camp, and I'm one of the people who have always been in that camp, that thinks you just can't get up there and be a leader unless you've done your apprenticeship. And they won't like to hear me saying this, but it takes you up to thirty-five years of age before you've done that apprenticeship.

As more and more young Aboriginal people finish school and continue to university there may be increasing conflict in these intergenerational relations. Sam Watson, whose own daughter Nicole is a lawyer with a developing public profile, expresses the ambivalence common to many of his generation:

> The young ones coming through, it's a different world now in many ways. All the young ones coming through now are far better educated and they're

going to do business in a different way. You've still got 85 per cent or 90 per cent of the community fighting the same battles that we fought back in the '60s, '70s and '80s, and we'll still keep on fighting those in the same way we've always fought them. But the younger people that come through now, they're the ones that are going to fight it through the boardrooms and through government committees and that sort of bullshit. That's their way, that's fine, you know. We all do what we've got to do.

Since the abolition of ATSIC, there is no national training ground in which emerging leaders can learn political skills and earn the stripes they apparently need to prove themselves. Kim Hill, for example, considers himself 'one of the fortunate ones' because he was part of 'the last batch of young people coming through that system'. As more young Aboriginal leaders emerge in coming years—from communities and from universities—one of the challenges for their elders and other senior people will be to let them go out into the world and achieve. At the moment, some older leaders—like Paul Briggs—worry that young leaders feel 'the broader world's not open to them', and will not make the most of the opportunities that are available to them. Paul argues that:

I don't think we've got a vision of how you expand the Aboriginal world, how you make it not so constrictive to young Aboriginal people's visions of where they fit . . . I think there's something there about the empower-ment of people to feel strong, confident, with the self-esteem as a people that allows the young people to go out and explore. At the moment we feel protective and if we've got one kid that is a lawyer then we hold on to them because they're so valuable. I think we suffocate kids like that.

Colleen Hayward also worries about the long-term implications of holding back emerging leaders:

It goes beyond the issue that the voices of young people won't be heard to a concern that their voices won't be heard because they will have stopped talking. I'm fearful of that. And I'm critical of people who say, 'No, no, look, you guys have got to earn your stripes first', because my next question would be, 'And how are you creating an environment that enables them to do that?'

Despite Colleen's fears, Geoff Scott remains confident that new young leaders will emerge, but he would dearly like older leaders to get beyond the view that 'they did it hard so why should you do it any easier', arguing that this attitude is 'immature' and not concerned with 'succession planning'. In the real or perceived absence of this sort of planning from the older generation, however, the younger generation is doing it for themselves.

The next generation

In the absence of consistent support from older leaders and activists, some younger people have set out to develop stronger peer support structures. Among the various Indigenous leadership programs available to young Indigenous people is the National Indigenous Youth Movement of Australia (NIYMA), a peer-support organisation formed in 1999 by Darren Godwell, Billy Gordon, Tanya Hosch, Mark Yettica Paulson and Gregory Phillips. Despite teething problems, NIYMA continues today, and is now supporting a new group of emerging leaders like Adele Cox, Eugenia Flynn and Tim Goodwin.

Members of NIYMA describe the group as being 'concerned with the survival, strength and *emergence* of future generations of our countrymen and women' (Phillips et al. 2003: 108). Participants in NIYMA like to clarify that the organisation is not about youth issues but rather, as Eugenia Flynn explains, about 'black issues but from a young perspective'. A key concept in NIYMA is the idea of 'safe space', which Eugenia Flynn explains is a commitment to the notion that 'when you do business together, or when you're in the support network, that space is safe from people yelling at you or heckling you . . . It doesn't mean you can't have disagreements but you do it in a respectful way.' In part, this safe space is intended to encourage in young people the 'self-belief that they are valued and important, and not isolated and alone' (Phillips et al. 2003: 110). Eugenia Flynn believes NIYMA is 'effective' in this regard, but she also feels that 'it can be really hard to find support for the organisation'. Nevertheless, Eugenia maintains that NIYMA is 'making change with a lot of the young people that are doing stuff in their communities'.

However, not all young people support the approach that NIYMA takes to issues of youth leadership in Aboriginal political culture. The view was put to me during the research for this book that the members of NIYMA are a group of self-appointed leaders who have not come out of communities and, in the words of one critic, are really 'leaders who have never led anything'. To these criticisms, Eugenia adds others who has heard, namely that they are 'young black professionals' or 'yuppies' or 'glamour blacks'. Eugenia wonders at the sentiment behind this criticism and asks:

> What's wrong with being a young black professional? Aren't we meant to be trying to move forward and celebrate success in any way, shape or form that it comes? I'm not saying that success means that you're rich or whatever but I think when people make those comments the value judgment there is that being successful is not what being a real black is about.

Larissa Behrendt also experiences this sort of criticism at times, but observes that there is 'more suspicion and jealousy' of younger people from 'people who have perhaps had a higher profile' than from 'people in the communities in which we work'.

Paul Briggs has been concerned with the lack of leadership opportunities for young people in Aboriginal communities, and remains worried that 'the channels for young people to have a view are not there' and that communities are 'not allowing Aboriginal kids to have a voice'. However, there are certainly some communities where work to develop the skills and capacity of younger people is starting to pay off. In some remote Northern Territory communities, successful programs—like the Mt Theo program at Yuendumu, for example—'support the development of positive and coherent youth identity, enabling young people to live a life of value and meaning in their own communities' (Ray 2007: 195). In western New South Wales, Sam Jeffries was concerned that no young people were taking up the spaces that were reserved for them on community councils. To counter this lack of participation, the Regional Assembly decided to get a group of young people from across the region together during school holidays and run a workshop on political engagement. Sam says he was 'quite amazed' at the number of young people who 'really showed an interest in the community governance environment in their own communities':

> And now that's had this whole impact of young people engaging with political parties, starting to see role models in their communities, and we're exposing them to the things that we're doing here . . . I mean, after

one meeting, we had kids who have had no exposure to public speaking or anything like that presenting to the Regional Assembly. I was just so amazed at the take up of young people.

As a result of the workshop, the Assembly now has a regional strategy for the engagement of young people and is developing a Youth Assembly that will feed into the Regional Assembly. The young people involved in the Youth Assembly will 'undertake a planning process around young people's needs and issues' that the Regional Assembly will eventually adopt as part of their broader planning process.

Such initiatives will bring comfort to other Aboriginal leaders and activists who already expend considerable energy mentoring and supporting younger people. Aden Ridgeway, for example, believes the youthful demographics of the Aboriginal population create a mandate to 'ensure young people are encouraged to step up and supported to take on that role' (quoted in Liddle 2006). Ridgeway himself feels that some of his more important achievements have been 'the small and quiet stuff with youth groups and local communities', insisting that 'young people are the future and I have tried to help them believe they can be whatever they want to be' (quoted in Cheatham 2005). Colleen Hayward is one of many who takes great pleasure in supporting emerging leaders, saying:

> I want to hear those voices. One of the greatest pleasures that I have at work is I've got a couple of young Aboriginal people on my staff that are a joy to work with. They're wonderful, they're bright and they're energetic, and they look at things in a different way, because they've got different experiences to what I have. I see my role as really providing a safe place for them to grow and to fertilise them and water them and all of that stuff. Every day I get to see them grow! . . . I need to let them know that they can leap off the abyss, but safely, because if it looks as though they're going to crash, I'm on the other end of the rope.

Securing the future

The focus of much political activism for older leaders and activists today is, as Henry Atkinson says, 'to try and secure a future for the younger generations and to make sure the country, the land, the water, the animals, insects are still there for the future generations'. Colleen Hayward argues passionately that fostering future leadership is the role of current leaders, arguing that a leader is not really a leader 'if when they go there's nobody there to step into their place'. Alison Anderson agrees, saying 'we need the young generation to keep coming up strongly'. At the same time, however, many older people display a degree of mistrust in, or even jealousy of, emerging leaders and there is often considerable tension between the generations. Younger people are demanding a right to speak, while also looking to their elders and seniors for support. In the absence of this support, however, Geoff Scott observes that many younger leaders and activists seem to have 'made the decision that they don't need those people to keep going'. Geoff also sees that, like the current generation of leaders, the next generation is 'not looking to be leaders. They're looking to make a difference.'

Regardless of their political and professional independence, however, young and emerging leaders still want encouragement from their elders, and they need support to ground their politics in culture. As the young people from NIYMA have argued:

> young Indigenous people need to know that their identity as a Black person is based in their spiritual connection to their culture . . . Indigenous young people have the self-evident right to be proud of who they are, and need to be able to decide for themselves what it means to be Black in a changing world. (Phillips et al. 2003: 110)

There are new challenges to intergenerational politics in this changing world, however, as political decision-making now occurs at a much faster pace than a generation ago. Patrick Dodson worries that intergenerational connections are being broken as 'a lot of the older people get left behind' in this 'faster world' where 'information is very speedy and decisions are required'. The older people preferred the politics of a time when, for decisions to be made, 'you needed to sit down around campfires and talk to people and camp there in that country' (Dodson 1998: 101). Accessing and utilising new technologies is providing younger people with new power in their communities, and proving a base for careers and training that further enhance their status. While these achievements are both necessary and laudable, they also have the inevitable consequence of further undermining Aboriginal social structures by continuing the erosion of the elders' traditional power (Mudrooroo 1995: 90). It is neither possible, nor desirable, to try

and stymie this evolution in Aboriginal political culture. To be effective leaders in the twenty-first century, young leaders need to combine
knowledge of culture and traditional governance with knowledge of
Western systems of governance (KALACC 2006: 43). It does, however,
seem important to understand these changing dynamics in their proper
historical context, and to understand the social consequences that flow
from these subtle and inexorable changes. As Anthony Philip Petrick
frets, in the new political order in Aboriginal communities, 'there is
not enough learning of culture . . . I am a bit afraid it's going to be
lost forever sometimes' (Petrick 1998: 106). In light of such fears, it is
necessary to recognise the significance of customary law in Aboriginal
political culture, the focus of the next chapter.

10
MEN, WOMEN AND CUSTOMARY LAW

Customary law has always been the backbone of Aboriginal society and culture. It provides guidelines on how to live, and rules for relations between and within families and language groups. It is grounded in an ancient and complex cosmology that is generally referred to as the Dreaming, which includes creation legends and parables passed from generation to generation through song, dance, art and story. But recognising customary law in contemporary times can seem complex and challenging for both Aboriginal and non-Aboriginal people. Colonisation has interrupted the inevitable evolution of Aboriginal custom and belief, instead pushing Aboriginal people to defend their threatened culture. At the same time, there has been extensive but poorly informed public debate about the recognition of customary law that has done much to muddy the water and demonise Aboriginal men.

Underpinning much of the often-hysterical public discussion about customary law is the very real issue of violence in Aboriginal communities and the extent to which contemporary violence has a basis in, or is justified by, aspects of customary law. Gender relations in Aboriginal political culture are deeply implicated in this discussion although, as Mick Dodson has pointed out, 'the vast majority of Aboriginal men condemn the violence that corrodes our communities' (Dodson 2007b). Although violence against women is not the only manifestation of violence in Aboriginal families and communities, it is prominent. Aboriginal women such as Boni Robertson and Judy Atkinson have been speaking and writing about gendered violence for many years with little political response. Despite women's activism on this issue, there is only periodic mainstream interest in it—for example, in 2003 after Mick Dodson gave a compelling speech on violence in Aboriginal communities at the National Press Club (Dodson 2003b). The speech received a huge amount of media attention, eventually prompting the then prime minister to hold a summit on Indigenous violence. Relief at this political intervention quickly evaporated, however, as no follow up to the summit's discussions was forthcoming. The issue again hit the headlines in 2006 when Alice Springs Crown Prosecutor, Nanette Rogers, appeared on ABC television to describe the 'culture of sexual assaults on children and violence against women' that she claimed was endemic to Central Australian Aboriginal communities (ABC 2006). Despite the fact that many of Rogers' claims had already been made by Aboriginal women in various reports, another media frenzy followed her appearance and eventually sparked the Northern Territory government to commission the inquiry that produced the *Little Children are Sacred* report.

In the meantime, debate on issues of violence, customary law and the status of women in Aboriginal society has continued. Many Aboriginal people reject the claim that customary law in any way allows for the abuse of women and children, yet this very defence has been used in courts of law. Media attention on the issue continues to point the finger at Aboriginal men,[1] further exacerbating social problems in many communities where women shoulder much responsibility while receiving little formal recognition. The populist view understands violence as a part of traditional Aboriginal culture. Many Aboriginal leaders and activists, however, instead see violence as a symptom of the historical disruption to Aboriginal society and the systems of customary law that regulated interpersonal behaviour. A July 2008 health summit held at Ross River in the Northern Territory and attended by nearly 400 Aboriginal men addressed precisely this issue. The summit issued the Inteyerrkwe Statement in which the men apologised for the 'hurt, pain and suffering' inflicted on Aboriginal women and children by Aboriginal men, calling for the 'love and support of our Aboriginal women to help us move forward' (Liddle 2008).

Violence in Aboriginal communities

There can be no doubting the fact that violence in Aboriginal communi ties is a devastating problem. Whether it is labelled domestic violence, family violence or community violence, it is evident that prolific violence in Aboriginal communities is tearing apart the fragile social fabric that in some areas has barely survived 220 years of colonisation. In his speech at the National Press Club, Mick Dodson suggested that there were 'very few Aboriginal families' not touched by the 'trauma, despair and damage' that violence creates (Dodson 2003b). Although statistics concerning violence are notoriously unreliable and often under-estimate the extent of the problem, data from the National Aboriginal and Torres Strait Islander Social Survey suggest that about one in four Indigenous people over the age of fifteen has been the victim of physical or threatened violence (discussed in Al-Yaman et al. 2006). The incidence of violence in Aboriginal communities is described as being 'disproportionately higher' than the same type of violence in the broader population (Memmott et al. 2001: 6) and it seems likely from the available evidence that the incidence of violence against Aboriginal women is higher than the incidence of violence against non-Aboriginal women, although violence against both groups remains a significant social problem. It is important to note, however, that being the victim of violence is not the experience of all Aboriginal women, nor is it the sum total of Aboriginal women's lives.

Debates about the causes of, and justification for, violence against women in Aboriginal communities produce vastly differing perspectives. While Aboriginal people understand contemporary violence in the context of Australia's colonial history, mainstream public debate tends to attribute this violence to Aboriginal culture and refocus public interest on individual behaviour. For Aboriginal people, the historical context is crucial to understanding both the social dynamics that underpin violence and the intergenerational processes that continue to produce it (Anderson 2002: 409). Without this context, simplistic policy responses continue to focus on internal community dynamics, pathologising communities and individuals and producing 'solutions' that treat the symptom rather than the cause of violent behaviour. This view, often supported by the belief that Aboriginal violence has its roots in customary law and traditional behaviour, is used to justify government action such as the Northern Territory intervention. In a discussion paper for the conservative

Bennelong Society, for example, social scientist Stephanie Jarrett concedes that 'there may be nothing "inherent" about "Aboriginality" that leads to greater levels of violence', but maintains that 'violence was and is prevalent within Aboriginal traditional culture, performing a central plank in maintaining law, and economic and power relations' (Jarrett 2006: 7). The playwright Louis Nowra also propounds this view in *Bad Dreaming*, his controversial contribution to this issue, where he argues that Aboriginal men's 'ancient and long-lasting' treatment of women displayed a 'consistent pattern' of being 'harsh, sexually aggressive . . . [and] misogynist' (Nowra 2007: 24). Both authors base their claims, in part, on the evidence of early settlers and their recorded observations of Aboriginal society. In light of these criticisms, it is worth remembering that physical punishment such as flogging was also a central component of the British colonial regime at the time of the invasion, and that violence—including sexual violence—against Aboriginal and non-Aboriginal women was not uncommon. Such behaviour is not described as part of 'traditional' British culture.

Critics of non-Aboriginal authors like Nowra maintain that: 'It is easy to make it look like Aboriginal people condone violence when you overlook all the Aboriginal voices that speak out against it and all the community initiatives started by Aboriginal people to combat it.' (Behrendt and Watson 2007) Many Aboriginal scholars espouse an alternate view of the place of violence in Aboriginal culture, suggesting that much contemporary violence is more likely the product of invasion and colonisation. Pallawah scholar Kyllie Cripps has argued that contemporary Indigenous family violence results from a complex mix of factors, amongst them policies and practices associated with colonisation including dispossession, cultural dislocation and the dislocation of families through removal, along with a range of other factors including marginalisation as a minority; direct and indirect racism; unemployment; welfare dependency; a past history of abuse; poverty; destructive coping behaviours; addictions; health and mental health issues; and low self-esteem and a sense of powerlessness (Cripps 2007: 8). Larissa Behrendt has argued that the sexual exploitation of Aboriginal women by white settlers produced a 'transferred misogyny' through which Aboriginal men were 'quick to learn that exploitation of black women was acceptable and quick to forget the status Aboriginal women held in their own communities' (Behrendt 2000: 364). Hannah McGlade makes a related

point, arguing that: 'Many Aboriginal men have internalised the patriarchal values and beliefs of the colonisers.' (McGlade 2001: 140) In our
interview, William Tilmouth expressed a similar opinion, arguing that:

> Violence is another learnt behaviour. Aboriginal men were told, 'Come over
> here and take control of your woman. She's going wild. What kind of a man
> are you to let your woman run wild like that?' And so they would be encour-
> aged to beat their women to show the white men they were in control. But
> nobody ever talked about the fact that that woman had just been raped by
> that white man and that she had been poured full of alcohol so that she
> could be raped.

Muriel Bamblett sees the exploitation and subordination of Aboriginal women by colonisers as a deliberate strategy to disempower
communities because 'women were the source of power and the ones
that could bring about change'. The way forward, in Muriel's eyes, is for
Aboriginal women to 'reclaim their traditional roles'.

So were women victimised in traditional culture? Although there can
be no way of ever answering this question definitively, there is a very
strong view among many Aboriginal leaders and activists that gender
relations in pre-contact Aboriginal society were healthy and balanced.
Further, they argue that this balance was enshrined in, and maintained by, customary law that recognised women's separate spheres of
responsibility to land and ceremony, now often referred to as 'women's
business'. These areas of responsibility meant that women were entitled
to influence the social, political and cultural affairs of their communities, with women elders generally exercising the same level of influence
as their male counterparts (KALACC 2006: 26; Behrendt 1995: 13).
While not everyone agrees with this view—Sam Watson, for example,
suggests that women in traditional Aboriginal society 'didn't have any
great equality'—many others argue that this gender balance existed and is
maintained in many areas today.[2] In our interview, Muriel Bamblett told
me she had spent time researching the question of whether women were
ever seen as 'subservient' to men in Aboriginal society. The evidence,
she says, confirms that 'women were never seen as being secondary to
men, everything was very equal in communities'. Alwyn McKenzie also
believes that the traditional culture of the Adnyamathanha people was
'a shared thing' in which 'men and women played a part, in different

roles, but equally'. Alwyn sees this as only logical, arguing that: 'Without each other they wouldn't have been able to survive.' Hannah McGlade maintains that Aboriginal women 'come from nations which value and respect the woman's role, rights and responsibilities in their cultures and communities' (McGlade 2001: 139). Indeed, it seems likely that the segregated roles and responsibilities accorded to men and women in much customary law provided women with a protected and enduring sphere of power in their communities.

There are many contemporary and well-understood social problems that contribute to ongoing violence in Aboriginal communities. Ted Wilkes highlights the impact of overcrowded housing as a significant factor in 'the abuse of our women and the abuse of our children and the domestic violence'. But overcrowding is just one symptom of the problems in many Aboriginal communities that have resulted from decades of under-investment coupled with the lack of autonomy discussed in Chapter 2. In too many communities, there is a seemingly inevitable progression from lack of autonomy and control to feelings of hopelessness and helplessness to alcohol and other substance abuse and finally a range of violent behaviours including domestic violence and other forms of assault, child abuse, and various forms of self-abuse including suicide. Judy Atkinson sees a link between what she describes as 'colonial impacts' and the sort of binge drinking by which many Aboriginal people 'self-medicate' to numb the pain of the 'trauma-inducing conditions' in which they live. This combination of circumstances promotes violence within the families and groups caught in these systems (Atkinson 2002: 67). This sort of violence is evident in dominated and dependent Indigenous communities all over the world (Trudgen 2000: 173). Given our knowledge of these circumstances, it is simplistic in the extreme to attribute behaviour that is in large part the result of relatively recent social trauma to a range of customary laws that have their basis in an ancient cosmology.

Understanding customary law

Before colonisation, the spiritual beliefs and practices that comprise Aboriginal cosmology were also the basis of governance and social control within and between language groups. Customary laws were understood to have been laid down by ancestral beings, and therefore had a sort of external authority that was later eroded and replaced by the settler-state

(Keen 1988: 18). More wide ranging than the Western conception of law, Aboriginal customary law embraces all that non Aboriginal people might describe as law, religion, philosophy, art and culture, and provides groups and individuals with precise and binding guidelines by which to manage relationships to others, to land and resources, and related rights and obligations (Brennan 1995: 143). The scope of customary law extends far beyond issues of promised wives, male authority and 'payback'—despite the mainstream media's overwhelming interest in only these factors—to include guidelines about, for example, land management, trespass and succession. Patrick Dodson describes customary law as 'an all-encompassing reality' with 'many obligations and responsibilities and structures of accountability'. Dodson regrets the fact that:

> Most people unfortunately have only ever thought of customary law from a punitive position. They've thought about it in terms of punishment, in terms of spearing someone through the leg as a consequence of some violation, or at other extremes of the aberrations that might arise under a promised marriage structure. (quoted in KALACC 2006: 15)

The significance of some aspects of customary law in the practice of criminal law has been keenly debated, with many courts attempting to clarify the use they should make of customary law, including how they should receive evidence about the content of such laws and what impact this should have on issues such as sentencing and the granting of bail (Brennan et al. 2005: 57). While these issues are clearly challenging, they should not excuse contemporary courts and governments from further effort to understand the place of customary law in mainstream political culture. As Lowitja O'Donoghue has argued:

> The long standing absence of meaningful official recognition of Aboriginal customary law has had a detrimental effect on all facets of Aboriginal community development and has substantially contributed to many of the social problems and varying degrees of lawlessness present today. The failure of successive governments to recognise customary law has resulted in the erosion of Aboriginal cultures. (O'Donoghue 1995)

Nevertheless, the use of customary law to defend violence against women and children has angered many Aboriginal leaders and activists.

A seminal report on violence in Aboriginal communities by Audrey Bolger describes three kinds of violence: alcoholic violence, traditional violence and 'bullshit traditional violence' (Bolger 1991: 50). This last category is violence against women, often fuelled by alcohol, which is later justified by reference to the traditional rights of men in Aboriginal society. Bolger suggests that these arguments have been so pervasive in some communities that some younger women now believe that wife beating is a traditional practice, leaving older women the task of rejecting this as a distortion and an abuse of their culture (Bolger 1991; Behrendt 2000: 363). Judy Atkinson suggests that it has been the 'colonisers' who have categorised much Aboriginal interpersonal violence as 'customary practice', even though Aboriginal people themselves regard this same behaviour as unacceptable and as a transgression of cultural norms (Atkinson 2002: 11–12). This distortion of Aboriginal customary law has been exacerbated in national debates in which, in Megan Davis's opinion, customary law is 'popularly viewed as Indigenous communities reliving the halcyon days of Indigenous culture practising brutal, traditional punishment such as wounding or tribal payback' (Davis 2006b: 129). Tom Calma has been unequivocal in his view: 'Aboriginal customary law does not condone family violence and abuse, and cannot be relied upon to excuse such behaviour. Perpetrators of violence and abuse do not respect customary law and are not behaving in accordance with it.' (ATSISJC 2006b: 10)

Rex Wild and Patricia Anderson also addressed this issue in the *Little Children are Sacred* report, where they argued that the claim that customary law is behind child sexual abuse is 'a dangerous myth as it reinforces prejudice and ignorance, masks the complex nature of child sexual abuse and provokes a hostile reaction from Aboriginal people that is not conducive to dealing with the problem' (Wild and Anderson 2007: 18). The report authors also note that they were not able to find any case where Aboriginal customary law had been used *and accepted* as a defence that would exonerate an accused perpetrator from their criminal responsibility for violent offences against women or children (Wild and Anderson 2007: 19).

Some of my interviewees were frank about their own struggles to make sense of the complexities involved in the recognition of customary law. Colleen Hayward, for example, suggested that there was a time in her life when she would have described herself as 'a great supporter of customary law'. At that time, Colleen held the belief that 'if particular communities wanted to determine for themselves that they wanted to invoke customary law for particular community offences then they should be allowed to do that without penalty'. Now Colleen is unequivocal:

> That's not my thinking, and it hasn't been for a long time. I think too much customary law has been bastardised. I think customary law is thrown up as a convenient excuse for unacceptable behaviour, especially with domestic violence and child sexual abuse. Those things are not part of our cultural heritage, and any hiding behind the label of customary law is cowardice and bullshit, quite frankly.

Colleen refers to one high-profile case to make her point. In that case, a fifty-year-old man had kidnapped a fifteen-year-old girl and forced her to have sex with him, claiming that she was 'promised' to him under customary law. When the girl's relatives came to check on her, she tried to leave and her assailant fired a gun into the air to frighten her family off. For Colleen, despite the man's use of customary law as a defence, there is nothing ambiguous in the case: 'She was raped! That's a rape! It's not anybody exercising their customary law, it is sexual assault. And quite frankly, when she is raped in a *house* as opposed to a humpy, held at *gunpoint*, by a bloke who drove a *vehicle*, you know, it's a bit of a stretch really, it's a bit of a stretch.' Colleen's point is that people who are not even living in ways that suggest a traditional lifestyle too often use customary law to defend their unacceptable behaviour. Jilpia Jones makes a similar point, saying: 'If you're going to talk about traditional law, you'd better act the part. That's what I say.'

Important to this debate is the recognition that customary law is not the same thing to all people, and nor is it fixed in time. Customary law has always varied from nation to nation, although many groups in close proximity to one another share similar understandings of laws related to the sharing of resources, travelling on one another's country and intermarriage. Further, while Aboriginal people extol the ancient and unchanging nature of their law, the reality is that many aspects of customary law, like all other legal systems, have evolved and continue to evolve in response to changing social conditions. As Alison Anderson has argued, customary law is 'part of a living culture, and like all living cultures, Aboriginal culture has the capacity to adapt and evolve in response to change' (Anderson 2003: 2). It follows, then, that customary law can and does evolve in response to growing understanding of human rights principles through what Megan Davis describes as 'the organic nature of customary law in Indigenous culture and the dynamic and shifting course of Indigenous law' (Davis 2006b: 129). Tom Calma also stresses that 'custom and law can adapt to general societal change' (ATSISJC 2006b: 12). Invasion and colonisation, however, have had the effect of disrupting the organic evolution of customary law, the protection of which has become a defence against an aggressive occupying culture. Ray Swan makes the point that Aboriginal people do need to 'contemporise them systems [of customary law] to meet today's laws', and recognises that 'a lot of pay back laws would be classed as inhumane these days, would go against human rights principles'. Still, Ray maintains that this can only be done by Aboriginal people themselves, arguing that, 'We as a people have got the right to contemporise that law'. Ted Wilkes agrees, suggesting that 'there are some traditional practices which should be rearranged so that we can live in a contemporary world with a different ideology'. But there are other aspects of law that Ted sees as offering no conflict with contemporary human rights standards or legal practice—for example, 'family ties and respect for your mother-in-law . . . eye contact, you're not to look in the eye of a certain woman. They're all real and you hold on to them.'

What is almost universally rejected by Aboriginal leaders and activists, however, is the use of customary law to defend violent and abusive behaviour, particularly that directed at women and children. Eddie Cubillo thinks that the use of customary law as a defence in these instances has made such law appear to be a 'mishmash that doesn't give a real good story out there to everyone'. Where this defence is offered by lawyers in a criminal court, Warren Mundine argues that:

It really puts us in a bad light. It's a problem of the adversarial legal system, which has been placed on top of us from England, where a defence lawyer uses every tool in his kit to get his defendants off . . . If you're having offender after offender going to the court and saying, 'This is my customary right,' it gives a very bad view of what Aboriginal customary law is.

Despite these reservations, however, many Aboriginal people still believe it is important to retain an awareness of cultural law in many legal proceedings. Warren suggests there are 'important things to be preserved', and that in many instances customary law 'explains why a person does things'. He clarifies:

> I'm not talking about sexual abuse of young girls or anything like this. I'm talking about a wider range of other issues where [a defendant may say] 'I don't understand why this is illegal.' Customary law helps explain that and I think that's fair enough. To say, 'I don't understand why I can't walk across this country. We've been walking across this country for thousands of years and now I've been arrested for trespass?' Then customary law explains why that person is doing that and then the courts are able to deal with that.

Tom Calma agrees that this distinction is important, and he rejects the view that 'Anglo-Australian views are the benchmark and everything else that doesn't fit within that is not acceptable'. Tom insists the legal system must 'respect other cultures and other practices and other belief systems', and that Aboriginal people should have access to the legal system but 'not to the exclusion of our own cultural beliefs'. This view is entirely consistent with the law as it is currently practised in most Australian courts, where it is already the case that cultural background, religious belief and many other aspects of an individual's personal circumstances are taken into account in determining both crime and punishment (Chesterman 2005: 244). To remove the courts' capacity to take customary law into account, as legislative reforms initiated by the Howard government have done in the federal legal sphere,[3] is to add yet another layer of discrimination and disadvantage to Aboriginal people negotiating the complexities of Australia's legal system. It also further disempowers those already suffering the erosion of their customary law.

Emasculating Aboriginal men

The sexual exploitation of Aboriginal women has been a horrific aspect of the colonisation of this country. As Larissa Behrendt has argued, 'The bodies of black women' have been seen as 'the spoils of colonial conquest' and Aboriginal women have suffered the 'double taint of subordinated race and a subordinated gender' (Behrendt 2000: 364). In many communities, however, it is remarkable to observe the sort of community power still exercised by Aboriginal women, especially given the levels of violence they still endure. Marcia Langton has suggested that the 'leadership and stability of women' are a 'feature of post-frontier Aboriginal society' (Langton 1997: 96). There is a growing recognition that colonial power has stripped men of their traditional areas of authority and allowed the dominant culture to take over the roles that men once fulfilled. As a result, many men are caught in a downward spiral of alcohol abuse, violence and early death. According to Richard Trudgen, many Yolngu men feel that 'they have nothing to live or work for. They feel there would be little change in their communities if they weren't there.' (Trudgen 2000: 170) And increasingly they are not there, absent due to imprisonment or alcohol abuse (Langton 1997: 108). As Trudgen also observes: 'In Aboriginal communities right around Australia, one thing is evident: where the people have lost control, the men are dead or dying. Many communities are run mainly by women. If you ask where the men are, they will inevitably say, "They drank themselves to death."' (Trudgen 2000: 170)

In contrast, many of my interviewees emphasised the role that women play in their communities. Sam Watson maintains that the Brisbane Murri community remains strong primarily because 'we've always been dominated by a steel circle of aunties' to whom 'you've got to show respect'. Sam points out that these women are strong both in the community and at the forefront of political struggle, attending 'all our big marches' where they 'lead us all the way. They've never allowed themselves to be dominated or to be intimidated. They've been our inspiration all the way through.' Eddie Cubillo suggests that women retain 'a lot of responsibility in culture and ceremonies', even where the authority structure is not matrilineal, and suggests that while 'the beliefs of the men always were dominant in our culture', women like Eddie's grandmother have land and 'are still matriarchs'. Larissa Behrendt also spoke of the role that women have played in her life and education, saying that as she was growing up she 'never doubted the influence and power of women within my own community':

> And not just because Eualeyai-Kamilaroi nations are matrilineal and we've got our own cultural stories for women. When I was a kid and Dad would drag me along to meetings, it would always be that the men would bellow and shout and carry on, and then at the end, the women would say, 'Okay, this is what we're going to do.'

Growing up surrounded by women like Roberta Sykes, Marcia Langton and Linda Burney, Larissa says it 'never occurred' to her that 'women weren't powerful within my own community . . . it always seemed to me that in our community women had an enormous amount of power'.

Others, however, suggest that the power of women and men still belongs in separate social spheres and that colonisation has upset the gender balance. Vince Coulthard, for example, maintains that in Adnya-mathanha society 'the women are responsible for family' while 'the men are protectors and hunters and are responsible for keeping our country'. However, Vince also makes an important distinction between this worldview and the Western 'breadwinner' family structure of women at home and men out in the world. Vince argues that:

> Keeper of family doesn't mean women's place is in the home. There's other things involved in being keeper of family. Like working with family and youth services, I mean they're an agency where I believe that women should play a very important role. And women's health areas, I mean when it comes to dealing with women and children, you need women to do that. You can't have a male person go along and nurse women, it's inappropriate. And vice versa, you can't have a woman go along nursing a male, particularly if they're the same skin group. That's wrong, it's inappropriate.

Regardless of precolonial differences in gender relations around the country, it is clear that colonisation has changed these relations greatly (Atkinson 2002: 37). In acknowledging that 'family violence' has become 'one of the scourges of contemporary Indigenous life', Tim Rowse asks whether some government policies have had the unintended consequence of raising tension between Aboriginal women and men (Rowse 2002: 152). Many Aboriginal people see the erosion of tra-ditional gendered spheres of power and influence as contributing to what Alwyn McKenzie sees as the 'emasculation' of Aboriginal men. While Alwyn acknowledges that there are many Aboriginal communities where certain men are extremely dominant, he also sees a more subtle and per-vasive dynamic at work, where unemployment means that men are 'not being a provider in the way they see other people in society providing for their families'. As a result, 'fellas haven't got confidence when they're sober and so they might have a few beers' and in the end 'take it out on their families'. Robbie Thorpe makes a similar point, suggesting that

Aboriginal men in Fitzroy are 'heavily dominated by the women' because 'men haven't got a role': 'The only role that men have got is working for the white man. There's no real Aboriginal leadership . . . There's no role for Aboriginal men. It's easy for the government to deal with women, but where the culture is in the men.'

There is no doubt that many Aboriginal women (and men) would disagree with Robbie regarding his claims that culture resides in Aboriginal men, but his point about men's lack of a clear role is an important one. In many communities, women have taken the reins and are the drivers of change at the local level where it seems that women's domestic authority has shown greater resilience in a postcolonial context (Keen 1988: 18). As one woman said to me during the course of researching this book: 'Women are the voices now, they're the movers and the shakers; it's the women that's making it work.' In the Marika family, for example, women claim that cultural strength now lies with them because 'the women are the stronger people' who now must 'help our brothers with our cultural survival' (Langani Marika, quoted in ABC 2003b). In urban and remote areas, women are now the holders of the genealogical knowledge that is essential to native title claims and are influential in behind-the-scenes negotiations between different interests during the claims process (Brock 2001: 12). Rex Wild and Patricia Anderson reported that it was 'a common theme in virtually all places visited by the Inquiry that Aboriginal men felt disempowered', while 'many Aboriginal women have been working hard for years to improve their communities' (Wild and Anderson 2007: 20). In many communities, it is the women who run programs like night patrols where they are active in trying to keep their families safe.

In this context, it is especially damaging that so much public debate on violence in Aboriginal communities has had the effect of further demonising Aboriginal men. Mick Dodson believes that the Northern Territory 'intervention' painted all Aboriginal men as 'drunkards and wife beaters and child rapists'. Tom Calma makes the same point, highlighting the ways in which Aboriginal men have been portrayed in the media as 'all being abusers' in ways that are 'really affecting a lot of Indigenous men'. Tom stresses that making this point is 'not to disregard the rights of women or children' in any way; rather, it is 'just a statement of fact' about something that is becoming 'a major pressure point in Indigenous society'. Eugenia Flynn has observed the hurt experienced by her male friends, a fact she finds 'really sad' because this media image has become 'another stress that's placed upon Aboriginal men and they have to deal with these stereotypes when they're not all like that'. The Northern Territory intervention has further exacerbated these dynamics, with the abolition of CDEP pushing previously employed men on to the dole. The impact in communities such as Maningrida is unlikely to be the one that is intended. As Ian Munro, Chief Executive of Maningrida's Bawinanga Aboriginal Corporation, has observed: 'If you take proud, dignified men who have been working all day, every day, and you remove three-quarters of their income and send them home at lunchtime to an overcrowded house that may well have children in it, how on earth can those children be safer than they formerly were?' (quoted in ABC 2007f) Such unplanned consequences would seem to be potentially disastrous for a program designed to reduce violence.

At the community level, one outcome of such poor policy will be that Aboriginal women, already leaders in their communities, will have to shoulder a greater burden of responsibility for family and community welfare. Unfortunately, as discussed below, this fact remains poorly recognised in terms of women's status in public affairs and in Aboriginal political culture more broadly, where women are often still marginalised from the institutional spheres of power (ATSIC 1995b: 96).

Women speaking up

Given the strong emphasis on women's power in both traditional culture and contemporary communities, it seems paradoxical that many women feel excluded from exercising political influence. Aboriginal political culture is often described by women as being very much a 'boys' club'. Jackie Huggins has had rather more experience of this form of exclusion than she might wish, pointing out that during her time in politics: 'There's always been the boys' club.' She has too often seen 'the boys ganging up against the women'. For Jackie, this issue was underscored during her work on the review of ATSIC. In the course of consultations for the review, Jackie says that she:

> felt this whole gender divide so strongly. *They* [men] would say it doesn't happen, but it was the men that had the power, and the men would say, 'Well, the women vote for us at elections, so therefore why do you need equal seats' and so forth . . . But at those meetings, the women would come

up to me afterwards and say, 'We're not happy, Jackie, but we can't speak out at this meeting. We can't say stuff in front of our men.'

Larissa Behrendt has also experienced the boys' club up close, telling me that at first she was 'surprised' and 'shocked' by what she saw:

I remember when I first started to go to [national] meetings, I'd often be the only woman in the room other than Marcia Langton and I used to see how exhausted she would be by the end of it. People would just enjoy winding her up as though that was more fun than talking about the important issues that were on the table. And she would leave the meetings exhausted. And I just had such an admiration for her because I thought it would have been so easy for her to just think, 'Stuff it, I don't need this aggravation,' but she never did that. She never let them keep her out of the room, she just kept on at it. And if she hadn't kept on at it, it would have been absolutely impossible for me to be in the room, or the other women who are there now.

Like many others, Geoff Scott believes that the old leadership that dominated the ATSIC board was 'rife with sexism' and was very 'degrading and demeaning of women'. Alison Anderson had the unique experience of being the only woman on the ATSIC board during its last term. Following the election of the board for that term, the returned chairman Geoff Clarke thanked 'all those Aboriginal females' who had voted, and who had 'given us a mandate, you've returned the traditional role to Aboriginal men' (quoted in Jopson 2002). Despite such overt sexism among her colleagues, however, Alison maintains that 'at no stage' did she feel intimidated, and argues that: 'It's about your own capacity to deal with these issues and stand up. You don't have a mandate from them to bow down to them or to please them. You're there with one mandate and one mandate only and that's the mandate of your people to make things better for them.'

Jilpia Jones is another who is not intimidated by what she too refers to as the 'boys' club', saying: 'If I've got something to say, I say it regardless of who that boy is because to me they're just little men. I respect them but they have to listen to what I've got to say.' Jilpia also thinks that there is 'going to be a generation change' that will see 'all these educated young women' transform the old gender relations in Aboriginal political culture. Younger women like Eugenia Flynn suggest that

Jilpia may be right and that the sexist culture of the national Aboriginal political scene may finally be changing. Eugenia still maintains that 'men just think differently', but she is also deeply appreciative of the fact that the men in NIYMA 'are really mindful of the fact that they're men and that sometimes they occupy more space physically and mentally and emotionally than women do'. Nevertheless, Eugenia says she has to constantly remind them that 'we need a female here and we need a female there and we need gender balance in this situation and that situation'. Eugenia tells me: 'Those sorts of things are going to make some people feel uncomfortable . . . Men probably don't realise that inherently the way the world is structured means that they have more power, and so they don't realise that they need to accommodate for women in that way, which they really do.'

Doubtless there are many Aboriginal men who do not see the need to address persistent gender inequities in Aboriginal culture. Tauto Sansbury is happy to 'throw the cat among the pigeons' by saying he is 'concerned about this focus on gender balance all the time', suggesting that sometimes a gender balance is arrived at 'just to make people happy'. Vince Coulthard also has reservations, suggesting that women who take on a public role 'may as well get up and speak as a non-Aboriginal person because they're not coming from an Aboriginal perspective'. Vince is particularly concerned when it comes to 'dealing with country', which in his view is something 'the male needs to do'. Gendered relations to land remain a source of tension in some areas of Australia where, despite a rise in the profile of women in the land claims process, men's evidence is still seen as more important in establishing traditional ownership (Toussaint et al. 2001: 165). Marcia Langton suggests that this view has been perpetuated by the 'established anthropological orthodoxy' that sees questions of descent and succession as primarily 'patrilineal, or at least determined by patrifiliation' (Langton 1997: 84–5). Despite vastly differing communities and circumstances, this view of landholding means that women throughout Australia have to deal with very similar issues in their struggle to have their rights in land recognised (Brock 2001: 17).

Aboriginal women have also struggled to have their leadership roles in their communities recognised on the governing bodies of community organisations, where women are still usually outnumbered by men (Hunt and Smith 2007: 9). Some organisations have been determined to address such imbalance, proving it is possible to do so. The Kimberley

Aboriginal Law and Culture Centre, for example, in a unanimous 1994 agreement by members, changed the organisation's constitution to enable the election of both a chairman and a chairwoman. They also decided to institute a 50/50 gender balance on the organisation's executive committee to more appropriately address women's cultural business (KALACC 2006: 115). Other efforts have not been so successful, however. In the 1980s, a delegation of women persuaded the Central Land Council to establish a Central Australian Women's Council. Meetings and consultations were held with women throughout the region, generating considerable enthusiasm. For example, Lena Cavanagh from Santa Teresa summed up the need for a women-only council:

> I want women to be as strong as the men. All the women can stand together and have a meeting. Men is too strong on the Council, got to be more Council ladies strong. All the women can have their own council. They can speak about their land if they want to. They don't have to stand back and let the men do all the talking. (quoted in CLC 1994: 34)

Despite this enthusiasm, however, the Commonwealth government refused to provide any additional funds to establish the women's council and the initiative faded away. In light of all that has happened in Central Australian communities in the intervening twenty years, one has to wonder whether things might have been different if women, already strong in their communities, had also had their roles recognised and formalised through a separate Land Council structure.

Given the sometimes overt nature of sexism experienced by Aboriginal women, it may seem surprising that more do not embrace a feminist philosophy. However, relations between Aboriginal women and the Australian women's movement have never been easy. For some women, the white women's movement has seemed irrelevant to the real struggles in Aboriginal women's lives. Aileen Moreton-Robinson has argued that, in struggles for self-determination, Aboriginal women are 'politically and culturally aligned' with Aboriginal men, in part because they 'share a common history of colonisation' (Moreton-Robinson 2005: 66). Similarly, in an article that first appeared in the feminist journal *Refractory Girl* in 1976, Pat O'Shane argued that: 'Sexist attitudes did not wipe out whole tribes of our people; sexist attitudes are not slowly killing our people today—racism did, and continues to do so!' (O'Shane 1993: 74)

Many Aboriginal women viewed white feminists as insensitive to their own role in Australia's colonial history and the implications of this in contemporary Aboriginal political culture. White women simply 'invited' Aboriginal women to join their movement (Goodall and Huggins 1992: 401–2) with its discourse of women's independence, seemingly unable to recognise 'the majority of Indigenous women who actively fight each day of their lives to keep their families and communities together' (Morris 1996: 203). As Jackie Huggins has argued:

> In asking Aboriginal women to stand apart from Aboriginal men, the white women's movement was, perhaps unconsciously, repeating the attempts made over decades by welfare administrators to separate Aboriginal women and use them against their communities. While there were Aboriginal women who were deeply aware of the politics of sexism, many reacted with anger at the limited awareness of racism shown by the white women's movement. (Huggins 1998: 27)

In our interview, Muriel Bamblett makes a similar point, saying that she 'wouldn't want to be in a position where I don't have men beside me and around me . . . I don't want to be walking up the street with my husband on one side of the street marching for men's rights and me marching for women.' Like many Aboriginal women, Muriel sees women's struggles for equality as indivisible from Aboriginal men's struggles, insisting that: 'It's not about men and women, it's about us equally reclaiming our culture and what our culture is.'

Scepticism about the women's movement, however, does not mean that Aboriginal women were or are disinterested in issues of gender equality in their communities. From Lilla Watson's point of view:

> There was and is no question that I support in strongest terms women's liberation, whether it be for black or white women . . . Black women's liberation also must be part and parcel of the whole liberation movement of black people in this country to sustain that movement, strengthen it, and hold it together. (Watson 1987: 51–2)

And, despite her own scepticism about organised feminism, Jackie Huggins is proud to be seen as 'very much a fighter for women's rights', telling me that she does not 'care what the guys think about me'. Jackie also wants to say to younger women attempting to deal with the sexism in Aboriginal political culture: 'Ride it through, stay strong, it'll pass. You get stronger in it too.' And there are certainly some young women who have learnt from feminism and who take this knowledge into their current work. One young woman I spoke to told me of an early job in a feminist organisation that she says 'opened up my mind tremendously' because she 'had to understand a bit about feminist theory' and was 'surrounded by all these really strong feminist women'. This experience gave her a framework through which she could begin to talk about her 'experiences as a woman and as a black woman and my experience as a black person', saying that 'all of a sudden' these experiences 'made sense'. In general, however, it seems simplistic and unproductive to view Aboriginal gender relations as a set of opposing men's and women's interests in a context where rights and obligations are inextricably entwined in a complex political culture (Toussaint et al. 2001: 160).

There are many Aboriginal people who would like to see the traditional gender balance between Aboriginal women and men restored. These traditions emphasise the separate spheres of men's and women's business. Jilpia Jones points out that 'women have got a role because women have their own laws, men have got their laws and there's mutual respect'. Henry Atkinson suggests that, in Yorta Yorta culture, 'women that have got knowledge of their culture and their land and are not afraid to speak out play an important part, as strong as the part the men play'. Important in this context is the need for 'women to speak about their own business' while the men 'may not even hear what that business is'. Ray Swan agrees, saying that women 'should play a big, important role'. Ray also emphasises the importance of 'men's business and women's business', and suggests that after discussing their own business in their separate spheres 'both men and women can come together at a higher level to bring up their issues together'. Ray maintains that this was the way that gender relations were managed 'before Aboriginal society was interfered with', and argues that 'it wasn't Aboriginal men who put Aboriginal women in the kitchen. It was the white manager.'

Customary law as a resource

It is not possible to make conclusive statements about intra-community violence in pre-invasion Aboriginal society. It is also not necessary to do so. Regardless of whether or not violence was a part of traditional society, it is an unacceptable practice today. Violent individuals need to be held accountable for their behaviour, and it cannot be acceptable to anyone—black or white—that customary law be abused as a form of defence. But the gender relations that underpin much violence are complex and inextricably tied to Australia's colonial past. Understanding these complexities, and their relationship to history, is an essential step in reducing the incidence of violence. As Tom Calma has argued in his role as Aboriginal and Torres Strait Islander Social Justice Commissioner: 'Family violence and abuse is about lack of respect for Indigenous culture. We need to fight it as Indigenous peoples, and rebuild our proud traditions and community structures so that there is no place for fear and intimidation.' (ATSISJC 2006b: 5) Calma also recognises that this process of rebuilding will require a 'multi-pronged approach' in which breaches of rights such as family violence are not tolerated, but which also ensures that communities are properly resourced and supported 'to increase their capacity to address these issues'. Calma insists: 'This is not an either/or choice . . .' (ATSISJC 2007a: 5)

In these struggles, customary law is a resource, not a problem. Recognition of customary law has the potential to strengthen Aboriginal community governance and may also help to alleviate the over-representation of Aboriginal people in Australia's gaols through the implementation of restorative justice mechanisms (Anderson 2002: 3). If aspects of customary law do perpetuate harmful practices, they can—and must—be challenged to adapt to new values and new understandings of human rights (ATSISJC 2006b: 52). At times, the struggle for greater equality between Aboriginal women and men will mean challenging traditional hierarchies and becoming free from archaic traditions. Such tensions are common in Indigenous movements the world over (Havemann 2000: 24–5). Nonetheless, it is not necessary to throw the baby out with the bath water. Restoring the traditions and authority structures of Aboriginal customary law may do much to restore self-esteem and pride for many people—particularly men, for whom colonisation has been a damaging and degrading experience. Too many Aboriginal people are still dealing with past trauma, and mourning the loss and destruction of their culture. As the next chapter will consider, revitalising Aboriginal culture will do much to heal these wounds.

11
MOURNING AND
RECONCILIATION

Over recent decades, Aboriginal leaders and activists have prioritised the telling of Australia's colonial history in an uncensored fashion. Public reports such as the Royal Commission into Aboriginal Deaths in Custody (RCIADIC 1991),[1] the Stolen Generations inquiry (HREOC 1997) and other efforts to foreground Aboriginal experiences have contributed to a new, if contested, awareness among the broader Australian community of the extent of past injustices. There is some awareness, too, of the extent of unresolved and ongoing trauma that is the legacy of our colonial past. The formal reconciliation process, discussed in Chapter 1, was intended to address these wrongs and to begin the healing process. Instead, there was a concerted effort by the Howard government to have our 'black' history labelled a 'black armband view of history'.[2] Howard himself consistently refused all demands that he apologise to Aboriginal people for past policies. Under Howard's leadership, the grass-roots movement to resolve these issues, most publicly expressed in the mass walk over the Sydney Harbour Bridge in 2000, degenerated into the so-called 'history wars', leaving questions of mourning, healing and a way forward fundamentally unresolved.

Given the struggles of the last decade, some Aboriginal leaders and activists have argued that it is time to move on from mourning the past to a more celebratory focus on the survival of Indigenous peoples and culture. As Martin Nakata has suggested, perhaps a new 'narrative of survival' will take Indigenous people further than a 'narrative of cultural loss' (Nakata 2004: 15). However, there are still many Aboriginal people who are unwilling or unable to celebrate or move on without the symbolic healing that was the focus of the reconciliation process. For Patrick Dodson, for example, the 'mourning period' can only come to an end when 'the proper protocols and practical arrangements have been carried out' (2000: 15). The failure to apologise for past injustices and to fully implement the recommendations of the final report from the Council for Aboriginal Reconciliation (CAR 2000) was a significant stumbling block in this process, finally overcome with the Rudd government's apology in February 2008. But, as Dodson also points out, moving through what he calls 'the mourning gate' is 'not about a fresh event, it is about a continuing state of being for the Government and the society' (2000: 15).

National days of celebration or commemoration often provide a focus for these issues. While 26 January, for example, is Australia Day for non-Aboriginal Australia, it is Survival Day or Invasion Day for Aboriginal people. For many Aboriginal people this day is, as Gary Foley has suggested, 'perpetually a day of mourning'. Michael Mansell has also argued that Australia Day 'should be abandoned as a day for celebration' because it meant Australians were celebrating 'the benefits to one race at the expense of another' (both quoted in Harvey 2005). Jackie Huggins has spoken of her own feelings about the day:

> It's a day of reflection and mourning, a time to think about what the invasion of their country meant for my ancestors, and on the terrible suffering that continues for many Indigenous Australians . . . It may seem strange that someone as optimistic as I am should use this day to focus on the negatives, but for one day each year I allow myself to think this way. (Reconciliation Australia 2006)

Many Aboriginal people, like Jackie, need time and space to remember and mourn the actions of the past. Tom Calma understands the significance of days like Survival Day and Sorry Day[3] for this process of mourning, although he worries that for many people this is also a process of 'reinforcing and reliving' feelings of loss that some people 'may have thought that they'd put behind them through healing processes'. Tom has publicly expressed his concern that events like the tenth anniversary of the *Bringing Them Home* report 'raised the ghosts of those experiences—the trauma, the grief and the memories—which, left unresolved, can re-traumatise people and create a "limbo" world in which they have not been able to go home' (quoted in *Koori Mail* 2007b). For too many Aboriginal people mourning seems to continue with no resolution, and with no real possibility for the healing that they need.

Mourning and healing

It has been over ten years since the 1997 release of *Bringing Them Home*, the report of the National Inquiry into the Separation of Aboriginal and Torres Strait Islander Children from Their Families. This seminal report documented the tragic and often horrific stories of the many thousands of Aboriginal children taken from their families—children who were subsequently institutionalised, sent into domestic service, adopted by white families, and in other ways denied their identities and their culture. The removal of children has become the most well-known aspect of assimiliation policy, aimed—at least in part—at destroying Aboriginal identity by educating Aboriginal children in non-Aboriginal homes and institutions (Bradley and Seton 2005: 38). The report, according to Mick Dodson, documented the 'deliberate theft' of Aboriginal cultural identity by removing the children from families and communities and by removing 'the next generations from their land' (Dodson 2007a: 4).

The taking of Aboriginal children from their families has been described as genocidal, although for some this language seems inflammatory in the Australian context: genocide belongs to Hitler and the Jews, not Australia and the Aborigines. But as Carmel Bird points out, one of the definitions of genocide is 'the forcible transferring of children of a group to another group'. Bird argues that: 'A state cannot excuse itself by claiming that the practice of genocide was previously lawful under its own laws or that its people did not (or do not) share the outrage of the international community.' (Bird 1998: 6) Regardless of one's assessment of the genocidal implications of child removal, the fact remains that Aboriginal children were unjustly taken from their families as a result of race-based policy, and that Aboriginal people are still experiencing the shockwaves of trauma from these acts today.

In the introduction to this book, I wrote of my own experiences of confronting the reality of the contemporary impact of past policies of child removal. Aboriginal people do not have to confront this fact; they live with it every day. Documented effects of child removal include:

- the grief of parents and family for the child or children removed;
- the interruption to family and community structure when children have been taken;
- the loss of identity, of rightful place in family, of ties with family, community and culture of the children removed;
- the anxiety of the search for family and identity;
- the turmoil, for all, of trying to fit each other back into each other's lives; and
- the pain and anger when this doesn't happen as it was hoped, or if it can't happen at all (Hermeston 2005: 480).

The trauma of past policies continues to affect a huge number of Aboriginal people. Aboriginal trauma expert Judy Atkinson has argued that policies of child removal have produced a group of:

profoundly hurt people living with multiple layers of traumatic distress, chronic anxiety, physical ill-health, mental distress, fears, depressions, substance abuse, and high imprisonment rates. For many, alcohol and other drugs have become the treatment of choice, because there is no other treatment available. (Atkinson 2002: 70)

It is also clear, as Carmel Bird has argued, that the 'complex, ongoing and compounding effects of the [child] separations' have produced an intergenerational 'cycle of damage' from which it is 'profoundly difficult to escape' (Bird 1998: 12). It is not possible, as Aden Ridgeway has pointed out, to 'treat the symptoms of dysfunction in isolation from the historic causes' (Ridgeway 2003: 189). Kevin Gilbert once observed that it is not possible to 'look down on black people while you understand the historical reasons that have reduced them to what they are' (Gilbert 2002: 11). As Jackie Huggins has argued: 'Grief, trauma and sorry business set the pace in too many of our communities. So much so that it can seem like we are in the midst of some endless war, where the calls bearing bad news never stop coming.' (Huggins 2007)

In a blistering speech to mark the tenth anniversary of the *Bringing Them Home* report, Lowitja O'Donoghue argued that Aboriginal people are still 'dying of despair' resulting from child removal, 'while those in power look the other way' (O'Donoghue 2007). Tom Calma has also suggested that the tenth anniversary combined with the first successful damages case by a member of the Stolen Generations[4] should remind all Australians that 'the reality of Australia's Stolen Generation is not a thing of the past. Its reverberations are felt every day in every Aboriginal community, in every capital city and in every regional centre by Aboriginal people of all walks of life and of all ages.' (quoted in Dornin 2007)

Concern with these issues was very high among the majority of my interviewees. Like many Aboriginal people, Geoff Scott recognises that the 'mourning issues'—by which he means the issues of deaths in custody and the Stolen Generations—'won't go away, not until they're acknowledged and dealt with'. Alwyn McKenzie told of his mother, who he says 'gets a bit tired of telling the stories; she's Stolen Generation and it hurts her all the time'. Robbie Thorpe spoke of the 'mental stress amongst Aboriginal people'. Paul Briggs suggested that Aboriginal people need to better understand 'what's happened to us over the last 200 years, the generational hand down of grief and trauma and its impact on the way in which Aboriginal people live'. Dr Marika also referred to 'intergenerational trauma and grief and suffering', and argued that Aboriginal people 'should be compensated for all those things, not marginalised'. Dr Marika had herself had personal experience of these impacts, telling me she had developed 'a lot of anxiety and mental depression' because of all the deaths in her family, leaving her unable to work or sleep. Her own premature death in May 2008 from a heart condition at the age of forty-nine added another devastating layer of grief to her Yirrkala community.

For many Aboriginal people, these traumas are also a part of their community's recent past, with experiences of dispossession still within their parents' memories and often even within their own lifetimes (Goodall 1996: 338). Marvyn McKenzie points out that 'there's a lot of people still living today who are still hurting from the impact from the things that have happened'. From his time working in the Northern Territory, Marvyn knows that there are people still alive there who remember 'that period when they was rounded up and shot'. Larissa Behrendt has recalled the way the past lives on in her family: 'I remember our elder, Granny Green (my own grandmother's cousin), taking me and my father across the paddocks and pointing out the spiritual places but also the sites of our more recent history where children were stolen or, as she would tell us in whispers, where massacres had taken place.' (Behrendt 2006: 6–7)

Tom Calma has also observed the continuing impact of recent history, noting in our interview that, in many communities, 'the history is still there, people are still there from the time that they were taken away'. Tom is frustrated that too often it is possible to 'just forget about those people and expect them to just fit in now'. Like many others, Tom acknowledges that until the 'psychological impacts' of trauma are addressed 'we're not going to have a more settled Aboriginal population'. Like Tom, Geoff Scott sees the effects of trauma in many Aboriginal people, and is frustrated that this is never properly addressed despite all the medical evidence that points to this need. Geoff argues that:

> Every sort of modern psychology will tell you trauma will keep coming back until people deal with it. You might put it out of your mind for a while, but it'll come back again. Strong people can do it, they can block out whole sections of their memory in life and move on. But the easier way is to be mature enough to say that yes, there were atrocities, there were the wrong things done. Admit it.

Judy Atkinson has argued that the 'layered trauma' that is the legacy of colonisation is today expressed in 'dysfunctional' and 're-traumatising', sometimes violent behaviour (Atkinson 2002: 24). However, not all Aboriginal people accept that past trauma explains or justifies current anti-social behaviour. Colleen Hayward, for example, accepts that her view will put her 'at odds' with other leaders and activists, but maintains that:

> I can understand that people who have been dispossessed—and that's all of us—racially abused, punished and damaged in the process of colonis-ation will feel the negative impact of those things. What I don't buy is [the argument] that how that manifests in your behaviour is outside your choice. Can I feel angry and really strong about something? Of course, I do! I mean I don't feel half-hearted about anything. Does that mean I'm going to go home and bash somebody that I'm supposed to love? Or abuse a child? Or damage somebody that I don't even know because I feel like I need to lash

out? Those are all unacceptable behaviours. Should people who are damaged in that way and lash out have ever been damaged? No, of course not. But what we do with that is our choice. That's true self-determination.

Noel Pearson has made a similar point, arguing that 'the wrongs of the past are not the reasons our people are in jail and our children in care'. In Pearson's view, Australia's brutal history 'might provide an explanation for the position we are in but it doesn't provide a solution'. Pearson urges other Aboriginal people to focus on the immediate problems in their communities, saying he could 'sit around and cry as much as I like about historical reasons for our situation' but that this will not provide answers to contemporary social issues (quoted in Hodder 2005: 19). Pearson insists that explanations for contemporary dysfunction that emphasise what he calls the 'structural violence of history' do not lend themselves to policy solutions today, arguing that 'we have to deal with what we face now' (Pearson 2007a: 53). Marcia Langton agrees, arguing that irrespective of historical trauma, Aboriginal people must take responsibility for their own behaviour, claiming that 'it is the practices of Aboriginal people themselves that transform mere poverty into a living hell' (Langton 2008a: 160).

Part of what Pearson and Langton are responding to is the charge of cultural relativism, or the suggestion that Aboriginal people should be treated differently before the law simply because they are Aboriginal. Marcia Langton has decried the response to Aboriginal dysfunction that takes account of past trauma as 'sentimental, blame-shifting nonsense' that 'dehumanises' Aboriginal people (Langton 2007). This is a complex and fraught argument. On the one hand, it can indeed be seen as racist to expect a different standard of behaviour from Aboriginal people than would be expected of non-Aboriginal people. From this perspective, one might demand that the criminal justice system, for example, should respond to Aboriginal offenders in precisely the same way as it would respond to non-Aboriginal offenders. But if one takes into account the well-documented intergenerational effects of trauma, this argument becomes less convincing. There is a difference between cultural relativism that is based in racist views about the innate predisposition of a people—a view that might see Aboriginal people as more 'savage' or somehow unable to stop themselves from committing violent crimes— or Pearson's view that a strong criminal justice response is required to

restore social norms in Aboriginal communities, and a view that recognises the pointlessness of responding to damaged people by subjecting
them to further damage in the prison system. Prison *cannot* respond
to the deep and unresolved rage that many Aboriginal people express
through their offending behaviour. Unless offenders are to be incarcer-
ated for life, they will return to their communities more damaged than
when they left. It is not cultural relativism to demand of Australian
society a more sophisticated response to this situation. It is certainly not
racist to suggest that governments should listen to what so many Aboriginal people themselves are asking for: the services and support they
need to heal, and a criminal justice system that incorporates successful
cultural models of restorative justice.

Instead of this response, however, there has been a fundamental failure
to properly recognise and mourn the losses experienced by Aboriginal
people during the last 220 years (Attwood 2005: 194). Irene Watson has
pointed out that Australia does not even have 'remembrance shrines' that
'recognise the demise of Aboriginal peoples'. Instead, Watson argues,
there is 'a mass denial that it even happened' (Watson 2007: 29). Amidst
the other traumas of colonisation, Aboriginal people have also experienced the 'denigration and destruction' of their traditional ceremonial
processes for healing from trauma. This means that the feelings of
distress that accompany loss and devastation remain as 'destructive forces
within the land and the people' (Atkinson 2002: 35). In the absence of
memorials, ceremony and the associated respect for Aboriginal trauma
and loss, for many Aboriginal people the pain continues.

What still hurts

Traumatic aspects of Australia's colonial history are often talked about as
though they were long ago. It would be nice—for Aboriginal and non-
Aboriginal people alike—to think that those times were indeed behind
us as a nation. Sadly, this is not true. The 2008 apology was an important step in the right direction but there is still a long way to go in this
regard. Our failure to properly address past harms and to resolve national
sentiment about our history means that it lives on in the present. We are
diminished as a nation by this failure, and Aboriginal people continue to
be wounded by racism and a lack of recognition in the present.

The so-called 'history wars', which erupted with the publication of
conservative historian Keith Windschuttle's book *The Fabrication of*

Aboriginal History (2002), caused considerable pain to Aboriginal people. Windschuttle attempted to discredit certain historical accounts of massacres of Aboriginal people, most notably the work of Henry Reynolds and Lyndall Ryan. His work was a response to critical historical accounts of Australia's colonial history that had emerged since the 1970s and had persuaded many Australians that stories of Australian nation-building were incomplete without acknowledgment of the suffering of Aboriginal people (Goot and Rowse 2007: 150). These critical accounts had 'struck at the heart' of Australian national identity, creating a 'crisis of legitimacy' and exposing Australia's failings to deal with our history in a just and moral way (Attwood and Magowan 2001: xv). Windschuttle's work found a receptive political audience, particularly in then prime minister John Howard who himself had insisted that Australian history should be told as a positive story, emphasising nation-building, and relegating past treatment of Aboriginal people to the status of an unfortunate 'blemish' (Sanders 2006: 50). Patrick Dodson has suggested that, from the viewpoint of advocates such as Howard and Windschuttle, the very existence of Aboriginal people in contemporary Australia has been an 'affront' to the nation's institutional foundations, weakening the capacity of the nation to celebrate its achievements through the fear that the 'issues of unfinished business between us would surface and detract from the moment' (Dodson 2000: 15).

The telling of Australian history remains deeply personal for many Aboriginal people. In Tony Birch's view, the most common response to Australia's colonial history has been one of 'official denial and collective and complicit amnesia' that has established a 'sanitised colonial memory' (Birch 2007: 108, 110). Lowitja O'Donoghue has suggested that the time for this sort of denialism is past, and has argued that governments must 'accept the history of this country . . . The history wars, they need to stop, the denials need to stop' (quoted in Parker 2007). Alwyn McKenzie describes Windschuttle's work as 'deflating', and expresses his pain at a white historian trying to 'make a lie out of stories that a lot of elder Aboriginal people have told from personal experience about atrocities that were committed'. Marvyn McKenzie is disturbed by the teaching of history in school that leaves Aboriginal people as 'the natives on the sidelines of history' when there is still 'truth that needs to be told'. Eugenia Flynn expresses the anger and frustration that so many Aboriginal people still feel at the failure to acknowledge their history. Without this acknowledgment, says Eugenia, 'you can't be healed':

> Sometimes you just get really angry like, 'Bloody hell, you people don't realise that everything that you have right now and the successes and the wealth that you enjoy comes off the backs of blacks!' People don't acknowledge that this was ours to begin with. It's like stealing someone's child or something and just refusing to acknowledge that ever happened.

The lack of recognition of colonial history is compounded by a feeling of marginalisation that many of my interviewees attributed to persistent racist attitudes in the wider Australian society. Muriel Bamblett, for example, expressed the view that white Australians 'aren't proud of us, they actually don't like us', and she particularly worries about the impact of these sentiments on Aboriginal kids in the playground. Songwriter Bob Randall has made a similar point, expressing his sadness that Australia is 'such a racist country. The majority of people who are here would rather see us not around any more.' (quoted in *Koori Mail* 2007b). The media are thought to be the most persistent culprit in perpetuating negative views of Aboriginal people, an issue raised by my interviewees in no uncertain terms. In Muriel Bamblett's view, the media are:

> the ones that persecute us, they're the ones depriving us of rights, they're the ones that are disempowering us. They actually make us hated in our own country . . . The only time you ever read anything it's bad . . . The media has to change and they have to be held accountable for what they're doing to Indigenous people in this country.

Dr Marika made the same point: 'We only hear all these negative things you know and all these negative comments . . . You know media is really bad, yeah. It has given the wider public a negative perspective of what Yolngu people are. They always pick on us, the Indigenous people of this country, the Aboriginal people.' Alwyn McKenzie agrees, expressing his view that 'the biggest enemy of Aboriginal people is the media', who 'always want a bad news story' while 'disregarding all of the good work over the years'. According to Alwyn: 'Papers like *The Australian* will just grab the headlines and see some small community where there might be petrol sniffing and that's the thing that they'll put in the paper and say, "That's the problem with Aboriginal people."'

Several of my interviewees also spoke of the sort of racism they have to confront individually in their daily lives. Eugenia Flynn is of the view that 'a lot of white Australians have fooled themselves into thinking that Australia isn't racist or that Australian people can't be racist' when the daily experience of many Aboriginal people tells a different story. Colleen Hayward agrees, recounting the story of a Friday night out with friends that ended in confrontation after a woman was 'loudly supportive of [Pauline] Hanson and Hanson's policies', spouting 'every negative stereotype that you could imagine'. For Colleen, the experience was:

> so abrasive and so offensive that I couldn't ignore it to enjoy my evening. And you toss up, do you say something? Do you leave? Do you ignore it? And as I'm deciding I don't think I can stay there any longer, this woman went to the loo, and I took the opportunity to follow her, and I said to her, 'Look, you don't know me, but I'm sitting in a bar trying to enjoy a drink as well, and you're there saying things about me, and you don't even know me! And I want you to know that when you say that Aboriginal people are like this and like that, that we don't work, that we don't shower, that we have no respect, that we're all alcoholic—you're talking about me, you're talking about my brothers and sisters, you're talking about my family, you're talking about my father, you're talking about my grandparents, and you need to know how hurtful that is.'

There are many, many such stories that are part of the daily lives of Aboriginal people: taxis that refuse to stop and pick up Aboriginal passengers, shop assistants who refuse service or falsely accuse Aboriginal customers of theft, real estate agents claiming that a rental property is no longer available once they have seen the colour of the prospective tenants' skin, verbal abuse in the streets, and so on. In March 2008, a group of sixteen Aboriginal women from Yuendumu in the Northern Territory who had travelled to Alice Springs to attend Royal Life Saving Society swimming classes were ordered to leave a hostel because of their skin colour. The women were deeply embarrassed, but angry enough to go public and demand an apology (ABC 2008). Experiences such as these are a constant, daily endurance test for many Aboriginal people all over Australia.

Yet it is in this context of ongoing racism and a denigration of their history that many Aboriginal people have chosen to take a more positive view and celebrate their survival. For many, there is an emphasis on the history of Aboriginal resistance, which several interviewees equated with white Australia's celebration of the ANZACs. Jilpia Jones responds to arguments about the 'black armband' view of Australia's history with the view that 'if that's what people say, they'd better get rid of the memory of Gallipoli'. Marvyn McKenzie also makes the point that ANZAC celebrations 'remember the thing that shaped your [white] culture, that shaped your character'. He argues that for Aboriginal people, 'our character was shaped when we resisted'. Indeed, survival and resistance have become an essential component of Aboriginality (Peters-Little 2000: 4). Mick Dodson has pointed out that Aboriginal people draw a different relationship with their past to the one that has been 'imposed' on them, arguing that 'one is an act of resistance, the other is a tool in the politics of domination and oppression' (Dodson 2003a: 40). Mudrooroo has also argued that those who 'fought long and hard have become part of our history' (Mudrooroo 1995: 194). Muriel Bamblett fears that aspects of this history of resistance will be lost because 'there's not even any attempt to preserve it and you know, it's slipping away every day'.

Another important reason for emphasising Aboriginal survival is the sheer difficulty of reliving pain and trauma through commemorations that emphasise mourning. Colleen Hayward thinks there needs to be a 'mix' of mourning and celebration, but stresses that for many people mourning is incredibly difficult:

> Sorry Day after Sorry Day after Sorry Day, I would see people bereft. The people telling their stories were bereft in terms of all of the memories and pain that was evoked . . . We can't pretend that bad things haven't happened but I think it needs to be combined with our hopes and aspirations and actions towards a positive future. It's got to be both.

Tom Calma also feels that it is important to emphasise 'the positive side' of Aboriginal lives in order to show the wider community 'that we are taking control of our own affairs'. Aden Ridgeway has suggested that Aboriginal people 'should be more willing to celebrate and learn from our successes' (Ridgeway 2003: 197). Alwyn McKenzie also sees the importance of celebrating 'achievements and our survival as opposed

217

to always talking about our losses and grief and stresses'. According to Alwyn, 'too much talking about grief's not going to do anybody any good'. While mourning is important, Alwyn also sees the need for leaders and activists to 'try and inspire our people too and tell them good stories'. Lowitja O'Donoghue has made a similar argument in the past, arguing that:

> it's vitally important for us to celebrate what we have managed to achieve on behalf of our communities—partly to revitalise our own commitment to the many tasks ahead, but also as an indication to the broader community that we continue to value the rights and entitlements we possess. We have to celebrate because sometimes there seems to be so little to celebrate in Indigenous affairs. (O'Donoghue 1997: 31)

Paul Briggs suggests that, while Aboriginal people 'don't celebrate enough', he also thinks: 'We're not celebrated enough either . . . Australian society doesn't celebrate Indigenous people.' Paul would like to see a future where celebrations of Aboriginal culture involve 'not only having Aboriginal people in a park on their own but the mainstream institutions engaging in the celebration of Indigenous identity'. This is an important point. Paul is expressing a desire felt by many Aboriginal people to move out of the margins of Australian society and celebrate and be celebrated as making an important contribution to the life of this country. There are many obstacles to seeing this desire fulfilled, but a significant one for Aboriginal people is the resolution of unfinished business.

Unfinished business

Mick Dodson has described the concept of unfinished business as being about 'confronting the legacy of the past and re-aligning the relationship between Aboriginal and Torres Strait Islander people and government and the peoples of Australia' (Dodson 2003c: 31). At its heart, this goal is simple. Aboriginal people seek what Geoff Scott describes as 'the lasting settlement of our outstanding issues':

> When they are settled, we'll be able to put those things behind us. While they're continuing to be attacked and ignored and not recognised, they will not go away because their impacts are with us today and people feel

them every day . . . I don't think they'll go away until you get that lasting settlement of the issues. For as long as you refuse to do it, for as long as government try and find the cheap, easy way out, it won't happen.

For many Aboriginal people, the making of a treaty or some other form of agreement between their nation or nations and the Commonwealth government would be a significant step towards resolving the unfinished business. A treaty may allow some form of redress for the sense of grievance and injustice that still runs so deep for many Aboriginal people (Brennan et al. 2005: 122). Mick Dodson has argued that the need for a treaty is based on the recognition that Aboriginal people 'have been injured and harmed throughout the colonisation process and just recompense is owed' (2003c: 33). Sam Watson maintains a passionate argument that until a treaty is signed 'between the so-called Australian government and the 500 tribal nations of this land', the Australian state remains illegitimate. In our interview, Sam argued that:

until that treaty is signed the history of the Australian Commonwealth and the States *cannot even begin*. The federation of the Australian colonies in 1901 should not have happened because there was no treaty signed by the invading white culture . . . To this day, to this moment, not one Aboriginal nation out of those 500 nations has ever ceded or surrendered sovereignty. So until that treaty is signed with those 500 nations, history cannot begin.

Robbie Thorpe agrees, telling me that a treaty is 'a healing thing' and arguing that it would 'create a foundation of law to grow from. If you want to grow on *terra nullius* you're not going to grow very far. You're going to be found out to be a racist, pariah state at the end of the day. So if you want to go down the proper channels where everyone is treated equally you've got to have a treaty.' For Henry Atkinson, the denial of native title to the Yorta Yorta only underscores the need for formal recognition of Aboriginal people's status. Henry would like to see 'some type of treaty that gives recognition to Indigenous Australians as being the traditional owners of this country. At the moment that's denied to us . . . So a treaty or sovereignty to this country. That's what I'd really like to see.'

Talk of a treaty or treaties has long been a part of Aboriginal political culture. Claims have taken various forms, some secessionist, some conciliatory. Some views have conflicted with others—for example, the NAC's announcement that it would negotiate a 'Makarrata',[5] rather than a treaty, was greeted with scorn by others, including Kevin Gilbert, who argued that a Makarrata was an unacceptable compromise, a mere 'agreement' between white government and 'rubbish men', in contrast to a treaty between sovereign nations (Gilbert 1980). Gilbert, in consultation with the Sovereign Aboriginal Coalition, went on to develop a draft treaty that called for the creation of a sovereign and autonomous Aboriginal state, which comprised a land base of 'not less than forty percent of the land mass of each "Australian State"' (Gilbert 1988: 53). Gilbert's draft was a central component of the Treaty '88 campaign. Also in 1988, the then prime minister, Bob Hawke, was presented with the Barunga Statement, and in response signed a statement in which he undertook to negotiate a treaty with Aboriginal people. Hawke reneged on this agreement, however, and the treaty did not come to pass. Despite efforts by ATSIC to revive the issue in the 1990s (see ATSIC 1995a), and by CAR at the Corroboree 2000 event, it was not possible to engage mainstream politicians in the debate during the term of the Howard government. During this time, discussion was reduced to what Lester-Irabinna Rigney describes as a 'bread versus freedom' debate (Rigney 2002), with the alleged symbolism of a treaty set in opposition to so-called 'practical reconciliation'.

In 2008, the question of treaty or other legal agreement, including the possibility of embedding the recognition of Aboriginal and Torres Strait Islander peoples in the body of the Australian Constitution, was revived in political debate during the Indigenous stream at the new prime minister's 2020 Summit. As a participant in that stream, I witnessed an emerging consensus on the issues of legal recognition, prefaced by a commitment to a national dialogue on the issue. The discussion was poorly reported, both in the final plenary of the Summit and in the media over the following days. There was no division between those wanting a treaty and those wanting constitutional reform. Indeed, at the end of the first day of the Summit the 100 Indigenous and non-Indigenous delegates had agreed on three priority areas, each of which went to the heart of the question of 'unfinished business'. These three priorities were:

1. Initiating a national dialogue towards formalising a legal basis for the relationship between Indigenous and non-Indigenous Australia. Whether this took the form of a treaty or other legal agreement, or reform to the body (as opposed to the preamble) of the Constitution was unresolved, although by the end of the second day a strong preference for Constitutional reform seemed to have emerged.

2. The creation of a reconstruction fund, perhaps based on a percentage of GDP, that would be directed towards the rebuilding of core services in Aboriginal communities, providing improved health and education initiatives and direct services to families and the development of an Aboriginal healing fund. This was linked to the establishment of an Aboriginal and Torres Strait Islander Productivity Commission to oversee expenditure of government funding and the relative outcomes in addressing disadvantage.

3. Prioritising the development of a new cultural framework for Australia that places Aboriginal culture at the centre through the creation of a Cultural Heritage Authority. New national symbols were suggested, including a new national holiday to commemorate the apology, along with prioritising the digitisation of Aboriginal language and culture to ensure its survival.

How the Rudd government responds to these priorities will have crucial implications well into the future for the health, well-being and status of Aboriginal people in Australia.

Reconciliation

Chapter 1 detailed the development and derailment of reconciliation under the Howard government, through which Aboriginal people's psycho-emotional needs for recognition and healing were neglected in favour of the so-called 'practical reconciliation' agenda (Altman and Hunter 2003: 14).[6] But can a government really derail a process that is essentially between peoples, a process aimed at 'the removal of enmity and the restoration of harmonious relations' (Pratt et al. 2001: 136)? Mick Dodson has said that he often hears people say that 'reconciliation is dead', a statement that he says he finds 'deeply irritating and a bit of a cop out' (Dodson 2007c). If reconciliation is to have any meaning in Australia it requires that, as a nation, we face up to our history in ways that will allow all of us to move forward, psychologically and politically

(Brennan et al. 2005: 122). We have not done this. Instead we continue, as David Cooper has argued, to 'paper over the darker aspects' of this history by 'shifting blame to those most affected' (Cooper 2005: 15).

The concept of reconciliation is deeply ambivalent for many Aboriginal people. Yuin elder Max Dulumunmun Harrison believes the word to be 'a falseness' and 'a lie' because 'there has never been a partnership in the first place to reconcile about' (quoted in McConchie 2003: 1). Les Malezer has suggested that reconciliation 'does not challenge the sentiment of the racist' (Malezer 2002). In one of the last interviews before his death, Kevin Gilbert expressed this view with force: 'What are we to reconcile ourselves to? To a holocaust, to massacre, to the removal of us from our land, from the taking of our land? The reconciliation process can achieve nothing because it does not at the end of the day promise justice.' (quoted in Mudrooroo 1995: 228) Irene Watson has asked similar questions more recently, wondering:

> what does reconciliation really mean? Will it provide homes for the homeless, food for the hungry, land for the dispossessed, language and culture for those hungry to revive from stolen and dispossessed spaces? How can you become reconciled with a state and its citizens who have not yet acknowledged your humanity, let alone your status as the first peoples of this conquered land? (Watson 2007: 20)

Today, Eugenia Flynn worries that reconciliation has become 'just about white Australians using it as a process to deal with their guilt', which she points out 'really takes from Indigenous people as much as historically white Australia has taken from Indigenous people': 'I think that the good elements of reconciliation are the acknowledgment of injustices and the commitment to moving forward. But I think the rest of it is just warm and fuzzy stuff that isn't going to effect any real change.'

Key to a meaningful process of reconciliation is what has been referred to as the 'unsettling' of non-Aboriginal Australia. One significant component of the unsettling that needs to occur is for non-Aboriginal Australians to come to appreciate the many ways in which they have benefited and continue to benefit from Aboriginal dispossession. Contemporary Australia has built much of its wealth, particularly in the pastoral and mining industries, on land 'that was stolen in sometimes vicious, illegal and deceitful actions' (Behrendt 2007b: 11). Klynton

Wanganeen argues that non-Aboriginal people 'may not have made those policies, they may not have made the decisions and they may not have done the dispossessing, but the rewards and everything that they have today is a direct result of that'.

Several of my interviewees emphasised their belief that a true reconciliation process could yet have the opportunity to change the country at a deep level by opening the hearts and minds of many non-Aboriginal people. Colleen Hayward feels strongly that even people with strong racist opinions 'need a chance to change their views'. Colleen's views echo Paul Briggs' sentiments about the need for reconciliation to go beyond the work of governments. Paul suggests that any relationship with government is 'unhealthy if it's devoid of any other levels of communication with Australian people'. Crucial in developing better relationships is what Paul calls 'cultural literacy', or a concerted effort to do away with the ignorance that 'underpins the relationships that Aboriginal people have with the broader community'—an ignorance 'fed by stereotypes and myths that have been handed down over generations'. Larissa Behrendt makes a similar point, suggesting that in this regard Australia has a long way to go to recover the lost ground of the Howard years:

> It's just such a crucial thing to be able to somehow educate and also open people's hearts to this idea. And I'm not sure that we know how to do that yet because I think there's been decades and decades of attempts to work on that and nothing has really broken through. There was a sense [in the 1990s] that people were becoming aware of this history and were taking it on board as part of the national story, but we couldn't be further from that today. So you have to really question how deep that commitment or interest or concern was when Paul Keating gave the Redfern Park speech[7] . . . How deep did that go into the community? It seems to me John Howard was able to delve much more deeply into the Australian psyche by reverting to [the idea of] the white man struggling against the elements than Keating was ever able to when he showed such leadership on reconciliation. And that's a tragedy.

What comes after sorry?

Another fundamental step in resolving unfinished business was the long-awaited apology from the Commonwealth government to members of the Stolen Generations. Despite the recommendations of *Bringing Them Home*, one of which was that all Australian governments should officially and publicly apologise to the Stolen Generations for the harms done by past policies, the Howard government consistently refused to give an official apology on behalf of the Australian parliament. Howard was unmoved by the thousands of people around the country who signed 'Sorry Books' as their own personal way of apologising, or by the making of an apology by all state parliaments. Eventually Howard compromised enough to work with then Senator Aden Ridgeway to craft a statement of 'regret', which was passed in the parliament in August 1999. For most Aboriginal people, however, this statement had little meaning given Howard's insistence that it was not an apology.

Many members of the Stolen Generations have articulated the importance of an apology. Val Wenberg, for example, stressed that: 'Sorry is very important to me . . . We are not free from past wrongs until we get a national apology. If we get that apology, my spirit can rest.' (quoted in *Koori Mail* 2005c). Kurijinpi Ivan McPhee expressed similar feelings, saying: 'And till today we still upset. We very, very feel upset that no one told us sorry.' (quoted in KALACC 2006: 129) Geoff Scott also saw that an apology was important in terms of recognition, arguing that 'a lot of the people in the Stolen Generations, all they want is acknowledgment that yes, this did happen'. Over time, however, it became clear that Aboriginal people would no longer accept an apology from Howard, a view reflected by several of my interviewees. Klynton Wanganeen expressed the view that an apology from the Howard government would have been 'useless' and 'hollow', telling me that if Howard 'wrote an apology, it wouldn't be worth the paper it's written on' because there would be 'no empathy or feeling behind it'. Alison Anderson made a similar point, asking:

> Why are we waiting for some whitefella to legitimise the fact that these atrocities happened? We know that, so let's move on . . . Why do you want John Howard to say sorry to you? Because all you're doing is you're getting it from the person that doesn't feel the pain, the person that didn't go through the pain. So why do you legitimise him as a person that will stand up and say sorry?

Many other Aboriginal people came to feel similarly ambivalent about the notion of an apology, and the importance such a statement had taken on in the national imagination. In response to these concerns, 2007 also saw the formation of a new national organisation that was set up as an alternative to the National Sorry Day Committee (NSDC). The group's convenor, Debra Hocking, said the new organisation was formed to highlight other priorities for Stolen Generation members, saying:

> While we acknowledge that we still do not have a formal apology by the Prime Minister, there are other aspects from the *Bringing Them Home* report that need addressing . . . We still have high respect and regard for the Sorry Day Committee, but I think that for the healing of this country, if we're going to be held up by one person refusing to give an apology, then it's holding us all back. (quoted in Boase 2007)

Despite these misgivings, however, the change of government in November 2007 put the issue of a national apology firmly back on the agenda, and on 13 February 2008 the newly elected prime minister, Kevin Rudd, made good on his election promise that he would make a formal apology to the Stolen Generations. During the first sitting of the new parliament, Rudd made a moving speech in the House of Representatives that produced an outpouring of emotion around the country. The key moment came early in the speech, with the central acknowledgment that:

> The time has now come for the nation to turn a new page in Australia's history by righting the wrongs of the past and so moving forward with confidence to the future. We apologise for the laws and policies of successive parliaments and governments that have inflicted profound grief, suffering and loss on these our fellow Australians. We apologise especially for the removal of Aboriginal and Torres Strait Islander children from their families, their communities and their country. For the pain, suffering and hurt of these Stolen Generations, their descendants and for their families left behind, we say sorry. To the mothers and the fathers, the brothers and the sisters, for the breaking up of families and communities, we say sorry. And for the indignity and degradation thus inflicted on a proud people and a proud culture, we say sorry. (Rudd 2008)

The apology was very well received, with Lowitja O'Donoghue describing it as 'wonderful, just magnificent', and Patrick Dodson putting the view that the event represented an 'epic gesture on the part of the Australian settler state to find accommodation with the dispossessed and colonised' (Dodson 2008b: 6). Marcia Langton argued that the apology would remove a 'canker' from 'the national dermis', thus allowing a 'brave new future' to open up (Langton 2008b: 221). For members of the Stolen Generations, the apology was particularly poignant. Noel Tovey expressed the view that listening to Rudd's speech was like 'this man was validating my 74 years of life' (Petty 2008: 15), while for Netta Cahill McCarthy the apology meant that 'people believe us, that this has happened and that we are not liars' (quoted in Parker 2008a).

But for some the apology was diminished by the government's refusal to accompany it with a compensation fund for victims of past policy (as recommended in the *Bringing Them Home* report), although there were a range of views on this question among Aboriginal leaders and activists. Some urged people to consider the apology and reparations as two separate issues. Mick Dodson, for example, argued that 'a parliamentary apology is one thing' but that reparations 'are another issue' that should be dealt with separately (quoted in *Koori Mail* 2007e). Marion Scrymgour agreed, claiming that the nation had 'one opportunity to get this right and I think the apology is the most symbolic and most important step in the healing process' (quoted in Ravens 2008). Michael Mansell was one of the most vociferous in arguing for the apology and reparations to be considered together, arguing that 'an absence of compensation is a contradiction of the apology' (quoted in *Coyne* 2008). But while not everyone agreed that an apology and reparations should go together, there seemed to be general agreement that reparations were required at some point, with Pat Dodson making precisely this point in a speech at the National Press Club immediately after the apology. Sam Watson suggested that the Rudd government needed to 'look at what the Tasmanian government and Victorian government have done' in setting up compensation funds, arguing that if a national fund (that would be of primary benefit to those in the Northern Territory) was not set up it would inevitably mean that compensation would be pursued through the courts (quoted in *National Indigenous Times* 2008b).

There can be absolutely no doubt that the apology was a crucial step in making amends for the past and at last beginning to heal some of the pain of our history. But as many Aboriginal people have remarked to me over the years, what really matters is what happens the day after.

We cannot imagine that one moment in time, whether it be the making of an apology or even the signing of a treaty, will be enough to address the continuing disadvantage and marginalisation experienced by so many Aboriginal people today. But these fundamental acts are, and will continue to be, essential for building new foundations in Indigenous Affairs. They are a starting point for a government committed to understanding the complexity of Aboriginal culture. As Muriel Bamblett argued in a 2007 speech:

> If we begin with listening we can relight the fire of reconciliation . . . Then the road to real reconciliation with its signposts of 'sorry' and 'treaty' can be travelled by all of us and the re-imagining of a new nation that respects and treasures the sovereignty and self-determination of its first peoples with justice and honour can begin. (Bamblett 2007)

The traumas of colonisation, including massacre, rape, starvation and introduced diseases through to policies that justified the removal of Aboriginal children from their families, are not resolved. They live on 'in the hearts, minds and souls of Aboriginal families whose ancestors survived these times' (Atkinson 2002: 64). Historian Bain Attwood emphasises the need for appropriate memorials, monuments and days of mourning through which black and white Australia can acknowledge a traumatic past and achieve a 'reinvestment in life' (Attwood 2005: 195). But Eugenia Flynn suspects that both Aboriginal and non-Aboriginal people are now wary of the reconciliation process, and that much trust has been eroded since 1996. She sees both groups avoiding confronting or unsettling each other, a problem she says is 'exactly what's in the way of moving forward'. This wariness means that, whatever approach is taken to further the reconciliation agenda, it must be pursued with generosity, patience, determination and creativity, with a central intent to replace the anger and despair experienced by many Aboriginal people every day with a strong sense of self-respect and autonomy (Fournier 2005: viii).

There is a sense of urgency in these issues that cannot be denied. Too many members of the Stolen Generations died without ever hearing an apology. Too many dispossessed elders have died without again walking on their country or being compensated for their loss. Long-term campaigners like Lowitja O'Donoghue have wondered 'why the struggle for justice has to be so hard for me and my people who are so scarred by the effects of our history and dispossession' (O'Donoghue 1997: 31). For Eugenia Flynn, these issues are personal. She says her vision for the future is a time when she and her family 'don't hurt any more':

> I don't want my dad, who's quite elderly now, to watch the news and get upset. He cries about the [intervention] stuff that is happening at the moment and for him to have worked so hard and for that to turn into nothing—it's heartbreaking, absolutely heartbreaking to see . . . Individually you hurt but as a community we're all hurting as well and it would be nice if we could be happy. That would be nice.

Geoff Scott makes the point that, at the Corroboree 2000 event at the Sydney Opera House, John Howard had the opportunity to 'change the nation'. Says Geoff, simply: 'He failed.' Yet in spite of setbacks like these, there is a persistent optimism among many Aboriginal leaders and activists that things must one day get better. Walmajari man Kurijinpi Ivan McPhee expressed these hopes thus:

> We're expecting government to say sorry to us. Stolen Generation, Reconciliation. All those things that we bin put it to government, government don't even recognise us. One day we'll have a good government to recognise us. It gonna take a long time. So far we just bin talking to a brick wall. (quoted in KALACC 2006: 73)

Perhaps we might yet have the government that Ivan imagines—a government that does have the courage to change the nation.

EPILOGUE:
LOOKING TO THE FUTURE

During the period in which this book was written, Australia celebrated a change of government. Towards the end of the election campaign the incumbent prime minister, John Howard, warned the nation that a change of government would change the country. The majority of Australia's Aboriginal population is hoping that he was right. The eleven and a half years that Howard was in office were an unmitigated disaster for Australia's Indigenous peoples, a period during which public sentiment and public policy looked backwards rather than forwards. Criticisms of his government's performance in this area have been extensively documented elsewhere (see, for example, Dodson 2004; Sanders 2005b; Maddison 2006) but as Lowitja O'Donoghue put it, Howard's record in Aboriginal affairs was, quite simply, 'woeful' (O'Donoghue 2007).

The new government led by Prime Minister Kevin Rudd may yet offer a more hopeful future for Aboriginal people, but that outcome is far from certain. The Rudd government not only inherited a troubled Indigenous Affairs portfolio, including the controversial Northern Territory 'intervention', but also faced the challenge that has met every other incoming prime minister in Australia's history. That challenge is to truly come to terms with Australia's past, to understand the impact of this past on Australia's Indigenous peoples, and to address the present-day ramifications of this past with courage, determination and a moral commitment to doing the right thing. The failure of past governments to

229

address the legacies of Australia's colonial history means that the current generation of non-Aboriginal Australians is enjoying the economic benefits of colonisation 'without the need to compensate, rectify, apologise, understand, recognise, reconcile or restructure relationships with Indigenous people' (Cronin 2007: 198). A new government is an opportunity to make these things right once and for all, but only time will tell whether the nation will seize this opportunity to deal with the unfinished business.

Expectations of Rudd and his government are high. Jawoyn woman Rachel Willika from Eva Valley in the Northern Territory took great heart from Rudd's election night commitment that he would govern for all Australians. Willika says: 'That Kevin Rudd, you can trust him. We trust him because he said he's going to be Prime Minister for all Australians . . . Now he is Prime Minister, Kevin Rudd can do something.' (Willika 2007) But exactly what a Rudd government will do over the long term remains to be seen. There have been so many false dawns for Aboriginal people in Australia, from the 1967 referendum to the promise of the 1992 *Mabo* decision. There have been moments, like the Hawke government's acceptance of the Barunga statement or Keating's Redfern Park speech, where it appeared that government and the Australian people were at last willing to engage and understand. Rudd's own apology to the Stolen Generations was another such moment. But Australia has seemed unable to grasp these moments and deliver the sort of real and lasting change that Aboriginal people so desperately need (Dodson 2000: 8). A new government is no guarantee of a better future, and Rudd's good intentions will almost certainly join the long list of past government failures if he, like so many before him, fails to come to terms with the complexity of Aboriginal political culture.

Finding a new voice

A better future for Aboriginal people in Australia does not rest with government alone. In order to make the most of the opportunities that a new government presents, Aboriginal leaders and activists must also take stock and rebuild. While Marcia Langton quite rightly emphasises that Aboriginal people were neither silenced nor passive during the Howard years (Langton 2008b: 228), it is also true that a key legacy of that period is the disarray in national representation created by the abolition of ATSIC. As Tauto Sansbury put it, Aboriginal politics got 'lost' during this time. Almost without exception, the people I interviewed for this book emphasised the need to focus on rebuilding their national representation and developing a strong national voice with which to speak to the new government. All the complexity that has been discussed in this book, however, makes this sort of rebuilding process infinitely more challenging. But as Alwyn McKenzie suggests, all these points of tension and complexity are crucially important. Alwyn insists that Aboriginal people must prioritise 'talking those things through and thrashing them out and coming up with compromise or ways through them or around them'. This is a process that belongs to Aboriginal people alone. Paul Briggs suggests that designing a future for Aboriginal people 'doesn't really need government intervention or support and it doesn't need government approval'. What it needs, according to Patrick Dodson, is a period of rebuilding a national leadership that will necessitate Aboriginal people going 'back to their roots' in order to 'acknowledge the inherent leadership that emerges out of culture' (quoted in KALACC 2006: 145).

Much discussion of the future of national representation for Aboriginal people has focused on the individuals who might be able to unite a new national organisation and generate a broad base of support. There is recognition that many of those in 'the old leadership' carry a lot of political baggage that will make them unpalatable to either Aboriginal people or the government of the day. However, there is also some recognition that there will never be a leader who has the unanimous support of the Aboriginal population. As Vince Coulthard asks, 'How are we going to find a person that each and every one of us Aboriginal people around Australia is going to be able to get down and support?' Vince argues that those who are prepared to stand up should be backed, suggesting that Aboriginal people must 'support them as best we can' while acknowledging that 'there's always going to be a few people who don't like what you do, that's the reality'. Klynton Wanganeen emphasises the need for Aboriginal leaders and activists to sort through some of these complexities behind closed doors in order to present a more united face. Klynton argues that:

> It has to be a debate that Aboriginal people have to agree to have and do it internally and disagree inside the ring. Have your disagreements there. Once you go outside the room we have to agree on the endpoint. We may disagree

on the steps that we need to take to get there but if we don't keep the end goal in sight, then we'll get sidetracked into our debates and fights against each other, which is how governments win against us.

One unanswered question is how and where these conversations might happen. Several of my interviewees spoke of the need to meet 'behind closed doors' in Aboriginal-only forums. Already, people have spent and continue to spend considerable sums of money out of their own pockets to get together with other leaders and activists to have these discussions. For these processes to go anywhere, however, Geoff Scott suggests that there needs to be a group of people who are 'independent of government' and who have 'credibility across the country' who are able to facilitate such a process 'for a year or two'. Geoff envisages a process to 'let the ideas filter through' that is organised by 'someone having the discipline and rigour to actually write it up and present it properly and feed it back'. Eugenia Flynn agrees that the 'ways of moving that forward really have to come from within the Indigenous community'. Eugenia also thinks that one of the 'silver linings' of the anger caused by the Northern Territory 'intervention' was that many Aboriginal people were 'really galvanised into action' in a way that was 'unifying us and helping us to move forward'.

A small population, like the Indigenous population in Australia, finds it harder to accommodate diversity and deal with disagreement than does a larger population. In a small population there is a tendency to individualise disagreements rather than acknowledge the inevitable diversity of views and ideology. People become divided and, as Irene Watson suggests, Aboriginal people tend to 'turn on each other' in a context where the small population size is compounded by the inter-generational impacts of colonisation (Watson 2007: 30). Noel Pearson has suggested that many Aboriginal people have 'internalised black American notions of political behaviour', meaning that everyone is cast as either 'an Uncle Tom on the right or a Malcolm X on the left'. Pearson believes that internalising these ideas of radicalism or sell-out limits Aboriginal capacity to negotiate difficult situations (1993: 184). Dr Marika saw Aboriginal people's continuing tendency to turn on one another as playing into mainstream political strategy, arguing that 'people have to be strong and solid together' because: 'When they divide us we're kind of scattered and fragmented and we can't think straight.'

Without a representative organisation, the fragmentation caused by political conflict only exacerbates the stress and frustration that many leaders and activists experience.

Some leaders and activists have suggested that parliamentary representation may offer an alternative form of representative voice for Aboriginal people. Although there are currently no Aboriginal people in our federal parliament,[1] Kim Hill hopes to one day take a seat in the federal senate because, he says, that is 'where they make laws'. At the same time, the notion of seeking representation in non-Aboriginal institutions of government is deeply conflictual for many Aboriginal people. Alison Anderson is one of five Aboriginal MLAs in the Northern Territory parliament.[2] In our interview, we discussed the ways in which she makes sense of two apparently conflicting positions: on the one hand as a member of a sovereign Aboriginal nation, and on the other as an Australian citizen representing other Aboriginal and non-Aboriginal citizens in parliament. Alison's position is that she is 'first and foremost an Indigenous Australian' who works to 'represent my people in this Parliament'. What helps her make sense of the potential conflict in her role is Aboriginal law:

> That's never changed over centuries after centuries, whereas the whitefella law is changed overnight in Parliament or with the stroke of a pen. Our law remains on the land and remains in the hearts of our people . . . It's really, really hard for me to understand the way whitefella politics works when I see the law written on the land, the hills and the trees and the rivers and on the sand dunes. Law that's never, ever changed.

For Alison, although these two laws are 'worlds apart', she carries her law with her into parliament, where she says:

> My law helps me translate in today's terms the importance of understanding Aboriginal poverty, the fact that the Aboriginal people are still suffering. So it's the really key factor still in my life . . . It's about, not necessarily changing the way Parliament operates, but it's about understanding that there's a different law also and there's a group of people that operate under a really, really different governance system.

From at least the 1930s, Aboriginal leaders and activists like Alison and Kim have expressed a desire for greater involvement in government and representation in parliament (Merlan 2005: 481). Today, however, there is a more ambivalent assessment of the capacity for parliamentary representation to actually deliver meaningful change. The Northern Territory MLAs, the largest group in any parliament in Australia, receive particular scrutiny in terms of their effectiveness, with many suggesting that their entry into both the ALP and the parliament itself has sapped some of their previous autonomy. Josie Crawshaw, for example, whose own nephew is one of the parliamentarians, suggests that the pressures on Aboriginal parliamentarians tend to silence them both on issues that affect Aboriginal people and on issues that affect their country and constituents. In many ways, they are forced to 'cooperate in their own oppression'. Eddie Cubillo expresses similar views, saying:

> You have six Indigenous people in there who I hoped were going to do tremendous things. But unfortunately, if you're in a party it's very hard to do what you personally would like to do. They're all quality people but they're just bound . . . I understand they're probably just as passionate about it as I am but they're hamstrung at the moment.

Not everyone shares these views. Tom Calma considers it a 'travesty' that there are no Aboriginal people in the federal parliament and argues that strategies must be developed to increase this representation because: 'The time for making decisions on behalf of Indigenous people are long gone.' (*Koori Mail* 2005d: 10)

While parliamentary representation interests some, the greater consensus among my interviewees was for a new national representative body outside of the nation's parliaments and outside of the control of government. Paul Briggs stressed that for Aboriginal people to 'have an identity in Australia' they 'still need a national voice'. Paul believes that many people feel 'under siege' without ATSIC, generating a 'sense of urgency' about creating a replacement. However, Paul also recognises that if a new representative body is going to be developed through consensus, 'it could take some time'. But he is optimistic that it will happen:

> I think that it will emerge, a process will emerge and a strategy will emerge that will give us a national voice again . . . But we have to do that not as a reactionary issue to the plays of the Commonwealth. It has to be based on

the views of Indigenous peoples and our ideas about future directions more than anything else.

For Mick Dodson, the key to any new representative organisation will be the method of selection for representatives, and that 'whatever method is chosen is chosen by the people'. Mick claims not to care whether that method is 'a secret ballot, full-on elections supervised by the Electoral Commission, tossing a coin, drawing straws, names out of a hat, or whether the elders do it' as long as there is 'a free and fully informed decision'. Mick also thinks that having different methods of selection in different parts of the country will be workable, stressing again that 'it's the choice of the method that's important, not the method of choice'. Mick argues that: 'Democracy often doesn't work for Indigenous groups. I think we get ourselves in all sorts of trouble, being too wedded to democracy as the only method of choosing your representative.' This view is echoed by Bunuba woman June Oscar, who thinks that democratically elected representatives often find themselves more concerned with their accountability 'to government and not to the cultural bosses' (quoted in KALACC 2006: 115). Ironically, this view was also once endorsed by Lowitja O'Donoghue, later appointed as Chair of the elected body ATSIC, who in 1976 argued in a report to government on the workings of the NACC that she did 'not support the concept of a nationally elected advisory body because *it is more likely to produce politicians than advisors*' (quoted in Department of Aboriginal Affairs 1976: 117, emphasis in original).

Still, elected representation remains important to many people. For some, there is a retrospective recognition of what ATSIC had to offer. John Maynard comments that, during ATSIC's tenure, 'everyone was just so busy attacking the bloody thing', but in its absence people have realised the benefit of a vehicle through which to elect representatives. Alwyn McKenzie understands that some aspects of a democratic election process can conflict with aspects of customary law and leadership, but he also believes that by the end of the ATSIC era people had adjusted. According to Alwyn, people in his old ATSIC region of Nulla Wimilla Kutja in South Australia had 'gotten used to a democratic process, they liked that'. There had been debates about other methods of selecting representatives but, says Alwyn, 'in the end they said it should be on a democratic basis' with the provision that voters 'should be able to hear their debates and see how good they are so it's not just a popular thing'.

Klynton Wanganeen believes that Aboriginal people 'have to have the debate about whether you want a democratic process or you want a prescriptive process':

> You can't have a democratic process and specify male, female, youth, elders. You have that debate first. If the debate determines that you want a democratic process, then you have to take what comes through a democratic process. If the outcome is you want to get that gender balance and the mix of youth and elderly, then you have to build in a prescriptive process that can cater for it in a semi-democratic way.

Klynton's preference is for what he calls a 'semi-democratic process' through which representation can ensure a 'gender, youth and elder balance'. Two points are important for Klynton in this process. The first is his conviction that once Aboriginal people have had the debate about the means of selecting representatives, then they must decide to 'make that decision work'. The other point is that while cultural differences should be recognised and represented at the local and regional level, once representation becomes aggregated at the state or national level differences must, to some extent, be put aside.

Others see the potential pitfalls of a return to elected leadership, pointing out that the ATSIC process sometimes meant that people were elected with only a small number of votes because the turnout in some areas was very low. There are calls to investigate other ways for communities to choose their representatives that may have a closer fit with traditional ways of selecting and endorsing leaders. Tom Calma agrees that there are other ways, and has floated his idea of a selection process by which a panel of 'eminent Indigenous people' calls for nominations. People who wish to put themselves forward 'not only have to nominate, they also have to stand up and justify why they should be in that position and how they are going to represent an Indigenous view'. Like others, however, Tom also stresses that whatever selection method is chosen, Aboriginal people then need to agree to back their representatives 'and not start to undermine them the day they step into the ruddy job'.

As discussed in Chapter 7, some interviewees—including Mick Dodson and Jackie Huggins—would like to see a model similar to the Canadian Assembly of First Nations. Mick sees a model such as this as an opportunity to develop a representative body that takes account of some of the complexity discussed in this book because its building blocks are local and regional, which builds diversity into the organisational structure from the ground up. According to Mick, the number of representatives a community would send to a regional assembly could be determined by the size of the community. It would also be possible to represent 'other interests' that would be important to a national body. So, according to Mick, the assembly model could provide:

> scope for youth assemblies, women's assemblies, elders' assemblies. You might even want an organisational assembly so all the organisations get involved. And those assemblies can send delegates to the national assembly, so, there's all sorts of ways of ensuring that not only you get a legitimate representation, but also you get legitimate interests represented . . . So there are ways you can think of to cater for the diversity of interests.

But while these possibilities are real, Klynton Wanganeen also believes that determining a new model will be a difficult process because he sees that, if a new model 'even remotely resembles ATSIC', it would 'get a flogging from the media and the government'. At the same time, however, Klynton suggests that if a new organisation is 'too far removed from ATSIC' it would 'get a flogging from the Aboriginal community'. The key will be to find a balance that 'shows you can build on the strengths that ATSIC had, but still have it linked to the grass roots of Aboriginal communities'.

There are also questions about what a new national representative body should do once it is created. Mick Dodson tells me he has strong views on this issue and argues for an organisation that is primarily an 'advocacy body' that 'should have the capacity to scrutinise governments at all levels, including their delivery of services to Indigenous people'. This advocacy would 'extend to the international arena in pursuing Indigenous rights and rights recognition'. A new body, according to Mick, should also have a research capacity, enabling it to provide sound, evidence-based policy advice to the government of the day. What Mick thinks that a new body should *not* do—a point made by several of my interviewees—is engage in service delivery or the funding of organisations. Many Aboriginal leaders and activists believe that ATSIC's downfall was primarily brought about by its service delivery role, muddling its function as a representative body that could scrutinise and criticise government with the work of government itself. All are eager to avoid such pitfalls again, and are determined to develop a more autonomous national body that can neither be created nor abolished by the government of the day.

In abolishing the NIC early in 2008, Jenny Macklin committed that the Rudd government would develop a new national representative body for Indigenous peoples. In July 2008, the Human Rights and Equal Opportunities Commission released a comprehensive discussion paper outlining the key issues to be faced in establishing a new body. The discussion paper focused on three key questions. First, what lessons can be learned from mechanisms for representing Aboriginal and Torres Strait Islander peoples at the national, state and territory or regional level that have previously existed or that are currently in place? Second, what lessons can be learned from mechanisms for representing Indigenous peoples that have been established in other countries? And third, what options are there for ensuring that a national Indigenous representative body is sustainable? (ATSISJC 2008c).

In response to the discussion paper the Rudd government announced a six month consultation process, beginning in July 2008, with the stated intent of allowing for 'widespread engagement with Aboriginal and Torres Strait Islander people across the country to gain feedback on the Indigenous community's aspirations and preferred model(s) for a national Indigenous representative body' (see FAHCSIA 2008). While some Aboriginal people expressed disappointment that the consultation process was to be led by government rather than Indigenous people, in general there was relief that work on developing a new representative body was at last moving forward.

A better future?

In a public lecture around the time of the Corroboree 2000 event to mark the end of the Decade of Reconciliation, Patrick Dodson asked the nation some hard questions:

> Will we again fail as a nation to grasp this opportunity to change the political architecture of this country? Will we again fail to rise above the mediocrity that ties us to seeking incremental change through short-term stopgap bureaucratic solutions? Or can we work towards realigning the relationship between us? (Dodson 2000: 8)

On that occasion, the nation did fail again, as it had failed so often before. A failure of heart, a failure of courage, and a fundamental failure to do what is morally right has left Australia floundering, condemning Aboriginal people in Australia to years, if not decades, of further suffering. In a 2008 speech marking the national apology, which he described as 'the moment when hope re-emerged', Dodson again emphasised our capacity to do much, much better:

> We as a nation should be capable of developing public policy that recognises the fact that Indigenous society—which draws on thousands of years of cultural and religious connection to Australian lands—has survived. We are capable of creating a relationship where the imperatives of Indigenous life are understood and respected by governments and institutionalised as part of good governance. (Dodson 2008a: 3, 6)

Until Australia is able to truly draw on this capacity, however, it will continue to flounder in its response to the demands of Aboriginal people while the rest of the world moves on. The gap in outcomes for Indigenous peoples in Australia and other countries is worsening and there is real reason to fear that the current policy settings here will further exacerbate this disparity. In September 2007 the long-awaited United Nations Declaration on the Rights of Indigenous Peoples was signed by 143 member nations. Australia was one of only four countries to vote against the declaration. The other abstainers—Canada, the United States and Aotearoa New Zealand—while far from perfect, all have more developed domestic protections for Indigenous rights than Australia has ever contemplated.

Megan Davis found her experience working on the Draft Declaration as a United Nations Fellow really underscored how 'backward' Australia is in this area when compared with other liberal democracies. Unlike other comparable countries, Australia has failed to reform state institutions in order to adequately include Aboriginal people. Their continued exclusion 'permeates all aspects of Aboriginal culture and contributes to the ongoing dislocation experienced by many Indigenous peoples within the Australian community'. This disturbing backwardness really 'hit home' for Davis during her time at the UN:

As I looked around the room at the representatives of 300 million Indigenous people worldwide in over 70 different countries, I heard them speak of having Treaty agreements; or Bills of Rights that protected them in law; constitutional recognition of first peoples, constitutional recognition of national parks, of consultation, of traditional languages and cultures; representative bodies such as Parliaments or assemblies or special dedicated seats for Indigenous peoples in political systems.

As most Indigenous participants in the room nodded their heads, I looked around at those participants who—like Indigenous Australians—really needed this Declaration. Who had nothing. There was a small group of us, most from extremely impoverished developing countries who had zero or limited protection. In Australia we have a *Racial Discrimination Act* that can be overridden with ease. We have a provision in our Constitution that may facilitate the making of laws to the detriment of Indigenous peoples simply because they are Indigenous. We have no federal Bill of Rights . . . We have no formal agreement with the state—no Treaty—and we have no Indigenous political representative body, constitutional recognition of our status as first peoples or the right to be consulted or indeed dedicated parliamentary seats.

Davis concluded that the political reality in Australia is that 'Indigenous rights are largely dependent upon the goodwill of the government of the day' (Davis 2006d). That situation may change in the future. The Rudd government announced its support for the Declaration of the Rights of Indigenous Peoples and in mid-2008 began seeking the views of Indigenous people in Australia on how it ought to formally indicate its endorsement of the declaration.

Australia's new government has the opportunity to demonstrate maximum goodwill by finally reforming our political institutions. While this book has highlighted the immense complexity of Aboriginal political culture, it is also important to remember that there are no real mysteries to finding a way forward. Aboriginal people understand these political complexities completely; they live them every single day. Properly listening to their views and their proposals, working in collaboration and partnership with them, and ultimately giving them the support and respect to become more autonomous is the only way for any government to proceed with any chance of success. Despite sometimes honourable intentions, every single government to date has failed to do what was needed. Jackie Huggins suggests that if the road to hell is paved with good intentions, then: 'Indigenous affairs is a full street directory of these roads.' (Huggins 2007) Political good intentions and goodwill alone will never be enough. As Alexis Wright has argued: 'Too many non-Indigenous people have tried to save us and have failed.' (2005: 107) Surely the time has come to let Aboriginal people save themselves.

Report after report, including the Royal Commission into Aboriginal Deaths in Custody (RCIADIC), the *Bringing Them Home* report, and most recently the *Little Children are Sacred* report, have made precisely this point. International evidence confirms that Indigenous communities begin their revival at the point where they acquire the sort of territorial autonomy that enables their political involvement in running their own affairs in areas such as health, education and economic development (Fournier 2005: vii). Returning the control of Aboriginal lives to Aboriginal people is the only way to avert disaster. We need, as a nation, to let go of the idea that self-determination was tried and failed, and accept that it was never tried at all. The alternative, as Alwyn McKenzie points out, is that: 'One of these days in some places the Aboriginal people are going to be gone from the country and that's going to be a loss to everybody.' Alwyn asks: 'Do you really want that? Or will you get together and start supporting Aboriginal people so that we can have that confidence of retaining our knowledge, our experiences and just assessing where we stand in the world?'

Paul Briggs believes that 'the biggest waste that's happening in Australia is the loss of Aboriginal lives and the waste of the energies of peoples trying to make a difference'. While resolving the unfinished business is most pressing for Aboriginal people, who are debilitated through the 'conflicted nature of living with two forms of sovereignty' (Brady 2007: 147), there are implications for the nation as a whole. It is in all of our interests to address what Megan Davis has described as 'the perennial footnote to Australia's claim that it has an excellent human rights record' (2006c: 47). Patrick Dodson has suggested that these unresolved issues create a 'spiritual malaise' that 'will continue to be a source of crippling national ambiguity, until such a time that we confront the reality of our relationship as two sovereign peoples inhabiting one land' (Dodson 2005: 3). More recently, he has proposed establishing a new national dialogue on the issues of unfinished business in order to develop a 'meaningful co-existence' between Indigenous and non-Indigenous Australia (Dodson 2008a: 32). As David Ross (1997) of the Central Land Council has argued, resolving past injustices as a basis of 'achieving just settlements' is definitely 'in the national interest' (1997: 126).

Early signs from the Rudd government have sent mixed messages to Aboriginal people. The profoundly important symbolism of the national apology has clashed with the failure to establish a compensation fund for victims of past policy; the commitment to 'Closing the Gap' by 2030 has clashed with the lukewarm response to the 2020 Summit proposals for constitutional recognition. It remains to be seen whether the Rudd government will do more than repeat the mistakes of previous Australian governments by responding to a complex political culture with simplistic and cowardly policy. With a fuller understanding of Aboriginal political culture governments cannot claim not to know, they should not fail to engage with Aboriginal people as the architects of their own futures, and they must not avoid the difficult issues. A treaty or some other form of agreement, political representation, compensation, land justice, an economic base, regional agreements, spending levels to address real need, proper recognition of culture and customary law—these issues are the starting points to providing Aboriginal people with the degree of political and economic autonomy that they need to regain personal dignity and control of their lives. They are complex solutions, as befits the complexity of contemporary Aboriginal politics. None of them is a silver bullet, none a 'solution'. By without any one of them, no policy response, no intervention, will ever succeed.

Given Australia's past history of failure in the field of Indigenous affairs, it may seem that a more hopeful future is merely fanciful. But these goals are no more than has been achieved in other comparable countries, and they are goals shared by Indigenous peoples all over the world. It is inevitable that *one day* an Australian government will also face up to this country's obligations to our Indigenous peoples and deal with the unfinished business. Whether this is the Rudd government or not, whether this happens in my lifetime or not, it surely must happen eventually. There is no doubt that Aboriginal people themselves will never give up their struggle towards these goals. Despite endless setbacks and disappointments, despite the failure of successive governments, they will never give up their belief in the possibility that one day they will be healthy, autonomous and free in their own land.

· NOTES

Intoduction

1   *A note on terminology:* Broadly speaking, Indigenous people are the original inhabitants of a territory that has been conquered by ethnically or culturally different groups and who subsequently have been incorporated into states that consider them inferior 'outsiders' (Maybury-Lewis 2003: 324). Throughout this book, the terms 'Indigenous people' or 'Indigenous peoples' are used to refer to all such groups including the combined groups of Aboriginal people and Torres Strait Islanders who make up Australia's Indigenous population. The primary focus of the book, however, is the Indigenous people of mainland Australia, who are here often referred to as 'Aboriginal people' despite the inadequacy of this term for capturing the distinct and diverse range of Indigenous nations and cultures that make up this population. The terms 'Indigenous' and 'Aboriginal' are capitalised because they are used as proper nouns to signify the political sovereignty of these groups.

2   Of course, even in writing about the complexity of Aboriginal political culture I am guilty of its simplification. There are many important issues that barely rate a mention in this book, not because I do not recognise their significance, but because I am only writing one volume of what could be an encyclopaedic set. There are some aspects of complexity that I have been forced to exclude. I have not, for example, focused at all on the differences between mainland Aboriginal people and Torres Strait Islanders. I was unable to get to Tasmania, and so have only been able to include the writings of Tasmanian Aboriginal leaders and activists and not interview material.

3   Since our interview, John has published this research in the book *Fight for Liberty and Freedom: The origins of Australian Aboriginal activism* (Maynard, 2007).

4   For more information on the alliance, see its website at www.nationalab
     originalalliance.org.
5   This was evident at the Rudd government's 2020 Summit held in April
     2008. As a fellow delegate in the Indigenous stream at the summit, I wit-
     nessed Noel Pearson's failure to engage first hand.
6   The 'trifecta' is a trio of minor charges frequently laid against marginalised
     young people. It begins with a verbal confrontation between police and
     a young person, which results in a charge of offensive language. As the
     young person struggles against the arresting officers, they are frequently
     charged with resisting arrest and assaulting police. The trifecta is often the
     first interaction a young person will have with the criminal justice system.

Chapter 1 A history of policy failure

1   *Terra nullius* did not in fact become a doctrine of Australian law until
     the *Mabo* judgment of 1992, when the High Court attributed it as legal
     doctrine (evidenced by Crown actions of the past) in order to refute it.
2   Many states had adopted assimilation policy earlier than this.
3   The sexual exploitation of children by non-Aboriginal mine workers was
     also discussed in the *Little Children are Sacred* report (Wild and Anderson
     2007: 64).
4   The Council of Australian Governments (COAG) trials, designed to
     coordinate services to Aboriginal communities through 'whole of gov-
     ernment' programs, were announced in April 2002. The trial sites were:
     Anangu Pitjantjatjara Yankunytjatjara (APY) Lands, South Australia;
     Australian Capital Territory; Cape York, Queensland; East Kimberley
     region, Western Australia; Murdi Paaki region, western New South Wales;
     northeast Tasmania; Shepparton region, Victoria; and Wadeye, Northern
     Territory. Each trial was led by one Australian government and one state
     government agency. Following highly critical independent reviews of
     progress under the trials, they were quietly abandoned in early 2007.
5   Trachoma causes scarring of the cornea and upper eyelid, leading to loss of
     vision. Spread by flies, clothing and hands, it is preventable with increased
     hygiene and cleanliness.
6   The town had no working petrol bowser, with a 90-kilometre round trip
     required to access the closest petrol supply.
7   *Wik* held that the granting of statutory interests did not necessarily result
     in the extinguishment of native title and that pastoral leases did not neces-
     sarily confer a right of exclusive possession.
8   Coined by historian Peter Read in the 1980s, the term 'stolen genera-
     tions' has, according to Robert Manne, taken on a similar significance for

Indigenous Australians as the term 'the Holocaust' has for Jews (Manne 2001b: 82).

9 The Howard government was in control of the Senate from 1 July 2005. In the Lower House, the legislation was supported by the Labor Opposition, apparently keen to avoid being 'wedged' in the run-up to a federal election.

Chapter 2 Autonomy and dependency

1 The intervention was estimated to require at least 700 new public servants to administer programs such as the quarantining of welfare payments.

2 This dynamic, essentially one of co-option, is certainly not unique to the Aboriginal rights movement. I have written elsewhere on the dangers of close relationships with apparently friendly government for the women's and environment movements—see Maddison and Edgar 2008.

3 Metal breastplates were initially presented to Aboriginal 'leaders' by colonial governments. These breastplates, also known as king plates, were intended to recognise men who were thought to have control over their people. Later pastoralists also gave them out to those Aboriginal men who 'served' them well. Many Aboriginal people today see breastplates as a symbol of dispossession, accepted only by those who accepted their subjugation to white governments.

Chapter 4 Tradition and development

1 Maccassan trading visits to northern Australia continued for a longer period than European settlement to date, only ending in 1907 when they were banned by federal legislation (National Oceans Office 2004).

2 Despite these legislative restrictions, the expenditure of these funds is essentially at the discretion of the federal Minister for Indigenous Affairs. In July 2007 it was reported in the *National Indigenous Times*, *The Age* and the *Financial Review* that the then Minister, Mal Brough, had approved a $100 000 payment from these funds to the Aboriginal cultural festival, The Dreaming, which is held at Woodford in Queensland. This was the first time in the history of the ABA that approval had been given for expenditure outside the Northern Territory. Woodford is in Brough's former electorate of Longman, the seat he lost in the November 2007 election.

3 An example of successful negotiation under the native title regime is the innovative statewide Indigenous Land Use Agreement in South Australia. For details, see Agius et al. (2007).

4 In April 2008 it was revealed that Northern Territory Chief Minister Paul Henderson had advised federal Indigenous Affairs Minister Jenny Macklin

that large numbers of Aboriginal people who had effectively been displaced by the emergency intervention were travelling to urban centres where they were 'creating unrest and straining police capacity', and that the intervention was having a 'perverse effect on urban communities' (Skelton 2008).

5   In light of this discussion, it is ironic that the community of Titjikala was forced to close its cultural tourism venture after the abolition of CDEP under the new intervention regime saw the venture lose its CDEP-funded workforce.

6   In 2007 Alcan was acquired by mining giant Rio Tinto.

7   The Japanese-owned natural gas company INPEX went ahead and installed a floating gas rig at the Maret Islands despite the concerns of traditional owners and allegations by the Kimberley Land Council that the development breached the *Native Title Futures Act* (ABC 2007b).

Chapter 5 Individualism and collectivism

1   In early 2008, it was reported that Mal Brough was working on a business deal involving a housing development in the Tiwi Islands, from which he was seeking to profit. Brough, who later lost his seat in the November 2007 election, was the Indigenous Affairs Minister responsible for orchestrating the Tiwi lease (*National Indigenous Times* 2008c).

2   This comment was made to me in a personal phone call unrelated to this book.

Chapter 6 Indigeneity and hybridity

1   This is a point also made by Attwood and Markus (2004: 250).

2   In some cases, 'passing' might not be about the deliberate hiding of Aboriginal identity, but may arise out of confusion in family history and a lack of certainty about Aboriginal ancestry. The former minister Mal Brough's cultural identity was a source of much speculation—and some humour—in this regard during the interviews for this book. Some were simply incredulous that Brough's sister identifies as, and is accepted as, Aboriginal while the former minister does not. For more information on Brough's situation, see Davies (2007).

3   Mudrooroo himself has become emblematic of some of the complexities surrounding Indigenous identity. Born Colin Johnson, Mudrooroo changed his name to Mudrooroo Narogin in 1988 and later to Mudrooroo Nyoongah. It remains unclear whether Mudrooroo was genuinely convinced of his Aboriginality, confused and uncertain, or whether he chose a path of deliberate deception. The question of his descent also remains unclear. Mudrooroo was challenged to prove his Aboriginality after his

sister claimed their father had been African–American and their mother white. Mudrooroo's response to these challenges to what he now calls his 'dubious genealogy' was to say: 'Am I to write a fictional life story as others have done to prove who I am? I never knew my father and even my mother is in doubt. So just see me as a mongrel and forget any other labels.' Gary Foley claims 'there are still numerous Aboriginal people in Australia . . . [including Foley] . . . who regard Mudrooroo as an Aboriginal person' (Foley 1997).

4   Tasmanian Aboriginal people have endured some particularly challenging issues to do with questions of Aboriginal identity. Mainstream accounts of Tasmanian colonial history insisted that 'full-blood' Aboriginal people became 'extinct' in the state with the death of Truganini in 1876. This claim is incorrect, evidenced by several vibrant and vocal Aboriginal communities in Tasmania, including the Palawa people, represented by well-known national activist Michael Mansell and the Tasmanian Aboriginal Centre. Mansell, however, has led the charge in challenging the Aboriginality of other groups, most particularly those known as the Lia Pootah people from the southeast of the state. These claims were tested in court, with mixed results, in 1998. For more information on this fraught and highly complex situation, see Ryan (1996), Everett (2000) and Sanders (2003).

Chapter 7 Unity and regionalism

1   Although this book is not dealing with issues unique to Torres Strait Islanders, it is worth noting here Martin Nakata's argument that even naming that group of islands was based on ignorance of inter-island politics and has 'effectively silenced territorial boundaries and political affiliations between and among the different tribal groups of the various islands' (Nakata 2003 [1994]: 133).

2   For details on the NAA's resolutions at the Alice Springs meeting, see the website: www.nationalaboriginalalliance.org.

3   In the late 1990s, a debate about regionalism and land councils was sparked by the Reeves review of the Northern Territory Land Rights Act (Reeves 1998). Aboriginal stakeholders and others raised concerns about some of Reeves' assumptions regarding regionalism. These concerns were documented in a response to the Reeves report produced by the Centre for Aboriginal Economic Policy Research (Altman et al. 1999).

4   For details of the development of the Noongar Nation and other regional governance examples from Western Australia, see Barcham (2006).

5   In November 2002, the Howard government announced yet another review of ATSIC. The review was intended to 'examine and make

recommendations to government on how Aboriginal and Torres Strait Islander people can in the future be best represented in the process of the development of Commonwealth policies and programs to assist them' (Ruddock 2002). In announcing the review the then minister, Phillip Ruddock, claimed that he wanted the process to 'strengthen ATSIC' as a 'unique organisation that is meant to give Indigenous people a genuine voice in policy making' (quoted in Sanders 2005b: 161). The review team (former Liberal MP John Hannaford, former Labor MP Bob Collins and Indigenous academic and activist Jackie Huggins) released its final report, *In the Hands of the Regions*, in November 2003, recommending structural change but emphatically not recommending that ATSIC be abolished. In March 2004, however, the then Opposition Leader, Mark Latham, announced that if elected he would abolish ATSIC and replace it with an unspecified directly elected national representative body (ALP 2004), a statement that was met with little public debate. Two weeks later, the government announced that it too would abolish the organisation, disregarding the fact that the review report had unambiguously supported continuing and strengthening ATSIC's mandate and functions (Jonas and Dick 2004: 7), instead suggesting that the decision was in accordance with the findings of the report. Documents related to the review, including submissions, have been archived in the National Library of Australia.

6   The Assembly of First Nations is the national, non-government organisation representing Canadian First Nations peoples. More information can be found on the Assembly's website at www.afn.ca.

Chapter 8 Community and kin

1   The Indigenous Community Governance Project (ICGP) is a partnership between the Centre for Aboriginal Economic Policy Research (CAEPR) and Reconciliation Australia that has been conducting research on Indigenous community governance with participating Indigenous communities and regional Indigenous organisations and other research partners since 2003.

2   The drift to towns and town camps continues today, and has been exacerbated by recent policy. There are reports, for example, that the new alcohol restrictions in the Northern Territory, which have not been accompanied by treatment and rehabilitation facilities, have prompted a new migration over the border into the South Australia community of Kupa Piti (discussed in ATSISJC 2008a).

Chapter 10 Men, women and customary law

1 The *Little Children are Sacred* report drew attention to the incidence of sexual assault perpetrated on Aboriginal children by non-Aboriginal men, including mine workers and individuals employed in Aboriginal communities in a range of support services. Early media coverage on the report was heavily focused on this issue; however, in subsequent days and weeks this concern was swept away by the announcement of the federal 'intervention', which refocused the blame on Aboriginal perpetrators.

2 It is probable that different Aboriginal nations afforded women different status and authority, as is still the case today.

3 In June 2006, following considerable media attention on the issue of violence and abuse in Aboriginal communities, the Howard government introduced legislation to prevent courts from considering customary law and cultural practices as mitigating factors in sentencing violent offenders. At the time, Aboriginal and Torres Strait Islander Social Justice Commissioner Tom Calma responded in the media that the legislation would 'do nothing to address the issue of violence' and 'may even make solving the problem harder' (Calma 2006).

Chapter 11 Mourning and reconciliation

1 The Royal Commission into Aboriginal Deaths in Custody (RCIADIC) was established in 1989 in response to public concern over the deaths in police custody and prisons of ninety-nine Aboriginal people between January 1980 and May 1989.

2 Black armbands as a symbol of mourning have been a feature of twentieth century Aboriginal politics in Australia (McKenna 1997). Shortly after his election in 1996, Howard made his position clear on this practice, and indeed this view of history, in a speech in which he stated: 'I profoundly reject the black armband view of Australian history. I believe the balance sheet of Australian history is a very generous and benign one.' (Howard 1996)

3 Sorry Day is commemorated on 26 May each year, the anniversary of the release of the *Bringing Them Home* report. In 2005 there was debate over the National Sorry Day Committee's decision to change the name of Sorry Day to the National Day of Healing. This move received a very mixed response, and after several months of criticism, including from groups representing members of the Stolen Generations, the committee apologised and reverted to the original name.

4 In August 2007 the South Australian Supreme Court awarded Bruce Trevorrow $775 000 in compensation for pain, suffering and false impris-

onment after he was taken from a hospital at the age of thirteen months and given to a white family by the South Australian Aborigines Protection Board. The South Australian government appealed the decision.Trevor-row died in June 2008, before the appeal was heard and before receiving his compensation.

5   Makarrata is a Yolngu word meaning 'coming together after a struggle' (Keon-Cohen 1981: 3), or the end of a period of disagreement or dispute. The term was, for a short time, used synonymously with the word 'treaty' between Indigenous Australians and the Australian government, although it was dropped after consultations by the NAC revealed that it was not generally supported by Aboriginal people around Australia, who preferred the term 'Treaty' (NAC 1981).

6   For a comprehensive history and analysis of Australia's formal reconcili-ation process, see Gunstone (2007).

7   On 10 December 1992, the then prime minister, Paul Keating, gave a landmark speech in Redfern that went further than any other political statement in Australia has done to acknowledge the wrongs of Australia's treatment of Aboriginal people. In 2007, ABC Radio National listeners voted the speech as their third most 'unforgettable speech'.

Epilogue

1   There have only ever been two Indigenous people in Australia's federal parliament. The first was Neville Bonner, a Liberal senator for Queensland from 1971 to 1983. The second was Aden Ridgeway, a Democrat senator for New South Wales from 1998 to 2005.

2   The 2008 election in the Northern Territory saw a reduction in the number of Aboriginal MLAs from six to five. Elliot McAdam, the ALP Member for Barkly, retired and Matthew Bonson, the ALP Member for the new electorate of Fong Lim, lost his seat. However, the seat of Braitling was won by Adam Giles, meaning that for the first time in Australian political history there would be Aboriginal members on opposite sides of a parliamentary chamber (Graham 2008).

BIBLIOGRAPHY

Aboriginal and Torres Strait Islander Commission (ATSIC) 1995a,
  *Recognition, rights and reform: A report to government on native title social
  justice measures*, Aboriginal and Torres Strait Islander Commission,
  Canberra

——1995b, *The final report of the evaluation of the effectiveness of ATSIC
  programs in meeting the needs of Aboriginal women and Torres Strait Islander
  women*, Aboriginal and Torres Strait Islander Commission, Office of
  Evaluation and Audit, Canberra

Aboriginal and Torres Strait Islander Social Justice Commissioner (ATSISJC)
  2006, *Submission to the Australian Senate Community Affairs Legislation
  Committee on the Aboriginal Land Rights (Northern Territory) Amendment
  Bill 2006 (Cth)*, 13 July

——2006b, *Ending family violence and abuse in Aboriginal and Torres Strait
  Islander communities—key issues*, Human Rights and Equal Opportunity
  Commission, Sydney

——2007a, *Social Justice Report 2006*, Human Rights and Equal Opportunity
  Commission, Sydney

——2007b, *Native Title Report 2006*, Human Rights and Equal Opportunity
  Commission, Sydney

——2008a, *Social Justice Report 2007*, Human Rights and Equal Opportunity
  Commission, Sydney

——2008b, *Native Title Report 2007*, Human Rights and Equal Opportunity
  Commission, Sydney

——2008c, *Building a sustainable national Indigenous representative body: Issues for
  consideration*, Human Rights and Equal Opportunity Commission, Sydney

Agius, Parry, Jenkin, Tom, Jarvis, Sandy, Howitt, Richie and Williams, Rhiân
  2007, '(Re)asserting Indigenous rights and jurisdictions within a politics
  of place: Transformative nature of native title negotiations in South
  Australia', *Geographical Research*, vol. 45, no. 2, pp. 194–202

Agius, Quenten 2006, Letter to the editor, *Koori Mail*, 1 March, p. 23

Ah Kit, John 1997, 'Land rights at work: Aboriginal people and regional economies', in *Our Land Is Our Life: Land rights—past present and future*, Galarrwuy Yunupingu (ed.), University of Queensland Press, St Lucia, pp. 52–63

Altman, Jon 2005, 'Development options on Aboriginal land: Sustainable Indigenous hybrid economies in the twenty-first century' in *The Power of Knowledge, the Resonance of Tradition*, eds Luke Taylor, Graeme Ward, Graham Henderson, Richard Davis and Lynley Wallis, Aboriginal Studies Press, Canberra, pp. 34–48

——2006, 'The future of Indigenous Australia: Is there a path beyond the free market or welfare dependency?', *Arena Magazine*, no. 84, August–September

——2007, *Alleviating Poverty in Remote Indigenous Australia: The role of the hybrid economy*, Topical Issue 2007/10, Centre for Aboriginal Economic Policy Research, Australian National University, Canberra

Altman, Jon, Buchanan, Geoff and Biddle, Nicholas 2006, 'The real "real" economy in remote Australia' in *Assessing the Evidence on Indigenous Socioeconomic Outcomes: A focus on the 2002 NATSISS*, Boyd Hunter (ed.), ANU E-press, Canberra, pp. 139–52

Altman, Jon and Hinkson, Melinda 2007 (eds) *Coercive Reconciliation: Stabilise, normalise, exit Aboriginal Australia*, Arena Publications, Melbourne

Altman, Jon and Hunter, Boyd 2003, *Monitoring 'Practical' Reconciliation: Evidence from the reconciliation decade, 1991–2001*, Research Paper no. 254/2003, Centre for Aboriginal Economic Policy Research, Australian National University, Canberra

Altman, Jon, Linkhorn, Craig and Clarke, Jennifer 2005, *Land Rights and Development Reform in Remote Australia*, Working Paper no. 276/2005, Centre for Aboriginal Economic Policy Research, Australian National University, Canberra

Altman, Jon, Morphy, Frances and Rowse, Tim 1999, *Land Rights at Risk? Evaluations of the Reeves Report*, Research Monograph no. 14, Centre for Aboriginal Economic Policy Research, Australian National University, Canberra

Altman, Jon and Whitehead, Peter 2003, *Caring for Country and Sustainable Indigenous Development: Opportunities, constraints and innovations*, Working Paper no. 20/2003, Centre for Aboriginal Economic Policy Research, Australian National University, Canberra

Al-Yaman, Fadwa, Van Doeland, Micke and Wallis, Michelle 2006, *Family Violence Among Aboriginal and Torres Strait Islander Peoples*, Cat. No. IHW 17, Australian Institute of Health and Welfare, Canberra

Anderson, Alison 2003, 'Women's rights and culture: An Indigenous woman's perspective on the removal of traditional marriage as a defence under Northern Territory law', *Indigenous Law Bulletin*, no. 31, bar.austlii.edu. au/au/journals/ILB/2004/31.html

Anderson, Ian 2002, 'Understanding Indigenous violence', *Australian and New Zealand Journal of Public Health*, vol. 26, no. 5, pp. 408–9

Anderson, Pat 2007, The Douglas Gordon Oration at the Public Health Association of Australia Annual Conference, Alice Springs, 25 September

Arabena, Kerry 2005, *Not Fit for Modern Australian Society: Aboriginal and Torres Strait Islander people and the new arrangements for the administration of Indigenous affairs*, Research Discussion Paper no. 16, Australian Institute for Aboriginal and Torres Strait Islander Studies, Canberra

Atkinson, Judy 2002, *Trauma Trails, Recreating Song Lines: The transgenerational effects of trauma in Indigenous Australia*, Spinifex Press, Melbourne

Attwood, Bain 2003, *Rights for Aborigines*, Allen & Unwin, Sydney

——2005, *Telling the Truth About Aboriginal History*, Allen & Unwin, Sydney

Attwood, Bain and Magowan, Fiona (eds) 2001, *Telling Stories: Indigenous history and memory in Australia and New Zealand*, Allen & Unwin, Sydney

Attwood, Bain and Markus, Andrew 1999, *The Struggle for Aboriginal Rights: A documentary history*, Allen & Unwin, Sydney

——2004, *Thinking Black: William Cooper and the Australian Aborigines' League*, Aboriginal Studies Press, Canberra

Austin-Broos, Diane 2008, *Arrernte Present, Arrernte Past*, University of Chicago Press, Chicago

Australian Broadcasting Corporation (ABC) 2003a, 'Interview with Gary Foley', *Late Night Live*, Radio National, 28 August, www.abc.net.au/rn/latenightlive/stories/2003/927329.htm

——2003b, 'Dynasties: Marika', *Dynasties*, ABC Television, 1 December, www.abc.net.au/dynasties/txt/s982601.htm

——2006, 'Crown prosecutor speaks out about abuse in central Australia', *Lateline*, ABC Television, 15 May, www.abc.net.au/lateline/content/2006/s1639127.htm

——2007a, 'Noel Pearson discusses the issues faced by Indigenous communities', *Lateline*, ABC Television, 26 June, www.abc.net.au/lateline/content/2007/s1962844.htm

——2007b, 'Land access deal worries traditional owners', *AM*, Radio National 24 August, www.abc.net.au/am/content/2007/s2013855.htm

——2007c, 'Maret Island drilling angers native title claimants', ABC Online, 5 October, www.abc.net.au/news/stories/2007/05/10/1919215.htm

——2007d, 'McArthur River mine ruling sidestepped', ABC Online, 2 May, www/abc.net.au/news/newsitems/200205/s1912609.htm

——2007e, 'Tiwi lease "hugely divisive"', *Message Stick* online, www.abc.net. au/message/news/stories/ms_news_2020312.htm

——2007f, 'Tracking the intervention', *Four Corners*, ABC Television, 5 November, www.abc.net.au/4corners/content/2007/s2082285.htm

——2007g, 'NT intervention will smash culture, say Aboriginal leaders', *The World Today*, ABC Radio, 7 August, www.abc.net.au/worldtoday/content/2007/s1998531.htm

——2008, 'Racism claims levelled at Alice Springs hostel', *AM*, Radio National, 11 March, www.abc.net.au/am/content/2008/s2185865.htm

Australian Labor Party 2004, Policy Statement: Opportunity and Responsibility for Indigenous Australians, 30 March, www.alp.org.au/media/0304/20007157

Bamblett, Muriel 2007, 'Relighting the fire of reconciliation', speech at the Self-determination, not invasion forum, Melbourne Town Hall, Melbourne, 10 December

Barcham, Manuhuia 2006, *Regional Governance Structures in Indigenous Australia: Western Australian examples*, Working Paper no. 1/2006, CIGAD Working Paper Series, Centre for Indigenous Governance and Development, Massey University, Palmerston North, New Zealand

Barnes, Damien 2004, 'After ATSIC—which way?', *Australian Indigenous Law Reporter*, vol. 8, no. 4, pp. 13–16

Barnett, Darrin 2005, 'No ATSIC, no black voice', *National Indigenous Times*, 3 February, p. 11

Bauman, Toni and Williams, Rhiân 2004, *The Business of Process: Research issues in managing Indigenous decision-making and disputes in land*, Research Discussion Paper no. 13, Australian Institute for Aboriginal and Torres Strait Islander Studies, Canberra

Bayet-Charlton, Fabienne 2003 [1994], 'Overturning the doctrine: Indigenous people and wilderness—being Aboriginal in the environmental movement', in *Blacklines: Contemporary critical writings by Indigenous Australians*, Michele Grossman (ed.), Melbourne University Press, Melbourne, pp. 171–80

Behrendt, Larissa 1995, *Aboriginal Dispute Resolution*, Federation Press, Sydney

——2000, 'Consent in a (neo)colonial society: Aboriginal women as sexual and legal "other"', *Australian Feminist Studies*, vol. 15, no. 33, pp. 353–67

———2003, *Achieving Social Justice: Indigenous rights and Australia's future*, Federation Press, Sydney

———2004, 'Election 2004: Indigenous rights and institutions', *Australian Review of Public Affairs*, 16 August, www.australianreview.net/digest/2004/08/behrendt.html

———2006, 'What lies beneath', *Meanjin*, vol. 65, no. 1, pp. 4–12

———2007a, 'The emergency we had to have', in *Coercive Reconciliation: Stabilise, normalise, exit Aboriginal Australia*, Jon Altman and Melinda Hinkson (eds), Arena Publications, Melbourne, pp. 15–20

———2007b, *Finding the promise of Mabo: Law and social justice for the first Australians*, The Mabo Oration 2007, presented at the Anti-Discrimination Commission, Queensland, www.adcq.qld.gov.au/ATSI/FindingthePromise.html

———2008, 'New body could be a long time coming', *National Indigenous Times*, 24 January, p. 24

Behrendt, Larissa and Watson, Nicole 2007, 'Good intentions are not good enough,' *The Australian Literary Review*, 2 May, p. 22

Bennell-Pearce, Roderick 2005, Letter to the editor, *National Indigenous Times*, 3 February, p. 16

Bennett, Scott 1989, *Aborigines and Political Power*, Allen & Unwin, Sydney

Beresford, Quentin 2006, *Rob Riley: An Aboriginal leaders' quest for justice*, Aboriginal Studies Press, Canberra

Bern, John and Dodds, Susan 2002, 'On the plurality of interests: Aboriginal self-government and land rights' in Duncan Ivison, *Political Theory and the Rights of Indigenous Peoples*, Paul Patton and Will Sanders (eds), Cambridge University Press, New York, pp. 163–79

Birch, Tony 2007, 'The "invisible fire": Indigenous sovereignty, history and responsibility', in *Sovereign Subjects: Indigenous sovereignty matters*, Aileen Moreton-Robinson (ed.), Allen & Unwin, Sydney, pp. 105–17

Bird, Carmel (ed.) 1998, *The Stolen Children: Their stories*, Random House, Sydney

Boase, Ken 2007, 'New group forms for tenth Sorry Day', *Koori Mail*, 17 January, p. 4

Bolger, Audrey 1991, *Aboriginal Women and Violence*, North Australian Research Unit, Australian National University, Darwin

Bradfield, Stuart 2004, 'Citizenship, history and Indigenous status in Australia: Back to the future or towards treaty?', in *Write/Up, Journal of Australian Studies*, Elizabeth Hartrick, Robert Hogg and Sian Supski (eds), no. 80, API Network and University of Queensland Press, St Lucia, pp. 165–76

——2005, 'White picket fence or Trojan horse? The debate over communal ownership of Indigenous land and individual wealth creation', *Land, Rights, Laws: Issues of Native Title*, vol. 3, Issues paper no. 3, Native Title Research Unit, Australian Institute of Aboriginal and Torres Strait Islander Studies, Canberra

——2006, 'Separatism or status quo? Indigenous affairs from the birth of land rights to the death of ATSIC', *Australian Journal of Politics and History*, vol. 52, no. 1, pp. 80–97

Bradley, John and Seton, Kathryn 2005, 'Self-determination or "deep colonising": Land claims, colonial authority and Indigenous representation', in *Unfinished Constitutional Business? Rethinking Indigenous self-determination*, Barbara A. Hocking (ed.), Aboriginal Studies Press, Canberra, pp. 32–46

Brady, Wendy 2007, 'That sovereign being: History matters', in *Sovereign Subjects: Indigenous sovereignty matters*, Aileen Moreton-Robinson (ed.), Allen & Unwin, Sydney, pp. 140–51

Brennan, Frank 1995, *One Land, One Nation: Mabo—towards 2001*, University of Queensland Press, St Lucia

Brennan, Sean 2006, 'Economic development and land council power: Modernising the *Land Rights Act* or same old same old?', *Australian Indigenous Law Reporter*, vol. 10, no. 4, pp. 1–34

Brennan, Sean, Behrendt, Larissa, Strelein, Lisa and Williams, George 2005, *Treaty*, Federation Press, Sydney

Briskman, Linda 2003, *The Black Grapevine: Aboriginal activism and the stolen generations*, Federation Press, Sydney

Brock, Peggy 2001, 'Aboriginal women, politics and the land', in *Words and Silences: Aboriginal women, politics and the land*, Peggy Brock (ed.), Allen & Unwin, Sydney, pp. 1–17

Brough, Malcolm 2006, 'Blueprint for action in Indigenous affairs', speech to the National Institute of Governance, Indigenous Affairs Governance Series, Canberra, 5 December, www.facsia.gov.au/internet/Minister3.nsf/content/051206.htm

——2007, 'National emergency response to protect children in the Northern Territory', media release, 21 June

Bunda, Tracey 2007, 'The sovereign Aboriginal woman', in *Sovereign Subjects: Indigenous sovereignty matters*, Aileen Moreton-Robinson (ed.), Allen & Unwin, Sydney, pp. 75–85

Burgmann, Verity 2003, *Power, Profit and Protest*, Allen & Unwin, Sydney

Byrne, Mark 2005, 'Reconciliation: Stalled, fermenting, or taken out the back and shot?', *New Matilda*, 30 November, www.newmatilda.com/

policytoolkit/policydetail.asp?PolicyID=229&CategoryID=12

Calma, Tom 2006, 'Knee-jerk response will create injustice for Aboriginal defendants', *Sydney Morning Herald*, 3 October, p. 13

——2007a, 'Maximising economic and community development opportunities through native title and other forms of agreement-making', paper presented at the National Native Title Conference 2007: Tides of Native Title, 6–8 June, Cairns

——2007b, 'Today's actions could be tomorrow's tragedy', media release, Human Rights and Equal Opportunities Commission, Sydney, 11 May, www.hreoc.gov.au/about/media/media_releases/2007/32_07.html

Cape York Institute 2004, *Strong families then strong communities*, Roundtable convened by Senator Jocelyn Newman, Old Parliament House, Canberra, www.capeyorkpartnerships.com

——2007, *From Hand Out to Hand Up: Cape York welfare reform project, design recommendations*, Cape York Institute for Policy and Leadership, Cairns

Carter, April 2005, *Direct Action and Democracy Today*, Polity Press, Cambridge

Central Land Council (CLC) 1994, *The Land is Always Alive: The story of the Central Land Council*, Central Land Council, Alice Springs

——2007, *From the Grassroots: Feedback from traditional landowners and community members on the Australian Government intervention*, an initial briefing paper, Central Land Council, Alice Springs, 19 December

Central and Northern Land Councils 1994, *Our Land, Our Life*, www.clc.org.au/media/publications/olol.asp

Charlesworth, Max 1984, *The Aboriginal Land Rights Movement*, Hodja Educational Resources, Richmond

Cheatham, Kirsten 2005, 'Aden looks to the future', *Koori Mail*, 18 May, p. 9

Chesterman, John 2005, *Civil Rights: How Indigenous Australians won formal equality*, University of Queensland Press, Brisbane

——2008, 'Forming Indigenous policy without representation will fail', *The Age*, 4 March, www.theage.com.au/cgi-bin/common/popupPrintArticle.pl?path=/articles/2008/03/03/1204402360867.html

Chesterman, John and Galligan, Brian, 1997, *Citizens Without Rights: Aborigines and Australian citizenship*, Cambridge University Press, Melbourne

Chittick, Lee and Fox, Terry 1997, *Travelling with Percy: A South Coast journey*, Aboriginal Studies Press, Canberra

Combined Aboriginal Organisations of the Northern Territory (CAO) 2007, *A proposed emergency response and development plan to protect Aboriginal children in the Northern Territory—a preliminary response to the Australian Government's proposals*, 10 July, www.snaicc.asn.au/news/NTAboriginalOrgsResponse.html

Coombs, H.C. and Robinson, Cathy, 1996, 'Remembering the roots: Lessons for ATSIC', in *Shooting the Banker: Essays on ATSIC and self-determination*, Patrick Sullivan (ed.), North Australia Research Unit, Australian National University, Darwin

Cooper, David 2005, 'Escaping from the shadowland: Campaigning for Indigenous justice in Australia', *Indigenous Law Bulletin*, vol. 16, no. 10, pp. 15–17

Cornell, Stephen 2004, 'Indigenous jurisdiction and daily life: Evidence from North America', paper presented at the National Forum on Indigenous health and the treaty debate: Rights governance and responsibility, University of New South Wales, 11 September

Council for Aboriginal Reconciliation (CAR) 2000, *Reconciliation—Australia's Challenge: Final report of the Council for Aboriginal Reconciliation to the Prime Minister and the Commonwealth Parliament*, Commonwealth of Australia, www.austlii.edu.au/au/other/IndigLRes/car/2000/16/index.htm

Coyne, Darren 2008, 'Waiting for an apology', *Koori Mail*, 16 January, p. 1

Cripps, Kyllie 2007, 'Indigenous family violence: From emergency measures to committed long-term action', *Australian Indigenous Law Review*, vol. 11, no. 2, pp. 6–18

Cronin, Darryl 2003, 'Indigenous disadvantage, Indigenous governance and the notion of a treaty in Australia: An Indigenous perspective', in *Treaty: Let's get it right!*, Hannah McGlade (ed.), Aboriginal Studies Press, Canberra, pp. 151–65

——2007, 'Welfare dependency and mutual obligation: Negating Indigenous sovereignty', in *Sovereign Subjects: Indigenous sovereignty matters*, Aileen Moreton-Robinson (ed.), Allen & Unwin, Sydney, pp. 179–200

Cunneen, Chris 2005, 'Consensus and sovereignty: rethinking policing in the light of Indigenous self-determination', in *Unfinished Constitutional business? Rethinking Indigenous self-determination*, Barbara A. Hocking (ed.), Aboriginal Studies Press, Canberra, pp. 47–60

Curry, Stephen 2004, *Indigenous Sovereignty and the Democratic Project*, Ashgate, Aldershot

Cutliffe, Tony 2006, *Left for Dead: An analysis of media, corporate and government complicity in the loss of Yorta Yorta identity in Victoria, Australia*, The Eureka Project, Melbourne

Davies, Julie-Anne 2007, 'All in the family', *The Bulletin*, 10 July, pp. 18–21

Davis, Megan 2003, 'International human rights law and the domestic treaty process', in *Treaty: Let's get it right!*, Hannah McGlade (ed.), Aboriginal Studies Press, Canberra, pp. 137–50

——2005, 'Aboriginal leadership and welfare reform: you're not the first, Nöel', *Online Opinion*, 8 September, www.onlineopinion.com.au/view. acp?article-166

——2006a, 'The "S" word and Indigenous Australia: A new variation of an old theme', *Australian Journal of Legal Philosophy*, no. 31, pp. 127–41

——2006b, 'Treaty, Yeah? The utility of a treaty to advancing reconciliation in Australia', *Alternative Law Review*, no. 31, pp. 127–36

——2006c, 'Recognition of Aboriginal and Torres Strait Islander rights', *Journal of Indigenous Policy*, no. 5, pp. 35–47

——2006d, 'Living in an abnormal democracy', *National Indigenous Times*, 30 November, p. 21

——2008, 'ATSIC and Indigenous women: Lessons for the future', *University of New South Wales Faculty of Law Research Series*, paper no. 9, law.bepress.com/unswwps/flrps08/art9

Davis, Richard 2005, 'Identity and economy in Aboriginal pastoralism', in *The Power of Knowledge, the Resonance of Tradition*, Luke Taylor, Graeme Ward, Graham Henderson, Richard Davis and Lynley Wallis (eds.), Aboriginal Studies Press, Canberra, pp. 49–60

de Costa, Ravi 2006, *A Higher Authority: Indigenous transnationalism and Australia*, UNSW Press, Sydney

de Heer, Rolf, with Reynolds, Molly 2007, 'A toxic mix', *Griffith Review*, no. 16, Winter, pp. 61–6

Dean, Bartholomew and Levi, Jerome (eds) 2003, *At the Risk of Being Heard: Identity, Indigenous rights and postcolonial states*, University of Michigan Press, Ann Arbor

Debelle, Penelope 2005, 'Clash of cultures', *The Age*, 30 July, www.theage.com. au/news/national/clash-of-cultures/2005/07/29/1122144018106.html

Department of Aboriginal Affairs 1976, *The Role of the National Aboriginal Consultative Committee: Report of the Committee of Inquiry*, Australian Government Printing Service, Canberra

Department of Families, Housing, Community Services and Indigenous Affairs (FAHCSIA) 2008, *Consultations for the Proposed National Indigenous Representative Body*, Department of Families, Housing, Community Services and Indigenous Affairs, Canberra, www.fahcsia.gov. au/internet/facsinternet.nsf/indigenous/repbody.htm

Dick, Tim 2007, 'Land rights in limbo', *Sydney Morning Herald*, 26 January, www.smh.com.au/news/national/land-rights-in-limbo/2007/01/26/1169788693377.html

Dillon, Michael 2007, 'Patent medicine and the elixir of home ownership', in *Coercive Reconciliation: Stabilise, normalise, exit Aboriginal Australia*, Jon

Altman and Melinda Hinkson (eds.), Arena Publications, Melbourne, pp. 223–30

Dodson, Michael 1997, 'Citizenship in Australia: An Indigenous perspective', *Alternative Law Journal*, vol. 22, no. 2, pp. 57–9

——2003a, 'The end in the beginning: Re(de)finding Aboriginality', in *Blacklines: Contemporary critical writings by Indigenous Australians*, Michele Grossman (ed.), Melbourne University Press, Melbourne, pp. 25–42

——2003b, 'Violence, dysfunction, Aboriginality', address to the National Press Club, Canberra, 11 June

——2003c, 'Unfinished business: A shadow across our relationships', in *Treaty: Let's get it right!*, Hannah McGlade (ed.), Aboriginal Studies Press, Canberra, pp. 30–40

——2004, 'Indigenous Australians', in *The Howard Years*, Robert Manne (ed.), Black Inc., Melbourne, pp. 119–43

——2006a, 'Put-down language', letter to the editor, *Koori Mail*, 5 July, p. 26

——2006b, 'Reconciliation: Taking the next step', speech to the Reconciliation: Taking the Next Step luncheon, 25 July, www.reconciliation.org.au/I-cms.isp?page=262

——2007a, 'Tides of native title', The 2007 Mabo Lecture, AIATSIS Native Title Conference, Cairns, 7 June

——2007b, 'A reply to populist politics on culture', *Alternative Law Journal*, vol. 32, no. 1, p. 3

——2007c, 'Whatever happened to reconciliation?', public lecture, Australian Catholic University, Melbourne, 20 June

Dodson, Michael and Smith, Diane 2003, *Governance for Sustainable Development: Strategic issues and principles for Indigenous Australian communities*, Discussion paper no. 250/2003, Centre for Aboriginal Economic Policy Research, Australian National University, Canberra

Dodson, Patrick 1997, 'Reconciliation in crisis', in *Our Land is Our Life: Land rights—past present and future*, Galarrwuy Yunupingu (ed.), University of Queensland Press, St Lucia, pp. 137–49

——1998, 'Memorable times and hard times', in *Take Power Like This Old Man Here: An anthology celebrating twenty years of land rights in central Australia*, Alexis Wright (ed.), IAD Press, Alice Springs, pp. 95–102

——2000, 'Beyond the mourning gate: Dealing with unfinished business', The Wentworth Lecture, AIATSIS, Canberra, 12 May

——2005, speech to the National Reconciliation Planning Workshop, Old Parliament House, Canberra, 31 May, www.reconciliation.org.au/i-cms.isp?page=110

——2007, 'A time for honest talk', *The Age*, 10 October, www.theage.com.au/news/opinion/patrick-dodson/2007/10/09/1191695905428.html

——2008a, 'Reconciliation', in *Dear Mr Rudd: Ideas for a better Australia*, Robert Manne (ed.), Black Inc. Melbourne, pp. 28–41

——2008b, 'After the apology', address to the National Press Club, Canberra, 13 February

Dodson, Patrick, Elston, Jacinta and McCoy, Brian 2006, 'Leaving culture at the door: Aboriginal perspectives on Christian belief and practice', *Pacifica*, no. 19, pp. 249–62

Dodson, Patrick and Pearson, Noel 2004, 'The dangers of mutual obligation', *The Age*, 15 December, www.theage.com.au/news/Opinion/The-dangers-of-mutual-obligation/2004/12/14/1102787075763.html

Dornin, Tim 2007, 'Compensation for Stolen Generation urgent: Calma', *National Indigenous Times*, 4 October, p. 8

Elder, Bruce 2003, *Blood on the Wattle: Massacres and maltreatment of Australian Aborigines since 1788*, expanded edition, New Holland Publishers, London

Epoch Times 2007, 'Alice Springs Aborigines reject federal funds', 23 May, en.epochtimes.com/news/7-5-23/55635.html

Everett, Jim 2000, 'Aboriginality in Tasmania', *Siglo: Journal for the arts*, vol. 12, p. 12

Fajans, Jane 2006, 'Autonomy and relatedness: Emotions and the tension between individualism and sociality', *Critique of Anthropology*, vol. 26, no. 1, pp. 103–19

Falk, Phillip and Martin, Gary 2007, 'Misconstruing Indigenous sovereignty: Maintaining the fabric of Australian law', in *Sovereign Subjects: Indigenous sovereignty matters*, Aileen Moreton-Robinson (ed.), Allen & Unwin, Sydney, pp. 33–46

Fernandes, Sanjay 2007, 'An interview with Gary Foley: History will judge Howard's reforms', *Online Opinion*, 28 August, www.onlineopinion.com.au/view.asp?article=6272

Flick, Isabel and Goodall, Heather 2004, *Isabel Flick: The many lives of an extraordinary Aboriginal woman*, Allen & Unwin, Sydney

Foley, Gary 1997, *Muddy Waters: Archie, Mudrooroo and Aboriginality*, Essay 10, the Koori History website, www.kooriweb.org/foley/essays/essay_10.html

——2007, 'The Australian Labor Party and the *Native Title Act*', in *Sovereign Subjects: Indigenous sovereignty matters*, Aileen Moreton-Robinson (ed.), Allen & Unwin, Sydney, pp. 118–39

Foster, Denise, Mitchell, Julia, Ulrik, Jane and Williams, Raelene 2005, *Population and Mobility in the Town Camps of Alice Springs*, a report

prepared by Tangentyere Council Research Unit, Desert Knowledge
Cooperative Research Centre, Alice Springs

Fournier, Jean T. 2005, 'Preface', in *Unfinished Constitutional Business?*
Rethinking Indigenous self-determination, Barbara A. Hocking (ed.),
Aboriginal Studies Press, Canberra, pp. vii–ix

Franklin, Mathew and Karvelas, Patricia 2008, 'Vow to help Aboriginal
urban poor', *The Australian*, 28 April, www.theaustralian.news.com.au/
story/0,25197,23607966-2702,00.html

Gaita, Raimond, 2007, 'Comment', *The Monthly*, August, pp. 10–14

Gardiner, Greg and Bourke, Eleanor A. 2000, 'Indigenous populations,
"mixed" discourses and identities', *People and Place*, vol. 8, no. 2,
pp. 43–52

Gardiner-Garden, John 2000, *The Definition of Aboriginality*, Research
Note 18, 2000–01, Parliamentary Library, Parliament of Australia,
www.aph.gov.au/LIBRARY/pubs/rn/2000-01/01RN18.htm

Gilbert, Kevin 1980, 'Makarrata: NAC sellout', *AIM Aboriginal-Islander-
Message*, no.13, p. 5, www.aiatsis.gov.au/lbry/dig_prgm/treaty/t88/
m0019849_a.rtf

——1988, *Aboriginal Sovereignty: Justice, the law and the land*, self-published,
Canberra, www.aiatsis.gov.au/lbry/dig_prgm/treaty/t88/m0066865_a/
m0066865_p1_a.pdf

——2002 [1973], *Because a White Man'll Never Do It*, Angus & Robertson
Classics, HarperCollins, Sydney

Giles, Tamara 2005a, 'Debate rages over Tent Embassy plans', *National
Indigenous Times*, 4 August, p. 3

——2005b, 'Last days in the political arena for Aden Ridgeway', *National
Indigenous Times*, 23 June, p. 9

Goodall, Heather 1996, *Invasion to Embassy: Land in Aboriginal politics in New
South Wales, 1770–1972*, Allen & Unwin, Sydney

Goodall, Heather and Huggins, Jackie 1992, 'Aboriginal women are
everywhere: contemporary struggles', in *Gender Relations in Australia:
Domination and negotiation*, Kay Saunders and Raymond Evans (eds),
Harcourt Brace Jovanovich, Australia

Goot, Murray and Rowse, Tim 2007, *Divided Nation? Indigenous affairs and
the imagined public*, Melbourne University Press, Melbourne

Gordon, Michael 2004, 'Give us some hope', *The Age*, December, p. 4

Gordon, Sue, Hallahan, Kay and Henry, Darrell 2002, *Putting the Picture
Together: Inquiry into Response by Government Agencies to Complaints
of Family Violence and Child Abuse in Aboriginal Communities*, WA
Department of Premier and Cabinet, Perth

Graham, Chris 2005, 'But wait, there's more', *National Indigenous Times*, 13 October, pp. 4, 7

———2006a, 'Give it back: Yunupingu demands return of Barunga statement', *National Indigenous Times*, 26 January, p. 9

———2006b, 'One for the true believers', *National Indigenous Times*, 21 September, p. 5

———2007a, 'PM's reign a "living nightmare": leaders', *National Indigenous Times*, 6 September, p. 6

———2007b, 'Brough, Pearson, Yunupingu rejected by Aboriginal voters', Crikey.com, 27 November

———2008, 'Black face off', *National Indigenous Times*, 11 August

Gunstone, Andrew 2007, *Unfinished Business: The Australian formal reconciliation process*, Australian Scholarly Publishing, Melbourne

Hannaford, John, Huggins, Jackie and Collins, Bob 2003, *In the Hands of the Regions: A new ATSIC*, Report of the review of the Aboriginal and Torres Strait Islander Commission, Department of Families, Community Services and Indigenous Affairs, Canberra, www.atsia.gov.au/Media/Reports/PDF/atsic_review_report.pdf0

Harvard Project on American Indian Economic Development 2008, *The State of Native Nations: Conditions under US policies of self-determination*, Oxford University Press, New York

Harvey, Jirra Lulla 2005, 'Looking forward, looking back', *Koori Mail*, 9 February, p. 26

Havemann, Paul 2000, 'Enmeshed in the web? Indigenous peoples' rights in the network society', in *Global Social Movements*, Robin Cohen and Shirin Rai (eds), Athlone Press, London, pp. 18–32

Hermeston, Wendy 2005, 'Telling you our story: How apology and action relate to health and social problems in Aboriginal and Torres Strait Islander communities', *Medical Journal of Australia*, vol. 183, no. 9, pp. 479–81

Hinkson, Melinda 2007, 'In the name of the child', in *Coercive Reconciliation: Stabilise, normalise, exit Aboriginal Australia*, Jon Altman and Melinda Hinkson (eds), Arena Publications, Melbourne, pp. 1–12

Hocking, Debra 2006, 'The long journey home: A reflection on the journey of healing', *Journal of Australian Indigenous Issues*, vol. 9, no. 2–3, pp. 93–102

Hodder, Steve 2005, 'A blunt message', *Koori Mail*, 13 July, p. 19

Howard, John 1996, Transcript of the Prime Minister-Elect the Hon. John Howard MP, press conference, Sydney, 4 March

———2000, Address to Corroboree 2000, Sydney Opera House, 27 May

———2005, Address to the National Reconciliation Planning Workshop, Old Parliament House, Canberra, 30 May

Howard, John and Vanstone, Amanda 2004, Transcript of the Prime Minister The Hon. John Howard MP Joint Press Conference with Senator Amanda Vanstone, Parliament House, Canberra, 15 April

Howard, Michael C. 1982, 'Aboriginal brokerage and political development in south-western Australia', in *Aboriginal Power in Australian Society*, Michael Howard (ed.), University of Queensland Press, St Lucia, pp. 159–83

Howard, Michael C. (ed.), 1982, *Aboriginal Power in Australian Society*, University of Queensland Press, St Lucia

Howitt, Richard 2001, *Rethinking Resource Management: Justice, sustainability and Indigenous peoples*, Routledge, London

Howitt, Richard, Connell, J. and Hirsch, P. 1996, *Resources, Nations and Indigenous Peoples: Case studies from Australasia, Melanesia and Southeast Asia*, Oxford University Press, Oxford

Howlett, Catherine 2006, 'Mining and Indigenous peoples: Which theory "best fits"?', paper presented to the Australasian Political Science Association Conference, University of Newcastle, 25–27 September

Huggins, Jackie 1998, *Sister Girl: The writings of an Aboriginal activist and historian*, University of Queensland Press, St Lucia

——2003, 'Always was, always will be', in *Blacklines: Contemporary critical writings by Indigenous Australians*, Michele Grossman (ed.), Melbourne University Press, Melbourne, pp. 60–5

——2007, Speech to the Garma festival, Gulkula, 4 August, www. reconciliation.org.au/downloads/156/HugginsGARMA.pdf

Hughes, Helen 2005, 'The economics of Indigenous deprivation and proposals for reform', *Issue Analysis*, no. 63, Centre for Independent Studies, Sydney, www.cis.org.au/IssueAnalysis/ia63/IA63.pdf

——2007, *Lands of Shame: Aboriginal and Torres Strait Islander 'homelands' in transition*, Centre for Independent Studies, Sydney

Hughes, Helen and Jenness, Warin 2005, 'A new deal for Aborigines and Torres Strait Islanders in remote communities', *Issue Analysis*, no. 54, Centre for Independent Studies, Sydney, www.cis.org.au/IssueAnalysis/ia54/IA54.pdf

Human Rights and Equal Opportunities Commission (HREOC) 1997, *Bringing Them Home: Report of the National Inquiry into the Separation of Aboriginal and Torres Strait Islander Children from Their Families*, Human Rights and Equal Opportunities Commission, Sydney

Hunt, Janet and Smith, Diane 2007, *Indigenous Community Governance Project: Year 2 research findings*, Working paper no. 36/2007, Centre for Aboriginal Economic Policy Research, Australian National University, Canberra

Ivanitz, Michele 2002, 'Democracy and Indigenous self-determination', in *Democratic Theory Today: Challenges for the 21st century*, April Carter and Geoffrey Stokes (eds), Polity Press, Cambridge, pp. 121–48

Janke, Terri and Quiggin, Robynne 2006, *Indigenous Cultural and Intellectual Property: The main issues for the Indigenous arts industry in 2006*, written for the Aboriginal and Torres Strait Islander Arts Board, The Australia Council, Sydney

Jarrett, Stephanie 2006, *Minority Rights Harm Aboriginal Women and Children*, Bennelong Society Occasional Paper, September, www.bennelong.com.au

Jeffries, Sam 2007, 'Rhetoric and reverse gear: Indigenous policy as a strategic afterthought', paper presented at the 4th National Indigenous Education Conference, *Aboriginal and Islander Health Worker Journal*, vol. 31, no. 1, pp. 22–7

Johns, Gary 2006, 'Social stability and structural adjustment', paper presented at *Leaving Remote Communities*, the Bennelong Society Sixth Annual Conference, Melbourne, 2 September, www.bennelong.com.au/conferences/pdf/Johns2006.pdf

Jonas, William and Dick, Darren 2004, 'The abolition of ATSIC: Silencing Indigenous voices?', *Dialogue*, no. 23, pp. 4–15

Jones, Delmos J. and Hill-Burnett, Jacquetta 1982, 'The political context of ethnogenesis: An Australian example', in *Aboriginal Power in Australian Society*, Michael C. Howard (ed.), University of Queensland Press, St Lucia, pp. 214–46

Jones, Jonathon 2002, 'Boomalli: To strike, to make a mark', in *Life in Gadigal Country*, Anita Heiss (ed.), Gadigal Information Service, Sydney, pp. 53–64

Jopson, Debra 2002, 'No change at top as Clark lays on the charm', *Sydney Morning Herald*, 20 December, www.smh.com.au/articles/2002/12/19/10 40174346664.html

Jull, Peter 2005, 'Not honesty to have it thus set down! Making national Indigenous policy', paper presented at the conference Peace, Justice and Reconciliation in the Asia-Pacific Region, University of Queensland, 1–3 April

Kauffman, Paul 1998, *Wik, Mining and Aborigines*, Allen & Unwin, Sydney

Keen, Ian (ed.) 1988, *Being Black: Aboriginal cultures in 'settled' Australia*, Aboriginal Studies Press, Canberra

Kelly, Paul 2004, 'Black leaders offer new accord', *The Australian*, 4 December, www.theaustralian.news.com.au/common/story_page/0,5744,11582580%255E601,00.html

Keon-Cohen, Bryan 1981, 'Makarrata legal issues', *Aboriginal Law Bulletin*, no. 1, pp. 2–3

Kidd, Rosalind 2007, *Hard Labour, Stolen Wages: National report on stolen wages*, Australians for Native Title and Reconciliation, www.antar.org. au/images/stories/PDFs/StolenWages/stolenwages.pdf

Kimberley Aboriginal Law and Culture Centre (KALACC) 2006, *New Legend: A story of law and culture and the fight for self-determination in the Kimberley*, Kimberley Aboriginal Law and Culture Centre, Fitzroy Crossing

Koori Mail 2005a, 'Agius warns on culture', 20 April, p.4

——2005b, 'Pearson warns on ownership', 2 November, p. 13

——2005c, 'Committee reverts to previous name', 21 September, p. 10

——2005d, 'Ridgeway's departure "a sad loss"', 29 June, p. 10

——2006, 'Exploring scenarios for life post-ATSIC', 11 October, p. 4

——2007a, 'People in positions of powerlessness engage in lateral violence', 28 February, p. 9

——2007b, 'Report anniversary a bittersweet time', 6 June, p. 41

——2007c, 'Garma signs resolution to stop "draconian" legislation in NT', 9 August, p. 3

——2007d, 'That's more like it!', 19 December, p. 1

——2007e, 'Sorry Day push for national apology', 19 December, p. 7

Langton, Marcia 1988, 'Medicine square', in *Being Black: Aboriginal cultures in 'settled' Australia*, Ian Keen (ed.), Aboriginal Studies Press, Canberra, pp. 201–25

——1997, 'Grandmothers' law, company business and succession in changing Aboriginal land tenure systems', in *Our Land Is Our Life: Land rights—past present and future*, Galarrwuy Yunupingu (ed.), University of Queensland Press, St Lucia, pp. 84–116

——1998, 'Cost-efficient, triple-documented ethnic cleansing', address to the International Museums Conference, Melbourne, October, www.faira.org. au/lrq/archives/199811/stories/cost-efficient.html

——2002, 'A new deal? Indigenous development and the politics of recovery', Dr Charles Perkins AO Memorial Oration, University of Sydney, 4 October

——2003 [1994], 'Aboriginal art and film: The politics of representation', in *Blacklines: Contemporary critical writings by Indigenous Australians*, Michele Grossman (ed.), Melbourne University Press, Melbourne, pp. 109–24

——2007, 'Stop the abuse of children', *The Australian*, 12 December, blogs. theaustralian.news.com.au/yoursay/index.php/theaustralian/comments/ stop_the_abuse_of_children

——2008a, 'Trapped in the Aboriginal reality show', *Griffith Review*, no. 19, pp. 145–62

———2008b, 'Indigenous Affairs', in *Dear Mr Rudd: Ideas for a better Australia*, Robert Manne (ed.), Black Inc., Melbourne, pp. 220–33

Liddle, John 2008, Interyerrkwe Statement, speech and press release, Aboriginal Male Health Summit, Central Australian Aboriginal Congress

Liddle, Kerryne 2006, 'What is the way forward?', *Koori Mail*, 26 April, pp. 8–9

Lippmann, Lorna 1981, *Generations of Resistance: The Aboriginal struggle for justice*, Longman Cheshire, Melbourne

Maaka, Roger and Fleras, Augie 2005, *The Politics of Indigeneity: Challenging the state in Canada and Aotearoa New Zealand*, University of Otago Press, Dunedin

McCausland, Ruth 2005a, 'So just who is sharing the responsibility in Indigenous policy?', *New Matilda*, 9 March, www.newmatilda.com/home/printarticle.asp?ArticleID=519

———2005b, 'Petrol bowsers for washing kids' faces: a "new conversation" in Indigenous policy', paper presented to the National Social Policy Conference, Sydney, July

McConchie, Peter 2003, *Elders: Wisdom from Australia's Indigenous leaders*, Cambridge University Press, Cambridge

McDonald, Gaynor 2001, '"Policy is for the policy makers": The cultural cost of different visions', paper presented to the National Social Policy Conference, Sydney 4–6 July

McDonald, Lindsey Te Ata o Tu and Muldoon, Paul 2006, 'Globalisation, neo-liberalism and the struggle for indigenous citizenship', *Australian Journal of Political Science*, vol. 41, no. 2, pp. 209–23

McGee-Sippel, Lorraine 2002, 'The 1988 Bicentennial march', in *Life in Gadigal Country*, Anita Heiss (ed.), Gadigal Information Service, Sydney, pp. 75–7

McGlade, Hannah 2001, 'Aboriginal women and the Commonwealth government's response to Mabo—an international human rights perspective', in *Words and Silences: Aboriginal women, politics and the land*, Peggy Brock (ed.), Allen & Unwin, Sydney, pp. 139–56

McIntosh, Ian 2003, 'Reconciling personal and impersonal worlds: Aboriginal struggles for self-determination', in *At the Risk of Being Heard: Identity, rights and postcolonial states*, B. Dean and J.M. Levi (eds.), University of Michigan Press, Ann Arbor, pp. 293–323

McKenna, Mark 1997, *Different Perspectives in Black Armband History*, Research paper 5 1997–98, Parliamentary Library, Parliament of Australia, www.aph.gpv.au/library/pubs/rp/1997-98/98rp05.htm

Macklin, Jenny 2008a, 'Closing the gap: Building an Indigenous future', address to the National Press Club, 27 February

——2008b, 'Out of the chaos', address to the Melbourne Institute Economic and Social Outlook Conference, Melbourne, 27 March

——2008c, 'Beyond Mabo: Native title and closing the gap', The Mabo Lecture, James Cook University, Townsville, 21 May, www.fahcsia.gov. au/internet/jennymacklin.nsf/content/beyond_mabo_21may08.htm

Maddison, Sarah 2006, 'A decade of lost opportunities: The Howard government and Indigenous policy', *Journal of Australian Indigenous Issues*, vol. 9, nos 2–3, pp. 5–26

Maddison, Sarah and Edgar, Gemma 2008, 'Into the lion's den: Challenges for not-for-profits in their relationships with government', in *Strategic Issues for the Not for Profit Sector*, Jo Barraket (ed.), UNSW Press, Sydney, pp. 188–211

Maher, Sid 2008, 'Council in $50m deal for camps', *The Australian*, 26 June, www.theaustralian.news.com.au/story/0,25197,23923525-5013172,00. html

Malezer, Les 2002, 'Reconciliation sounds OK but "No", Thanks!', *Crossings*, vol. 7.1 asc.uq.edu.au/crossings/7_1/index.html

Manne, Robert 2001a, *The Barren Years: John Howard and Australian political culture*, Text Publishing, Melbourne

——2001b, 'In denial: the stolen generation and the Right', *Quarterly Essay*, Issue 1

——2007, 'Pearson's gamble, Stanner's dream: The past and future of remote Australia', *The Monthly*, August, pp. 30–40

Mansell, Michael 2003, 'Citizenship, assimilation and a treaty', in *Treaty: Let's get it right!*, Hannah McGlade (ed.), Aboriginal Studies Press, Canberra, pp. 5–17

——2005, 'Why Norfolk Island but not Aborigines?', in *Unfinished Constitutional Business? Rethinking Indigenous self-determination*, Barbara A. Hocking (ed.), Aboriginal Studies Press, Canberra, pp. 82–92

——2007, 'The political vulnerability of the unrepresented', in *Coercive Reconciliation: Stabilise, normalise, exit Aboriginal Australia*, Jon Altman and Melinda Hinkson (eds.), Arena Publications, Melbourne, pp. 73–84

Marika, Dr 1999, 'The 1998 Wentworth lecture', *Australian Aboriginal Studies*, no. 1, pp. 3–9

Martin, David 1999, 'The Reeves Report's assumptions on regionalism and socio-economic advancement', in *Land Rights at Risk? Evaluations of the Reeves Report*, Jon Altman, Frances Morphy and Tim Rowse (eds), Research Monograph no. 14, Centre for Aboriginal Economic Policy

Research, Australian National University, Canberra, pp. 155–66

——2005, 'Rethinking Aboriginal community governance', in *Community and Local Governance in Australia*, Paul Smyth, Tim Reddell and Andrew Jones (eds), UNSW Press, Sydney, pp. 108–27

Maybury-Lewis, David 1997, *Indigenous Peoples, Ethnic Groups and the State*, Allyn and Bacon, Boston

——2003, 'From elimination to an uncertain future: changing policies towards Indigenous peoples', in *At the Risk of Being Heard: Identity, rights and postcolonial states*, B. Dean and J.M. Levi (eds), University of Michigan Press, Ann Arbor, pp. 324–34

Maynard, John 2007, *Fight for Liberty and Freedom: The origins of Australian Aboriginal activism*, Aboriginal Studies Press, Canberra

Memmott, P., Stacy, R., Chambers, C. and Keys, C. 2001, *Violence in Indigenous Communities*, Commonwealth Attorney-General's Department, Canberra

Merlan, Francesca 2005, 'Indigenous movements in Australia', *Annual Review of Anthropology*, vol. 34, pp. 437–94

Moreton-Robinson, Aileen 2003, 'Introduction: Resistance, recovery and revitalisation', in *Blacklines: Contemporary critical writings by Indigenous Australians*, Michele Grossman (ed.), Melbourne University Press, Melbourne, pp. 127–31

——2005, 'Patriarchal whiteness, self-determination and Indigenous women: The invisibility of structural privilege and the visibility of oppression', in *Unfinished Constitutional Business? Rethinking Indigenous self-determination*, Barbara A. Hocking (ed.), Aboriginal Studies Press, Canberra, pp. 61–73

——2007, 'Writing off Indigenous sovereignty: The discourse of security and patriarchal white sovereignty', in *Sovereign Subjects: Indigenous sovereignty matters*, Aileen Moreton-Robinson (ed.), Allen & Unwin, Sydney, pp. 86–104

Moreton-Robinson, Aileen (ed.) 2007, *Sovereign Subjects: Indigenous sovereignty matters*, Allen & Unwin, Sydney

Morgan, George 2006a, *Unsettled Places: Aboriginal people and urbanisation in New South Wales*, Wakefield Press, Kent Town

——2006b, 'Aboriginal politics, self-determination and the rhetoric of community', *Dialogue*, no. 25, pp. 19–29

Morgan, Sally 1987, *My Place*, Fremantle Arts Centre Press, Fremantle

Morris, Barry 1988, 'Dhan-gadi resistance to assimilation', in *Being Black: Aboriginal cultures in 'settled' Australia*, Ian Keen (ed.), Aboriginal Studies Press, Canberra, pp. 33–64

Morris, Linda 2007, 'A new faith for Kooris', *Sydney Morning Herald*, 4 May, p. 9

Morris, Lynette 1996, 'Black sistas: Indigenous women and the welfare', in *D.I.Y. Feminism*, Kathy Bail (ed.), Allen & Unwin, Sydney

Morrissey, Michael 2006, 'The Australian state and Indigenous people 1900–2006', *Journal of Sociology*, vol. 42, no. 4, pp. 347–54

Morrissey, Philip 2003, 'Aboriginality and corporatism', in *Blacklines: Contemporary critical writings by Indigenous Australians*, Michele Grossman (ed.), Melbourne University Press, Melbourne, pp. 52–9

Mudrooroo 1995, *Us Mob: History, culture, struggle. An introduction to Indigenous Australia*, HarperCollins, Sydney

——2003, 'The global nomad', available at: www.mudrooroo.com/4574.html

Mulgan, Richard 1998, 'Citizenship and legitimacy in post-colonial Australia', in *Citizenship and Indigenous Australians: Changing conceptions and possibilities*, Nicolas Peterson and Will Sanders (eds), Cambridge University Press, Melbourne, pp. 179–95

Murdoch, Lindsay 2007, 'Sole survivor sitting on a $5b fortune', *Sydney Morning Herald*, News Review, 14 July, p. 7

Myers, Fred 1991, *Pintupi Country, Pintupi Self: Sentiment, place and politics among Western Desert Aborigines*, University of California Press, Berkeley

——2005, 'Unsettled business: Acrylic painting, tradition and Indigenous being', in *The Power of Knowledge, the Resonance of Tradition*, Luke Taylor, Graeme Ward, Graham Henderson, Richard Davis and Lynley Wallis (eds), Aboriginal Studies Press, Canberra, pp. 3–33

Nakata, Martin 2003 [1994], 'Better', in *Blacklines: Contemporary critical writings by Indigenous Australians*, Michele Grossman (ed.), Melbourne University Press, Melbourne, pp. 132–44

——2004, 'Indigenous Australian studies and higher education', The Wentworth Lecture, Australian Institute of Aboriginal and Torres Strait Islander Studies, Canberra

National Aboriginal Conference 1981, 'Makarrata: Some ways forward', position paper presented to the World Council of Indigenous Peoples, Canberra, available at: www1.aiatsis.gov.au/exhibitions/treaty/nac/m0031095_a.pdf

National Indigenous Council (NIC) 2006, *Report to Government, December 2004 to December 2005*, in author's collection

——2007, *Report to Government, January to December 2006*, in author's collection

National Indigenous Times 2007, 'Heartbreak Hill', 23 August, pp. 16–18

——2008a, 'Community consultation: Macklin', 24 January, p. 3

——2008b, 'Speech moving, but not far enough', 21 February, p. 7

——2008c, 'Brough's Tiwi dealings warrant scrutiny: Calma', 21 February, p. 3

National Oceans Office 2004, *Living on Saltwater Country: Review of literature about Aboriginal rights, use, management and interests in northern Australian marine environments,* National Oceans Office, Hobart, www.environment. gov.au/coasts/mbp/publications/pubs/saltwater-lit-review.pdf

NSW Aboriginal Child Sexual Assault Taskforce (2006), *Breaking the Silence: Creating the future, addressing child sexual assault in Aboriginal communities in NSW,* NSW Attorney-General's Department, Sydney

Niezen, Ronald 2003, *The Origins of Indigenism: Human rights and the politics of identity,* University of California Press, Berkeley

Nowra, Louis 2007, *Bad Dreaming: Aboriginal men's violence against women and children,* Pluto Press, Melbourne

O'Donoghue, Lowitja 1995, 'Customary Law as a vehicle for community empowerment', speech delivered at the Forum on Indigenous Customary Law, Parliament House, Canberra, 18 October

——1997, 'Something to celebrate', in *Our Land is Our Life: Land rights—past present and future,* Galarrwuy Yunupingu (ed.), University of Queensland Press, St Lucia, pp. 28–32

——2007, speech to mark the Tenth Anniversary of the *Bringing Them Home Report,* Great Hall of Parliament, Canberra, 24 May

O'Shane, Pat 1993, 'Aboriginal women and the women's movement', in *Refracting Voices: Feminist perspectives from Refractory Girl,* Southwood Press, Marrickville

——1998, 'Aboriginal political movements: Some observations', 13th Frank Archibald Memorial Lecture, University of New England, Publications Office, University of New England, Armidale, 14 October

Palmer, Kingsley 2005, 'Dependency, technology and governance', in *The Power of Knowledge, the Resonance of Tradition,* Luke Taylor, Graeme Ward, Graham Henderson, Richard Davis and Lynley Wallis (eds), Aboriginal Studies Press, Canberra, pp. 101–15

Paradies, Yin 2006, 'Beyond black and white: Essentialism, hybridity and Indigeneity', *Journal of Sociology,* vol. 42, no. 4, pp. 355–67

Parker, Kirstie 2007, 'New hope for Aust's Stolen Generations', *Koori Mail,* 15 August, p. 11

——2008a, 'Sorry "the first battle"', *Koori Mail,* 13 February, p. 9

——2008b, 'Equal by 2030', *Koori Mail,* 26 March, p. 1

Parker, Siv 2006, 'Under pressure', *Koori Mail,* 16 August, pp. 1, 6

Parliamentary Debate, House of Representatives 1999, Motion of Reconciliation, 26 August

——2000, Questions without Notice: Aboriginals: Stolen Generations, 3 April, 14 August

Pascoe, Bruce 2007, 'Australians in denial . . .', *Online Opinion*, 21 May, www.onlineopinion.cm.au/print.asp?article=5858

Paul, Mandy and Gray, Geoffrey (eds) 2002, *Through a Smoky Mirror: History and native title*, Native Title Research Series, Aboriginal Studies Press, Canberra

Pearson, Noel 1993, 'From remnant title to social justice', *Australian Quarterly*, vol. 65, no. 4, pp. 179–84

——2000a, *Our Right to Take Responsibility*, self published

——2000b, 'The light on the hill', The Ben Chifley Memorial Lecture, Panthers Leagues Club, Bathurst, 12 August

——2005, *The Cape York Agenda: Fundamental transformation through radical reform*, Cape York Institute for Policy and Leadership, Cairns, www.cyi.org.au/WEBSITE%20uploads/Documents/Cape%20York%20 Agenda%20final.pdf

——2006a, 'New approaches to Indigenous policy: The role of rights and responsibilities', public seminar, Cape York Institute for Policy and Leadership, Cairns, 6 July

——2006b, 'Layered identities and peace', Earth Dialogue, Brisbane Festival, 23 July

——2007a, 'White guilt, victimhood and the quest for a radical centre', *Griffith Review*, no. 16, pp. 3–58

——2007b, 'More Uncle Toms than meet the eye', *The Australian*, 28 July, p. 24

——2007c, 'An end to the tears', *The Australian*, 23 June, pp. 17, 22

Pearson, Noel and Kostakidis-Lianos, Lara 2004, 'Building Indigenous capital: Removing obstacles to participation in the real economy', Cape York Institute for Policy and Leadership, Cairns

Peters-Little, Frances 2000, *The Community Game: Aboriginal self definition at the local level*, Research Discussion Paper no. 10, Australian Institute for Aboriginal and Torres Strait Islander Studies, Canberra

Peterson, Nicolas 1998, 'Welfare colonialism and citizenship: Politics, economics and agency', in *Citizenship and Indigenous Australians: Changing conceptions and possibilities*, Nicolas Peterson and Will Sanders (eds), Cambridge University Press, Melbourne, pp. 101–17

——1999, 'Reeves in the context of the history of land rights legislation: Anthropological aspects', in *Land Rights at Risk? Evaluations of the Reeves Report*, Jon Altman, Frances Morphy and Tim Rowse (eds), Research Monograph no. 14, Centre for Aboriginal Economic Policy Research, Australian National University, Canberra, pp. 25–32

Peterson, Nicolas and Sanders, Will (eds) 1998, *Citizenship and Indigenous Australians: Changing conceptions and possibilities*, Cambridge University Press, Melbourne

Petrick, Anthony Phillip 1998, 'Sorting things out', in *Take Power Like This Old Man Here: An anthology celebrating twenty years of land rights in central Australia*, Alexis Wright (ed.), IAD Press, Alice Springs, pp. 105–7

Petty, Anna 2008, 'After 30 years of denial come tears of relief', *Sydney Morning Herald*, 14 February, p. 15

Phillips, Gregory, Goodwin, Timothy, Coates, Dameeli, More, Seleneah and Yettica-Paulson, Mark, on behalf of NIYMA 2003, 'A story of emergence: NIYMA's view on a treaty', in *Treaty: Let's get it right!*, Hannah McGlade (ed.), Aboriginal Studies Press, Canberra, pp. 107–17

Pratt, Angela, Elder, Catriona and Ellis, Cath 2001, '"Papering over differences": Australian nationhood and the normative discourse of reconciliation', in *Reconciliation, Multiculturalism, Identities: Difficult dialogues, sensible solutions*, Mary Kalantzis and Bill Cope (eds), Common Ground Publishing, Melbourne, pp. 135–48

Ravens, Tara 2007, 'NT child report authors "betrayed" by federal government', *National Indigenous Times*, 9 August, p. 3

——2008, 'NT govt under fire for compo stance', 24 January, p. 4

Ravens, Tara and Peters, Dennis 2007, 'Aboriginal land to become nuclear waste site', *The Australian*, 25 May, www.theaustralian.news.com.au/printpage/0,5942,21793355,00.html

Ray, Tristan 2007, 'Youth well-being in Central Australia', *Coercive Reconciliation: Stabilise, normalise, exit Aboriginal Australia*, Jon Altman and Melinda Hinkson (eds), Arena Publications, Melbourne, pp. 195–203

Reconciliation Australia 2006, 'Australia Day and reconciliation?', media release, 25 January, www.reconciliation.org.au/downloads/157/Australia_Day.pdf

Reeves, John 1998, *Building on Land Rights for the Next Generation: The Review of Aboriginal Land Rights (Northern Territory) Act 1976*, ATSIC, Canberra

Reilly, Alexander 2001, 'Land rights: From past to present to absent', *Alternative Law Journal*, vol. 26, no. 3, pp. 143–4

Reilly, Alex, Behrendt, Larissa, Williams, George, McCausland, Ruth and McMillan, Mark 2007, 'The promise of regional governance for Aboriginal and Torres Strait Islander Communities', *Ngyia: Talk the law*, vol. 1, Governance in Indigenous Communities, pp. 126–66

Reynolds, Henry 1982, *The Other Side of the Frontier: Aboriginal resistance to the European invasion of Australia*, Penguin, Ringwood

——1998, 'Sovereignty', in *Citizenship and Indigenous Australians: Changing conceptions and possibilities*, Nicolas Peterson and Will Sanders (eds), Cambridge University Press, Melbourne, pp. 208–15

Ridgeway, Aden 2003, 'Mabo ten years on—small step or giant leap?', in *Treaty: Let's get it right!*, Hannah McGlade (ed.), Aboriginal Studies Press, Canberra, pp. 185–97

——2005, 'Addressing the economic exclusion of Indigenous Australians through native title', The Mabo Lecture, National Native Title Conference, Coffs Harbour, 3 June

Rigney, Lester-Irabinna 1999, 'Internationalization of an Indigenous anticolonial cultural critique of research methodologies: A guide to indigenist research methodology and its principles', *Wicazo Sa Review*, vol. 14, no. 2, Emergent Ideas in Native American Studies, pp. 109–21

——2002, 'Bread verses freedom: Treaty and stabilising Indigenous languages', paper presented at the National Treaty Conference, National Convention Centre, Canberra, 29 August, available at pandora.nla.gov.au/pan/14130/20051121-0000/www.treatynow.org/conference.html

——2003, 'Indigenous education, languages and treaty: The redefinition of a new relationship with Australia', in *Treaty: Let's get it right!*, Hannah McGlade (ed.), Aboriginal Studies Press, Canberra, pp. 72–87

Rimmer, Matthew 2007, 'A right of resale? Indigenous art under the hammer', ABC News Opinion, online, 27 July, www.abc.net.au/news/stories/2007/07/27/1989699.htm

Ring, Graham 2006, 'Stormclouds build over black Australia', *Arena Magazine*, no. 85, pp. 7–8

Rintoul, Stuart 2002, 'The third wave', *The Australian*, 2 March, pp. 19–25

——2004, 'Long Walk over, longer journey ahead', *The Australian*, 4 December

Ross, David 1997, 'Future directions: It's all about rights!', *Our Land Is Our Life: Land rights—past present and future*, Galarrwuy Yunupingu (ed.), University of Queensland Press, St Lucia, pp. 125–36

Rowley, Kevin, O'Dea, Kerin, Anderson, Ian, McDermott, Robyn, Saraswati, Karmananda, Tilmouth, Ricky, Roberts, Iris, Fitz, Joseph, Wang, Zaimin, Jenkins, Alicia, Best, James, Wang, Zhiqiang and Brown, Alex 2008, 'Lower than expected morbidity and mortality for an Australian Aboriginal population: 10-year follow-up in a decentralised community', *Medical Journal of Australia*, vol. 188, no. 5, pp. 283–7

Rowse, Tim 1992, *Remote Possibilities: The Aboriginal domain and the administrative imagination*, North Australia Research Unit, Australian National University, Darwin

——1993, *After Mabo: Interpreting Indigenous traditions*, Melbourne University Press, Melbourne

——1998, 'Indigenous citizenship and self-determination: the problem of shared responsibilities', in *Citizenship and Indigenous Australians: Changing conceptions and possibilities*, Nicolas Peterson and Will Sanders (eds), Cambridge University Press, Melbourne, pp. 79–100

——2001, 'Democratic systems are an alien thing to Aboriginal culture…', in *Speaking for the People: Representation in Australian Politics*, Marian Sawer and Gianni Zappalà (eds), Melbourne University Press, Melbourne, pp. 103–33

——2002, *Indigenous Futures: Choice and development for Aboriginal and Islander Australia*, UNSW Press, Sydney

——2005, 'The politics of being practical: Howard and his quiet revolution in Indigenous affairs', Speech to the Brisbane Institute, www.brisinst.org.au/resources/rowse_tim_indigenous.html

Royal Commission into Aboriginal Deaths in Custody (RCIADIC) 1991, *National Report*, vol. 1, Australian Government Publishing Service, Canberra

Rudd, Kevin 2008, Apology to Australia's Indigenous Peoples, House of Representatives, Parliament House, Canberra, 13 February, www.pm.gov.au/media/Speech/2008/speech_0073.cfm

Ruddock, Phillip 2002, 'ATSIC Review Panel Announced', media release, 12 November, www.atsia.gov.au/Media/atsicreview/media.html#ATSIC%20Review%20Panel%20Announced

Russell, Peter H. 2005, *Recognising Aboriginal Title: The Mabo case and Indigenous resistance to English-settler colonialism*, UNSW Press, Sydney

Ryan, Lyndall 1996, *The Aboriginal Tasmanians*, 2nd edn, Allen & Unwin, Sydney

Sanders, Will 1998, 'Citizenship and the Community Development Employment Projects scheme: Equal rights, difference and appropriateness', *Citizenship and Indigenous Australians: Changing conceptions and possibilities*, Nicolas Peterson and Will Sanders (eds), Cambridge University Press, Melbourne, pp. 141–53

——2003, *The Tasmanian Electoral Roll Trial in the 2002 ATSIC Elections*, Discussion paper no. 245/2003, Centre for Aboriginal Economic Policy Research, Australian National University, Canberra

——2004, 'Prospects for regionalism in Indigenous community governance', *Dialogue*, no. 23, pp. 56–61

——2005a, *Housing Tenure and Indigenous Australians in Remote and Settled Areas*, Discussion paper no. 275/2005, Centre for Aboriginal Economic Policy Research, Australian National University, Canberra

——2005b, 'Never even adequate: Reconciliation and Indigenous affairs',
in *Howard's Second and Third Governments: Australian Commonwealth
Administration 1998–2004*, C. Aulich and R. Wettenhall (eds), UNSW
Press, Sydney, pp. 152–72

——2006, 'Indigenous affairs after the Howard decade: Administrative
reforms and practical reconciliation or defying decolonisation?', *Journal of
Australian Indigenous Issues*, vol. 9, nos. 2–3, pp. 43-51

SBS 2005, 'Nuclear waste dump', *Living Black*, SBS Television, 14 November

Schwab, Jerry 1988, 'Ambiguity, style and kinship in Adelaide Aboriginal
identity', in *Being Black: Aboriginal cultures in 'settled' Australia*, Ian Keen
(ed.), Aboriginal Studies Press, Canberra, pp. 77–96

Seidel, Peter 2004, 'Native title: The struggle for justice for the Yorta Yorta
Nation', *Alternative Law Journal*, vol. 29, no. 2, pp. 70–96

Senate Standing Committee on Environment, Communications, Information
Technology and the Arts 2007, *Indigenous Art: Securing the future*, www.
aph.gov.au/Senate/committee/ecita_ctte/indigenous_arts/report/report.
pdf

Senate Standing Committee on Legal and Constitutional Affairs 1983,
*200 Years Later: The feasibility of a compact or 'Makarrata' between the
Commonwealth and Aboriginal people*, Australian Government Printing
Service, Canberra

Shaw, Wendy 2007, *Cities of Whiteness*, Blackwell Publishing, Malden

Skelton, Russell 2008, 'NT intervention "creating unrest" in big towns',
The Age, 26 April, www.theage.com.au/news/national/nt-intervention-
creating-unrest-in-big-towns/2008/04/25/1208743253119.html

Smith, Barry 1989, *The Concept of 'Community' in Aboriginal Policy and Service
Delivery*, NADU, Darwin

Smith, Diane 1996, 'From cultural diversity to regionalism: The political
culture of difference in ATSIC', in *Shooting the Banker: Essays on ATSIC
and self-determination*, Patrick Sullivan (ed.), North Australia Research
Unit, Australian National University, Darwin

——2007, 'Networked governance: Issues of process, policy and power in
a West Arnhem Land region initiative', *Ngiya: Talk the Law*, vol. 1,
Governance in Indigenous Communities, pp. 24–51

Stephenson, Peta 2007, *The Outsiders Within: Telling Australia's Indigenous–
Asian story*, UNSW Press, Sydney

Stokes, Geoffrey 2002, 'Australian democracy and Indigenous self-
determination, 1901–2001', in *Australia Reshaped: 200 years of
institutional transformation*, Geoffrey Brennan and Francis G. Castles
(eds), Cambridge University Press, Cambridge, pp. 181–219

Stokes, Geoffrey 2005, 'Why we went to Canberra', *Koori Mail*, 23 March, p. 24

Sutton, Peter 1999, 'The Reeves Report and the idea of the "community"', in *Land Rights at Risk? Evaluations of the Reeves Report*, Jon Altman, Frances Morphy and Tim Rowse (eds), Research Monograph no. 14, Centre for Aboriginal Economic Policy Research, Australian National University, Canberra, pp. 39–51

——2001, 'The politics of suffering: Indigenous policy in Australia since the 1970s', *Anthropological Forum*, vol. 11, no. 2, pp. 125–73

Taffe, Sue 2005, *Black and White Together: FCAATSI, The Federal Council of Aborigines and Torres Strait Islanders 1958–1973*, University of Queensland Press, St Lucia

Tangentyere Council 2004, *Tangentyere Council Annual Report*, Tangentyere Council, Alice Springs

Taylor, Louise 2003, 'Who's your mob? The politics of Aboriginal identity and the implications for a treaty', in *Treaty: Let's get it right!*, Hannah McGlade (ed.), Aboriginal Studies Press, Canberra, pp. 88–99

Taylor, Luke, Ward, Graeme, Henderson, Graham, Davis, Richard and Wallis, Lynley (eds) 2005, *The Power of Knowledge, the Resonance of Tradition*, Aboriginal Studies Press, Canberra

Tilmouth, Bruce 'Tracker' 1998, 'Introduction', in *Take Power Like This Old Man Here: An anthology celebrating twenty years of land rights in central Australia*, Alexis Wright (ed.), IAD Press, Alice Springs, pp. ix–xii

Tilmouth, William 2007, 'Saying no to $60 million', in *Coercive Reconciliation: Stabilise, normalise, exit Aboriginal Australia*, Jon Altman and Melinda Hinkson (eds), Arena Publications, Melbourne, pp. 231–8

Tonkinson, Robert 2007, 'Aboriginal "difference" and "autonomy" then and now: Four decades of change in a Western Desert society', *Anthropological Forum*, vol. 17, no. 1, pp. 41–60

Toussaint, Sandy, Tonkinson, Myrna and Trigger, David 2001, 'Gendered landscapes: The politics and processes of inquiry and negotiating interests in land', in *Words and Silences: Aboriginal women, politics and the land*, Peggy Brock (ed.), Allen & Unwin, Sydney, pp. 157–74

Townsend, Hamish 2006, 'No bush telegraph on land rights reform', *National Indigenous Times*, 24 August, p. 3

Trigger, David 2005, 'Mining projects in remote Aboriginal Australia: Sites for the articulation and contesting of economic and cultural futures', in *Culture, Economy and Governance in Aboriginal Australia*, Diane Austin-Broos and Gaynor McDonald (eds), Sydney University Press, Sydney, pp. 41–62

Trudgen, Richard 2000, *Why Warriors Lie Down and Die: Towards an understanding of why the Aboriginal people of Arnhem Land face the greatest crisis in health and education since European contact*, Aboriginal Resource and Development Services, Darwin

Tully, James 2000, 'The struggles of Indigenous peoples for and of freedom', in *Political Theory and the Rights of Indigenous Peoples*, Duncan Ivison, Paul Patton and Will Sanders (eds), Cambridge University Press, New York, pp. 36–59

Vadiveloo, Jane 2006, *Town Camps and Alice Springs: A background paper*, in author's collection

Vanstone, Amanda 2005a, 'Beyond conspicuous compassion: Indigenous Australians deserve more than good intentions', speech to the Australian and New Zealand School of Government, Australian National University, 7 December, www.atsia.gov.au/Media/former_minister/speeches/2005/07_12_2005_ANZSOG.aspx

——2005b, 'Message from the Minister', in *Australian Government Feature: Indigenous Affairs – Sharing Responsibility*, www.indigenous.gov.au/rpa/koori_mail_ins.pdf

Walter, Maggie 2007, 'Indigenous sovereignty and the Australian state: Relations in a globalizing era', in *Sovereign Subjects: Indigenous sovereignty matters*, Aileen Moreton-Robinson (ed.), Allen & Unwin, Sydney, pp. 155–67

Watson, Irene 2002, 'Aboriginal laws and the sovereignty of *Terra Nullius*', *Borderlands e-journal*, vol. 1, no. 2, www.borderlandsejournal.adelaide.edu.au/vol1no2_2002/watson_laws.html

——2007, 'Settled and unsettled spaces: Are we free to roam?', in *Sovereign Subjects: Indigenous sovereignty matters*, Aileen Moreton-Robinson (ed.), Allen & Unwin, Sydney, pp. 15–32

Watson, Lilla 1987, 'Sister, black is the colour of my soul', in *Different Lives: Reflections on the women's movement and visions of its future*, Jocelynne Scutt (ed.), Penguin, Ringwood, Victoria

Webber, Jeremy 2000, 'Beyond regret: Mabo's implications for Australian constitutionalism', in *Political Theory and the Rights of Indigenous Peoples*, Duncan Ivison, Paul Patton and Will Sanders (eds), Cambridge University Press, New York, pp. 60–88

Whittaker, Mark 2007, 'A town like Wadeye', *Weekend Australian Magazine*, 3–4 November, pp. 22–30

Wild, Rex, and Anderson, Patricia 2007, *Ampe Akelyernemane Meke Mekarle: Little children are sacred*, Report of the Northern Territory Board of

Inquiry into the protection of children from sexual abuse, www.nt.gov. au/dcm/inquirysaac/pdf/bipacsa_final_report.pdf

Willika, Rachel 2007, 'My NT community faces quarantined Christmas', ABC Opinion Online, 17 December, www.abc.net.au/news/ stories/2007/12/17/2120415.htm

Wilson, Ashleigh and Hodge, Amanda 2005, 'PM's new deal for blacks', *The Australian*, 7 April, p. 1

Windschuttle, Keith 2002, *The Fabrication of Aboriginal History, Volume One: Van Diemen's Land 1803–1847*, Macleay Press, Sydney

Woodward, Edward 1973, *Aboriginal Land Rights Commission: First report*, Australian Government Printing Service, Canberra

——1974, *Aboriginal Land Rights Commission: Second report*, Australian Government Printing Service, Canberra

Wootten, Hal 2004, 'Self-determination after ATSIC', *Dialogue*, no. 23, pp. 16–24

Wright, Alexis 2005, 'Embracing the Indigenous vision', *Meanjin*, vol. 65, no. 1, pp 104–8

——2007, 'Indigenous dreamers thwarted by fear', ABC News Opinion, online, 13 July, www.abc.net.au/news/stories/2007/07/13/1977989.htm

Young, Elspeth 2005, 'Rhetoric to reality in sustainability: Meeting the challenges in Indigenous cattle station communities', in Luke Taylor, Graeme Ward, Graham Henderson, Richard Davis and Wallis Lynley (eds), *The Power of Knowledge, the Resonance of Tradition*, Aboriginal Studies Press, Canberra, pp. 116–29

Young, Iris Marion 2000, 'Hybrid democracy: Iroquois federalism and the postcolonial project', in *Political Theory and the Rights of Indigenous Peoples*, Duncan Ivison, Paul Patton and Will Sanders (eds), Cambridge University Press, New York

Yu, Peter 1997, 'Multilateral agreements: A new accountability in Aboriginal affairs', in *Our Land Is Our Life: Land rights—past present and future*, Galarrwuy Yunupingu (ed.), University of Queensland Press, St Lucia, pp. 168–80

Yunupingu, Galarrwuy 2007, 'The challenge begins', *The Australian*, 21 September, www.theaustralian.news.com.au/story/0,25197,22453431-7583,00.html

Yunupingu, Galarrwuy (ed.) 1997, *Our Land Is Our Life: Land rights—past, present and future*, University of Queensland Press, St Lucia

INDEX

extended families 85, *see also* collectivism
external sovereignty 47

Fabrication of Aboriginal History 213–15
family identities 153
Family Responsibility Commission 21
Federal Council for the Advancement of
    Aborigines and Torres Strait Islanders
    127
Federal Court, overturns Noongar decision
    137–8
feminism 202–4
Fleras, Augie 45
Flick, Isabel 110
Flynn, Eugenia
    as emerging leader 180–1
    biography xvi
    on dependency 40–1
    on elders 175, 177–8
    on gender roles 201
    on 'history wars' 214–15
    on identity 105
    on Islam 113
    on jealousy 100
    on male demonisation 198–9
    on need for national body 232
    on racism 215–16
    on reconciliation 222, 226
    on separatism 36–7
    on the future 227
Foley, Gary
    on Australia Day 207
    on autonomy 30
    on class issues 116
    on collectivism 85
    on dysfunctional communities
        146
    on economic autonomy 39
    on leadership 169–70
    on *Native Title Act* 133
    on Noel Pearson 97–8
Fraser Coalition Government 6
funding, inadequacy of 157–8
future for Indigenous people 181–3,
    229–42

gangs in Wadeye 151–2
Garma Festival 15
'gatekeeper' families 157
gender issues in traditional culture 185–
    205, *see also* men; traditional culture;
    women
genealogical knowledge 198
generational change 165–84, 200–1
gerontocracy, *see* elders; leadership

Gilbert, Kevin
    Living Black vii
    on Aboriginality 103, 106–7
    on dependency 30–1, 41–2
    on leadership 97, 169
    on Makarrata 220
    on reconciliation 222
    on removal of children 208
    on reserves 148
    opposes citizenship 57
Githabul native title 134
Godwell, Darren 180
Goodwin, Tim 180
Gordon, Billy 180
Gordon, Sue 108
Gove land rights case 70, 89
government, *see also names of
        administrations, e.g.* 'Howard Coalition
    government'
    definition of indigeneity 111
    gender equality promoted by 197
    inquiry into role of NACC 107
    mistrust of xl
    opposition to land rights 65
    parliamentary representation 233–5
    relations with 223
    supports mining industry 71
Graham, Chris 18, 137
Gray, Bill 21
Griffiths, Rick 35
Gulpilil, David 85–6
Gurindji walk-off 5, 128

handouts, *see* welfare dependency
Hannaford, John 7
Harrison, Max Dulumunmun 222
Havnen, Olga 20
Hawke Labor Government
    agrees to negotiate treaty 220
    Barunga statement 230
    Indigenous policies 6–7, 10–11
    inequality rises during xl
    land rights legislation 70
Hayward, Colleen
    biography xvi
    non-Aboriginal family members 117
    on Aboriginality 109
    on ATSIC 34, 139, 140
    on citizenship rights 56
    on commemorative days 217
    on customary law 192–3
    on diversity xli
    on education policy 57–8
    on generational change 179,
        182

on historical trauma 211–12
on home ownership 94
on identity 118
on internal disputes 142
on leadership 177–8
on media stereotypes xxix
on racism 216, 223
on sovereignty 48, 51
Herron, John 12
High Court
  legal decisions 45–6
  Mabo judgment 46, 89
  Wik decision 10
  Yorta Yorta claim 120
Hill, Kim
  biography xvii
  on authenticity 117
  on elders 176
  on jealousy 99–100
  on kin obligations 86
  on land ownership 155
  on leadership 100
  on mining 71
  on native title 134
  on nuclear waste dump 77
  on parliamentary representation 233
  on police involvement 152–3
  political education of 179
'history wars' 206, 213–15
Hocking, Debra
  on Aboriginality 109
  on 'authenticity' 115
  on NSDC 225
home ownership 88–95
homelands 158–63
Hosch, Tanya 180
House of Representatives Standing
  Committee on Aboriginal Affairs 2–3
housing, overcrowded 190
Howard Coalition Government, *see also*
  Brough, Mal; Howard,
  John; Northern Territory intervention
attitude to collectivism 87–8
'bread versus freedom' debate 220
defeat of 229
directs resources from urban areas 67
Indigenous policies xl, 7–12, 221, 223,
  227
influences on 130
Northern Territory intervention 12–18
'practical reconciliation' 115
recalcitrance of xxxii–xxxiv, 224
removes customary law defence 195
suspicions of 38
view of history 206, 214

Howard, John, *see also* Howard Coalition
  Government; Howard Coalition
  government
lack of response from xxxii–xxxiv
on NT 'intervention' xxv
refusal to apologise 12
Wadeye speech 89–90
Howard, Michael 98
HREOC discussion paper 40
Huggins, Jackie 7
advocates assembly model
  141
biography xvii
on Aboriginality 122
on Australia Day 207
on dependency 40
on elders 171–2
on feminism 203–4
on generational change 165–6
on Indigenous affairs 240–1
on kinship relations and land 153–4
on leadership 168
on media pressure xxx
on need for economic base 66
on need for education xxxviii
on need for national body 129–30, 138,
  236–7
on passing as white 110
on removal of children 208
on sexism 199–200
on skin colour 108–9
Hughes, Helen 90, 160–1
human rights 11, 83–4, *see also* civil rights
  campaigns
Human Rights and Equal Opportunity
  Commission 238
humanitarian intervention 41
Hunt, Janet 95–6, 149
hybrid economy 73
hybridity 103–23

identities 104–10
imprisonment 213
In the Hands of the Regions 7
incompetence, perceived 1, 157
Indigeneity, defining 103–23
Indigenous Australians, *see* Aboriginal
  Australians
Indigenous Community Governance
  Project 43, 149
Indigenous Coordination Centres 9
'Indigenous estate' 88–9, *see also* land
  rights
Indigenous Land Corporation 69
Indigenous Land Tenure Principles 91

New South Wales Aboriginal Child Sexual
  Assault Taskforce 13
New South Wales, native title claims 134
New Zealand 80
Niezen, Ronald 124
nine-point plan 19
ninety-nine-year leases, *see* leasehold
  arrangements
non-Indigenous Australians
  cultural dominance of 172
  family relations with 116–17
  mistrust of xl, 37
  passing as 110
  readiness to negotiate with xxxi–xxxii
  'unsettling' 222
  view of Aboriginals 215–16
  view of traditional culture 64–5
Noongar native title 137–8
Noonkanbah mine 70
north-south divide 107, 128–35
Northern Land Council 6, 71, 77–8
Northern Territory
  Aboriginal MLAs 233–4
  emblematic of Aboriginal communities
    128
  legislation for mining industry
    71
  opposition to land rights in 65
  Woodward commission 149
Northern Territory Board of Inquiry into
  the Protection of Aboriginal Children
  from Sexual Abuse 13
Northern Territory intervention 12–18
  costs of xl
  John Howard on xxv
  leasehold arrangements under 95
  male demonisation by 199
  responses to xxxv, 126
  under Rudd government 20–1, 229–30
Nowra, Louis 188
NSW Aboriginal Child Sexual Assault
  Taskforce 13
NSW native title claims 134
NT, *see* Northern Territory; Northern
  Territory intervention
nuclear waste dump 77

O'Donoghue, Lowitja
  clash with Noel Pearson 98
  on autonomy 42
  on customary law 191
  on 'history wars' 214
  on leadership 100
  on national body 235
  on positivism 218

on removal of children 209
on reparations 226–7
on Rudd apology 225–6
Oodgeroo Noonuccal xxiv
'orbiting' 121
Oscar, June 235
O'Shane, Pat 46, 127, 202
ownership of land, *see* land rights

pan-Aboriginal organisations, *see* national
  organisations
Paradies, Yin 99, 123
parliamentary representation 233–5
'passing for white' 110
pastoral industry 6, 68–9, 146
paternalism 26, 41–3, *see also*
  protectionism
Paulson, Mark Yettica 177, 180
pay back laws, *see* customary law
Pearson, Noel
  attacks middle class 116
  criticisms of 129–30
  ignores requests for interview xxvii
  influence on Howard Government 90
  leadership role xxxv–xxxvi, 97–8
  on Aboriginality 121–2
  on autonomy 27
  on dependency 29–30, 41–2
  on development 72
  on historical trauma 212
  on identity 111
  on leasehold arrangements 92–3
  on modernisation 104
  on native title claims 120–1
  on Northern Territory intervention 17
  on 'orbiting' 87–8
  on political issues 132
  on radicalism 232
  on sovereignty 46
  Port Douglas meeting xxxii
peer support programs 180
penal system 213
peoplehood issues 46
Perkins, Charles 132–3
Peters-Little, Frances
  on assimilation 5
  on community 146–7, 163
  on 'gatekeeper' families 157
Petrick, Anthony Phillip 151, 167–8, 184
Phillips, Gregory 180
Pintupi people 153
Pitjantjatjara people 79
police involvement
  demand for 152–3
  in communities 163

on ATSIC 34–5
on autonomy 41
on citizenship 54
on elders 175
on gender equality 189
on gendered leadership 196
on generational change 178–9
on reparations 226
political education of 169
Wave Hill strike 5, 128
welfare dependency 24–6, 31–2
as media stereotype xxix
control via 42
economic development and 67–8
Wenberg, Val 224
Western Australia
education policy 57–8
native title in 134
regionalism in 137–8
Western Australian Aboriginal Child Health Survey 118
Western culture 172, *see also* non-Indigenous Australians
'white Australians', *see* non-Indigenous Australians
Whitlam Labor Government 6, 26–7, 148
wife beating 192
Wik decision 10
Wilcox, Murray 137
Wild, Rex
on autonomy 42
on customary law 192
on male disempowerment 198
on NT intervention 15
Wilkes, Ted
biography xxi
cultural education 168
on CDEP 67
on community 147
on development 80–1
on education policy 174
on generational change 169
on housing issues 190
on mining 72
on priorities 54–5
on traditional culture 118–19

Willika, Rachel 230
Windschuttle, Keith 213–15
Wiradjuri native title 134
women, *see also* gender issues in traditional culture
power held by 195–6
violence against 187
women's business 189
Woodward commission into land rights 149
Work for the Dole 14, 67–8
Wright, Alexis 21, 43
wulula 28

Xstrata 71

Yanner, Murandoo 177
Yirra statement 137
Yirrkala voting patterns 18–19
Yolngu people
bark petition 5, 127–8
economic autonomy for 80
leadership of 97
leasehold arrangements made by 93–4
males feel powerless 196
mining on land held by 70–1
trade by 64
Yorta Yorta land claim 120, 134, 219
Yorta Yorta people 204
Young, Iris Marion xli, 47
Youth Assembly 182
Yu, Peter 21, 133
on economic issues 80
on homelands movement 160
on regionalism 136
on right to negotiate 66
Yuendumu women 216
Yungngora community 70
Yunupingu, Galarrwuy
leasehold arrangements made by 93–4
Mala Elders group 40
on autonomy 43
on diversity xxix
recognised as 'landowner' 71
supports NT intervention 18